# Doctrine & Covenants Commentary

Volume One: Sections 1 – 34

Philip M. Hudson

Copyright 2017 by Philip M. Hudson.
The book author retains sole copyright to his contributions to this book.

Published 2017.
Printed in the United States of America.

All rights reserved.

No portion of this book may be reproduced, stored in a retrieval system,
or transmitted in any form or by any means – electronic, mechanical, photocopy,
recording, scanning, or other – except for brief quotations in
critical reviews or articles, without the prior written permission of the author.

ISBN 978-1-943650-57-6

Library of Congress Control Number 2017944349

Google images.

Published by BookCrafters, Parker, Colorado.
www.bookcrafters.net

# Table of Contents

Preface..........................................................................................................1

Introduction..................................................................................................5

Acknowledgements.....................................................................................11

Section 1......................................................................................................15

Section 2......................................................................................................27

Section 3......................................................................................................33

Section 4......................................................................................................39

Section 5......................................................................................................49

Section 6......................................................................................................59

Section 7......................................................................................................77

Section 8......................................................................................................89

Section 9......................................................................................................97

Section 10..................................................................................................103

Section 11..................................................................................................119

Section 12..................................................................................................135

Section 13..................................................................................................143

Section 14..................................................................................151

Section 15..................................................................................159

Section 16..................................................................................163

Section 17..................................................................................167

Section 18..................................................................................175

Section 19..................................................................................197

Section 20..................................................................................213

Section 21..................................................................................249

Section 22..................................................................................261

Section 23..................................................................................267

Section 24..................................................................................275

Section 25..................................................................................281

Section 26..................................................................................287

Section 27..................................................................................291

Section 28..................................................................................301

Section 29..................................................................................311

Section 30..................................................................................353

Section 31..................................................................................359

Section 32..................................................................................365

Section 33..................................................................................369

Section 34..................................................................................383

Author's Note..................................................................................................393

About the Author........................................................................................403

Also by the Author.....................................................................................405

# Preface

In the Book of Mormon account of Ammon by the Waters of Sebus, "every man that lifted his club to smite Ammon, he smote off their arms with his sword; for he did withstand their blows by smiting their arms with the edge of his sword, insomuch that they began to be astonished, and began to flee before him; yea, and they were not few in number; and he caused them to flee by the strength of his arm." (Alma 17:37).

Mormon may have included this episode in his abridgment because he knew that in our day we would face our own "Lamanites by the Waters of Sebus." We all have the same primal needs and the focus of our concern should be on the potential loss of our energy, vitality, and ultimately our eternal lives. It just may be that it was to address these very needs that the Lord provided us with the book of Doctrine & Covenants.

Perhaps our moments of greatest challenge will come when we are placed in compromising social situations and are tempted to homogenize our standards. Maybe it will be when we are climbing the ladder of success and are influenced to scramble over those who we think are in our way impeding our progress. It might be when we are alone with our computer, surfing the web, and we are more prone to visit sites of questionable value. It may come at the end of the month when we are reconciling our checkbook and are creatively attempting to balance our budget, but have not yet paid our tithing. It may be when we have not completed our home teaching, visiting teaching, or have not attended the temple in a while, and worldly concerns clamor for our time and attention. In all these situations, familiarity with the principles and doctrines that have been definitively addressed in the Doctrine & Covenants will allow us to move forward with purpose.

The Lord said: "That which the Spirit testifies unto you even so I would that ye should do in all holiness of heart, walking uprightly before me, considering the end of your salvation, doing all things with prayer and thanksgiving, that ye may not be seduced by evil spirits, or doctrines of devils, or the commandments of men." (D&C 46:7). The "Lamanites by the Waters of Sebus" standing in the way of our progress are those frightful apparitions that only come into focus when we take our minds off our goals. These ruffians influence us to lower our sights, compromise our standards, and achieve our objectives far too easily. If we are gliding smoothly and effortlessly through life with little expenditure of energy, we are probably going downhill, as the "Waters of Sebus" rush on by. Because our personal progress takes effort, we have been given the revelations in our latter-day scriptures to help us to avoid the pitfalls and potholes in the road that lies before us, to surmount the obstacles to our progression that lie in our path, and to climb to new heights of achievement.

In a real sense, the Doctrine & Covenants infuses us with "the power of God unto salvation," that we might be the architects of our own fate. (Romans 1:16). We have been endowed with the skills and the materials to build either a shanty or a temple in which to live our lives. Which one it will be depends on us. The outcome hinges largely on our perspective that is shaped by our familiarity with the principles of the gospel and doctrines of the kingdom. If we can face the "Lamanites" by the Waters of Sebus" in our lives with the understanding, faith, and courage that come from our familiarity with and reliance upon the scriptures, "we shall be strengthened and comforted, and spared the torment which accompanies the mistaken idea that all suffering comes as chastisement for transgression." (Marion G. Romney, C.R., 10/64).

As is so poignantly illustrated many times in the Doctrine & Covenants, bad things happen to good people, and life can be unpredictable. There are uncertainties with which each of us must deal, but if our footings are secure and our foundation is solid, we will be able to successfully adapt to every circumstance, and even use adversity to our advantage. Fanatics are those who lose sight of their objectives and redouble their efforts. We, on the other hand, remember the counsel of Paul, who was familiar with adversity: "Work out your own salvation," he said, "with fear and trembling" before the Lord. (Philippians 2:12).

As we face "Lamanites" by our own "Waters of Sebus," we remember that our triumphs will come by design, by the strength of our own will, and by our reliance on the Lord. We thank Him for His foresight; that he provided us with the fortification of latter-day revelation, that we might be better prepared to deal with "Lamanite" encounters. Thanks to Him, we think pro-actively, rather than retroactively. He empowers us to direct the course of the circumstances in which we find ourselves, as well as the eventual outcomes. We may not be able to control everything that unfolds in our lives, but we have at least been given the tools to influence personal consequences, even as we rely upon Him as the ultimate source of our strength.

Inaction is a manifestation of failure by default, a capitulation of our destiny to forces we believe to be beyond our control. If we roll over and turn belly-up to "Lamanites" when they menacingly surround and threaten us, we have virtually guaranteed defeat. Our flocks will be scattered and the Good Shepherd disappointed.

"Now the king will slay us," wailed the servants of Lamoni. (Alma 17:28). Our Lord and Master will not take our lives, however. We are very capable of doing that on our own. It is we who will exchange our birthright for a mess of pottage, who will forfeit our eternal lives if we allow "Lamanites" to overcome us, by neglecting the clear voice of warning in the scriptures.

Life is enough of a pressure cooker, as it is, without introducing the unneeded additional stress that is the consequence of unfamiliarity with the ordinances, covenants, and commandments. If we ignore the latter-day prophecies reassuring us that, no matter what might come, there is a power great enough to envelop us within the embrace of the Lord, we deny ourselves a supernal source of comfort and joy. It is true that many events "remain to (be) overcome through patience (in order to) receive a more exceeding and eternal weight of glory." (D&C 63:66). But the Lord reassured Joseph Smith: "Be patient in afflictions, for thou shalt have many. Endure them, for, lo, I am with thee, even until the end of thy days." (D&C 24:8). In the meantime, "in everything (we) give thanks, waiting patiently on the Lord," even in the face of destruction at the hands of fierce "Lamanites." (D&C 98:1-2). We "seek the face of the Lord always, that in patience (we) may possess (our) souls, and… have eternal life." (D&C 101:38).

King Lamoni's people were astonished at Ammon's response to the Lamanite threat, because in the Land of Nephi the people of King Lamoni had not yet learned how to draw upon the power of God. When his servants returned to his court to testify of the things they had seen Ammon do, "he was astonished exceedingly, and said: Surely, this is more than a man. Behold is this not the Great Spirit?" (Alma 18:1-2). Intuitively, they must have known that the Great Spirit was capable of mighty works, but now they were faced with the possibility that He had transferred His power to Ammon, for how else could he perform such great miracles? They had never considered that they, too, might be capable of withstanding the onslaughts of the formidable bands of Lamanites roaming the land and trolling for unsuspecting shepherds tending their flocks. The blessing of the Doctrine & Covenants helps us to overcome these feelings of temporal and spiritual inadequacy. Because of this body of scripture, we will never be left alone to face "Lamanites by the Waters of Sebus."

# Introduction

Members of the church do not have a lock on covenants. You say tomāto, I say tomáto. You say potāto, I say potáto. Broadly speaking, a covenant is a historical term for a treaty or other agreement. It is a legal term, particularly restricting the use of property; for example, Conditions, Covenants, and Restrictions, or C.C.&R.s, define the parameters relating to financial instruments. The U.N. uses the term, as in its International Covenant on Civil and Political Rights. The P.L.O. uses it as well, as in The Palestinian National Covenant of 1964, that outlined the aims of the Palestine Liberation Organization. So does the I.R.A., as in The Ulster Covenant of 1912, that protested against British home-rule. Covenants also define a series of solemn agreements believed by many to exist between God and Israel. The foundation of the Torah is the belief that God chose the Children of Israel, and made His Covenant with them. Israel is commonly called His Covenant People.

The Latter-day Saint concept of religious "covenants" or agreements we make with God piggy-backs on Israel's relationship with HIm, that goes back at least to Abraham. Today, with the restoration of the gospel, members of the church make a number of covenants with the Lord. There are baptismal covenants, sacramental covenants, the Oath and Covenant of The Priesthood, and several temple covenants. Because of the Great Apostasy, Latter-day Saints view these religious contracts in a way that is peculiar to their beliefs, and that others within Christian denominations may find strange.

Latter-day Saints believe that covenants are received only by revelation from God. They believe they are binding, and since He is a party to every gospel covenant, that they must necessarily come through a portal of two-way communication with Deity that is loosely described as inspiration, and more specifically defined as revelation. No-one can therefore enter into such covenants without direct interaction with God. It follows that the only ones who can make covenants with Him are members of the Church of Jesus Christ, who have taken a lot of heat over the doctrine, but nevertheless steadfastly maintain their belief in latter-day revelation. (See the 7th Article of Faith).

Latter-day Saints go to a great deal of effort to make covenants with God, that they believe are integral to His Plan and are necessary to bring to pass our exaltation and eternal life, which are its ultimate goals. They feel the intensely personal tug of covenants, believing that covenants tell us, as nothing else can, about the attributes of God and how to be ushered into His presence.

Covenants reveal His parenting style. He is our Father, and could give us everything He has, but what He is, we must earn for ourselves, as we struggle to overcome adversity and gain self-mastery. Covenants are our bridge supports over the unfathomable gulf that exists between mortality and eternity. More than any other things, it is our covenants that help us to narrow the focus of our efforts to become as He is. This is why covenants are so important to Latter-day Saints. Their vision of the divine destiny of all of the children of God explains the purpose of the covenants we make with Him.

If it were not possible to become as God is, Latter-day Saints believe that covenants would be unnecessary. This provides insight into why the world doesn't immediately understand why we make covenants with God, and particularly why the temple is poorly understood and largely unappreciated by those outside the faith. But, it also suggests the direction our teaching should follow. As Joseph Smith observed: "Reading the experience of others, or the revelation given to them, can never give us a comprehensive view of our condition and true relation to God. Knowledge of these things can only be obtained by experience through the ordinances of God set forth for this purpose." (H.C., 6:50).

The flow of the Doctrine & Covenants carries us toward a greater appreciation that the covenants we make with God reflect His attributes. For example, God is moral, so He gives us the Covenant of Chastity. (See D&C 132:41). He has charity, so He commands us to love Him and each other. (See D&C 121:45). God is disciplined, so He gives us the Law of Obedience. (See D&C 89:18). Because He is a righteous steward, He gives us the Law of Consecration. (See D&C 42:32).

Because He loves His less fortunate children, He gives us the Law of the Fast. (See D&C 109:15-16). Because His is a perfected, resurrected body, He gives us the Word of Wisdom. (See D&C 89). Because He is omniscient, He gives us the commandment to seek knowledge. (See D&C 130:19). In consequence of the Gift of His Son, He gives us the Law of Sacrifice. (See D&C 97:8). Because He rested from His labors on the seventh day, He gives us the Law of the Sabbath. (See D&C 68:29).

Within the pages of the Doctrine & Covenants lies a formula that establishes our relationship with God, permitting Him to lawfully and legitimately bestow specific blessings, while continuing to honor the influence of agency or free will. We all receive the right to guidance from the Holy Ghost. (See D&C 121:26). Worthy men receive the right to hold the priesthood. (D&C 13:1). Women may receive the opportunity to exercise power in the administration of priesthood ordinances in the temple. They also receive rights, privileges, blessings, and responsibilities that specifically relate to femininity. (See D&C 76:24). Entire families receive the blessings of the priesthood relating to eternal life in the Celestial Kingdom. (D&C 132:22-23).

The principles that were first introduced in the Doctrine & Covenants extend to all members of the church with the power to put them beyond the reach of the adversary. Obedience gives them the priesthood and spiritual power necessary to overcome evil and obtain exaltation. The Prophet Joseph Smith explained: "Salvation consists of a man's being placed beyond the power of his enemies, meaning the enemies of his progression, such as dishonesty, greediness, lying, immorality, and other vices." (Sermon delivered at the Nauvoo temple site on May 21, 1843. Sources: Joseph Smith diary (Willard Richards), Howard and Martha Jane Knowlton Coray Notebook, Franklin D. Richards "Scriptural Items," and James Burgess Notebook. See "Teachings," p. 297-298).

The Doctrine & Covenants promises us: "The gates of hell shall not prevail against you; yea, and the Lord God will disperse the powers of darkness from before you, and cause the heavens to shake for thy good, and His name's glory." (D&C 21:6). The gates of hell mark the entrance to the so-called spirit prison of the unjust, where unenlightened souls are allowed to go, to work out their own salvation and to await the day of their deliverance from the iron grip of Satan. (See "Doctrines of the Gospel Student Manual, (2000), p. 87–89, D&C 76:73, 88:97-102, Alma 40:11-14, & Moses 7:57).

The Doctrine & Covenants teaches us about responsibilities relating to the relationship we establish with God. We learn about our duty to keep His commandments. We learn about our missionary accountability, as we realize how the Lord promised Abraham that through his descendants the gospel would be taken to all the earth. Even today, as the Restoration continues to unfold. because of the Doctrine & Covenants we are continually learning about the fullness of the gospel, or The New and Everlasting Covenant, including the covenants made at our baptisms, at our ordinations to the Melchizedek Priesthood, during the administration of the sacrament, and in the temple.

The Doctrine & Covenants alludes to the promises we make with God that are ordained by His everlasting authority. Because the Plan dates from before the foundation of the world, we can be sure that our covenants will never be changed. He gave this same covenant to Adam, Enoch, Noah, Abraham, and other prophets, during individual gospel dispensations. The Lord only calls it the New and Everlasting Covenant because each time the gospel is restored after being taken from the earth due to apostasy, it is new to the people who receive it. (See Jeremiah 31:31-34 & Ezekiel 37:26).

In the Doctrine & Covenants, we learn about the "contract provisions" of the New and Everlasting Covenant. We agree to repent, to be baptized, and to receive the Holy Ghost, the endowment, and the covenant of marriage in the temple. We agree to follow and obey Christ to the end of our lives. Heavenly Father, in turn, promises us that we will receive exaltation in the Celestial Kingdom. (See D&C 132:20-24). The magnitude of that promise is hard for us to understand, but the Doctrine & Covenants gives us greater clarity, even as we look through a glass, darkly. (See 1 Corinthians 13:12).

The Doctrine & Covenants helps us to better understand that the commandments are for our benefit, and that, in faith, we may enjoy the blessings and beauties of heaven and earth. We may live, once again, in His presence, to partake of His love, compassion, might, majesty, power, greatness, glory, knowledge, wisdom, dominions, and exaltations.

In the Doctrine & Covenants, we learn that our Father in Heaven established His Covenant that we might be released from our bondage to sin, and be set free to take advantage of all the features of the Plan of Salvation. Without His Covenant made on our behalf, the Plan would have been frustrated. We are thrilled to know that covenants have set us free from the bands of death. We believe the words of King Benjamin, who said: "There is no other name given whereby salvation cometh, therefore, I would that ye should take upon you the name of Christ, all you that have entered into the covenant with God." (Mosiah 5:8).

Our covenants set us free to reach our potential, and we rejoice that we have been born again. Truly did Benjamin declare that those who enter into the Covenant "are born of him." (Mosiah 5:7). The Lord revealed to Joseph Smith, as recorded in the Doctrine & Covenants, that there is a priesthood that "administereth the gospel and holdeth the key of the mysteries of the kingdom, even the key of the knowledge of God. Therefore, in the ordinances thereof, the power of godliness is manifest." We are grateful for the Lord's book of commandments, for "without the ordinances thereof, and the authority of the priesthood, the power of godliness is not manifest unto men in the flesh." (D&C 84:19-21).

In order to better understand our covenants and their relationship to the events that surround us, we have learned to view Israel from at least three different perspectives. These allow us to appreciate the influence that her physical and spiritual qualities as a chosen people have had upon us. Membership in the Lord's church allows us to adopt covenants that increase many-fold our capacity to change the world in preparation for the Second Coming. In one sense, Latter-day Saints may simply be viewed as those in whom the blood of Israel flows. But a second perspective explores the expanding influence of those who have come out of the Gentile nations of the earth, who in doing so have made covenants with God to forsake the world and join His chosen people. As Paul taught the elect of God who had anciently become Israelites by adoption: "Ye are all the children of God by faith in Christ Jesus. For as many of you as have been baptized into Christ have put on Christ. There is neither Jew nor Greek, there is neither bond nor free, there is neither male nor female: for ye are all one in Christ Jesus. And if ye be Christ's, then are ye Abraham's seed, and heirs according to the promise." (Galatians 3:26-29).

A third point of view embraces those whose ancestors have occupied the Holy Land since biblical times. Many descendants of Abraham have deeply rooted ties that will surely figure prominently in the events surrounding the fulfillment of prophecy in the Last Days, such as those that relate to the gathering of Israel, and to preaching the gospel.

Some voices yet remain silent, while others are stridently vocal, but all the world has witnessed how Israel has been "gathered home to the lands of (her) inheritance, (to be) established in all (her) lands of promise." (2 Nephi 9:2). Israel, that has been scattered throughout the world, intuitively recognizes her need to make covenants with her God and Father. In fact, of this glorious day of restoration and gathering, a Nephite prophet said: "The Lord. . . has covenanted with all the house of Israel," that "the time comes that they shall be restored to the true church and fold of God," and that "they shall be gathered home to the lands of their inheritance, and shall be established in all their lands of promise." (2 Nephi 9:1-2).

Bruce R. McConkie declared: "Now I call your attention to the facts, set forth in these scriptures, that the gathering of Israel consists of joining the true church; of coming to a knowledge of the true God and of his saving truths; and of worshiping him in the congregations of the Saints in all nations and among all peoples. Please note that these revealed words speak of the folds of the Lord; of Israel being gathered to the lands of their inheritance; of Israel being established in all their lands of promise; and of there being congregations of the covenant people of the Lord in every nation, speaking every tongue, and among every people when the Lord comes again." (Mexico City Area Conference, 8/1972).

What better way could there be to come to a knowledge of God and of His saving truths, and to participate in the gathering of His chosen people, than by studying the canon of scripture found in His Doctrine & Covenants?

# Acknowledgements

In this commentary, I have attributed quotations to original authors whenever possible, as well as when I have editorialized their thoughts. In many cases, however, my language will naturally reflect the teachings of leaders and members of The Church of Jesus Christ of Latter-day Saints.

The list of those who have contributed their ideas to the construction of this commentary is endless. As I have collected my own thoughts, I have realized how heavily I have borrowed from the towering examples of those who, over the years, have been my mystical mentors, my sensible chaperones, my spiritual guides, my surrogate saviors, my compassionate critics, and everything in between.

They are my avatars, the manifestations of deity in bodily forms, my na'vi, the visionaries who communicate with God on a level to which I can only aspire, and my tsaddik, whom I esteem as the interpreters of biblical law and scripture. They are my divine teachers incarnate.

They have shown me the way, stretched my mind, reinforced my faith, strengthened my testimony, lifted my spirits, helped me to discover my wings, provided of their means, given immaterial support, emboldened me with words of encouragement, cheered me on with wise counsel, taught me humility, been there to steady me, soothed my troubled soul, stepped in to nurture me, led me to fountains of living water, wet my parched lips with inspired counsel, bound up my wounds, offered listening ears, and extended open arms.

Every teacher, student, classmate, business associate, friend, mentor, ordinance worker, temple patron, family member, priesthood and relief society brother, sister, or leader, with whom I have come in contact has influenced me. Every author, poet, journalist, essayist, thespian, satirist, and lyricist with whom I have become familiar has moved me in some positive way. I have tried to find the silk purse in every sow's ear, and the silver lining in every cloud.

If I have been given a lemon, I have done my best to follow the recipe for lemonade. I have learned not to cry because it's over, but to smile because I was privileged to have had the experience. I have discovered how to see the opportunity in every difficulty, and I have found that when I keep my face to the sun, the shadows will always be behind me.

I have come to know that there is so much good in the worst of us, and so much bad in the best of us, that it hardly behooves any of us to talk about the rest of us. I try to keep tempests in their teapots where they belong, and to keep adversity in perspective. I have witnessed the awesome power of change, that so often comes like a flash of lightning and a clap of thunder. I have seen others shrink in fear, but I have always tried to retain a grip on the assurance that after the storm, flowers will bloom. ("I Ching").

I remember the joyful anticipation of the optimistic little boy, who, when faced with the daunting task of shoveling up an enormous pile of manure in a horse stall near his home, enthusiastically set about his task with the exclamation: "There's got to be a pony in there, somewhere!"

Well did the poet teach: "No man is an island, entire of itself. Every man is a piece of the continent; a part of the main. If a clod be washed away by the sea, Europe is the less, as well as if a promontory were, as well as if a manor of thy friends or of thine own were. Any man's death diminishes me, because I am involved in mankind. Therefore, never send to know for whom the bell tolls. It tolls for thee." (John Donne).

Even now, when I think of the multitude of angels thinly disguised as my family, friends, and peers who have ministered to my needs, I remember the words of Sir Isaac Newton, who, when pressed to reveal the great secret behind his accomplishments, simply replied: "I stood on the shoulders of giants."

Of course, at the end of the day, I alone am responsible for the editorial content of this volume. I hope my interpretation of principles will cultivate your interest to dig deeper into the themes woven into the tapestry of these scriptures, by studying first-hand their related doctrines, and by simultaneously seeking inspiration from the Spirit. My only goal is to help you to expand your insights into the foundation truths and celestial guideposts that I have attempted to identify and explore within this commentary, that have been inspired by my love of the Doctrine & Covenants.

One last thought: I am well-aware of the potential problems associated with the use of a commentary when studying the scriptures. Elder Dallin Oaks of the Quorum of The Twelve very insightfully wrote the following: "Latter-day Saints know that learned or authoritative commentaries can help us with scriptural interpretation, but we maintain that they must be used with caution. Commentaries are not a substitute for the scriptures any more than a good cookbook is a substitute for food. (When I refer to "commentaries," I refer to everything that interprets scripture, from the comprehensive book-length commentary to the brief interpretation embodied in a lesson or an article, such as this one.)

One trouble with commentaries" he continued, "is that their authors sometimes focus on only one meaning, to the exclusion of others. As a result, commentaries, if not used with great care, may illuminate the author's chosen and correct meaning but close our eyes and restrict our horizons to other possible meanings. Sometimes those other, less obvious meanings can be the ones most valuable and useful to us as we seek to understand our own dispensation and to obtain answers to our own questions. This is why the teaching of the Holy Ghost is a better guide to scriptural interpretation than even the best commentary." ("Scripture Reading and Revelation," "Ensign," 1/1995).

It is with this wise counsel in mind that I close this Acknowledgement, and offer this Commentary to you, for your enjoyment and edification.

# Section One
## (The Lord's preface to the other revelations).

A man was sleeping in his hotel room on a cold winter night, when he was awakened by the smell of smoke and a voice shouting, "John, John, Get up!" He jumped out of bed, threw on his robe, and went to the door. When he opened it, a blast of hot air almost knocked him over. Slamming the door shut, he went to his bed, and climbed back in, saying to himself, "It must be a false alarm. My name isn't John!" This simple story illustrates how dangerous it would be to fail to recognize that the Doctrine & Covenants has been written for each of us.

The Doctrine & Covenants "is a collection of divine revelations and inspired declarations given for the establishment and regulation of the kingdom of God on the earth." But it is different from other scripture. "It is unique because it is not a translation of an ancient document, but is of modern origin and was given of God through his chosen prophets for the restoration of his holy work and the establishment of the kingdom of God on the earth in these days." ("Explanatory Introduction to The Doctrine & Covenants").

Joseph Fielding Smith, Jr. declared: "In my judgment, there is no book on earth yet come to man as important as the book known as the Doctrine & Covenants, with all due respect to The Book of Mormon, and the Pearl of Great Price. The book of Doctrine & Covenants to us stands in a peculiar position above them all. The Doctrine & Covenants contains the word of God to those who dwell here now. It is our book." ("Doctrines of Salvation," 3:198-199).

The Old Testament spans 3,600 years of history, from approximately 4,000 B.C. to 400 B.C., and the New Testament just 100 years. The Book of Mormon chronicles more than 1,000 years of history, but the bulk of the Doctrine & Covenants was recorded in just 24 years, from 1823, to 1847. Seventy seven of the revelations came in a three year period while Joseph Smith was working on his translation of the Bible.

There are at least 15 different ways in which revelation was received, in the Doctrine & Covenants. (See "How the Revelations in the Doctrine and Covenants Were Received and Compiled." "Ensign," 1/1985).

General revelations given for the benefit of the church and of the world.
Revelation given to others, through the Prophet Joseph Smith.
General revelations given for the benefit of the priesthood.
Revelation given to the Prophet for his instruction.
Revelation given through the Urim & Thummim.
Explanation of passages found in other scripture.
Words spoken by heavenly messengers.
Minutes of special church meetings.
Inspiration sent through letters.
Words spoken in prayers.
Historical narratives.
Official declarations.
Translations.
Prophecies.
Visions.

Section 1 was actually the 66th revelation received and recorded by Joseph Smith, but it is placed first in the Doctrine & Covenants because it is the Lord's Preface to the Book of Commandments. "Behold, this is mine authority, and the authority of my servants, and my preface unto the book of my commandments, which I have given them to publish unto you, O inhabitants of the earth." (V. 6). The Doctrine & Covenants is the only book in existence that bears the honor of a preface dictated by the Lord Jesus Christ Himself. Section One establishes the authority of the revelations that follow.

Section 1 was initially the preface to the Book of Commandments. This revelation was given in response to the prophet's inquiry as to whether the Book of Commandments should be published. When the press that was to have published the work was destroyed by a mob in 1835, the book was reconfigured in expanded form as the Book of Doctrine & Covenants.

"Hearken, O ye people of my church," said the Lord. (V. 1). Hear, and obey! For "the voice of the Lord is unto all men." (V. 2, see v. 4, 6, 11, & 34). This book is not only for members of The Church of Jesus Christ of Latter-day Saints. Its messages are intended for all of Father's children throughout the world. "There is no eye that shall not see, neither ear that shall not hear, neither heart that shall not be penetrated." (V. 2).

Those who reject the glad tidings, "the rebellious, shall be pierced with much sorrow." (V. 3). A principal reason, after all, for the Restoration was so that "the voice of warning (might) be unto all people." (V. 4).

The Lord indicated that there are at least six reasons why those living in the Last Days should "fear and tremble." (V. 7). (1) The Lord declared that His promises should be fulfilled, for the great and terrible day of the Lord is at hand. (2) Those with the authority of the priesthood are to be given the power to go forth "unto the inhabitants of the earth" and (3) there to "seal both on earth and in heaven, the unbelieving and rebellious" for judgment. (V. 8). (4) At that day, the Lord will "come to recompense unto every man according to his work, and measure to every man according to the measure which he has measured to his fellow man." (V. 10). These principles show us the manner by which God will judge us, and they also give new meaning to the Golden Rule.

IIn the Doctrine & Covenants, the warning is given at least 90 times to "prepare ye, prepare ye for that which is to come, for the Lord is nigh." (V. 12). Clearly, another important reason for the publication of the book was (5) to prepare the world for the coming judgment. God is infinitely patient and long-suffering, but the world has exceeded the limits of Justice, and even in love, God can no longer forbear. "And the anger of the Lord is kindled, and his sword is bathed in heaven, and it shall fall upon the inhabitants of the earth." (V. 13). This metaphor, also used by Isaiah, symbolizes the powerful judgments and destruction to be visited upon the wicked. "For my sword shall be bathed in heaven: behold, it shall come down upon Idumea, and upon the people of my curse, to judgment." (Isaiah 34:5).

During His mortal ministry, the Lord told His disciples that He would "send forth his angels, and they shall gather out of his kingdom all things that offend, and them which do iniquity; and shall cast them into a furnace of fire: there shall be wailing and gnashing of teeth. Then shall the righteous shine forth as the sun in the kingdom of their Father." (Matthew 13:41-43). Rid of the telestial influence of the wicked, the righteous would be free to come forth in the glory of the Celestial Kingdom of God.

Therefore, another reason (6) for the publication of the Doctrine & Covenants was to give the wicked one last chance to respond to the voice of the Lord, for they who will not hear His voice, "neither the voice of his servants, neither give heed to the words of the prophets and apostles," will ultimately "be cut off from among the people." (V. 14). This warning applies equally to members and non-members of the church, as does the denouncement of the unrighteous in the following verse.

"For they have strayed from mine ordinances, and have broken mine everlasting covenant." (V. 15). Joseph Smith once declared that "this generation is as corrupt as the generation of the Jews that crucified Christ." (H.C., 5:68). If this is an accurate description of behavior in the early years of the nineteenth century, it must be an absolute condemnation of the world today, as we embark upon a new millennium.

Today, idolatry is rampant. The world, as well as those who have made covenants with God, but who have then turned their back on Him, seek "not the Lord to establish his righteousness, but every man walketh in his own way, and after the image of his own god, whose image is in the likeness of the world, and whose substance is that of an idol, which waxeth old and shall perish in Babylon, even Babylon the great, which shall fall." (V. 16).

The devil, who fancies himself the prince of darkness and the god of this world, (J.S.T. John 14:3, 2 Corinthians 4:4, D&C 1:16, 11:28, & 3 Nephi 11:14), rules in the earth by the manipulation of those who worship idols. He thus delights in both idols and idol worshipers. (See 2 Nephi 9:37). John Taylor taught that the priesthood of those who honor their covenants "is the legitimate rule of God and is the only legitimate power that has a right to rule upon the earth, and when the will of God is done on the earth, as it is done in heaven, no other power will bear rule." (J.D., 5:187).

Those who fight against Zion are unfaithful to gospel principles and have thus prostituted themselves. (See 2 Nephi 10:16). Such individuals and institutions are characterized as being "the whore of the earth" in the sense that they are corrupt and are idol worshipers. Those who are not with God are against him. (See Moroni 7:13-17). Surely, Joseph Smith lamented as had Ezekiel, who saw that Covenant Israel had allowed herself to be led into spiritual bondage, until she was "as the heathen, as the families of the countries, to serve wood and stone." (Ezekiel 20:32).

In our day, Babylon has become firmly entrenched in the world. She is "the great whore that sitteth upon many waters, with whom the kings of the earth have committed fornication." (Revelation 17:1-2). To some extent, all of the governments of the earth are corrupt, are unfaithful to their heavenly mandate, and have figuratively committed fornication with the whore.

One of the terrible consequences of the fascination with Babylon of those who have lost their covenant consciousness is spiritual insensitivity. Isaiah foresaw the Last Days, when he wrote: "Stay yourselves, and wonder; cry ye out, and cry: they are drunken, but not with wine; they stagger, but not with strong drink. For the Lord hath poured out upon you the spirit of deep sleep, and hath closed your eyes: the prophets, and your rulers, and seers hath he covered. And the vision of all is become unto you as the words of a book that is sealed." (Isaiah 29:9-11).

In consequence of the great power exerted by Satan in the Last Days, and "knowing the calamity which should come upon the inhabitants of the earth," the Lord chose Joseph Smith to be His spokesman, "and spake unto him from heaven, and gave him commandments." (V. 17). At least seven specific reasons why He did so can be identified in the next ten verses.

(1). The Lord selects those who are humble and worthy, and then He tutors them. (V. 18). (2). He chooses "the weak things of the world." (V. 19). As Spencer W. Kimball once stated: "Christianity did not go from Rome to Galilee. It was the other way around. In our day, the routing is from Palmyra to Paris, not the reverse." (C.R., 4/1978).

(3). It is the Lord's hope that "every man might speak in the name of God the Lord, even the Savior of the world." (V. 20). Certainly, this is one of the most powerful evidences of both the Apostasy and the Restoration, that the authority to invoke the name of God is only bestowed by Him in specific time periods called "dispensations," and then rests with His children who become His priesthood servants.

(4). Because of the ministry of Joseph Smith and others, faith has increased to the point that the Covenant that God made with Abraham has now been reestablished. (V. 21 & 22). With the Covenant in place, it has become possible for the fulness of the gospel to be "proclaimed by the weak and the simple unto the ends of the world, and before kings and rulers." (V. 23). The strength of the gospel is its theology, which will bear up under the scrutiny of even the most powerful minds on earth.

We may expect grammatical errors in the revelations, until they are discovered and corrected. These are not the mistakes of God. In addition, some who oppose the church feel that changes in syntax in some of the revelations proves that Joseph Smith didn't really receive revelation. But just the opposite is true. He was the recipient the revelations. Although he was untutored in grammar and poetic expression, he knew what he had received. He edited them before they were published, so that the wording of each would accurately reflect the thoughts, impressions, and the inspiration the Lord had given him.

In any event, we have a clear declaration from Deity regarding His acceptance of the receipt of His word and will. (5). "Behold, I am God and have spoken it; these commandments are of me, and were given unto my servants in their weakness, after the manner of their language, that they might come to understanding. And inasmuch as they erred, it might be made known; And inasmuch as they sought wisdom they might be instructed; And inasmuch as they sinned they might be chastened, that they might repent; And inasmuch as they were humble they might be made strong, and blessed from on high, and receive knowledge from time to time." (V. 24-28).

(6). It was because of his humility that Joseph Smith was blessed to receive "the record of the Nephites," and the "power to translate through the mercy of God, by the power of God, the Book of Mormon." (V. 29). "And he has translated the book, even that part which I have commanded him, and as your Lord and your God liveth it is true." (D&C 17:6).

(7). It was because of his worthiness that Joseph Smith was given the "power to lay the foundation of this church, and to bring it forth out of obscurity and out of darkness, the only true and living church upon the face of the whole earth, with which I, the Lord, am well pleased, speaking unto the church collectively and not individually." (V. 30).

The reality of the apostasy and the subsequent restoration of priesthood authority are well documented in the scriptures and in the history of the church. No other church has the authority of the priesthood, that is necessary to bind and ratify the covenants we make with God. No other organization has the power to break the death grip of Satan, who would drag our souls down to hell in an instant, if he were given the opportunity to do so. No other organization has the full and unabridged support of "the only living and true God." (D&C 20:19).

"Of the other churches, we do not say they are wrong, so much as we say they are incomplete." (Boyd K. Packer, C.R., 10/1964). All the branches of the House of Israel, as well as the Gentiles who were grafted in, had become corrupted by the time the gospel was restored to the earth, in 1830. As Zenos lamented: "And now, behold, notwithstanding all the care with which we have taken of my vineyard, the trees thereof have become corrupted, that they bring forth no good fruit." (Jacob 5:46).

Ignorance is at the root of apostasy from the truth. If we suffer from a shallow understanding of basic principles of the gospel, the devil will seize upon our weaknesses. Members of the church require the solid foundation of understanding provided by the Doctrine & Covenants to successful resist his pervasively evil influence. This body of scripture provides us with a greater understanding of the special protection that is provided by the Melchizedek Priesthood, and by the endowment of spiritual power that is received only in the Lord's House. Its elucidation of clear and explicit principles provides those who are seeking the truth and who invite the Spirit into their lives with firm and abiding testimonies of the doctrines of the kingdom, the Plan of Salvation, and the Savior.

In the Middle Ages, during the height of the Great Apostasy, leaders like Charlemagne complained of illiterate monks, but could have been speaking of our own day: "What pious devotion had faithfully prompted in their hearts, their uneducated tongues could not put into words without stumbling." According to the historian Will Durant: "Hardly a Bible existed that was not riddled with the gross errors of untutored copyists." (Thomas Bulfinch, "The Age of Chivalry," p. 61). That confusion, which dragged on for hundreds of years and pervasively infected the Christian churches of Joseph Smith's day, has been summarily swept aside by the publication of The Book of Mormon, The Pearl of Great Price, and The Doctrine & Covenants, and the subsequent understanding of the revelations, by faithful members of The Church of Jesus Christ of Latter-day Saints.

One consequence of the apostasy from truth is an emasculated priesthood devoid of legitimate authority. "There is no regularly constituted church on earth," lamented the reformer Roger Williams, "nor any person authorized to administer any church ordinance; nor can there be until new apostles are sent by the Great Head of the Church for Whose Coming I am seeking." (Quoted by William Cullen Bryant, in "Picturesque America," p. 502).

In their efforts to clarify their consideration of Christ, even well-meaning individuals are cut adrift without the anchor of a reliable canon of scripture. They are often "simply multiplying mirrors and studying angles without increasing the light." (B.H. Roberts, "The Truth, The Way, The Life," p. 263). Of the apostate sects of Christendom, Emerson wrote: "The clergy are like as peas. I cannot tell them apart. It is the old story again. Once we had wooden chalices and golden priests. Now we have golden chalices and wooden priests." ("Lectures and Biographical Sketches," p. 180).

Even a superficial study of the activities of the architects of the Reformation reveals that their common purpose was to rediscover the power of God and revitalize the church with His authority. For example, John Wesley wrote: "The real cause why the extraordinary gifts of the Holy Ghost are no longer to be found in the Christian Church, is because the Christians have been turned heathens again, and have only a dead form left." ("Wesley's Works," Volume 7, Sermon 89, p. 26-27)

Machiavelli also criticized the prevailing religious authority "Had Christianity been preserved according to the ordinances of the Founder," he declared, "the people would have been far more united and happy that they are." (Will Durant, "The Reformation," p. 16). Jesus Christ, foresaw the Apostasy, recognized its reality, and in the Sacred Grove initiated decisive steps to usher in a Restoration that continues to this day. The book of Doctrine & Covenants is clear evidence of His continuing involvement in that process.

His attachment to the fortunes of the Saints may be traced to the fact that He "cannot look upon sin with the least degree of allowance." (V. 31). The terrible thing about hardening our hearts in disobedience to law is that understanding of "the word" is withheld, which leaves us vulnerable to the devil's influence. The scriptures identify the consequences of disobedience in very plain language. The effect of sin on those who have previously been taught the principles of the gospel in plainness is that the guidance of the Spirit is withdrawn, and they are left alone to grope in darkness. Guilt causes them to shrink from church activity, and in the absence of the Spirit, they have no claim on blessings, prosperity, or preservation.

Tragically, feeling uncomfortable in proximity to spiritual experiences, the unrepentant withdraw to lifestyles devoid of such associations. Thus begin downward spirals that gains momentum as sinful practices, more easily committed, become entrenched. Even worse, those who do this, "the same cometh out in open rebellion against God." (Mosiah 2:37). "Thus saith the Lord concerning all those who know my power, and have been made partakers thereof, and suffered themselves through the power of the devil to be overcome, and to deny the truth and defy my power: They are they who are the sons of perdition." (D&C 76:31-32). God hates the unrepentant disobedient because of what it does to them. Only if they are untainted by sin, can "the righteous shine forth as the sun in the kingdom of their Father." (Matthew 13:41-43).

For "he that repents and does the commandments of the Lord shall be forgiven." (V. 32). The Atonement sets us free from the terrible consequences of sin. Therefore, the Restoration of the gospel, with its laws and ordinances, was essential, that the Plan might once again become fully operational.

We can choose our own actions, but we cannot choose to escape their consequences The Law of the Harvest is immutable. "The decrees of God are unalterable; therefore, the way is prepared that whosoever will may walk therein and be saved." (Alma 41:8). We cannot "be restored from sin to happiness." (Alma 41:10). Justice is the unalterable decree of God which declares that both righteousness and sin dictate their own consequences. "He that repents not, from him shall be taken even the light which he has received; for my Spirit shall not always strive with man, saith the Lord of Hosts." (V. 33).

Once again, the Lord is "willing to make these things known unto all flesh." (V. 34). For He is "no respecter of persons." (V. 35). Our spirituality is not related to an office or a calling in the church, but is daily living the gospel of Jesus Christ. "God is mindful of every people, whatsoever land they may be in; yea, he numbereth his people, and his bowels of mercy are over all the earth." (Alma 26:37). "And he inviteth them all to come unto him and partake of his goodness; and he denieth none that come unto him, black and white, bond and free, male and female; and he remembereth the heathen; and all are alike unto God, both Jew and Gentile." (2 Nephi 26:33).

His mercy breaks the barrier of death, and offers the hope of eternal family life to all who have ever lived on the earth. God is absolutely non-discriminatory as He deals with His children. Sooner or later, all will either accept or reject the invitation to enter into a covenant relationship with Him. Ultimately, the principle of agency will either deify us or damn us. The day has come for us to choose, for peace has been taken from the earth, and the devil has power over his own dominion. (V. 35).

However, as He binds the influence of Satan, "the Lord shall (exert His) power over his saints, and shall reign in their midst, and shall come down in judgment upon Idumea, or the world." (V. 36). Anciently, Idumea, or Edom, was a non-Israelite nation south of the Salt Sea. Traveling through that land symbolized to the prophetic mind our pilgrimage through a wicked world.

Therefore, a merciful God has given us the guidance represented by the Doctrine & Covenants. "Search these commandments," He declared, "for they are true and faithful, and the prophecies and promises which are in them shall all be fulfilled." (V. 37). "Faith in the gospel is much like a living organism," taught John Widtsoe. "To be healthy and vigorous, it must be fed. If starved, it sickens, weakens, and may die. Loss of faith may always be traced to neglect, mistreatment, and sin. The food of faith is simple but imperative. Knowledge of the gospel must be maintained and increased by regular, continuous study. It is an erroneous assumption to think that knowledge of the gospel comes, as it were, with breathing, while to secure academic knowledge requires toil." ("Evidences and Reconciliations").

Spiritual illumination comes from a study of the scriptures and of the words spoken by the servants of God, for, as the Lord declared: "Whether by mine own voice or by the voice of my servants, it is the same." (V. 38). "These words are not of men nor of man, but of me," He declared, "wherefore, you shall testify they are of me and not of man. For it is my voice which speaketh them unto you; for they are given by my Spirit unto you, and by my power you can read them one to another; and save it were by my power you could not have them. Wherefore, you can testify that you have heard my voice and know my words." (D&C 18:34-36).

When we read the words of the Doctrine & Covenants under the influence of the Spirit, we are hearing the voice of the Lord, as well as reading His words. The Savior said: "Learn of me, and listen to my words; walk in the meekness of my Spirit, and you shall have peace in me." (D&C 19:23). "For behold, and lo, the Lord is God, and the Spirit beareth record, and the record is true, and the truth abideth forever and ever. Amen." (V. 39). Truth is at the very foundation of faith, and is the catalyst that motivates us to action. Truth is deed. The horizon of our knowledge extends only as far as our action. This is why works are an important companion to vital, active faith. (See James 2:17 & Matthew 5:16). Faith without action has no life-generating or sustaining power, because alone it is impotent. The Doctrine & Covenants is an excellent vehicle to allow us to generate that power unto salvation.

# Section 2

## (The First Revelation, received from an angel, prior to the organization of the church).

In September, 1823, the angel Moroni gave Joseph Smith the following counsel: "Wherever the sound (of the marvelous work) shall go it shall cause the ears of men to tingle, and wherever it shall be proclaimed, the pure in heart shall rejoice, while those who draw near to God with their mouths, and honor him with their lips, while their hearts are far from him, will seek its overthrow, and the destruction of those by whose hand it is carried. Therefore, marvel not if your name is made a derision, and had as a by-word among such, if you are the instrument in bringing it, by the gift of God, to the knowledge of the people." ("The Messenger and Advocate," 1:5, 2/1835).

According to his mother, Lucy Mack Smith, Moroni also warned Joseph: "You are but a man. Therefore, you will have to be watchful and faithful to your trust, or you will be overpowered by wicked men; for they will lay every plan and scheme to get the plates away from you, and if you do not take heed continually, they will succeed." ("History of Joseph Smith," p. 110).

Satan clearly understood the importance of the restoration of keys and authority to the earth, and used every means within his power to destroy Joseph Smith and thwart his mission. Today, those who bear the priesthood in The Church of Jesus Christ of Latter-day Saints need to recognize that they are all marked men. Satan has hired assassins whose sole purpose is to destroy faith, particularly of those who have received the covenants of the temple.

Little wonder, then, that Joseph was cautioned so strongly, for the prophecy concerning the coming of Elijah that comprises Doctrine & Covenants Section 2 was the first revelation he received and is one of the most carefully documented prophecies of all time, appearing in all four of the Standard Works. (Malachi 4:5-6, 3 Nephi 24 & 25, J.S.H. 1:36-39, and D&C 2 & 110). In fact, John Widtsoe said: "The beginning and the end of the gospel is written in Section 2 of the Doctrine &

Covenants. It is the keystone of the wonderful gospel arch, and if that center stone should weaken and fall out, the whole gospel structure would topple down in unorganized doctrinal blocks." ("Doctrine & Covenants Institute Student Manual," Section 2).

The section in its entirety reads: "Behold, I will reveal unto you the Priesthood, by the hand of Elijah the prophet, before the coming of the great and dreadful day of the Lord. And he shall plant in the hearts of the children the promises" or covenants "made to the fathers," that is to say, Abraham, Isaac, and Jacob, "and the hearts of the children shall turn" or bind "to their fathers. If it were not so," if the sealing power of the priesthood were not restored, "the whole earth would be utterly wasted at his coming" because the Plan of Salvation would be thwarted. This is the curse mentioned in Malachi 4:6.

In Joseph Smith History, (The Pearl of Great Price), the prophecy reads: "Behold, I will reveal unto you the Priesthood by the hand of Elijah the prophet, before the coming of the great and dreadful day of the Lord. ... And he shall plant in the hearts of the children the promises" or covenants "made to the fathers," that is to say, Abraham, Isaac, and Jacob, "and the hearts of the children shall turn" or bind "to their fathers. If it were not so," if the sealing power of the priesthood were not restored, "the whole earth would be utterly wasted at his coming." (J.S.H. 1:38-39).

Malachi wrote (in the Old Testament): "Behold, I will send you Elijah the prophet before the coming of the great and dreadful day of the Lord: And he shall turn the heart of the fathers to the children, and the heart of the children to the fathers, lest I come and smite the earth with a curse." (Malachi 4:5-6).

The Lord (in The Book of Mormon) quoted Malachi during His ministry among the Nephites: "Behold, I will send you Elijah the prophet before the coming of the great and dreadful day of the Lord; And he shall turn the heart of the fathers to the children, and the heart of the children to their fathers, lest I come and smite the earth with a curse." (3 Nephi 25:6).

The wording of Malachi in the Bible is identical to 3 Nephi 25:5-6 in The Book of Mormon, but differs from that in the Doctrine and Covenants and the Pearl of Great Price, which are also identical. When Moroni quoted the prophecy to Joseph Smith when he appeared in his bed chamber in 1823, his alterations from the Bible and Book of Mormon texts were probably for emphasis and clarification, rather than for correction, to help Latter-day Saints to better understand the prophecy.

Section 2 was placed in the Doctrine & Covenants in 1870, at the direction of

Brigham Young. If the revelations in the Doctrine & Covenants were structured in chronological order, it would be the first, inasmuch as it was received on September 21, 1823. The beginning of the ministering of angels in this dispensation began in the evening on that date, when the Angel Moroni appeared to Joseph Smith in his bed chamber. As the Restoration progressed, such communication from the heavens flowed steadily. (See Moroni 7:22-29, & 37). For example, through the Prophet Joseph Smith in an epistle to the Saints, the Lord later promised to all those who are pure vessels bearing the priesthood that had been restored: "Thy confidence (shall) wax strong in the presence of God; and the doctrine of the priesthood shall distil upon thy soul as the dews from heaven. The Holy Ghost shall be thy constant companion, and thy scepter an unchanging scepter of righteousness and truth; and thy dominion shall be an everlasting dominion, and without compulsory means it shall flow unto thee forever and ever." (D&C 121:45-46).

The Lord elaborated on this promise when He said: "And, behold, and lo, this is an ensample unto all those who were ordained unto this priesthood, whose mission is appointed unto them to go forth. And this is the ensample unto them, that they shall speak as they are moved upon by the Holy Ghost. And whatsoever they shall speak when moved upon by the Holy Ghost shall be scripture, shall be the will of the Lord, shall be the mind of the Lord, shall be the word of the Lord, shall be the voice of the Lord, and the power of God unto salvation." (D&C 68:1-4).

This prophecy of Malachi concerning keys and covenants was fulfilled almost 13 years after it was received by Joseph Smith, on a day that fortuitously happened to coincide with the Passover. Of that experience, Joseph said: "Another great and glorious vision burst upon us; for Elijah the prophet, who was taken to heaven without tasting death, stood before us, and said: Behold, the time has fully come, which was spoken of by the mouth of Malachi – testifying that he (Elijah) should be sent, before the great and dreadful day of the Lord come – To turn the hearts of the fathers to the children, and the children to the fathers, lest the whole earth be smitten with a curse. Therefore, the keys of this dispensation are committed into your hands; and by this ye may know that the great and dreadful day of the Lord is near, even at the doors." (D&C 110:13-16).

During the Paschal Service each year, the door in Jewish homes is left open, and a place is set at the table with a vacant chair. This is done in order to be ready to admit Elijah so that, as the forerunner of the Messiah, he might partake of the Passover Feast. This he literally did on Sunday, April 3, 1836, but it was in the Kirtland Temple, and not in Jewish homes.

It was necessary that Elijah be the one to restore the priesthood authority of the sealing power. Those who hold the priesthood officiate by the authority they possess, but only when directed to do so by those who hold the keys relating to that particular priesthood power. Although Moses, Elijah, and Jesus conferred keys of authority on Peter, James, and John on the Mount of Transfiguration, the Lord reserved for Elijah the responsibility to restore the keys of the sealing power to Joseph Smith in the Last Days.

As Joseph Fielding Smith, Jr. taught: Elijah "held the keys of the authority to administer in all the ordinances of the priesthood, and without this authority that is given, the ordinances could not be administered in righteousness." ("Doctrines of Salvation," 2:113). Many prophets had held similar keys, but the reason that Elijah was reserved for his mission to Joseph Smith was that he was the last prophet to hold the keys of the priesthood, or the fullness of the power of the priesthood. God specifically sent him to deliver these keys relating to the sealing power so that those who would subsequently bear the priesthood could authoritatively bind the Latter-day Saints by covenant to the ordinances of the gospel, consistent with the overall objectives of the Plan of Salvation.

From the time that Elijah fulfilled his latter-day mission, the keys of the priesthood have been held in their fullness only by the Presidents of The Church of Jesus Christ of Latter-day Saints. When Joseph Smith conferred the keys of the sealing power upon Brigham Young, he was at that time the President of the Council of The Twelve. Parley P. Pratt said: "This last key of the priesthood is the most sacred of all, and pertains exclusively to the First Presidency of the church, without whose sanction and approval or authority, no sealing blessing shall be administered pertaining to things of the resurrection and the life to come." ("Millennial Star," 5:151).

The day when the Lord comes will be at once "great and dreadful." (Malachi 4:5). For the righteous, it is the day when Christ will come in power and glory; for the unrighteous, it is when He will take vengeance upon the wicked. The Doctrine & Covenants version of the prophecy emphasizes the Covenant made anciently with Abraham, Isaac, and Jacob. The Priesthood keys that Elijah delivered to the Prophet Joseph Smith made the blessings associated with obedience available to faithful Saints in the Last Days. For example, sealers in the temples derive their authority directly from the First Presidency of the Church.

As Malachi pointed out, if they are unprepared to meet Christ, the whole population of the earth will be wasted, or destroyed, at the Second Coming. To circumvent this calamity, the sealing power was given to the Presidency of the Melchizedek Priesthood, which "administereth the gospel and holdeth the key of the mysteries of the kingdom, even the key of the knowledge of God. Therefore, in the ordinances thereof, the power of godliness is manifest. And without the ordinances thereof, and the authority of the priesthood, the power of godliness is not manifest unto men in the flesh, for without this no man can see the face of God, even the Father, and live." (D&C 84:19-22).

Even though for almost three millennia the Jews have waited in vain for Elijah to join the Paschal Feast on the Passover, the purposes of God have not been thwarted. The Latter-day fulfillment of the prophecy of Malachi testifies: "No power on earth or hell can overthrow or defeat that which God has decreed. Every plan of the Adversary will fail, for the Lord knows the secret thoughts of men, and sees the future with a vision clear and perfect." (Joseph Fielding Smith, Jr., "Church History and Modern Revelation," 1:26).

The principles that are addressed in Section 2 of the Doctrine & Covenants are extremely important to the Saints in the Last Days; in fact, the three-fold mission of the church to preach the word, perfect the Saints, and redeem the dead revolves around Section 2. From the time that the revelation was received in the evening of September 21, 1823, it has been recognized as an affirmation of the Lord Jesus Christ that He would redeem Israel. In the Dispensation of The Fulness of Times, the House of the Lord has once again become a dominant feature of the church and kingdom, and is a tangible confirmation of the fulfillment of prophecy and of the restoration of the priesthood keys of authority.

# Section 3

## (Received prior to the organization of the church).

At least 8 sections of the Doctrine & Covenants (3, 6, 7, 11, 14, 15, 16, & 17) were received by the means of the Urim and Thummim, a device that seems to have been unneeded after Joseph received the Melchizedek Priesthood, in June 1829. The added endowment of the priesthood, combined with Joseph's expanding experience in receiving revelation through the channel of the Holy Ghost, may explain this.

This revelation was "given to Joseph Smith the Prophet, at Harmony, Pennsylvania, July 1828, and relates to the loss of 116 pages of manuscript translated from the first part of The Book of Mormon, that was called the 'Book of Lehi.' The Prophet had reluctantly allowed these pages to pass from his custody to that of Martin Harris, who had served for a brief period as scribe in the translation of The Book of Mormon." (Superscript to Section 3). Section 3 stands as a testament to the basic honesty of Joseph Smith.

Speaking later of the loss of the pages of translation, Joseph Smith said: "And they have never been recovered unto this day." (H.C., 1:21). His mother recorded in her journal: "I well remember that day of darkness," when it became evident that the manuscript was gone for good. "The heavens seemed clothed with blackness and the earth shrouded with gloom." (Lucy Mack Smith, "The History of Joseph Smith, by His Mother," Chapter 25).

"The works, and the designs, and the purposes of God cannot be frustrated, neither can they come to naught." (V. 1). God knows all things. (See 2 Nephi 9:20). He knows the end from the beginning. (See 1 Nephi 9:6). He is the same yesterday, today and forever. (See 1 Nephi 10:18). Past, present, and future are ever before His eyes. (See D&C 130:7). He can prepare for any eventuality, since He is omniscient. (See 2 Nephi 9:20).

As Joseph Smith explained to the Reverend John Wentworth: "No unhallowed hand can stop the work from progressing. Persecutions may rage, mobs may combine, armies may assemble, calumny may defame, but the truth of God will go forth boldly, nobly, and independent, until it has penetrated every continent, visited every clime, swept every country and sounded in every ear, until the purposes of God shall be accomplished and the Great Jehovah shall say the work is done." (H.C., 4:540).

"For God doth not walk in crooked paths, neither doth he turn to the right hand nor to the left, neither doth he vary from that which he hath said, therefore, his paths are straight, and his course is one eternal round." (V. 2). "No power on earth or hell can overthrow or defeat that which God has decreed. Every plan of the adversary will fail, for the Lord knows the secret thoughts of men, and sees the future with a vision clear and perfect, even as though it were in the past." (Joseph Fielding Smith, Jr., "Church History and Modern Revelation," 1:26). "O how great the holiness of our God! For he knoweth all things, and there is not anything save he knows it." (2 Nephi 9:20). If this were not so, "he would cease to be God, and man could not have faith in him." (Joseph Fielding Smith, Jr., "Doctrines of Salvation," 1:7-10).

But God is in every sense perfect. And so, "it is not the work of God that is frustrated, but the work of men. For although a man may have many revelations, and have power to do many mighty works, yet if he boasts in his own strength, and sets at naught the counsels of God, and follows after the dictates of his own will and carnal desires, he must fall and incur the vengeance of a just God upon him." (V. 3-4).

Jacob explained that true learning must be accompanied by access to the Spirit. (2 Nephi 9:28, see 1 Corinthians 2:24, 2 Timothy 3:7, D&C 3:4, 88:4, & 123:12). He taught that an appeal to vanity is the devil's way of turning our minds against the Plan of Salvation. (See 2 Nephi 14:27, 28:4, & 28:14). He warned against the pitfalls of intellectual apostasy. (See 2 Nephi 9:42, & Colossians 2:8).

2 Nephi 9:29 is a hokmah that Jacob employed to drive the point home: "But to be learned is good, if they hearken unto the counsels of God." (See "The Way of The Intellectuals," in "An Approach to The Book of Mormon," Chapter 27).

In Joseph's first interview with Moroni, his mother recorded that he had been given specific counsel. "You are but a man," cautioned the angel. "Therefore, you will have to be watchful and faithful to your trust or you will be overpowered by wicked men; for they will lay every plan and scheme to get the plates away from you, and if you do not take heed continually, they will succeed." ("History of Joseph Smith," p. 110). Now the Lord reminded Joseph: "How strict were your commandments; and remember also the promises which were made to you, if you did not transgress them." (V. 5).

"And behold, how oft you have transgressed the commandments and the laws of God, and have gone on in the persuasions of men." (V. 6). Joseph was only 24 years of age when he lost the manuscript. By his own later admission, in his youth he had been "left to all kinds of temptations" and had mingled "with all kinds of society" and "frequently fell into many foolish errors, and displayed the weakness of youth, and the foibles of human nature," which led him "into divers temptations, offensive in the sight of God." (J.S.H. 1:28).

But he had been particularly susceptible to the influences of Martin Harris, who was "23 years his senior, a prominent and wealthy farmer, and one of the few who believed his story and supported him with both money and labor. There would have been tremendous inner pressure for Joseph to want to show his appreciation to Martin Harris. His faith in God was absolutely firm, but he lacked experience in trusting his untried friend in his constant pleadings." ("Doctrine & Covenants Commentary," p. 19).

From the Lord's perspective, it was easy to chasten Joseph: "For, behold, you should not have feared man more than God. Although men set at naught the counsels of God, and despise his words, yet you should have been faithful and he would have extended his arm and supported you against all the fiery darts of the adversary; and he would have been with you in every time of trouble." (V. 7-8).

James E. Talmage taught: "Our Heavenly Father has a full knowledge of the nature and dispositions of each of His children, a knowledge gained by long observation and experience in the past eternity of our primeval childhood; a knowledge compared with which that gained by earthly parents through mortal experience with their children is infinitesimally small. By reason of that surpassing knowledge, God reads the future of men individually and of men collectively as communities and nations. He knows what each will do under given conditions, and sees the end from the beginning. His foreknowledge is based on intelligence and reason; He foresees the future as a state which naturally and surely will be; not as one which must be because He has arbitrarily willed that it should be." ("The Great Apostasy," p. 20).

Therefore, the Lord declared: "Behold, thou art Joseph and thou wast chosen to do the work of the Lord, but because of transgression, if thou art not aware thou wilt fall." (V. 9). God does not pre-ordain our fate, except conditionally. (See D&C 130:20). To bring Joseph to a heightened state of awareness of his transgression, the Lord told him: "Repent of that which thou hast done which is contrary to the commandment which I gave you, and thou art still chosen, and art again called to the work." (V. 10).

The only payment required for the gift of forgiveness is "the heart and a willing mind." (D&C 64:34). The only thing that we must give up are our sins. As Alma had counseled his son Corianton: "Only let your sins trouble you, with that trouble which shall bring you down unto repentance." (Alma 42:29). Through his experience, Joseph learned to give himself completely to the Lord. Never again would he be persuaded by men to deviate from his course. The lesson was well learned; he knew the Lord was speaking the truth, when He said: "Except thou do this, thou shalt be delivered up and become as other men, and have no more gift." (V. 11).

Joseph had committed a serious sin. He had delivered the sacred record "into the hands of a wicked man who (had) set at naught the counsels of God, and (had) broken the most sacred promises which were made before God, and (had) depended upon his own judgment and boasted in his own wisdom." (V. 12-13). Martin Harris was a victim of his own pride, that was for him a crippling personality trait. By association, Joseph was in peril as well.

But the Lord had confidence in the abilities of the 24 year old, who through adversity would yet develop his spiritual muscles and fulfill his calling as the Prophet of the Restoration. The work of the Lord would not be frustrated; as the Lord explained: "For this very purpose are these plates preserved, which contain these records - that the promises of the Lord might be fulfilled, which he made to his people; and that the Lamanites might come to the knowledge of their fathers, and that they might know the promises of the Lord, and that they may believe the gospel and rely upon the merits of Jesus Christ, and be glorified through faith in his name, and that through their repentance they might be saved." (V. 19-20).

The Book of Mormon was written "unto the remnant of the House of Israel." (Title Page to The Book of Mormon). It was written for the benefit of "the Nephites, and the Jacobites, and the Josephites, and the Zoramites, through the testimony of their fathers. And this testimony shall come to the knowledge of the Lamanites, and the Lemuelites, and the Ishmaelites." (V. 17-18).

Under the best conditions, "the Lord called his people Zion, because they were of one heart and one mind, and dwelt in righteousness; and there was no poor among them." (Moses 7:18). In Book of Mormon times "there was a great division among the people" who were differentiated by religious affiliation rather than by race. (4 Nephi 1:35). "The true believers in Christ, and the true worshippers of Christ, (among whom were the three disciples of Jesus who should tarry) were called Nephites, and Jacobites, and Josephites, and Zoramites. And it came to pass that they who rejected the gospel were called Lamanites, and Lemuelites, and Ishmaelites." (4 Nephi 1:37-38).

Jacob 1:13 also makes a distinction regarding the divisions among the children of Lehi. "The people which were not Lamanites were Nephites." But within this group of Nephites were "Jacobites, Josephites, Zoramites, Lamanites, Lemuelites, and Ishmaelites." Likewise, among the Lamanites were counted those who "were a compound of Laman and Lemuel, and the sons of Ishmael, and all who had dissented from the Nephites." (Alma 43:13).

Inasmuch as 2 Nephi 5:5-6 reports that "all those who would go" went with Nephi when he departed into the wilderness from the Land of Their First Inheritance, it is plausible to assume that this group included descendants of Laman, Lemuel, and Ishmael, who are called "Lamanites, Lemuelites, and Ishmaelites" in verse 13. Additionally, note the absence of a reference in this verse to "Samites," consistent with the blessing given to Sam by Lehi, wherein he was told his posterity would be included with Nephi's. For Lehi "spake unto Sam, saying: ...Thy seed shall be numbered with his seed; and thou shalt be even like unto thy brother." (2 Nephi 4:11, see D&C 3:17).

In the Last Days, there would be no such distinctions between members of The Church of Jesus Christ of Latter-day Saints. They would be "no more strangers and foreigners, but fellowcitizens with the Saints, and of the household of God." (Ephesians 2:19).

# Section 4

## (Received prior to the organization of the church).

"Now behold, a marvelous work is about to come forth among the children of men." (V. 1). Of course, this refers to both the restoration of the gospel of Jesus Christ, and the publication of The Book of Mormon. These events were critical to the success of the Plan of Salvation as it relates to the human family in the Last Days. The Lord seldom intervenes directly in our lives. Generally, He works through individuals who serve others. Therefore, the Lord cautioned those who would embark upon a course of devotion to God: "See that ye serve him with all your heart, might, mind and strength, that ye may stand blameless before God at the last day." (V. 2). He requires that His servants be totally committed to the work, without reservation. (See Matthew 6:24). The Master called His disciples to a higher plane of spirituality and to a commitment to selfless consecration of effort. He advised them: "Lay up for yourselves treasures in heaven, where neither moth nor rust doth corrupt, and where thieves do not break through nor steal." (3 Nephi 13:19-20). The key is to lose ourselves in service, even as we let our light shine before men. (See 3 Nephi 12:16).

Every member of The Church of Jesus Christ of Latter-day Saints is a missionary, by virtue of their baptismal covenant. "Therefore," said the Lord, "if ye have desires to serve God, ye are called to the work." (V. 3). "My understanding," declared George Albert Smith, "is that the most important mission that I have in this life is first, to keep the commandments of God, and second, to teach them to my Father's children who do not understand them." (C.R., 10/1916).

As those enlisted in the missionary army of Jesus Christ continue to focus their attention on their brothers and sisters who have not been exposed to the gospel, they will be brought into harmony with the attributes of their Father in Heaven, whose concern is for the eternal welfare of all of His children. "And ye shall be even as I am, and I am even as the Father, and the Father and I are one," said the Savior to the Three Nephites. (3 Nephi 28:10).

"For behold, the field is white already to harvest; and lo, he that thrusteth in his sickle with his might, the same layeth up in store that he perisheth not, but bringeth salvation to his soul." (V. 4). In the Book of Alma, Ammon metaphorically described the harvest to illustrate for his brethren how thousands had been gathered through their missionary efforts. "Behold, the field was ripe," he said, "and blessed are ye, for ye did thrust in the sickle, and did reap with your might, yea, all the day long did ye labor; and behold the number of your sheaves!" (Alma 26:5). His party had come up out of the Land of Zarahemla into the highlands of Nephi to bring a message of love to their brethren the Lamanites. In its absence, they "would still have been racked with hatred (against the Nephites), and they would also have (remained) strangers to God." (Alma 26:9).

"And faith, hope, charity and love, with an eye single to the glory of God, qualify him for the work." (V. 5). The standard of the world is: "Seeing is believing." But seeing is not only irrelevant to the acquisition of faith, it is often the wrong message that is being presented. The advertising milieu of Madison Avenue testifies that this is all too true. Harold B. Lee taught: "You must learn to walk to the edge of the light, and then a few steps into the darkness; then the light will appear and show the way before you." (Boyd K. Packer, "What is Faith?" p. 42). This is the way faith is developed and strengthened.

There are probably three classic definitions of faith in the scriptures. The first is that "faith is not to have a perfect knowledge of things; therefore if ye have faith ye hope for things which are not seen, which are true." (Alma 32:21). This is correct in the ultimate sense. In Alma's usage, the verse might more clearly read: "Faith is not to have a perfect knowledge of things <u>gained through one's own experiences</u>." In the context in which Alma taught this principle to his Zoramite audience, it is important to remember that Korihor's demand for a sign had been the condition for his faith, since he trusted only his physical senses. The rational approach is the enemy of faith. Some things need to be believed to be seen.

Secondly, "faith is the substance of things hoped for, the evidence of things not seen." (Hebrews 11:1). In this context, faith is not to receive a sign from heaven. As Alma told the Zoramites, "If a man knoweth a thing he hath no cause to believe, for he knoweth it." (Alma 32:18). No exercise of faith is necessary to receive a sign from heaven. When the sign is given, one might have a sure knowledge of the event, but no expenditure of faith has been made to produce it. Under proper circumstances, though, "by doing our duty, faith increases until it becomes perfect knowledge." (Heber J. Grant, C.R., 4/1934). Initially, faith is to believe what we do not see, and the reward of faith is to see what we believe.

Thirdly, "faith is things which are hoped for and not seen; wherefore, dispute not because ye see not, for ye receive no witness until after the trial of your faith." (Ether 12:6). It is important to remember that in matters of faith the Lord is not on trial. At the Bar of Justice, the Judge will receive the evidence that had been the substance of that which had been provided for the development of our faith, and our previous acceptance or rejection of that proof will determine our reward or punishment. The trials that we face in mortality are eminently fair.

Hope in Christ is to have the assurance of peace, that the direction of our lives is on course, and that the Lord is pleased with, and approves of, our efforts. As Mormon said, hope is born of faith. "Behold, I say unto you that ye shall have hope through the atonement of Christ and the power of his resurrection, to be raised up unto life eternal, and this because of your faith in him according to the promise." (Moroni 7:41). Hope is not trust in some wildly improbable promise, nor is it a high stakes gamble. It is the inevitable result of well-founded faith, when one is "meek and lowly of heart," or in a position to recognize and act upon the particles of their faith. (Moroni 7:43).

With a foundation of faith and hope, Mormon revealed to his son how charity follows the qualities of faith and hope, and is the supreme characteristic of the Lord's disciples. (Moroni 7:44-48). He taught: "If a man be meek and lowly in heart, and confess by the power of the Holy Ghost that Jesus is the Christ," with a sure hope born of faith, "he must needs have charity. (Moroni 7:44, see 2 Nephi 33, & Ether 12:32).

"And charity suffereth long (or is the quality of patience), and is kind (or is characterized by sensitivity toward others, and is empathic), and envieth not (or is less concerned with telestial trinkets and more focused on celestial sureties), and is not puffed up, (or is humble), seeketh not her own (or is selfless), is not easily provoked (but reflects poise under provocation), thinketh no evil (or has no secret agenda to follow), and rejoiceth not in iniquity (but is repulsed by sin), but rejoiceth in the truth, beareth all things, believeth all things, hopeth all things, endureth all things" or is drawn toward the light, and is continually open to that which is good. (Moroni 7:45).

Without these qualities, our progression stops. "If ye have not charity, ye are nothing, for charity never faileth. Wherefore, cleave unto charity, which is the greatest of all (the spiritual gifts), for all things must fail (without it)." (Moroni 7:46). It is the greatest of all the qualities of God Himself, Who is the possessor of all spiritual gifts.

"Charity is the pure love of Christ, and it endureth forever, and whoso is found possessed of it at the last day, it shall be well with him." (Moroni 7:47, see Ether 12:34). Charity can motivate us to Christian service, and in doing so it also prepares us to be like God, so that we will feel comfortable in His Presence. As such, it is a gift which is bestowed upon the faithful by the grace of God.

"Remember faith, virtue, knowledge, temperance, patience, brotherly kindness, godliness, charity, humility, (and) diligence." (V. 6). We do this, Peter wrote, "that we might be partakers of the divine nature." (2 Peter 1:4). When God said: "Let us make man in our image, after our likeness," He meant not only that we should have the same physical characteristics as our Parents, but the same spiritual qualities, as well. (See Moses 2:26). Like-minded individuals seek each other out, are drawn to each other, and have a natural affinity for each other. "For this end was the law given," to prepare us to believe in Christ, "and we are made alive in Christ because of our faith." (2 Nephi 25:25).

Alma recognized the virtue of the word, or its incredible power to touch the hearts of the people. An example from the life of the Savior illustrates this principle. During His earthly ministry, Jesus was filled with the Spirit of God, and so it was natural that the spiritually hungry were drawn to Him. In Him, they satisfied their yearnings. Jesus, in turn, being a wellspring of the Spirit, sensed each moment when need drew upon that reserve: "And a certain woman, which had an issue of blood twelve years...when she had heard of Jesus, came in the press behind, and touched his garment. For she said, If I may touch but his clothes, I shall be whole. And straightway she felt in her body that she was healed. And Jesus, immediately knowing in himself that virtue had gone out of him, turned him about and said, Who touched my clothes?" (Mark 5:25-30).

This episode is meaningful because it gives assurance that in a wonderfully complete manner, God is sensitive to our needs and to our prayers, however small or insignificant they may seem to us. He does hear us, because in conformity to spiritual law, we draw upon the life force, or the virtue, that is the Spirit of God. Every time we call upon God, we are, in effect, touching His garment.

"No man knoweth of (God's) ways, save it be revealed unto him." (Jacob 4:8). John Taylor echoes this verse. He said: "No matter what ability and talent (we) may possess, all must come under this rule if they wish to know the Father and the Son. If knowledge of them is not obtained through revelation it cannot be obtained at all." ("The Gospel Kingdom," p. 112). The light and knowledge we receive of God is given by revelation, which is a principle that is so basic that it almost requires no definition, because it speaks to our spirits.

Wo unto those who are enslaved by drunkenness, and by selfish indulgence. "Wo unto them that rise up early in the morning, that they may follow strong drink, that continue until night, and wine inflame them!" (2 Nephi 15:11). Those who are intemperate are blinded to the work of the Lord that is before their very eyes. "They regard not the work of the Lord, neither consider the operation of his hands." (2 Nephi 15:12). They are captive because they have no knowledge of God. "Their honorable men are famished, and their multitude dried up with thirst." (2 Nephi 15:13).

Their condition is contrasted to God's exalted state. "Therefore, hell hath enlarged herself, and opened her mouth without measure; and their glory, and their multitude, and their pomp, and he that rejoiceth, shall descend into it. And the mean (or common) man shall be brought down, and the mighty man shall be humbled, and the eyes of the lofty shall be humbled." (2 Nephi 15:14-15). But "the Lord of Hosts will be exalted in judgment, and God that is holy shall be sanctified in righteousness." (2 Nephi 15:16).

The Lord is patient and long-suffering, and yet extends His arm of mercy long after the faint-hearted have given up. When Elijah complained to the Lord that "the children of Israel have forsaken thy covenant, thrown down thine altars, and slain thy prophets with the sword; and I, even I only, am left; and they seek my life to take it away," He responded: "Yet I have left me seven thousand in Israel, all the knees which have not bowed unto Baal, and every mouth which hath not kissed him." (1 Kings 19:14 & 18).

Joseph Fielding Smith, Jr. declared: "The greatest crime in all this world is to lead men and women away from true principles." (C.R., 4/1951). The following story illustrates the level of brotherly kindliness, human decency, and concern that is expected of each of us, and particularly of members of the church.

Before Fiorello La Guardia became mayor of New York City, he was a magistrate. One day there appeared before him a man accused of stealing a loaf of bread. Upon questioning, the man explained that he'd committed the crime to feed his family, for they were starving. Whereupon, La Guardia dismissed the case, and sentenced all present in the courtroom to pay a fine for living in a city where a man needed to steal to feed his family.

The Lord illustrated the gospel principle of concern for the welfare of others, when He said: "I am the bread of life: He that cometh to me shall never hunger; and he that believeth on me shall never thirst." (John 6:35). In the Eternal Court of Justice, what will be the penalty for our failure to provide others with the Bread of Life, or for feeding them stale, or moldy, or otherwise unwholesome bread?

Lyman Abbott said: "The brotherhood of man is an integral part of Christianity no less than the Fatherhood of God; and to deny the one is no less infidel than to deny the other." ("Christianity and Social Problems," p. 369). Said Thomas Carlyle: "The mystic bond of brotherhood makes all men one," echoing the words of Epictetus: "The universe is but one great city, full of beloved ones, divine and human, by nature endeared to each other."

The covenants we make with our Father in Heaven introduce us to Godliness because they reflect His attributes. God is moral, so He gives us the Covenant of Chastity; He has charity, so He commands us to love Him and each other. God is disciplined, so He gives us the Law of Obedience; because He is a righteous steward, He gives us the Law of Consecration. Because He loves His less fortunate children, He gives us the Law of the Fast. Because His is a perfected, resurrected body, He gives us the Word of Wisdom. Because He is omniscient, He gives us the commandment to seek knowledge. In consequence of the Gift of His Son, He gives us the Law of Sacrifice. Because He rested from His labors on the seventh day, He gives us the Law of the Sabbath.

God is our Father, and He is perfect in every way. He could give us everything He has, but what He is, we must earn for ourselves, as we struggle to overcome adversity and gain self-mastery. Our covenants help us to focus our efforts to become as He is. This is the purpose of the covenants we make with Him. If it were not possible to become as God is, covenants would be unnecessary.

The only motive strong enough to encourage the exercise of self-control required by the gospel of Jesus Christ is love of God and each other. There is a contrast between those who are stiff-necked, and those who have humility. The latter enjoy the companionship of the Holy Spirit or Holy Ghost, "which maketh manifest unto the children of men, according to their faith." (Jarom 1:4). Perhaps a stiff neck prevents us from looking up to Heavenly Father for guidance, over to priesthood leaders for counsel, around to seek out those in need, or down in an attitude of humility.

Joseph F. Smith declared: "No man need fear in his heart when he is conscious of having lived up to the principles of truth and righteousness as God has required it at his hands, according to his best knowledge and understanding." (C.R., 4/1903). When we are diligent in our obedience, our agency enjoys its greatest expression. This is one of the hardest things for the unconverted to understand.

"Ask, and ye shall receive; knock, and it shall be opened unto you." (V. 7). Wo unto those who do not feel the need to receive instruction from God. (See 2 Nephi 28:27). The Savior taught: "He that receiveth my law, and doeth it, the same is my disciple." (D&C 41:5). Blessings that follow true discipleship have a performance cost. "Blessed are those which hunger and thirst after righteousness, for they shall be filled." (Matthew 5:6). Receiving the Law of Christ seems to be an ongoing process. As the Psalmist wrote: "Thou preparest a table before me in the presence of mine enemies; thou anointest my head with oil; my cup runneth over." (Psalms 23:5).

The challenge of individuals and society is not that they receive too much revelation, but that they receive too little. They also look in all the wrong places. Throughout the Bible, the prophets repeatedly warned Israel against dalliances with astrologers, exorcists, familiar spirits, magicians, sorcerers, and witches, and in participating in divinations, enchantments, and other activities that solicit the intervention of evil spirits. Isaiah mocked those who relied on such, when he said: "Thou art wearied in the multitude of thy counsels. Let now the astrologers, the stargazers, the monthly prognosticators, stand up, and save thee from these things that shall come upon thee. Behold, they shall be as stubble; the fire shall burn them; they shall not deliver themselves from the power of the flame; there shall not be a coal to warm at, nor fire to sit before it." (Isaiah 47:13-14).

On one occasion the Prophet Joseph Smith asked: "Does it remain for a people who never had faith enough to call down one scrap of revelation from heaven, and for all they have now are indebted to the faith of another people who lived hundreds and thousands of years before them, does it remain for them to say how much God has spoken and how much he has not spoken?" (H.C., 11:17-18).

Another time, he declared: "We shall at last have to come to this conclusion, whatever we may think of revelation, that without it we can neither know nor understand anything of God, or the devil." (H.C., 3:391-392). The doctrine of The Book of Mormon attests to that fact. By the Spirit, Nephi taught revelatory truths about both God and the devil that are startling, but are vital to our understanding if we are to negotiate successfully the dangerous passage through mortality.

Joseph Smith said: "I thank God that I have got this old book (as he held up the Bible) but I thank him more for the gift of the Holy Ghost. I have got the oldest book in the world, but I (also) have the oldest book in my heart, even the gift of the Holy Ghost." ("Teachings," p. 349).

The Lord explained the process to Joseph Smith. He asked: "He that is ordained of me and sent forth to preach the word of truth by the Comforter, in the Spirit of truth, doth he preach it by the Spirit of truth or some other way? And if it be by some other way it is not of God. And again, he that receiveth the word of truth, doth he receive it by the Spirit of truth or some other way? If it be some other way it is not of God." (D&C 50:17-20). As Paul taught, the key to gospel knowledge is personal revelation, and "let him be accursed who preaches any other gospel." (Galatians 1:8-12). "That which is of God is light; and he that receiveth light, and continueth in God, receiveth more light: and that light groweth brighter and brighter until the perfect day." (D&C 50:24).

# Section 5
## (Received prior to the organization of the church).

This revelation was given in response to the request of Martin Harris to be one of the Three Witnesses. Harris had repented of his folly, reported in D&C 3:2, in July 1828. Now, he desired "a witness at (the Lord's) hand." (V. 1).

Those whom the missionaries teach are converted, not by witnessing miracles, or by the examination of records, but by the Spirit. If the world had physically handled the plates, it would have proven nothing. All the records, including those from which The Book of Mormon were translated, are now in the possession of God, Who said: "I (will) preserve the words which thou hast not read, until I shall see fit in mine own wisdom to reveal all things unto the children of men." (2 Nephi 27:22).

When He decides that the time is right, He will reveal "many great and important things pertaining to the kingdom of God." (9th Article of Faith). But He will do it in His own way, very likely through the instrumentality of His prophet, who is the presiding authority of His church. The undeserved and unsupportable ridicule that the church has suffered at the hands of its detractors through the years suggests that it is very unlikely that He would ever offer up the sacred records themselves to be scrutinized, analyzed, criticized, and rationalized by pompous doctors and professors of religion clothed in the robes of the false priesthood, and cloistered in the ivory towers of academia.

"Hugh Nibley argued: "You cannot prove the genuineness of any document to one who has decided not to accept it. When a man asks for proof we can be pretty sure that proof is the last thing in the world he really wants. His request is thrown out as a challenge, and the chances are that he has no intention of being shown up. After all these years, the Bible itself is still not proven to those who do not choose to accept it. So The Book of Mormon as an 'unproven' book finds itself in good company." ("An Approach to The Book of Mormon," p. 2).

However, with the reaffirmation of the Law of Witnesses, the Lord once again has chosen the weak things of the world to "stand as (witnesses) of these things." (V. 3). Joseph had made a covenant with God that he would sustain that law, and so would not show the plates to unauthorized persons, no matter what their intentions might have been. In the meantime, Joseph was admonished to focus all his energies on his "first gift" and complete the inspired translation of the records with which he had been entrusted. (V. 4).

For "woe shall come unto the inhabitants of the earth," said the Lord, "if they will not hearken unto my words." (V. 5). "Wo" is a condition of deep suffering that is the result of misfortune and affliction, or grief and calamity. Our lives are days of probation, of testing, or of putting to the proof our declared values. The gospel of "repentance is (always available) unto them that are under condemnation and under the curse of a broken law." (Moroni 8:24).

If we successfully complete our probationary trial, we shall escape the ordained consequences of disobedience. Therefore, the Lord told Joseph that it would be critical that "hereafter (he should) be ordained and go forth and deliver (the Lord's) words unto the children of men," that the gospel might be written in their hearts. (V. 6).

The Savior said: "If they will not believe my words, they would not believe you, my servant Joseph, if it were possible that you should show them all these things, which I have committed unto you." (V. 7). The Lord will not indulge the prurient interest of those who only want theological titillation to satisfy their wicked and adulterous curiosity. "Critics of the Book of Mormon often remark sarcastically that it is a great pity that the golden plates have disappeared, since they would conveniently prove Joseph Smith's story.

Of course, they would do nothing of the sort. The presence of the plates would only prove that there were plates, and no more. It would not prove that Nephites had written them, or that an angel had brought them, or that they had been translated by the gift and power of God, and we can be sure that scholars would quarrel about the writing on them for generations without coming to any agreement, exactly as they have done with the Bible. If Joseph Smith had retained possession of the plates following his translation, it would have had a very disruptive effect on the progress of the Restoration, and it would have proven nothing.

On the other hand, a far more impressive claim is put forth when the whole work is given to the world in what is claimed to be a divinely inspired translation. In this case, any cause or pretext for disagreement and speculation about the text is reduced to an absolute minimum. It is a text for all the world to read and understand, and (as a gift of God) it is far more miraculous than any gold plates would be." (High Nibley, "An Approach to The Book of Mormon," p. 17-18). To sum it up, Heavenly Father is more interested in converting than in convincing, more concerned with faith than fault-finding, more involved in pure and undefiled religion than in cold and hard rationalism, drawn more to testimony than to those who trash His word, more impressed with meekness than with murmuring, and finds humility rather than hubris more effective in building character. He is less impressed by those who let intellect do for intelligence.

"Oh, this unbelieving and stiff-necked generation. Mine anger is kindled against them." (V. 8). It may be that stiff-neckedness is characterized by a skin so thick and rigid that extraordinary means become necessary to penetrate it in order to touch the spirit. Jarom drew a contrast between those who are stiff-necked, and those who have faith. The latter, he wrote, have access to the Holy Spirit or Holy Ghost, "which maketh manifest unto the children of men, according to their faith." (Jarom 1:4). Perhaps a stiff neck prevents us from looking up to Heavenly Father for guidance, over to priesthood leaders for counsel, around to seek out those in need, or down in an attitude of humility and prayer.

Only when our hearts are softened, does the whole meaning of the Law snap into focus: It is the Atonement, "every whit pointing to that great and last sacrifice; (which) will be the Son of God." (Alma 34:14). He brings "salvation to all those who (should) believe on his name; this being the intent of this last sacrifice." The blood of the Savior will redeem all who exercise "faith unto repentance." (Alma 34:15.)

"Thus, mercy can satisfy the demands of justice, and encircles them in the arms of safety, while he that exercises no faith unto repentance is exposed to the whole law of the demands of justice" and the anger of the Lord; "therefore only unto him that has faith unto repentance is brought about the great and eternal plan of redemption" offered by a compassionate God. (Alma 34:6). Because of His infinite love, and His desire to be merciful to His children, the Lord assured Joseph: "This generation shall have my word through...the testimony of three of my servants, whom I shall call and ordain, unto whom I will show these things, and they shall go forth with my words that are given through you." (V. 10-11).

The witnesses, the Lord said, "shall know of a surety that these things are true, for from heaven will I declare it unto them. I will give them power that they may behold and view these things as they are." (V. 12-13). With power from above, they were charged with the responsibility to testify to the world, precisely because the state of the wicked is so terrible, inasmuch as they live outside the protective vale of redemption. "So complete is the darkness prevailing in the minds of these spirits," said Bruce R. McConkie, "so wholly has gospel light been shut out of their consciences, that they know little or nothing of the Plan of Salvation. Hell is literally a place of outer darkness, that hates light, buries truth, and revels in iniquity." ("Mormon Doctrine," p. 551-552, see 2 Nephi 28:16).

But, just as Isaiah had done, these Latter-day witnesses would "wait upon the Lord," and trust in His strength. (2 Nephi 18:17). Isaiah had contrasted his role as a witness with the false messages the people were then receiving from evil sources. They were in the habit of consulting with "familiar spirits" or diviners of the occult, and with "wizards that peep and mutter," in the manner of sorcerers and necromancers who used ventriloquism to call forth so-called "messages" from departed spirits. (2 Nephi 18:19). Isaiah's descriptions aptly describe the machinations of the wicked in the Last Days.

In effect, Isaiah was asking if it were not better for the people to "seek unto their God for the living to hear from the dead." (V. 19). They should look to the teachings of the law, and to the testimony of living witnesses. "If they speak not according to this word, it is because there is no light in them." (V. 20).

If men and women do not speak from the vantage point of authority, it is because they do not have the Spirit. Such individuals are "hardly bested," or hard pressed, and "hungry," or spiritually malnourished. In this condition, they tend to "fret themselves," or to be enraged, and curse God. (V. 21). Such individuals "shall look unto the earth and behold trouble, and darkness, dimness of anguish, and shall be driven to darkness." (V. 22).

Even as the wicked grope about blindly, the Lord described the Restoration as "the beginning of the rising up and the coming forth of my church out of the wilderness - clear as the moon, and fair as the sun, and terrible as an army with banners." (V. 14, see Song of Solomon 6:10). The Savior indicated to the Nephites that in the day when the latter-day Restoration would burst upon the world stage, it would be of such significance "that kings (would) shut their mouths." (3 Nephi 21:8). Its destiny would be to become the greatest power the world has ever known. "For in that day," declared the Savior, "shall the Father work a work, which shall be a great and marvelous work among them." (3 Nephi 21:9).

"And the testimony of three witnesses will I send forth of my word." (V. 15, see D&C 6:28). "The (external) evidence that will prove or disprove The Book of Mormon does not exist. When, indeed, is a thing proven? Only when an individual has accumulated in his own consciousness enough observations, impressions, reasonings, and feelings to satisfy him personally that it is so. The same evidence that convinces one expert may leave another completely unsatisfied. The impressions that build up the definite proof are themselves nontransferable." (Hugh Nibley, "Since Cumorah," p. viii). That compelling testimony, that comes only from a spiritual witness, may only be described as great and marvelous.

For "whosoever believeth on my words," promised the Lord, "them will I visit with the manifestation of my Spirit; and they shall be born of me, even of water and of the Spirit." (V. 16). There are three levels of witness: Joseph Smith the Prophet, the Three Witnesses, and the unimpeachable Witness of the Spirit. By the power of these separate and individual witnesses, "every member of the church is entitled to know that God our Heavenly Father lives. They are also entitled to know that Jesus Christ is the Savior and Redeemer of the world, and that He has opened the door for us, that we, through our individual acts, may receive salvation and exaltation and dwell once again in the presence of our Heavenly Father." (Henry D. Taylor, C.R., 4/1971).

However, "seeing, even the Savior, does not leave as deep an impression in the mind as (does the third tier of witness, that is) the testimony of the Holy Ghost. The impressions on the soul that come from the Holy Ghost are far more significant than a vision. It is where spirit speaks to spirit, and the imprint upon the soul is far more difficult to erase." (Joseph Fielding Smith, Jr., "Seek Ye Earnestly," p. 213-214).

Nevertheless, Joseph was told: "You must wait yet a little while, for ye are not yet ordained." (V. 17). He would not receive the authority of the priesthood until May and June, 1829. A leader of the Reformation in America, Roger Williams, had over a century earlier prophetically written: "There is no regularly constituted church on earth, nor any person authorized to administer any church ordinance; nor can there be until new apostles are sent by the Great Head of the church, for Whose Coming I am seeking." (William Cullen Bryant, "Picturesque America," p. 502).

The priesthood authority for which Roger Williams yearned can be both a blessing and a curse, for the testimony of those who have been born again will "go forth unto the condemnation of this generation if they harden their hearts against them." (V. 18). "For a desolating scourge shall go forth among the inhabitants of the earth, and shall continue to be poured out from time to time, if they repent not, until the earth is empty, and the inhabitants thereof are consumed away and utterly destroyed by the brightness of my coming." (V. 19).

From a strictly rational perspective, one writer of the modern age, has written: "I suspect that AIDS may not be nature's pre-eminent display of power. Whether the human race can actually maintain a population of five billion or more without a crash with a hot virus remains an open question. The answer lies hidden in the labyrinth of tropical ecosystems. AIDS is the revenge of the rain forest. It may be only the beginning." (Richard Preston, "The Hot Zone," p. 408-409).

In the Last Days, "plagues shall go forth, and they shall not be taken from the earth" until the Lord has completed His work. (D&C 84:97). "And thus, with the sword and by bloodshed the inhabitants of the earth shall mourn; and with famine, and plague, and earthquake, and the thunder of heaven, and the fierce and vivid lightning also, shall the inhabitants of the earth be made to feel the wrath, and indignation, and chastening hand of an Almighty God, until the consumption decreed hath made a full end of all nations." (D&C 87:6). As Brigham Young declared, when people refuse the gospel, their "land will eventually become desolate, forlorn, and forsaken" as nature refuses her bounties.

Abba Eban observed: "As Isaiah understood, there can be no redemption for man unless he conquers self-deification. He must abandon the worship of his own creations, and liberate himself from his lust for power, avarice, domination, and the cult of the state. There can be no redemption until man recognizes his moral obligations as transcendent and divine.

No form of government," he declared, "no level of material well-being, will save man. He will be redeemed only when 'towers fall, and Jerusalem triumphs over Babylon. What is at stake, finally, is not only intelligence, but feeling. Man has to change his heart. Salvation, the prophets tell us, is preconditioned by repentance. Therefore, the redeeming act of God waits upon man's initiative." ("My People: The Story of The Jews," p. 59-60).

In the Last Days, as the Spirit is withdrawn, "there shall be heard of fires, and tempests, and vapors of smoke in foreign lands; and there shall also be heard of wars, rumors of wars, and earthquakes in divers places." (Mormon 8:29-30). These are conditions with which Moroni was intimately familiar. He knew that the wrath of God requires the destruction of the wicked, and that our day would be frighteningly similar to the last days of the Nephites. Perhaps it is because the scriptures speaks to our common feeling that they are so convincing.

David O. McKay taught: "Every person who lives in this world wields an influence, whether for good or for evil. It is not what he says; it is not what he does. It is what he is. Every person radiates what he or she really is. It is what we are and what we radiate that affects the people around us. As individuals, we must think nobler thoughts. We must not encourage vile thoughts or low aspirations. We shall radiate them if we do. If we think noble thoughts, if we encourage and cherish noble aspirations, there will be that radiation when we meet people, especially when we associate with them." ("Man May Know for Himself," p. 108).

"Act now, before it is too late, urged Spencer W. Kimball. "Now is the time to chart the course of action you will follow tomorrow and next week and next year. Now is the time to commit yourself to be as Abraham, to follow the Lord, to refuse to procrastinate, to repent of those sins you have committed, to begin to keep those commandments you have been failing to live. Determine now to attend priesthood and sacrament meetings every Sabbath, to pay your tithing faithfully, sustain in very deed the programs of the church, visit the temple often, give service in the organizations, and keep your actions constructive, your attitudes wholesome. Remember that Abraham sought for his appointment to the priesthood. He did not wait for God to come to him; he sought diligently through prayer and obedient living to learn the will of God. Here, then, is the challenge the Lord gives every returned missionary, every single man and woman, every father and mother in the church: 'Go ye, therefore, and do the works of Abraham." (D&C 132:32). ("Ensign," 6/1975). The means of escape is the gospel of Jesus Christ. Keep the commandments, and avoid punishment. (See Alma 37:13).

In his entreaty to Joseph to be obedient, the Lord acknowledged the reality that His prophet was only 23 years old at the time, and he was inclined to place his confidence in his elders. "And now I command you, my servant Joseph, to repent and walk more uprightly before me, and to yield to the persuasions of men no more." (V. 22).

One of the terrible consequences of our fascination with Babylon is spiritual insensitivity. Isaiah foresaw the Last Days, when he wrote: Stay yourselves, and wonder; cry ye out, and cry: they are drunken, but not with wine; they stagger, but not with strong drink. For the Lord hath poured out upon you the spirit of deep sleep, and hath closed your eyes: the prophets, and your rulers, and seers hath he covered. And the vision of all is become unto you as the words of a book that is sealed." (Isaiah 29:9-11).

When the Lord commanded Joseph: "Repent and walk more uprightly before me, and yield to the persuasion of men no more," He knew His young prophet could do so with total and unwavering commitment. (V. 21). "Be firm in keeping the commandments wherewith I have commanded you," the Lord continued, "and if you do this, behold I grant unto you eternal life, even if you should be slain." (V. 22).

Perhaps this was a foreshadowing. Joseph may have begun to realize that he would some day be required to seal his testimony with his own blood. (See Hebrews 9:16-17). Joseph would later write: "I know what I say. I understand my mission and business. God Almighty is my shield, and what can man do if God is my friend. I shall not be sacrificed until my time comes. Then I shall be offered freely." ("Teachings," p. 274).

We read that, at times during the history of the Jaredites, "all the prophets who prophesied of the destruction of the people (were) put to death." (Ether 11:5). Before their martyrdom, "they had testified that a great curse should come upon the land, and also upon the people, and that there should be a great destruction among them, such as one as never had been upon the face of the earth, and their bones should become as heaps of earth upon the face of the land except they should repent of their wickedness." (Ether 11:6). Wars, contentions, famines and pestilence followed, "such as one as never had been known upon the face of the earth." (Ether 11:7).

Then and now, "God doth not walk in crooked paths, neither doth he turn to the right hand nor to the left, neither doth he vary from that which he hath said, therefore his paths are straight, and his course is one eternal round." (D&C 3:2). In other words, it is ordained that identical results always flow from the same causes.

Having established the standard of commitment that He would require from His Special Witnesses, the Lord said concerning Martin Harris: "He exalts himself and does not humble himself sufficiently before me; but if he will bow down before me, and humble himself in mighty prayer and faith, in the sincerity of his heart, then will I grant unto him a view of the things which he desires to see." (V. 24).

An appeal to vanity is Satan's way of turning our minds against the Plan of Salvation. "I" and "Mine" are usually accompanied by an unbended knee. Neal Maxwell wrote: "To the humble, the simpleness and the easiness of the way are glad realities; to the crowded, ego filled minds of proud men, the sudden burst of light from a spiritual sunrise is irritating rather than awesome, and causes them to blink rather than to stare in reverent awe." ("That My Family Should Partake," p. 82). The counsel specifically given to Martin Harris is applicable to all: "Beware of pride, lest ye become as the Nephites of old." (D&C 38:39).

"And then (Martin Harris) shall say unto the people of this generation: Behold I have seen the things which the Lord hath shown unto Joseph Smith, Jun., and I know of a surety that they are true, for I have seen them, for they have been shown unto me by the power of God and not of man. And I the Lord command him, my servant Martin Harris, that he shall say no more unto them concerning these things, except he shall say: I have seen them, and they have been shown unto me by the power of God." (V. 25-26).

At the beginning of The Book of Mormon, The Testimony of Three Witnesses reads in part: "Be it known unto all nations, kindreds, tongues, and people, unto whom this work shall come: that we, through the grace of God the Father, and our Lord Jesus Christ, have seen the plates which contain this record.... Wherefore we know of a surety that the work is true.... And they have been shown unto us by the power of God, and not of man." (The Testimony of Three Witnesses).

The Lord warned Joseph: "There are many that lie in wait to destroy thee from off the face of the earth; and for this cause, that thy days may be prolonged, I have given unto thee these commandments." (V. 33). Two years later, the Lord declared to Joseph: "Let them, therefore, who are among the Gentiles flee unto Zion, and let them who be of Judah flee unto Jerusalem, unto the mountains of the Lord's house. Go ye out from among the nations, even from Babylon, from the midst of wickedness, which is spiritual Babylon." (D&C 133:12-14).

For the wicked "shall surely gather together against thee, (but they) shall fall." (3 Nephi 22:15). In effect, the Lord was saying not to worry, for he would always be there to offer rest for the weary. "No weapon that is formed against thee shall prosper," He reassured the Nephites, "and every tongue that shall revile against thee in judgment thou shalt condemn." (3 Nephi 22:17). The message that the Lord delivered to the Nephites must have been comforting to Joseph, who knew that those words would "be of great worth unto (him) in the last days; for in that day (he would) understand them; wherefore, for (his) good (had the Lord) written them." (2 Nephi 25:7-8). "And if thou art faithful in keeping my commandments," Joseph was promised, "thou shalt be lifted up at the last day." (V. 35).

# Section 6
## (Received prior to the organization of the church).

Doctrine & Covenants Sections 6, 8, 9, and 10 help to define, describe, explain, and illustrate the spirit of revelation. In Section 6, the Lord spoke to Oliver Cowdery through Joseph Smith in order to assure him that he had, in fact, been receiving revelation. Verses 1-5 are identical to D&C 12:1-5, and D&C 14: 1-5. Verses 1-9 are identical to D&C 11:1-9. The repetition only stresses the universal importance of these verses. (See Mosiah 5:1-3).

"A great and marvelous work is about to come forth among the children of men." (V. 1). Moroni urged those who read The Book of Mormon to recognize how merciful God has been to His children from the time of Adam to the present day. (Moroni 10:3). As we ponder this in our hearts, it is easier to understand why God would give us such "a marvelous work and a wonder" as a companion body of scripture to the Bible, to testify independently that Jesus is the Christ, the Savior of the World. (Isaiah 29:14).

Moroni taught how beautiful in its simplicity is The Book of Mormon test of authenticity. The way of the world is to scrutinize from every rational angle, to organize committees charged with the responsibility to analyze data, compile reports, develop hypotheses and paradigms, reach compromise, and finally publish conclusions. But "O that cunning plan of the evil one! O the vainness, and the frailties, and the foolishness of men! When they are learned they think they are wise, and they hearken not unto the counsel of God, for they set it aside, supposing they know of themselves, wherefore, their wisdom is foolishness and it profiteth them not. And they shall perish. But to be learned is good if they hearken unto the counsels of God." (2 Nephi 9:29-30).

An appeal to vanity is Satan's way of turning our minds against the Plan of Salvation. (See 2 Nephi 14:22, 28:4 & 14). "I" and "Mine" are usually accompanied by an unbended knee. Neal Maxwell wrote: "To the humble, the simpleness and the easiness of the way are glad realities; to the crowded, ego filled minds of proud men, the sudden burst of light from a spiritual sunrise is irritating rather than awesome, and causes them to blink rather than to stare in reverent awe." ("That My Family Should Partake," p. 82).

The approach that Moroni suggested, however, that is necessary to come to a knowledge of the truth of all things, is one of meekness, lowliness of heart, and humility. It is truly wonderful that in our day of rational societal pessimism, this fresh approach should be suggested as the critical key to understanding.

"Behold, the field is white already to harvest; therefore, whoso desireth to reap let him thrust in his sickle with his might, and reap while the day lasts, that he may treasure up for his soul everlasting salvation in the kingdom of God." (V. 3). The Lord numbers His children by their willingness to accept covenants. The missionary efforts of members of the church in the conversion process is really quite simple. Just find those who are the elect, and teach them by the Spirit. "And ye are called to bring to pass the gathering of mine elect," declared the Lord, "for mine elect hear my voice and harden not their hearts." (D&C 29:7).

When the missionaries are faithful, their continuing focus of attention on their spiritually hungry brethren will eventually bring them into complete harmony with the attributes of Heavenly Father, Whose concern is for all of His children. "And ye shall be even as I am, and I am even as the Father, and the Father and I are one," said the Savior. (3 Nephi 28:10).

"Therefore, if ye will ask of me you shall receive; if you will knock it shall be opened unto you." (V. 5). The Lord does not ask us to subvert the way in which we express our faith. He only asks that we establish a spiritual rapport with Him by developing a relationship that is initiated, and then sustained, through intimate conversation. We do not draw near to God by constructing eloquent prayers or elaborate edifices in which to recite them by rote.

The world's misconception of the nature of God is characterized by its secularization of the divine model, and was first represented by the ancient ziggurat of Babel, that the people constructed in the false hope that the top thereof would reach all the way to heaven. (See Genesis 11:4). But Heavenly Father's children cannot find Him that way.

Missionaries in all ages have been shocked by the distorted understanding of those who are spiritually illiterate. B.H. Roberts related an experience he had as a young elder while serving in the Southern States Mission: "As Brother Palmer and I stepped into the church," he recalled, "we found the pastor engaged in prayer, and what was my surprise to hear him say: 'O Lord, help us to understand that we have enough of Thy word; that the canon of scripture is full. Help us to believe, O Lord, that the awful voice of prophecy will no more be heard; help us to believe that revelation has ceased, that Thou wilt no more speak to man.' Well, thought I, there is a wide difference between the ideas contained in that person's prayer and what we are going to preach!" (Quoted in "Defender of The Faith," p. 108).

Expressions of false doctrine pepper memorized prayers with the elements of apostasy. Some believe that God is a Spirit. Others believe in their pre-destination. For many, Sunday is the only day of worshipful prayer. Their weekday activities are uninfluenced by belief in God, for whatever faith they possess lies dormant. When religious thoughts are confined to the Sabbath, they can become sterile, or devoid of vitality. Their expressions may be impotent, or without power. With this in mind, James taught: "Faith without works is dead, being alone." (James 2:14). Such a stylistic ritual in prayer is astonishing to those who are accustomed to conversations with God that are on more intimate levels.

As Truman Madsen so keenly observed: "At one level, we all indulge the daily clichés and more or less mean them: 'Forgive us,' or Help us to overcome our weaknesses.' At a deeper level, we voice actual present feelings, even when they are raw, ugly, miserable ones: 'Father, I feel awful,' or 'I am racked with anxiety.' But there is an even deeper level, the inmost of which often defies words, even feeling words. This level may be likened to what the scriptures call 'groanings which cannot be uttered.' (Romans 8:26). Turned upward, they become the most powerful prayer-thrusts of all. There is a wordless center in each of us." ("Christ & The Inner Life," p. 17-18).

"Seek not for riches, but for wisdom, and behold, the mysteries of God shall be unfolded unto you, and then shall ye be made rich." (V. 7). Temporal wealth is by far the number one criterion of success when measured by the standard of the world, but the Lord explains here that religious truth that can only be known by revelation is more valuable, because it has the power to propel us toward eternal life in the Kingdom of God.

"You shall be the means of doing much good in this generation." (V. 8). There is a timelessness to the question: How can we to establish the church? Neal A. Maxwell said: "In the Last Days, discipleship will be lived in crescendo." (C.R., 10/1985). Our actions will swell the chorus of voices shouting "Hallelujah," and will significantly hasten the millennial reign of the Lord. B.H. Roberts once said: "The Latter-day Saints are the white hot sparks struck off the Divine Anvil of God," destined to kindle a fire that will burn brightly to celestialize the earth, so that it might worthily receive its rightful King.

True disciples commit the Thirteen Articles of Faith to life, as well as to memory, and actively practice their religion. John Taylor observed: "There are some Christian people in this world who, if a man were poor or hungry, would say, let us pray for him. I would suggest a little different regimen for a person in this condition; rather take him a bag of flour and a little beef or pork. A few such comforts will do him more good than your prayers." (Quoted in "Companion to The Old Testament," p. 192). As Edward Bulwer-Lytton observed: "When a person is down in the world, an ounce of help is better than a pound of preaching." Socrates taught that we must know ourselves. Cicero believed that we must control ourselves. But the principles of the gospel embrace a higher standard wherein we give of ourselves. Those who establish the church are committed to internalize the demands of discipleship in just this way.

It is for this reason that Joseph and Oliver were commanded: "Say nothing but repentance unto this generation; keep my commandments, and assist to bring forth my work, according to my commandments." (V. 9). All teaching should be geared to motivate us to repentance. "Behold," said the Lord, "this is my doctrine - whosoever repenteth and cometh unto me, the same is my church." (D&C 10:67).

"Behold thou hast a gift, and blessed art thou because of thy gift. Remember it is sacred and cometh from above." (V. 10, see v. 25). Oliver's was the gift of revelation and the gift of Aaron, to be a spokesperson for the Prophet. (See D&C 89:3). The fulfillment of the exercise of this gift occurred on April 30, 1830, when Oliver Cowdery preached the first public discourse in this dispensation.

"And if thou wilt inquire, thou shalt know mysteries which are great and marvelous; therefore thou shalt exercise thy gift, that thou mayest find out mysteries, that thou mayest bring many to the knowledge of the truth, yea, convince them of the error of their ways." (V. 11). The key to our understanding of the mysteries of God is the spiritual illumination of our minds.

On the subject of secular Christianity and the New Dispensation, B.H. Roberts once wrote: "In their efforts to clarify (their consideration of Christ) they were often simply multiplying mirrors and studying angles without increasing the light. The New Dispensation brought a flood of light that did not simply replace the darkness, but illuminated elements and principles, and their relationships, that heretofore had been (only) dimly perceived." ("The Truth, The Way, The Life," p. 263).

This revelation must have given Oliver Cowdery a much clearer understanding of the role of the living prophet, seer, and revelator. To his dismay, however, Oliver would learn that people often "will not seek wisdom, neither do they desire that she should rule over them!" Under those circumstances, "how blind and impenetrable are the understandings of the children of men." (Mosiah 8:20).

On the college portals in Moorish Granada (1300 – 1492) were inscribed these lines: "The world is supported by four things, the learning of the wise, the justice of the great, the prayers of the good, and the valor of the brave." The casualties of every gospel dispensation are those who try to let intellect do for intelligence. Such learned ones suppose that they can judge both the truth and the morality of the word of the Lord and of His prophets. In a society of Saints, however, people will gain knowledge and skill by both study and faith, and will not confuse the two.

Oliver was cautioned: "Make not thy gift known unto any save it be those who are of thy faith. Trifle not with sacred things." (V. 12). The rational approach of the world around us is the enemy of faith. Thus, secular humanism and other similar latter day ideologies that compete with gospel principles for our attention destroy faith and are devilish doctrines, subtle though they may be. They are abominable to God because they attempt to thwart the successful implementation of His Plan of Salvation for those who have the faith to believe.

The Savior cautioned the Nephites: "Give not that which is holy unto the dogs, neither cast ye your pearls before swine, lest they trample them under their feet, and turn again and rend you." (3 Nephi 14:6). What could be more sanctified than Jesus Christ, the Holy One of Israel. The seraphim surrounding the throne of God cried one "unto another, and said: Holy, holy, holy, is the Lord of Hosts; and the whole earth is full of his glory." (2 Nephi 16:2). "In the language of Adam, Man of Holiness is his name, and the name of his Only Begotten is the Son of Man (of Holiness), even Jesus Christ." (Moses 6:57).

The point is, that when dealing with topics of the most sacred nature, that by very definition portray Jesus Christ as their centerpiece, it is very important to treat them with the utmost respect. As the Lord taught Joseph Smith: "That which cometh from above is sacred, and must be spoken with care, and by constraint of the Spirit and in this there is no condemnation." (D&C 63:64).

J.S.T. Matthew 7:9-11 records the words of the Savior: "Go ye into the world, saying unto all, repent, for the kingdom of heaven has come nigh unto you. And the mysteries of the kingdom ye shall keep within yourselves; for it is not meet to give that which is holy unto the dogs; neither cast ye your pearls unto swine, lest they trample them under their feet. For the world cannot receive that which ye, yourselves, are not able to bear; wherefore ye shall not give your pearls unto them, lest they turn again and rend you."

When we realize that the mysteries of the kingdom are the saving principles and ordinances of the gospel of Jesus Christ that can only be spiritually discerned, we better understand why those who are unprepared to receive that which is before them would ignore the Light of Christ or the influence of the Holy Ghost. They would figuratively trample the principles, the ordinances, and the Savior Himself, under their feet.

"Even the very God of Israel do men trample under their feet," wrote Nephi. "I say, trample under their feet, but I would speak in other words - they set him at naught, and hearken not to the voice of his counsels." (1 Nephi 19:7). "These are they who are not valiant in the testimony of Jesus; wherefore, they obtain not the crown over the kingdom of our God." (D&C 76:79). "To be valiant in the testimony of Jesus is to take the Lord's side on every issue. It is to think what He thinks, to believe what He believes, to say what He would say, and to do what He would do." (Bruce R. McConkie, C.R., 10/1974).

"There is no gift greater than the gift of salvation." (V. 13). The Prophet Joseph Smith said that salvation consists of our being placed beyond the power of our enemies, meaning the enemies of our progression, such as dishonesty, greediness, lying, immorality, and other vices. (Sermon delivered at the Nauvoo temple site on May 21, 1843. (Sermon delivered at the Nauvoo temple site on May 21, 1843. Sources: Joseph Smith diary (Willard Richards), Howard and Martha Jane Knowlton Coray Notebook, Franklin D. Richards "Scriptural Items," and James Burgess Notebook. See "Teachings," p. 297-298). There is no greater expression of empowerment than to internalize these characteristics of the divine model.

"As often as thou hast inquired (of me) thou hast received instruction of my Spirit." (V. 14). In a variety of ways, Heavenly Father has always provided direction for His children. The Nephites first were given the Rod of Iron, or the word of God, that would lead them along a strait and narrow path directly to the Tree of Life. (1 Nephi 19-20, & 30). Soon thereafter, they were given the "Liahona," which is an old word from the language of the fathers, needing to be interpreted by Alma as "a compass." (Alma 37:38).

Speaking to our day, he taught: "It is as easy to give heed to the word of Christ (our compass) which will point you to a straight course to eternal bliss, as it was for our fathers to give heed to this compass, which would point unto them a straight course to the promised land. Do not let us be slothful (or move slowly) because of the easiness of the way. Look to God, and live." (Alma 37:38-47).

In all ages of the world, God has raised up prophets to testify of His existence, of His Son, the Redeemer of the World, and of His Plan of Happiness. "Surely the Lord God will do nothing, but he revealeth his secret unto his servants the prophets." (Amos 3:7). Yes, "there is a God in heaven that revealeth secrets, and maketh known...what shall be in the latter days." (Daniel 2:28).

The Lord said of Joseph Smith and Sidney Rigdon: "For by my Spirit will I enlighten them, and by my power will I make known unto them the secrets of my will - yea, even those things which eye has not seen, nor ear heard, nor yet entered into the heart of man." (D&C 76:10). The Latter-day Saints believe "all that God has revealed, all that He does now reveal, and we believe that He will yet reveal many great and important things pertaining to the Kingdom." (8th Article of Faith).

Is the way easy or is it difficult? For the Israelites in the Wilderness of Sinai, it was only necessary that they look upon the Brazen Serpent, the staff of Moses, typifying Christ. "And as many as should look upon that serpent should live, even so as many as should look upon the Son of God, with faith, having a contrite spirit, might live, even unto that life which is eternal." (Helaman 8:13-16)

Today, our trials are no more sophisticated. Noah preached of the Flood. Ezra Taft Benson warned of a flood of pornography that is inundating the world. Moses wrote of the bondage of Israel in Egypt, and Gordon B. Hinckley of the temporal bondage of financial indebtedness, and of the spiritual bondage that comes when we offer up our agency as a sacrifice to the popular idols of the day. Elijah rebuked those who worshiped Baal. Our leaders caution us against spiritual death that comes from the worship of our contemporary gods of wood and of stone. Joseph endured seven years of famine in Egypt. The First Presidency has counseled us since 1937 to have our year's supply, reminding us that Noah preached for 100 years before the floods came.

The Nephites wrote about the depravations of the Band of Gadianton. Today, the Lord cautions us against "the evils and designs which do and will exist in the hearts of conspiring men in the last days." (D&C 89:4). The Old Testament condemned murder; our priesthood leaders expose the deception and damnable heresy of "pro-choice." The dietary code of the Law of Moses set the Israelites apart from their neighbors, just as our Word of Wisdom does for the Saints today. The Apostles warned of unnatural affection, while our prophets condemn "alternative lifestyles" as deviant behavior of the most abominable nature.

The message is the same. "We talk of Christ, we rejoice in Christ, we preach of Christ, we prophesy of Christ, and we write according to our prophecies, that our children may know to what source they may look for a remission of their sins." (2 Nephi 25:26). Christ was, is, and shall ever be "the way, the truth, and the life" of this world. (John 14:6).

"I did enlighten thy mind." (V. 15). Joseph Smith described his and Oliver Cowdery's baptismal experience in these words: "Our minds being now enlightened, we began to have the scriptures laid open to our understandings, and the true meaning and intention of their more mysterious passages revealed unto us in a manner which we never could attain to previously, nor ever before had thought of." (J.S.H. 1:74).

"There is none else save God that knowest thy thoughts and the intents of thy heart." (V. 16). It must have been of great comfort to both Oliver and Joseph, to learn this truth about the nature of God. As Joseph Fielding Smith, Jr. declared: "No power on earth or hell can overthrow or defeat that which God has decreed. Every plan of the adversary will fail, for the Lord knows the secret thoughts of men, and sees the future with a vision clear and perfect, even as though it were in the past." ("Doctrines of Salvation," 1:7-10). "O how great the holiness of our God!" cried Jacob. "For He knoweth all things, and there is not anything save he knows it. Else He would cease to be God, and man could not have faith in him." (2 Nephi 9:20).

Those who are not anchored to the Rock of Jesus Christ, who lack the implicit faith that He is in control of every situation, are built upon a satanic sandlot. Such telestial turf is the devil's domain, and when we venture onto it, we risk losing our way. For such individuals, the gaping gates of hell are open to receive them. The quicksand of secular humanism and other false ideologies lies ready to suck the unwary into the underworld of the adversary.

But Oliver was cautioned that he could gain traction by being "diligent." He was cautioned: "Stand by my servant Joseph, faithfully, in whatsoever difficult circumstances he may be for the world's sake. Admonish him in his faults, and also receive admonition of him. Be patient; be sober; be temperate; have patience, faith, hope and charity." (V. 18-19).

The Lord declared that Oliver must hold fast to the rod of iron. Joseph later gave the assurance that "no unhallowed hand can stop the work from progressing; persecutions may rage, mobs may combine, armies may assemble, calumny may defame, but the truth of God will go forth boldly, nobly, and independent, until it has penetrated every continent, visited every clime, swept every country, and sounded in every ear, 'til the purposes of God shall be accomplished and the Great Jehovah shall say 'The work is done.'" ("The Wentworth Letter," H.C., 4:540).

"Be faithful and diligent in keeping the commandments of God, and I will encircle thee in the arms of my love." (V. 20). It must have been an indescribable experience for Oliver to know on such a deeply personal level that his Savior knew him, and loved him.

Melvin J. Ballard related an experience that might be shared by all those who have received the covenants and hope to enjoy the companionship of the Second Comforter. He said: "I found myself one evening in the dreams of the night in the sacred building, the temple. After a season of prayer and rejoicing, I was informed that I should have the privilege of entering into one of those rooms, to meet a glorious Personage, and, as I entered the door, I saw, seated on a raised platform, the most glorious Being my eyes have ever beheld or that I ever conceived existed in all the eternal worlds. As I approached to be introduced, he arose and stepped towards me with extended arms and he smiled as he softly spoke my name. If I shall live to be a million years old, I shall never forget that smile. He took me in his arms and kissed me, pressed me to his bosom and blessed me, until the marrow of my bones seemed to melt. When he had finished, I fell at his feet, and as I bathed them with my tears and kisses, I saw the prints of the nails in the feet of the Redeemer of the world. The feeling that I had in the presence of Him who hath all things in his hands, to have his love, his affection and his blessing was such that if I ever can receive that of which I had but a foretaste, I would give all I am, all that I ever hope to be, to feel what I then felt." ("Sermons and Missionary Experiences of Melvin Joseph Ballard," p. 156).

The pure love of Christ is an unconditional acceptance of others that is expressed in the following sentiment: "Wouldn't it be nice if, as we tuck our children into bed after particularly stressful days, we could say something like this: I've been watching you, and you are about the most special human being I've ever met. I'm proud to wear your name. I know we had an argument today, but that was behavior. It's the person I love. It's behavior I got bothered with, but not you. I love you unconditionally, not based on achievement, but on you and your potential. I love you very much." (Anonymous).

Jesus Christ is "the light which shineth in darkness, and the darkness comprehendeth it not." (V. 21). The Master called His disciples to a higher plane of spirituality and to a commitment to selfless consecration of effort. He said: "Lay not up for yourselves treasures upon earth, where moth and rust doth corrupt, and thieves break through and steal; But lay up for yourselves treasures in heaven, where neither moth nor rust doth corrupt, and where thieves do not break through nor steal." (3 Nephi 13:19-20). The key is to lose ourselves in service, even as we let the reflected light of Christ shine before our friends and neighbors. (See 3 Nephi 12:16).

The Savior taught: "The light of the body is the eye. If, therefore, thine eye be single, thy whole body shall be full of light." (3 Nephi 13:22). Elsewhere, He promised: "There shall be no darkness in you, and that body which is filled with light comprehendeth all things." (D&C 88:67). He continued: "But if thine eye be evil, thy whole body shall be full of darkness. If, therefore, the light that is in thee be darkness, how great is that darkness!" (3 Nephi 13:23). The influence of Satan that gripped Joseph in the Sacred Grove before his deliverance by God illustrates just how overwhelming that intense darkness can be.

Joseph wrote: "I was seized upon by some power which entirely overcame me, and had such an astonishing influence over me as to bind my tongue so that I could not speak. Thick darkness gathered around me, and it seemed to me for a time as if I were doomed to sudden destruction.... I was ready to sink into despair and abandon myself to destruction - not to an imaginary ruin, but to the power of some actual being from the unseen world." (J.S.H. 1:15-16). We are also reminded of those who lost their way in mists of darkness, in Lehi's Vision of The Tree of Life. (See 1 Nephi 8:23).

"Did I not speak peace to your mind?" (V. 23). Oliver had caught a glimpse of the peace that can bring us into the Rest of the Lord, into a sacred sanctuary from the cares and concerns of the world. (See D&C 20:69). Even as he found himself in the midst of the children of men, who were riotously living telestial lives of the most carnal and sensual nature, Oliver had been able to taste of the goodness of God, and experience the peace that surpasseth understanding. (See Philippians 4:7). "What greater witness can you have than from God?" asked the Lord. (V. 23).

"There are records which contain much of my gospel, which have been kept back because of the wickedness of the people." (V. 26). Mormon said that he could not write "the hundredth part of the things of (his) people." (Words of Mormon 1:5, see Jacob 3:13, & Helaman 3:14). Even though Joseph wrote in his history that the plates at the Hill Cumorah were deposited in the earth in a box fashioned out of stone, other sources indicate that there were many more plates at that site. (See Helaman 3:15). Brigham Young declared that there was a whole room, with plates stacked high against the walls. Together, he said that they would comprise several wagon loads. (J.D. 19:38).

President Young recorded in his journal: "When Joseph got the plates, the angel instructed him to carry them back to the Hill Cumorah, which he did. Oliver says that when he and Joseph went there, the hill opened, and they walked into a cave, in which there was a large and spacious room." Miraculous forces were at work here, for the hill literally opened up before them, and revealed a depository much larger than the simple stone box familiar to Latter-day Saints when visualizing the scene.

President Young continued in his journal: "They laid the plates on the table; it was a large table that stood in the room. Under this table there was a pile of plates as much as two feet high, and there were altogether in this room more plates than probably many wagon loads; they were piled up in the corners and along the walls." ("Readings in L.D.S. Church History," 1:326, quoted in "A Companion to Your Study of The Book of Mormon," p. 21).

"You shall assist in bringing to light, with your gift, those parts of my scriptures which have been hidden because of iniquity." (V. 27). There may be several levels of meaning to this verse. First, the wicked may have the scriptures before their eyes, and yet not recognize them for what they are. Our twenty-first century culture tends to intensify this myopic view. We "tend to fill space, as if what we have, what we are, is not enough. Being affluent, we strangle ourselves with what we can buy, things whose opacity obstructs our ability to see what is really there." (Gretel Erlich, "Under Wyoming's Skies," "The Atlantic Magazine"). Secondly, even the wicked may be familiar with the scriptures, but with understanding that is amiss, because they have wrested them in a twisted and perverted way. Thirdly, the availability of the scriptures may be restricted by God because of widespread unrighteousness.

"And now, behold, I give unto you, and also unto my servant Joseph, the keys of this gift, which shall bring to light this ministry; and in the mouth of two or three witnesses shall every word be established." (V. 28). In 1829, in just over six weeks, Joseph Smith translated the plates on which was recorded the thousand year history of the Nephites. During that process, "through strenuous effort in exercising faith and with the operation of the inspiration of God upon his mind, Joseph obtained the thought represented by the Nephite characters, understood it in the Nephite language, and then expressed it in the language such as he was master of, which language was reflected and held in vision in the Urim and Thummim until written by the scribe. The language used was brightened, illuminated, and dignified by the spiritual light that radiated throughout his mind." (Ivan Barrett, "Joseph Smith and The Restoration," p. 83).

When the work was completed, rather than showing the plates to the world, the Lord re-introduced the Law of Witnesses. When translating The Book of Mormon,

Joseph Smith learned that there were to be special witnesses of the work he was performing. "The book shall be hid from the eyes of the world, that the eyes of none shall behold it save it be that three witnesses shall behold it, by the power of God, besides him to whom the book shall be delivered; and they shall testify to the truth of the book and the things therein. And there is none other which shall view it, save it be a few according to the will of God, to bear testimony of his word unto the children of men." (2 Nephi 27:12-13, see D&C 17).

Ultimately, there would be eleven witnesses in all. To three of these, God Himself declared that the plates were a true record, and an angel showed them the plates, as well. Eight of the eleven witnesses, including all three to whom God had spoken, eventually left the restored church and were either excommunicated or disfellowshipped for conduct unbecoming members, but none ever denied his testimony.

One left this sworn statement: "I will say once more to mankind, that I have never at any time denied (my) testimony or any part thereof. I also testify to the world, that neither Oliver Cowdery nor Martin Harris ever at any time denied their testimony. They both died reaffirming the truth of the divine authenticity of the Book of Mormon." (Sworn Statement of David Whitmer, made less than a year before his death, and quoted in "Readings in L.D.S. Church History," 1:62).

"In the mouth of as many witnesses as seemeth him good will (God) establish his word." (2 Nephi 27:14). Chapter 5 in the Book of Ether serves this purpose as a personal message from Moroni to Joseph Smith concerning the plates and the Three Witnesses. He wrote: "And in the mouth of three witnesses shall these things be established; and the testimony of three, and this work, in the which shall be shown forth the power of God and also his word, of which the Father, and the Son, and the Holy Ghost bear record - and all this shall stand as a testimony against the world at the last day." (Ether 5:4).

In spite of mounting physical evidence, it was the opinion of Joseph Fielding Smith, Jr., that "the Lord does not intend that The Book of Mormon, at least at the present time, shall be proved true by any archaeological findings. The book of Mormon is itself a witness of its truth." ("Answers to Gospel Questions," 2:196). By comparison, archaeological correlation with biblical scriptures has not created faith among Christians. However, for those who already possess faith, pilgrimages to the Holy Land, as well as to the Lands of The Book of Mormon, strengthen existing religious conviction.

"Verily, verily, I say unto you, if they reject my words, and this part of my gospel and ministry, blessed are ye, for they can do no more unto you than unto me. And even if they do unto you even as they have done unto me, blessed are ye, for you shall dwell with me in glory." (V. 29-30). It would be wrong to assume that the more righteous we are, the less we will suffer. The promise is that we will be blessed even though the blessing may be the strength to endure suffering. All suffer. The difference is that the wicked must suffer the consequences of sin, in addition to the suffering that is a part of our mortal experience. (See D&C 121:7). Marion G. Romney once said: "If we can bear our afflictions with understanding, faith, and courage, we shall be strengthened and comforted and spared the torment that accompanies the mistaken idea that all suffering comes as a chastisement for transgression." (C.R., 10/1964).

Joseph Smith may have understood in this verse that he would ultimately be required to seal his testimony with his own blood. He had received the counsel of Moroni that "wherever the sound (of the marvelous work) shall go it shall cause the ears of men to tingle, and wherever it shall be proclaimed, the pure in heart shall rejoice, while those who draw near to God with their mouths, and honor him with their lips, while their hearts are far from him, will seek its overthrow, and the destruction of those by whose hands it is carried. Therefore, marvel not if your name is made a derision, and had as a by-word among such, if you are the instrument in bringing it, by the gift of God, to the knowledge of the people." (Quoted in "Joseph Smith & The Restoration," p. 14).

We now know all too well that "martyrdom is not a thing of the past only, but of the present and of the future, for Satan has not yet been bound, and the servants of the Lord will not be silenced in this final age of warning and judgment. There are forces and powers in the world today, which would silence the tongue and shed the blood of every true witness of Christ in the world, if they had the power and means to do it." (Bruce R. McConkie, "Mormon Doctrine," p. 469).

"Where two or three are gathered together in my name...there will I be in the midst of them." (V. 32). This revelation was given on April 7, 1829, one year before the formal organization of the church. After receiving this instruction, Joseph and Oliver became increasingly aware of the need to hasten their work so that the church might be established.

As they translated The Book of Mormon, they learned that the Book of Moroni, in particular, consisted of appendices to the text that carefully documented essential basic ordinances found in the true church of Christ. The fact that these were recorded at all by Moroni attested to the necessity of a formal church organization to administer the ordinances, even though in The Book of Mormon very little was written about such a body. In any case, "these ordinances are not empty, passive rituals; rather, they bind us to receive the promises and blessings of the gospel by means of covenants of action between ourselves and the Lord." ("Doctrinal Commentary on The Book of Mormon," 4:319). The ordinances also attest to the nature of God, and illustrate that His church is founded on unchanging principles, and that the requirements for obtaining salvation are the same for all.

Another reason Joseph would have wanted a church organization would have been to introduce to others the kind of priesthood directed teaching he had experienced when translating The Book of Mormon. The goal of such teaching is to introduce to the elect the principles of the gospel, the covenants of God, and the ordinances of the priesthood, and to instruct the Saints so that they may learn how God has provided for them, that they might have the power to keep their promises. When we learn how to do this, we will be transformed into a Zion society. Certainly, where two or three are gathered in the name of Christ, His spirit is there to enlarge their understanding.

Of these ordinances, and particularly of the endowment, Joseph F. Smith wrote: "We entered into covenants with the Lord that we will keep ourselves pure and unspotted from the world. We have agreed before God, angels, and witnesses, in sacred places, that we will not commit adultery, will not lie, that we will not steal or bear false witness against our neighbors, or take advantage of the weak, that we will help and sustain our fellow men in the right, and take such a course as will prove most effectual in helping the weak to overcome their weaknesses and bring themselves into subjection to the requirements of heaven. We cannot neglect, slight, or depart from the spirit, meaning, intent and purpose of these covenants and agreements that we have entered into with our Father in Heaven, without shearing ourselves of our glory, strength, right and title to His blessings, and to the gifts and manifestations of His Spirit." ("Improvement Era," 8/1906). It would be difficult to more clearly compose a statement explaining the need for establishing a covenant relationship with God administered by a formal church organization.

"Whatsoever ye sow, that shall ye also reap." (V. 33). We can choose our own actions, but we cannot choose to escape their consequences. "The decrees of God are unalterable; therefore, the way is prepared that whosoever will may walk therein and be saved." (Alma 41:8). Our natural tendency seems to be to make mistakes, violate law, and suffer the consequences. It must be one of our critical lessons during mortality to deal with opposition, exercise agency, and experience the natural and inevitable positive and negative consequences of independent action.

"Let earth and hell combine against you, for if ye are built upon my rock, they cannot prevail." (V. 34). Central to the operation of the Plan of Salvation is complete and unequivocal dependence upon God. On the one hand, the sons of men "do not desire that the Lord their God, who hath created them, should rule and reign over them; notwithstanding his great goodness and his mercy towards them, they do set at naught his counsels, and they will not that he should be their guide." (Helaman 12:6). But when the righteous, whose lives are built upon the bedrock of the gospel of Jesus Christ, meet the opposition that is a part of mortality, foundation principles will prevail.

"Look unto me in every thought; doubt not, fear not." (V. 36). "In the armory of thought man forges the weapons by which he destroys himself," said Spencer W. Kimball. "He also fashions the tools with which he builds for himself heavenly mansions of joy and strength and peace. Between these two extremes are all grades of character, and man is their maker and their master. Man is the master of thought, the shaper of condition, environment, and of destiny." ("The Miracle of Forgiveness," p. 103).

King Benjamin had told his people that there are many ways to commit sin. (Mosiah 4:29). There is a rule, however, that is the foundation for purposeful living, and the order of counsel is significant. When we have been taught the truth, and with a firm knowledge of that which is good, we must take care to watch our thoughts, words, and deeds. (See Mosiah 4:30, & Alma 12:14).

"In the armory of thought, we forge the weapons by which we destroy ourselves," said Spencer W. Kimball. "We also fashion the tools with which we build for ourselves heavenly mansions of joy and strength and peace. Between these two extremes are all grades of character, and we are their maker. We are the masters of thought, the shapers of condition, environment, and of destiny." ("The Miracle of Forgiveness," p. 103).

When we are taught correct principles, we are left to govern our own behavior, according to the light and knowledge we have received. (See D&C 58:26). Usually, the Lord gives us the overall objectives to be accomplished and some guidelines to follow, but He expects us to work out most of the details ourselves. These are developed through study and prayer, and the promptings of the Spirit.

"Behold the wounds which pierced my side, and also the prints of the nails in my hands and feet; be faithful, keep my commandments, and ye shall inherit the kingdom of heaven." (V. 37). This is probably a figurative expression, for there is no evidence that Christ actually manifested himself to Joseph and Oliver at this time. However, to behold such would certainly have qualified them as special witnesses of Christ, and would also prepare them for the miraculous manifestations that followed.

When the resurrected Lord manifested Himself to the Nephites, they were so overwhelmed by His appearance and by His declaration that "it had been prophesied among them that (He) should show himself unto them after his ascension into heaven," that they fell to the earth. (3 Nephi 11:12). But the Savior invited them to rise, and feel the tokens in His hands and his feet, that they might know that He was "the God of Israel, and the God of the whole earth, and (had) been slain for the sins of the world." (V. 14, see Zechariah 13:6, & D&C 45:51-52). With these tokens, Christ confirmed that He is the God of this earth.

It must have taken some time, but the multitude did come forth, "and did feel the prints of the nails in his hands and in his feet; and this they did do, going forth one by one until they had all gone forth, and did see with their eyes and did feel with their hands, and did know of a surety and did bear record, that it was he, of whom it was written by the prophets, that should come." (3 Nephi 11:15). Mormon went to great length to verify that these people "had witnessed for themselves" that it was the Redeemer of Israel Who stood before them. (3 Nephi 11:16). Joseph and Oliver must have had manifestations of equal intensity.

# Section 7

## (A translation of a record written and hidden up by the Apostle John, received prior to the organization of the church)

"The revelation is a translated version of the record made on parchment by John and hidden up by himself." (Superscript). It was the content of the parchment, and not necessarily the parchment itself, that was revealed to Joseph and Oliver. The biblical account is sketchy, and incomplete. Either John did not make a full record of the event in His Gospel, or the current version has been altered. Evidently, the Lord thought it important that Joseph Smith have the more detailed account of His interview with John, and so He gave him this revelation, in April 1829.

John Taylor told the Saints that during Joseph's formative years, "not only had the principles of the gospel (been) developed but (he) was conversant with the parties who officiated as the leading men in former ages." (J.D., 20:174-175). He had communication "not only with the Lord, but also with the ancient apostles and prophets." (J.D., 21:94). "Nephi and others of the ancient prophets who formerly lived on this continent came to him." (J.D. 7:374). George Q. Cannon said: "If you will read the history of the church from the beginning, you will find that Joseph was visited by various angelic beings. He doubtless also had visits from Nephi, and it may be, from Alma and others." (J.D., 13:47).

"Joseph received instructions from the Lord by inspiration and by visitation from heavenly personages. The angel Moroni communicated with him often. Each year in September, Joseph visited the Hill Cumorah, and the angel enlightened him concerning his labors with the ancient record. Many ancient prophets and apostles appeared to Joseph during his formative years, imparting knowledge and furnishing him direction. Personalities who had once lived on the Western Hemisphere and had contributed to the record Joseph was to receive appeared and acquainted him with particulars about the people mentioned in the golden book. Nephi, Alma, Mormon, and the disciples chosen by the Savior when he appeared to the ancient Americans were among those who revealed themselves to him. These heavenly personages made their appearance to him before he received the Nephite record in September, 1827." (Ivan Barrett, "Joseph Smith & The Restoration," p. 68).

His mother said that Joseph "would describe the ancient inhabitants of this continent, their dress, mode of traveling, and the animals upon which they rode; their cities, their buildings, with every particular; their mode of warfare; and also their religious worship. This he would do with as much ease, seemingly, as if he had spent his whole life among them." (Lucy Mack Smith, "History of Joseph Smith," p. 83).

The New Testament account of the Lord's interview with John reads: "Peter seeing him saith to Jesus, Lord, and what shall this man do? Jesus saith unto him, If I will that he tarry till I come, what is that to thee? Follow thou me. Then went the saying abroad among the brethren, that that disciple should not die: yet Jesus said not unto him, He shall not die; but, If I will that he tarry till I come, what is that to thee? This is the disciple which testifieth of these things, and wrote these things: and we know that his testimony is true." (John 21:21-24). As the angel later told John, when he was in exile on Patmos: "Thou must prophesy again before many people, and nations, and tongues, and kings." (Revelation 10:11). Interestingly, no revisions to any of these verses were made by the Prophet in the Joseph Smith Translation of the Bible!

"And the Lord said unto me: John, my beloved, what desirest thou? For if you shall ask what you will, it shall be granted unto you." (V. 1). "A favorite theme of Brigham Young was that the dominion God gives to us is designed to test us and enable us to show to ourselves, our fellows, and all the heavens just how we would act if entrusted with God's power." (Hugh Nibley, "Subduing The Earth," p. 89-90). In the Book of Helaman, for example, the Lord told Nephi that because he had been unwavering, he would be made "mighty in word and in deed, in faith and in works." (Helaman 10:5). He was given the unlimited power of God, because he could be trusted to do exactly as God would do in similar circumstances.

Joseph Smith clearly taught that the exercise of priesthood power is based solely upon the principles of righteousness. If, in the capacity of the priesthood, we "undertake to cover our sins, or to gratify our pride, our vain ambition, or to exercise control or dominion or compulsion upon the souls of the children of men, in any degree of unrighteousness," the authority of our priesthood is taken from us. (D&C 121:34-37).

"You are, and always will be, independent in that stage of development to which your voluntary decisions and divine powers have led," taught Truman Madsen.

"There are limits all along the way to what you can be and do. But you are not a billiard ball. No power in the universe can coerce your complete assent or dissent. This thesis on capacity translates Bergson's metaphor into breath-taking fact: 'The universe is a machine for the making of gods.'" ("Eternal Man," p. 18, see Henri Bergson, "Two Sources of Morality and Religion," p. 306).

It was the desire of John to be translated, and so he asked the Lord: "Give me power over death, that I may live and bring souls unto thee." (V. 2). The two most important days of your life are the day you were born, and the day you find out why. When John had been "born again," he became a son of God. His life would never be the same, for he was changed through faith on the Lord Jesus Christ. (See Mosiah 5:7).

John was promised that he would be permitted to "tarry until (the Lord would) come in (His) glory." (V. 3). This refers to the translation of John. For most of our scriptural understanding of the doctrine of translation, we must turn to 3 Nephi Chapter 28 in The Book of Mormon. The setting was in Zarahemla, at a meeting between the resurrected Lord and his twelve "disciples." (3 Nephi 28:1).

The Savior asked the Twelve: "What is it that ye desire of me, after that I am gone to the Father?" (3 Nephi 28:1). Nine of them asked that they might have a speedy resurrection to eternal glory in the Celestial Kingdom of God, after their mortal ministry had been completed. (3 Nephi 28:2). The Savior granted their request, and promised them that after they reached the age of seventy-two, they should come to him. (3 Nephi 28:3). The significance of that age, by the way, is unknown.

Then the Savior turned to the three remaining disciples, and asked what was their desire. Perhaps they felt embarrassed to ask Him, for they might have felt their request to be selfish, and so "they sorrowed in their hearts." (3 Nephi 28:5). But He knew their thoughts, inasmuch as their desire was the same as that of John the Beloved. (3 Nephi 28:6).

Then Jesus introduced to the Nephites the doctrine of translation. The Latter-day Saints are a "peculiar people" in part because they believe in this doctrine. (See "Teachings," p. 170-171). He told the three disciples: "Ye shall never taste of death." (3 Nephi 28:7, see D&C 42:45 & 47). They would continue to live as mortal beings, and would eventually die, but would "never endure the pains of death," but when Christ would come in His glory, they would "be changed in the twinkling of an eye from mortality to immortality." (3 Nephi 28:8). Since "the sting of death is sin," translated beings in particular are able to avoid any unpleasant side effects of the transition from mortality to immortality. (1 Corinthians 15:56),

"Translated beings are still mortal, and will have to pass through the experience of death, although this will be instantaneous. Translated beings have not passed through death, that is, they have not had the separation of the spirit and the body." (Joseph Fielding Smith, Jr., "Answers to Gospel Questions," 1:165, 2:46). Probably all those who were translated before the resurrection of Christ were resurrected themselves at that time. (See D&C 133:54-55). Those who have been translated since His resurrection will "be changed in the twinkling of an eye," when Jesus comes to earth as the millennial Christ.

"Millennial man will live in a state akin to translation. His body will be changed so that it is no longer subject to disease or death, as we know it, although he will be changed in the twinkling of an eye to full immortality when he is a hundred years of age." (Bruce R. McConkie, "The Millennial Messiah," p. 644).

The Savior said that translated beings would enjoy other gifts as well. "And again, ye shall not have pain while ye shall dwell in the flesh, neither sorrow save it be for the sins of the world." (3 Nephi 28:9). These gifts would be important for these special missionaries, because they had been commissioned by the Savior Himself to "bring the souls of men unto (Him) while the world shall stand." (3 Nephi 28:9). In other words, missionary work was to be their full time activity until the Second Coming.

A fulness of joy comes in the Resurrection (See D&C 93:33), but missionary work can point us toward the same quality of happiness. (See D&C 93:20). The Savior told these disciples: "And for this cause ye shall have fulness of joy; and ye shall sit down in the kingdom of my Father; yea, your joy shall be full." (3 Nephi 28:10). There is no mistaking here the importance of missionary work in the eyes of Jesus Christ. Because of their desire to continue their missions on the earth, He said: "Therefore, more blessed are ye." (3 Nephi 28:7).

Their continuing focus of attention on their less fortunate brethren would eventually bring them into complete harmony with the attributes of their Father in Heaven. "And ye shall be even as I am, and I am even as the Father, and the Father and I are one." (3 Nephi 28:10).

After touching the nine disciples with His finger, the Savior departed. (3 Nephi 28:12). Then, the three were "caught up into heaven, and saw and heard unspeakable things. (3 Nephi 28:13). 3 Nephi 28:36 makes very clear that verses 13-23 speak of the three disciples. These three were forbidden to "utter the things which they saw and heard." (3 Nephi 28:14). They had likely received an endowment of spiritual and priesthood power akin to that received in the House of The Lord.

"Whether they were in the body or out of the body, they could not tell, for it did seem unto them like a transfiguration," which is a special change in appearance and nature wrought upon a person by the power of God. (3 Nephi 28:15, see v. 38-39). This transformation is from a lower to a higher state of being, resulting in a more exalted, impressive, and glorious condition. "No man hath seen God at any time in the flesh, except quickened by the Spirit of God" in the attitude of translation. (D&C 67:11, see D&C 76:19-20).

It was in this sense that Moses wrote: "But now mine own eyes have beheld God; but not my natural, but my spiritual eyes, for my natural eyes could not have beheld; for I should have withered and died in his presence; but his glory was upon me; and I beheld his face, for I was transfigured before him." (Moses 1:11). Thus, a difference between translation and transfiguration is that the latter seems to be more temporary. (See 3 Nephi 28:37-40).

Exodus records that Moses went up on Mount Sinai to speak with Jehovah. "And the glory of the Lord abode upon mount Sinai.... And the sight of the glory of the Lord was like devouring fire on the top of the mount in the eyes of the children of Israel." (Exodus 24:16-17). And when Moses came down from mount Sinai... behold, the skin of his face shone." (Exodus 34:29-30, see Mosiah 13:5-6, Helaman 5:36, D&C 110:3 & J.S.H. 1:32).

To Mormon, as he abridged this account made by Nephi, it seemed that the Three Nephites had been "changed from this body of flesh into an immortal state, that they could behold the things of God." (3 Nephi 28:15). "And now, whether they were mortal or immortal, from the day of their transfiguration, I know not." (3 Nephi 28:17, see v. 36).

The last five verses of 3 Nephi 28 are a postscript, added by Mormon some time later, which explains what the Lord told him in response to his question about the Three Nephite disciples. Mormon had inquired of the Lord to know their state of existence, and he was told "that there must needs be a change wrought upon their bodies, or else it needs be that they must taste of death." (3 Nephi 28:37). In other words, the Lord confirmed to Mormon that there was, indeed, a difference between these translated beings and normal mortals.

"Therefore, that they might not taste of death there was a change wrought upon their bodies, that they might not suffer pain nor sorrow save it were for the sins of the world." (3 Nephi 28:38). Not only would they not grow older, but while tarrying in this special state they would no longer experience the challenges of adversity normally associated with mortality.

"Now this change was not equal to that which shall take place at the last day; but there was a change wrought upon them, insomuch that Satan could have no power over them, that he could not tempt them; and they were sanctified in the flesh, that they were holy, and that the powers of the earth could not hold them." (3 Nephi 28:39). Indeed, to say that they were like other mortals would be a gross understatement.

In their sanctified state, they remain to this day on the earth, but enjoy complete power over Satan. Although endowed with the power of God, they adhere to the principles of the Prime Directive and will not interfere in the course of human events to change history, but will always allow agency to rule in the affairs of men. Their mission is to bring souls unto Christ. They will not allow Satan to thwart their mission as long as those to whom they minister do not willfully rebel and reject their invitation.

Therefore, "they did go forth upon the face of the land, and did minister unto all the people, uniting as many to the church as would believe in their preaching; baptizing them, and as many as were baptized did receive the Holy Ghost." (3 Nephi 28:18). In a demonstration of their power over the evil men of the earth, when "they were cast into prison by them who did not belong to the church...the prisons could not hold them, for they were rent in twain. And they were cast down into the earth; but they did smite the earth with the word of God, insomuch that by his power they were delivered out of the depths of the earth; and therefore they could not dig pits sufficient to hold them." (3 Nephi 28:19-20).

Satan clearly understood the power and potential influence of these Three Nephites, and he tried desperately to stop their ministry before it had even begun. Perhaps they had been foreordained to this mission under the hands of Heavenly Father Himself, while yet in the pre-earth existence. Perhaps Satan knew of their future ministry from that time, and in response to that knowledge had caused the people to stone to death Nephi's brother Timothy. (See 3 Nephi 19:4 & 3 Nephi 7:19).

But it was all futile. No power on earth could destroy them. Timothy had been raised from the dead by the power of the priesthood. By the way, we do not know the names of the Three Nephite disciples who tarried, nor do we know if Timothy was one of them. (See 3 Nephi 28:25). But we do know that three times were they "cast into a furnace and received no harm. And twice were they cast into a den of wild beasts; and behold they did play with the beasts as a child with a suckling lamb, and received no harm." (3 Nephi 28:21-22).

The Three Nephites ministered to those who needed the gospel the most. Even though they had been mistreated, and even abused, they did not lose sight of their mission statement, which was to bring souls unto Christ, to partake of His Divine Nature, enjoy the blessings of the gospel, and receive the ordinances of salvation, that they might enter into the covenants of exaltation.

Therefore, "they did go forth among all the people of Nephi, and did preach the gospel of Christ unto all the people upon the face of the land, and they were converted unto the Lord, and were united into the church of Christ, and thus the people of that generation were blessed, according to the word of Jesus." (3 Nephi 28:23, see 4 Nephi 1:1). Once again, we are given an example of the way the Savior operates in our affairs. He rarely intervenes directly, but gives priesthood assignments to His faithful servants, and then allows them to work in behalf of their brethren. Sacrifice has its rewards, for the scriptures testify that "after much tribulation come the blessings." (D&C 58:4).

The Three Nephites will remain on the earth as translated beings "until the judgment day of Christ; and at that day they (will) receive a greater change," to be resurrected "into the kingdom of the Father to go no more out, but to dwell with God eternally in the heavens." (3 Nephi 28:40).

The Three Nephites will remain on the earth as translated beings "until the judgment day of Christ; and at that day they (are) to receive a greater change," to be resurrected "into the kingdom of the Father to go no more out, but to dwell with God eternally in the heavens." (3 Nephi 28:40).

Mormon's experience with the Three Nephites was direct and personal, for he wrote: "I have seen them, and they have ministered unto me." (3 Nephi 28:26, see Mormon 8:11). Perhaps the Spirit witnessed to him, or perhaps they revealed to Mormon, that they would minister to the Gentiles, and among them "a great and marvelous work (would be) wrought by them, before that judgment day." (3 Nephi 28:27 & 32).

Mormon also learned that the Three Nephites would minister among the Jews and among "all the scattered tribes of Israel, and unto all nations, kindreds, tongues and people, and (would) bring out of them unto Jesus many souls, that their desire (might) be fulfilled, and also because of the convincing power of God which (would be) in them." (3 Nephi 28:28-29). Their ministry, it would seem, has known no bounds, as it has ranged over the earth through two millennia.

"And they are as the angels of God, and if they shall pray unto the Father in the name of Jesus they can show themselves unto whatsoever man it seemeth them good. Therefore, great and marvelous works shall be wrought by them." (3 Nephi 28:30-31).

Returning to the account revealed to Joseph and preserved for us in D&C Section 7, we read that John was told by the Lord that he would have a similar power to "prophesy before nations, kindreds, tongues and people." (V. 3, see Revelation 10:11). This was primarily accomplished through the Book of John and the Book of Revelation, but he also spoke to the Lost Ten Tribes of Israel." (See D&C 77:14). Perhaps he has also ministered to many others through the centuries, whose faith was kindled to question the Great Apostasy and who, with the additional light and knowledge provided by John, yearned for a restoration of primitive Christianity, worked tirelessly to bring it to pass, and were often martyred for their efforts.

Roger Williams was a leader of the Reformation in America, who lived well over a century before Joseph Smith. He prophetically wrote: "There is no regularly constituted church on earth, nor any person authorized to administer any church ordinance; nor can there be until new apostles are sent by the Great Head of the church, for Whose Coming I am seeking." (William Cullen Bryant, "Picturesque America," p. 502).

Thomas Jefferson said of the religion builders of his day: "They have so distorted and deformed the doctrines of Jesus, so muffled them in mysticisms, fancies and falsehoods, have caricatured them into forms so inconceivable, as to shock reasonable thinkers. Happy in the prospect of a restoration of primitive Christianity, I must leave to younger persons to encounter and lop off the false branches which have been engrafted into it by the mythologists of the middle and modern ages." ("Jefferson's Complete Works," 7:210 & 257).

The desire of John was to correct these errors in doctrine, and to do "a greater work yet among men than what he (had) before done." (V. 5). John's labors would be greater than had been his former work. Vaughn Featherstone once said that in the church we need those who can stand the heat of the refiner's fire, which is a celestial fire. He said that it is the destiny of these disciples to become an army of God, and that when the force is assembled, the enemy will be delivered into its hands. Certainly, John has been working behind the scenes for many centuries to muster the troops, to encourage and exhort them to persevere, and to act proactively as the battle lines are drawn against the legions of the adversary.

Because his work would present greater challenges than any he had ever before faced, he would be made "as a flaming fire and a ministering angel" by the Lord. (V. 6). Fire and smoke are frequently employed in the scriptures to depict the glory of God. In the language of Joseph Smith, "God Almighty Himself dwells in eternal fire; flesh and blood cannot go there, for all corruption is devoured by that fire. Our God is a consuming fire. Immortality dwells in everlasting burnings. ("Teachings," p. 367, see Deuteronomy 4:24, & Hebrews 2:29).

John shall minister to those who "shall be heirs of salvation who dwell on the earth." (V. 6). In the Bible, the bishops of the seven Asiatic churches were addressed as "angels." In this context, angel means "messenger," and is almost synonymous with "apostle," which also means "messenger." In this sense, John would exercise his mantle of authority to minister among men. "And as I said unto mine apostles, even so I say unto you, for you are mine apostles, even God's high priests.... Behold I send you out to reprove the world of all unrighteous deeds." (D&C 84:63 & 87). To reprove is to "convict." When we are taught correctly, our faith convicts us of our sins, and motivates us to repent, that we might merit salvation through the Atonement.

To Peter, the Lord said: "And I will make thee to minister for him and for thy brother James," in other words, to minister to the needs of his brethren, "and unto you three I will give this power and the keys of this ministry until I come." (V. 7). In the apostolic ministry, Peter, James, and John were the presiding authorities of the church. As such, Peter explained in his second epistle that they had been given "all things that pertain unto life and godliness, through the knowledge of him that hath called us to glory and virtue; whereby are given unto us exceeding great and precious promises; that by these ye might be partakers of the divine nature." (2 Peter 1:1, 3 & 4).

To both Peter and John, the Lord said: "Ye shall both have according to your desires, for ye both joy in that which ye have desired." (V. 8). Jesus revealed something of His character, and taught a marvelous lesson as well, when He declared: "And now, behold, my joy is great, even unto fulness." (3 Nephi 27:30). Here is a key to an understanding of the Lord as Savior and Redeemer. He did the work His Father gave to Him, because He loved us so much. By doing so, He received a fulness of joy. The message He has left with us is that if we follow His lead, we too can enjoy this consummate reward for missionary work well done, which is the ultimate work of salvation and is the work of pure, unselfish love.

Mahatma Gandhi once said: "My life is my message." (Response to a journalist's question about what his message to the world was, in "Mahatma: Life of Gandhi, Chapter 13). He could declare this without hypocrisy, because he was true to principles that were moral and ethical constants, that were to him as the guiding stars which would lead him to the safe haven that Judeo-Christians would call "heaven." The Savior held Himself up as the Prototype of the perfection which is an attainable goal for each of us. His gospel holds the key that opens the door to our personal progress. His divine intervention in our affairs breaks down every barrier that would otherwise doom our efforts to failure.

# Section 8

(Received prior to the organization
of the church).

Sections 8 and 9 discuss how revelation operates. To receive knowledge, you must "ask in faith, with an honest heart, believing that you shall receive." (V. 1). Perhaps the most dramatic spiritual manifestation that was the result of one seeking wisdom from God, was that which was received by Joseph Smith in the Sacred Grove. He had read in James 1:5-6: "If any of you lack wisdom, let him ask God, that giveth to all men liberally, and upbraideth not; and it shall be given him. But let him ask in faith, nothing wavering." He learned that wisdom which leads to salvation comes from God by revelation.

The following, written by an active, faithful member of The Church of Jesus Christ of Latter-day Saints, relates to the receipt of revelation and is quite remarkable. He wrote: "I felt I had received some revelation before. However, I saw that random revelation was not sufficient. To be a rock, a bastion of surety, revelation must be something on which one can count and receive in every occasion of real need. I began to seek it actively. I prayed, I fasted, I lived the gospel as best I knew. I was faithful in my church duties. I tried to live up to every scruple which my conscience enjoined upon me. And dependable revelation did come. Intermittently, haltingly at first, then steadily, over some years it finally came to be a mighty stream of experience. I came to know that at any time of day or night, in any circumstance, for any real need, I could get help. That help came in the form of feelings of encouragement when things seemed hopeless. It came in ideas to unravel puzzles that blocked my accomplishment. It came in priesthood blessings which were fully realized. It came in whisperings of prophecy which were fulfilled. It came in support and even anticipation of what the General Authorities of the church would say and do in general conference. It came in the gifts of the Spirit, as the wonders of eternity were opened to the eyes of my understanding. That stream of spiritual experience is today for me a river of living water that nourishes my soul in every situation. It is the most important factor of my life. If it were taken away, all that I have and am would be dust and ashes. It is the basis of my love, life, understanding, hope, and progress. My only regret is that though this river is so wonderful, I have not been able to take full advantage of it as yet. My life does not yet conform to all that I know. But now I do know; I do not just believe." (Chauncey Riddle, "Sunstone," 5/1988).

In particular, Oliver Cowdery wanted to know about "the engravings of old records, which are ancient." (V. 1). When Mormon chronicled the events of the ministry of Jesus among the Nephites, he wrote that those in the Last Days would receive The Book of Mormon "to try their faith, and if it shall so be that they shall believe these things then shall the greater things be made manifest unto them. And if it so be that they will not believe these things then shall the greater things be withheld from them, unto their condemnation." (3 Nephi 26:9-10). In 1829, Oliver was being placed on "scripture probation," to see if he would accept and utilize that with which he had been entrusted. The Lord was putting him on notice that because His people were a scripture possessing people, they were to be a scripture reading, scripture literate, and scripture obedient people, as well.

The Lord revealed to Oliver: "I will tell you in your mind and in your heart, by the Holy Ghost, which shall come upon you and which shall dwell in your heart." (V. 3). "This is the spirit of revelation." (V. 4). "That which is of God is light; and he that receiveth light, and continueth in God, receiveth more light; and that light groweth brighter and brighter until the perfect day." (D&C 50:24).

"Strait is the gate, and narrow is the way, which leadeth unto life, and few there be that find it." (3 Nephi 14:14). When our hearts are set upon temporal things only, spirituality is weakened until the things of God are no longer a part of our daily lives. We ought to "lay aside the things of this world, and seek for the things of a better." (D&C 25:10).

But what are we to do? How can we find the truth? Where can we turn for guidance and direction? Is there no one on the earth to help us, who has been authorized to speak in the name of God? Have the heavens closed? Are they silent? Are we to be left alone, to wander to and fro, like flotsam and jetsam on the sea of life? Does God answer our prayers? Has revelation ceased?

The Savior's instruction in Third Nephi - The Book of Nephi, confirms that the source of gospel knowledge is revelation, and "if any man preach any other gospel unto you than that ye have received, let him be accursed." (Galatians 1:9, see D&C 50:13-20).

The Savior warned against "false prophets, who come to you in sheep's clothing, but inwardly they are ravening wolves." (V. 15, see Matthew 7:15). Critics have used this scripture to attack the church, claiming that it speaks directly of the President and Prophet. This is quite a claim, coming as it does from a people "who never had faith enough to call down one scrap of revelation from heaven, and for all they have now are indebted to the faith of another people who lived hundreds and thousands of years before them. Does it remain for them to say how much God has spoken and how much he has not spoken?" (Joseph Smith, H.C., 2:17-18).

If their claim were reasonable, where then are the true prophets alluded to in Christ's warning? They must exist, for "Adam's revelation did not instruct Noah to build his ark; nor did Noah's revelation tell Lot to forsake Sodom; nor did either of these speak of the Exodus. These all had revelations for themselves, and so had Isaiah, Jeremiah, Peter, Paul, John, and Joseph Smith." (John Taylor, "Gospel Kingdom," p. 34).

God exists in the present tense; as Rufus Jones suggested, He is the Great I Am, and not the Great He Was. ("A Flash of Eternity," newspaper article). In the Doctrine & Covenants, the Lord testified that Joseph Smith was given "power from on high, by the means which were before prepared, to translate The Book of Mormon; which contains a record of a fallen people, and the fulness of the gospel of Jesus Christ to the Gentiles and to the Jews also; which was given by inspiration and is confirmed to others by the ministering of angels, and is declared unto the world by them - Proving to the world that the holy scriptures are true, and that God does inspire men and call them to his holy work in this age and generation, as well as in generations of old; Thereby showing that he is the same God yesterday, today, and forever." (D&C 20:8-12).

Something wonderful surrounds our testimonies of the living Prophet, Seer, and Revelator of The Church of Jesus Christ of Latter-day Saints. Over 150 years ago, John Greenleaf Whittier said of "these modern prophets, I discovered, as I think, the great secret of their success in making converts. They speak to a common feeling; they minister to a universal want. They speak a language of hope and promise to the weak, weary hearts, tossed and troubled, who have wandered from sect to sect, seeking in vain for the primal manifestations of the divine power." (Quoted in "A Mormon Conventicle," p. 461, and in "Howitt's Journal in the Millennial Star," 1848, p. 302-3).

A key was given by the Savior in the following verses. (V. 16-20). "By their fruits ye shall know them." (V. 20). Do these prophets, or teachers who speak in the name of the Lord, bless the lives of their people? Is their doctrine edifying and uplifting? Do they encourage a religion that promotes chastity, morality, and fidelity to family values? Do they hold dear the sanctity of life, and the rights of the unborn? Do they believe that moral agency is an eternal principle vital to the successful completion of our probation on earth? Do they believe in obeying, honoring, and sustaining the law of the land? Do they believe in being honest, true, chaste, benevolent, virtuous, and in doing good to others? Do they believe all things, hope all things, have they endured many things and hope to be able to endure all things? If there is anything virtuous, lovely, or of good report or praiseworthy, do they seek after these things? (See Philippians 4:8, & the 13th Article of Faith).

This was to be Oliver's gift. (V. 4 & 5). He was given the gift to receive revelation by the power of the Holy Ghost. But this was not all. The Lord told him: "You have another gift, which is the gift of Aaron." (V. 6). This was the gift and responsibility to be a scribe, and a spokesman for the Prophet Joseph Smith. It was a sacred trust, for as the Lord said: "There is no other power, save the power of God, that can cause this gift of Aaron to be with you." (V. 7).

"No power shall be able to take it away out of your hands, for it is the work of God." (V. 8). "No power on earth or hell can overthrow or defeat that which God has decreed. Every plan of the adversary will fail, for the Lord knows the secret thoughts of men, and sees the future with a vision clear and perfect, even as though it were in the past." (Joseph Fielding Smith, Jr., "Church History and Modern Revelation," 1:26).

"Therefore, whatsoever you shall ask me to tell you by that means, that will I grant unto you, and you shall have knowledge concerning it." (V. 9). Oliver was poised to understand the doctrine of Christ in even greater detail. This great blessing is always reserved for the faithful. Nephi had mourned "because of the unbelief, and the wickedness, and the ignorance, and the stiffneckedness of men; for they will not search knowledge, nor understand great knowledge, when it is given unto them in plainness, even as plain as word can be." (2 Nephi 32:7). His concern was justified, particularly because his focus was not only on his own brethren, but also on the world in the Last Days.

Today, many lack the desire to change, and are swept to and fro by powerful currents churning up a filthy froth in an unsettling sea of mediocrity. Within the gospel framework, our lives are dynamic and changing, but they are structured and predictable. Our knowledge increases, along with our responsibility and commitment to obedience. As our testimonies of Christ swell, faith intensifies our desire to repent. In this sense, when our lives are in harmony with gospel principles, we are in a constant state of improvement leading to perfection. Becoming Christ-like is our ultimate, incredible journey. We are moving along on the pathway to perfection. It is the road less traveled, but the rewards make completing the trip worth the effort.

"Remember that without faith you can do nothing; therefore ask in faith. Trifle not with these things; do not ask for that which you ought not." (V. 10). For if you "ask anything that is not expedient for you, it shall turn unto your condemnation." (D&C 88:65). As Mormon had written: "I judge that ye have faith in Christ because of your meekness; for if ye have not faith in him then ye are not fit to be numbered among the people of his church." (Moroni 7:39). He was like wise old Tevya, in The Fiddler on The Roof, who told his daughters: "In Anatevka, God knows who you are, and what you may become." (Sheldon Harnick).

One who had the opportunity to be present when Joseph Smith prayed for guidance said of the experience: "There was no ostentation, no raising of the voice as by enthusiasm, but a plain conversational tone, as a man would address a present friend. It appeared to me as though, in case the veil were taken away, I could see the Lord standing facing His humblest of all servants. It was the crowning example of all the prayers I ever heard." (Quoted in Hyrum & Helen Mae Andrus, "They Knew the Prophet," p. 52).

The Lord asked that we "use not vain repetitions." (3 Nephi 13:7). Alma taught that when "your prayer is vain, (it) availeth you nothing, and ye are as hypocrites who do deny the faith." (Alma 34:28, see Mosiah 4:16-27). Thoughtless repetition in prayer suggests faithlessness. This is why such prayers are ineffectual.

If we are full of faith, however, we will ask only for those blessings that we ought to have, for Heavenly Father "knoweth what things (we) have need of, before (we) ask him." (3 Nephi 13:8, see Matthew 6:8). Moreover, Christ has said: "If ye are purified and cleansed from all sin, ye shall ask whatsoever you will in the name of Jesus and it shall be done. But know this, it shall be given you what you shall ask." (D&C 50:29-30).

"Ask...that you may translate and receive knowledge from all those ancient records which have been hid up, that are sacred; and according to your faith shall it be done unto you." (V. 11). The Book of Mormon was translated by Joseph Smith, with Oliver Cowdery acting as scribe, in just six weeks, between April 7, 1829, and the first week of June, 1829. The translation was unlike that of any other text, because it was accomplished "through the mercy (and) power of God." (D&C 1:29). This is as specific an explanation as is found regarding just how Joseph Smith translated the plates. During his lifetime, he tended to let the record speak for itself. It was appropriate that he do so, because when we understand that it is an inspired translation, we are drawn to the book itself, and without distraction can put to the test the challenge left by Moroni: "And when ye shall receive these things, I would exhort you that ye would ask God, the eternal Father, in the name of Christ, if these things are not true; and if ye shall ask with a sincere heart, with real intent, having faith in Christ, he will manifest the truth of it unto you, by the power of the Holy Ghost." (Moroni 10:4).

Jesus Christ Himself testified that The Book of Mormon is true. "He translated the book, even that part which I have commanded him, and as your Lord and your God liveth it is true." (D&C 17:6, See D&C 19:26). As if to confirm that His influence was instrumental in the work of translation, the Lord reminded Oliver Cowdery that it was He that had earlier spoken to him. (V. 12). "Did I not speak peace to your mind concerning the matter?" the Lord asked. "What greater witness can you have than from God?" (D&C 6:22). Oliver had learned that the Spirit is quiet, unobtrusive, and peaceful, and that "the Lord moves in mysterious ways, His wonders to perform. He plants His footsteps in the sea, and rides upon the storm. Deep in unfathomable mines of never failing skill, He treasures up His bright designs, and works His sovereign will. Ye fearful saints, fresh courage take; the clouds ye so much dread are big with mercy and shall break in blessings on your head. Judge not the Lord by feeble sense, but trust Him for His grace. Behind a frowning providence He hides a smiling face. His purposes will ripen fast, unfolding every hour. The bud may have a bitter taste, but sweet will be the flower. Blind unbelief is sure to err, and scan His work in vain. God is His own interpreter, and He will make it plain." (William Cowper, 1773).

# Section 9
## (Received prior to the organization of the church).

This revelation, received in April 1829, teaches that each of us should perform the assignments given us according to our talents and abilities, and that we should not seek to do the work of others, unless asked to do so. In this section, Oliver Cowdery "is admonished to be patient, and is urged to be content to write, for the time being, at the dictation of the translator, rather than attempt to translate." (Superscript).

He was directed by the Lord: "Continue" in the work of translation as scribe, "until you have finished this record." (V. 1). In fact, he did just that, and The Book of Mormon translation was completed in just six weeks, between April 7, 1829, and the first week of June, 1829. One is reminded of the revelatory experience of Handel, when he created "The Messiah" in just 24 days, comprising 259 pages of musical score. The notes came to him so quickly that he could barely keep up as he scratched out the oratorio on whatever paper was handy. After he had written the "Hallelujah Chorus" in a fervor of divine inspiration, he exclaimed that he had "seen all heaven before him." At the end of the manuscript, in acknowledgement of his own puny efforts, he wrote the letters "SDG" – Soli Deo Gloria / "To God alone the glory."

Oliver had as much to do, and more. In this revelation, he was told that there were "other records" that would also require translation. (V. 2). The work that he was called to do was "to write for (the Lord's servant) Joseph," as a scribe. (V. 4). In all his work, he would remember Soli Deo Gloria.

Nephi saw that "these last records, which thou hast seen among the Gentiles, shall establish the truth of the first, which are of the twelve apostles of the Lamb, and shall make known the plain and precious things which have been taken away from them, and shall make known to all kindreds, tongues, and people, that the Lamb of God is the Son of the Eternal Father, and the Savior of the world; and that all men must come unto him, or they cannot be saved." (1 Nephi 13:40). In so many words, Nephi foresaw and emphasized the tremendous importance of the additional scripture that Joseph and Oliver would introduce to the world in the Last Days.

After all, God is interested in other nations, besides the Jews: "Know ye not that there are more nations than one? Know ye not that I, the Lord your God, have created all men, and that I remember those who are upon the isles of the sea; and that I rule in the heavens above and in the earth beneath; and I bring forth my word unto the children of men, yea, even upon all the nations of the earth?" (2 Nephi 29:7). These other scriptures serve as a second witness of Christ. "Know ye not that the testimony of two nations is a witness unto you that I am God, that I remember one nation like unto another. Wherefore, I speak the same words unto one nation like unto another. And when the two nations shall run together, the testimony of these two nations shall run together, also." (2 Nephi 29:8).

The scriptures are the basis upon which God shall judge the world. "For I command all men, both in the east and in the west, and in the north, and in the south, and in the islands of the sea, that they shall write the words which I speak unto them; for out of the books which shall be written I will judge the world, every man according to their works, according to that which is written." (2 Nephi 29:11).

Because Joseph Smith recognized that translations do not reflect with absolute accuracy the original words and intentions of writers, he wrote in the Wentworth Letter: "We believe the Bible to be the word of God as far as it is translated correctly." (8th Article of Faith). He observed that "our latitude and longitude can be determined in the original Hebrew with far greater accuracy than in the English version. There is a grand distinction between the actual meaning of the prophets and the present translation." ("Teachings," p. 290-91).

He also commented on the Bible's incompleteness: "It was apparent that many important points touching the salvation of men, had been taken from the Bible, or lost before it was compiled" ("Teachings," p. 10-11). He later said: "Much instruction has been given to man since the beginning, which we do not possess now. ("Teachings," p. 61). He also said: "I believe the Bible as it read when it came from the pen of the original writers. Ignorant translators, careless transcribers, or designing and corrupt priests have committed many errors." ("Teachings," p. 327).

He thus summarized: "Through the kind providence of our Father, a portion of His word which He delivered to His ancient Saints has fallen into our hands [and] is presented to us with a promise of a reward if obeyed, and with a penalty if disobeyed." ("Teachings," p. 61).

"The Bible is interpreted and understood by Latter-day Saints through four important means: (1) other LDS scriptures, that enrich and give perspective to our understanding of biblical teachings; (2) statements of modern prophets and apostles on the meaning of some biblical passages; (3) the Joseph Smith Translation of the Bible; and (4) personal revelation through the gift of the Holy Ghost, that enhances our comprehension of the scriptures. Consequently, Latter-day Saints are left with information about the meaning of many difficult passages that have divided the entire Christian world for two millennia." ("L.D.S. Infobase on The Bible").

"Although the K.J.V. was Joseph Smith's English Bible, he did not regard it as a perfect or official translation; this is why he studied Hebrew and undertook the task of producing an inspired revision of the scriptures. Twenty-first century church leaders have given a variety of reasons for the continued use of the K.J.V.: it was the common translation in use in the English-speaking world at the time of the Restoration; its language prevails in all the standard works; a large number of passages in the Book of Mormon, which parallel the Bible, were translated into the English style of the K.J.V.; the Joseph Smith Translation of the Bible (J.S.T.) was based on the K.J.V., with 90 percent of the verses unchanged. All Latter-day prophets have used the K.J.V., and using the K.J.V. in all church publications has made it possible to standardize annotations and indices." (L.D.S. Infobase on The Bible).

"You have not understood," chided the Lord. "You have supposed that I would give it unto you, when you took no thought save it was to ask me." (V. 7). Nephi similarly cautioned against being "at ease in Zion," or being spoon-fed gospel knowledge without intellectual or spiritual challenge. (2 Nephi 28:24). If we are gliding smoothly and effortlessly through life, we can be pretty sure that we are going downhill, because progress takes effort, as we climb to new heights of achievement.

Blessings that follow true discipleship have a performance cost. "Blessed are those which hunger and thirst after righteousness, for they shall be filled. (Matthew 5:6). Receiving the Law of Christ seems to be an ongoing process, and so the challenge of individuals and society is not that they receive too much revelation, but that they receive too little. They also look in all the wrong places.

Throughout the Bible, the prophets repeatedly warned Israel against dalliances with astrologers, exorcists, familiar spirits, magicians, sorcerers, and witches, and in participating in divinations, enchantments, and other activities that solicit the intervention of evil spirits. Isaiah mocked those who relied on such, when he said: "Thou art wearied in the multitude of thy counsels. Let now the astrologers, the stargazers, the monthly prognosticators, stand up, and save thee from these things that shall come upon thee. Behold, they shall be as stubble; the fire shall burn them; they shall not deliver themselves from the power of the flame; there shall not be a coal to warm at, nor fire to sit before it." (Isaiah 47:13-14).

"You must study it out in your mind," the Lord taught Oliver. "Then you must ask me if it be right, and if it is right I will cause that your bosom shall burn within you; therefore, you shall feel that it is right." (V. 8). "It is impossible to advance in the principle of truth," declared Lorenzo Snow, "to increase in heavenly knowledge, except we exercise our reasoning faculties and exert ourselves...to the utmost of our ability." (J.D., 18:48).

The Lord explained the process to Joseph Smith. He asked: "He that is ordained of me and sent forth to preach the word of truth by the Comforter, in the Spirit of truth, doth he preach it by the Spirit of truth or some other way? And if it be by some other way it is not of God. And again, he that receiveth the word of truth, doth he receive it by the Spirit of truth or some other way? If it be some other way it is not of God." (D&C 50:17-20).

As Paul taught, the key to gospel knowledge is personal revelation, and "let him be accursed who preaches any other gospel." (Galatians 1:8-12). "That which is of God is light; and he that receiveth light, and continueth in God, receiveth more light: and that light groweth brighter and brighter until the perfect day." (D&C 50:24). Proverbs counsels us: "Trust in the Lord with all thy heart, and lean not unto thine own understanding." (Proverbs 3:5).

But we must also remember that there is no revelation where there is no student. Perspiration must precede inspiration. With this in mind, Emerson wrote: "Truth comes only to the prepared mind." But when it does, it warms the bosom, for the Spirit of God burns like a fire.

"But if it be not right, you shall have no such feelings, but you shall have a stupor of thought that shall cause you to forget the thing which is wrong." (V. 9). The first issue of "The Times and Seasons" contained a lead editorial to the Elders: "Be careful that you teach not for the word of God the commandments of men," it cautioned, "nor the doctrine of men, nor the ordinances of men, for no man's opinion is worth a straw." As Moses observed: "Now for this cause I know that man is nothing, which thing I never had supposed." (Moses 1:10).

"Stand fast in the work wherewith I have called you." (V. 14). Wo unto those who deny the Lord and put their trust in man. In the scriptures, the "arm" is a symbol of power, and so the "arm of flesh" will be a curse to those who rely on it, for they will find that the support of the devil and his angels will be a millstone around their necks at the last day, when they are abandoned and will be left alone to be dragged screaming "down to hell." (Alma 30:60).

We lose power whenever our priorities are out of order. This is why it is necessary for the Lord to clarify His gospel in different dispensations. He wants our perspective to be crystal clear, so that we can focus on principles of perfection that are validated by the Spirit, and have the power of the priesthood at all times.

His power stems from love, in contrast to the elusive and transient counterfeit that has no substance and is driven by greed, avarice, lust, and the unrighteous desire for dominion. It is not difficult to see the fingerprints of Satan, smeared all over the programs, policies, pronouncements, and parties that promote petty, provincial, and personal agendas.

Disciples of Christ do not have the option to walk "in (their) own ways, and after the image of (their) own god." (D&C 1:16). What a blessing it is to know that when we discover what the Lord wants of us, all we need to do is stand our ground and put our shoulder to the wheel. As Brigham Young declared: " I never count the cost of anything. I just find out what the Lord wants me to do, and I do it."

# Section 10
## (Received prior to the organization of the church).

"Herein the Lord informs Joseph of alterations made by wicked men in the 116 manuscript pages from the translation of the Book of Lehi, in The Book of Mormon. These manuscript pages had been lost from the possession of Martin Harris, to whom the sheets had been temporarily entrusted. The evil design was to await the expected retranslation of the matter covered by the stolen pages, and then to discredit the translator by showing discrepancies created by the alterations. That this wicked purpose had been conceived by the evil one, and was known to the Lord even while Mormon, the ancient Nephite historian, was making his abridgment of the accumulated plates, is shown in The Book of Mormon (The Words of Mormon 1:3-7)." (Superscript).

Martin Harris had broken his promise to show the manuscript to only five people; therefore the Lord designated him a "wicked man." (V. 1). At the same time, Joseph had lost the gift of translation; therefore, his "mind became darkened." (V. 2). Through repentance, and after a season of real soul-searching, Joseph again earned the Lord's favor, and the gift was restored to him. (V. 3). In doing so, the Lord admonished him: "See that you are faithful and continue on unto the finishing of the remainder of the work of translation as you have begun." (V. 4).

The real tragedy in life is when we set our sights too low, easily reaching our objectives but accomplishing little, having nothing to show for our consistently timid efforts. The Lord challenged Joseph to rise to the occasion, to step up to the plate, and to boldly endure to the end of his mortal mission.

Then, Joseph received the same counsel that had been given by King Benjamin. (See Mosiah 4:27). "Do not run faster or labor more than you have strength and means provided to enable you to translate; but be diligent unto the end." (V. 4). This suggests that we should pace our progress. There is a difference between being anxiously engaged, and in being overanxiously engaged, thus falling into the trap of being under-engaged. Brigham Young understood this, when he taught:

"All organized existence is in progress either to an endless advancement in eternal perfections, or back to dissolution. There is no period in all the eternities wherein organized existence will become stationary, that it cannot advance in knowledge, wisdom, power, and glory." (J.D., 1:349).

"Pray always," Joseph was told, "that you may come off conqueror; yea, that you may conquer Satan, and that you may escape the hands of the servants of Satan that do uphold his work." (V. 5). When we pray to the Father continually, we are not likely to lose sight of our utter dependence on Him for both our temporal and spiritual welfare, nor will we forget from Whom both our talents and blessings flow. "True prayer consists more in the feeling that rises from the heart and from the inward desire of our spirits, to supplicate the Lord in humility and faith, that we may receive His blessings." (Joseph F. Smith, "Gospel Doctrine," p. 219).

Unfortunately, Satan and his servants were actively seeking to foil the work of the Restoration that Joseph Smith had begun: "Behold, they have sought to destroy you; yea, even the man in who you have trusted has sought to destroy you." (V. 6). In these verses, the Lord explained to Joseph that they schemed to overthrow the work in the following ways: Martin "sought to take away the things wherewith (he had) been entrusted; and he...also sought to destroy (Joseph's) gift." (V. 7).

"Wicked men" had taken the manuscript, "that which was sacred," seeking to alter the words which had already been translated. (V. 8-10). In doing so, they would have changed the meaning of and corrupted the translation. (V. 11). It was the cunning plan of the devil himself to "destroy this work" by thus discrediting the translation of the plates. (V. 12-13). Thereby, the wicked hoped to "get glory of the world." (V. 19).

Satan's primary objective is to thwart our progression. In Moroni's day, and in our own, he will "rage in the hearts of the children of men, and stir them up to anger against that which is good. And others will he pacify, and lull them away into carnal security, and thus the devil cheateth their souls, and leadeth them away carefully down to hell. And behold, others he flattereth away, and telleth them there is no hell, and thus he whispereth in their ears until he grasps them with his awful chains from whence there is no deliverance." (2 Nephi 28:20-22).

He is the master of disguise, and of techniques whereby he might lead unsuspecting but weak-willed individuals "by the neck with a flaxen cord, until he bindeth them with his strong cords forever." (2 Nephi 26:22). He is able to accomplish this because "their hearts are corrupt, and full of wickedness and abominations; and they love darkness rather than light, because their deeds are evil." (V. 21). Therefore, they will not seek the guidance and direction that the Lord is anxious to provide. Thus, "Satan stirreth them up, that he may lead their souls to destruction," or spiritual death. (V. 22).

But, the Lord assured Joseph, the efforts of the wicked to foil the work of the Restoration would "turn to their shame and condemnation in the day of judgment." (V. 23). They would ultimately be held accountable for their actions. "Satan spreads the counterfeit coin of false doctrine. Beware of this spurious currency; it will purchase for you nothing but disappointment, misery, and spiritual death." (Joseph F. Smith, "Juvenile Instructor," 9/1902).

That which is offered by Satan has always been over-zealously promoted by the unenlightened and poorly informed. It has passionate advocates, but they all miss the mark, and without exception they ultimately fail, no matter how much attention or financial support they may have received. Mormon's editorial comment in the Book of Alma is most perceptive and universally applicable: "And thus we see that the devil will not support his children at the last day, but doth speedily drag them down to hell." (Alma 30:60).

The adversary finally betrays his followers because he cannot deliver on his promises. His enticements lead Father's children into conceptual cul de sacs, religious roundabouts, and doctrinal dead ends from which there is no exit except retreat. His cunning caresses entice the weak to plunge into a perceived freedom that is really a bottomless pit of misery. In a perverted and twisted way, "the devil seeks that all men might be miserable like himself." (2 Nephi 2:27).

Satan has always raged "in the hearts of men, and stir(ed) them up to anger against that which is good." (2 Nephi 30:20). But sometimes he pacifies us, and lulls us into a false sense of worldly security, making us believe that we are gaining something when we are really losing. He does this very subtly, so as not to awaken our senses to the reality of what is really happening. (2 Nephi 30:21).

He seems to move us from brilliant, dazzling white, through every shade of grey, to that fathomless black which, by subtraction, is the absence of every good thought, word, deed, or worthy principle. He flatters us, and whispers that he does not exist, which leads us to judge ourselves as deserving of peace and plenty without really having earned the reward. (2 Nephi 30:22).

Meanwhile, as C.S. Lewis wrote: "Little people, like you and me, if our prayers are sometimes granted beyond all hope and probability, had better not draw hasty conclusions to our own advantage. If we were stronger, we might be less tenderly treated. If we were braver, we might be sent, with far less help, to defend far more desperate posts in the great battle." ("The World's Last Night," p. 10-11).

Satan uses every strategem in his playbook, that he might stir up our "hearts to anger against this work." (V. 24). He says to the weak-willed: "Deceive and lie in wait to catch, that ye may destroy; behold, this is no harm. And thus he flattereth them, and telleth them that it is no sin to lie. And thus he flattereth them, and leadeth them along until he draggeth their souls down to hell; and thus he causeth them to catch themselves in their own snare. And thus he goeth up and down, to and fro in the earth, seeking to destroy the souls of men." (V. 25-27). "Thus, Satan thinketh to overpower your testimony in this generation," the Lord told Joseph, "that the work may not come forth." (V. 33). But, said the Lord: "I will not suffer that they shall destroy my work; yea, I will show unto them that my wisdom is greater than the cunning of the devil." (V. 43).

The Words of Mormon help to explain just how powerful His wisdom is. Written by Mormon on the Small Plates of Nephi about 385 A.D., his insert was intended to be a bridge between the body of the Small Plates of Nephi, comprising the First Book of Nephi through the Book of Omni, and Mormon's own abridgment of the Large Plates of Nephi that starts with the Book of Mosiah.

Even though Mormon's abridgment of the Book of Lehi, from the Large Plates of Nephi, was included with all the other records, he must have known that Joseph Smith's manuscript translation up to the Book of Mosiah would, in some way, be corrupted. Therefore, he went to great pains to include this transitional book on the last leaf of the record comprising the Small Plates of Nephi.

Speaking of the loss of the manuscript translation of the Book of Lehi, the Lord declared to Joseph Smith that "the works, and the designs, and the purposes of God cannot be frustrated, neither can they come to naught." (D&C 3:1). He adequately prepares for any and every eventuality, inasmuch as He is omniscient. He knows the end from the beginning. (See 1 Nephi 9:6). He is the same yesterday, today, and forever. (See 1 Nephi 10:18). Past, present, and future are ever before His eyes. (See D&C 130:7). "With God, all things are possible." (Matthew 19:26).

God the Father, Mormon taught, knows all things, "being from everlasting to everlasting." (Moroni 7:22). Eternity spans the time from uncreate intelligence, through our spiritual development as children of our Heavenly Father, on into mortality, and finally to our reunion with Him in the resurrection. God is in every sense perfect. Faith, hope and charity define His attributes in absolute perfection. If we were to model our behavior after any individual, it would be Christ, Who in every quality is One with the Father. This is why Mormon taught that "in Christ there should come every good thing." (Moroni 7:22)

We are completely helpless to alter the progress, or affect the outcome, of any of God's activities. It was when Moses realized his utter dependence upon God that he exclaimed: "Now, for this cause I know that man is nothing, which thing I never had supposed." (Moses 1:10). Our debt to God is total and complete. King Benjamin asked his people: "Can ye say aught of yourselves? I answer you, Nay. Ye cannot say that ye are even as much as the dust of the earth; yet ye were created of the dust of the earth; but behold, it belongeth to him who created you." (Mosiah 2:25).

Jesus Christ counseled: "Remember, remember that it is not the work of God that is frustrated, but the work of men." (D&C 3:3). Joseph Fielding Smith, Jr. declared: "No power on earth or hell can overthrow or defeat that which God has decreed. Every plan of the adversary will fail; for the Lord knows the secret thoughts of men, and sees the future with a vision clear and perfect, even as though it were in the past." ("Church History and Modern Revelation," 1:26). Jacob clearly understood this, when he wrote: "Oh, how great the holiness of our God. For he knoweth all things, and there is not anything save he knows it." (2 Nephi 9:20). Else He would cease to be God, and man could not have faith in Him.

Joseph Smith explained to John Wentworth: "No unhallowed hand can stop the work from progressing. Persecutions may rage, mobs may combine, armies may assemble, calumny may defame, but the truth of God will go forth boldly, nobly, and independent, until it has penetrated every continent, visited every clime, swept every country, and sounded in every ear; till the purposes of God shall be accomplished, and the Great Jehovah shall say 'The work is done.'" (H.C., 4:540).

"The truth is, that after the thousands of attacks, and scores of books that have been published, not one criticism has survived, and thousands have borne witness that the Lord has revealed to them the truth of this marvelous work." (Joseph Fielding Smith, Jr., "Church History and Modern Revelation," 1:28-29).

At the opening of every dispensation of the gospel, Satan has made a frontal assault against the advent of truth. He deceived many of the sons and daughters of Adam and Eve in the first gospel dispensation. At the beginning of the Mosaic Dispensation, "Satan came tempting him saying: Moses, son of man, worship me." (Moses 1:12). In the days of Jesus, Satan had the audacity to attack the Master Himself. (Luke 4:1-13). We learn from the Prophet Joseph Smith that Satan was also present at and contested the opening of the Dispensation of The Fulness of Times. (J.S.H. 1:15).

Satan tried very hard to frustrate the work of translation of the plates delivered into the hands of Joseph Smith. He knew that the Church of Jesus Christ could not be organized until the publication of The Book of Mormon. But the Lord had anticipated his every move, and had provided a duplicate record, in the form of the Small Plates of Nephi.

Mormon was about to deliver to his son Moroni the record which he had been making. He had finalized his abridgment of the Large Plates of Nephi from the Book of Lehi through the Book of Mormon chapter 7. This was a comprehensive effort that chronicled almost 1,000 years of Nephite history. Mormon had witnessed the last great battles between the Nephites and the Lamanites, and the record of his people was completed, having been abridged by him from the Large Plates of Nephi onto the Plates of Mormon.

Mormon recorded: "And it came to pass that when we had gathered in all our people in one to the land of Cumorah...I made this record out of the plates of Nephi, and hid up in the hill Cumorah all the records which had been entrusted to me by the hand of the Lord, save it were these few plates which I gave unto my son Moroni." (Mormon 6:6).

Mormon hoped that his son Moroni would at least be able to document the outcome of the final conflict between the Nephites and Lamanites. "And it is many hundred years after the coming of Christ that I deliver these records into the hands of my son;" he wrote, "and it supposeth me that he will witness the entire destruction of my people. But may God grant that he may survive them, that he may write somewhat concerning them, and somewhat concerning Christ, that perhaps some day it may profit them." (Words of Mormon 1:2).

As a resurrected being, Moroni would bring the gospel contained in The Book of Mormon to the knowledge of the descendants of Lehi. Whoever the remnant of the seed of Lehi actually is, the scriptures tell us that they will be taught the gospel, "and they shall be restored to the knowledge of Jesus Christ, which was had among their fathers." (2 Nephi 30:5). Spencer W. Kimball confirmed: "The day of the Lamanites is here!" (C.R., 10/1960). As the curtain rises in the Last Days, and the children of Israel find themselves on center stage, the signs of the times will be revealed, unfolding a drama of all-encompassing proportion.

Then shall "their scales of darkness begin to fall from their eyes," and "they shall be a pure and a delightsome people." (2 Nephi 30:6). Before the 1978 revision of the English language scriptures, this verse was rendered "white" as opposed to "pure," to emphasize, by contrast, the concept of "spiritual blackness." In any event, the quality of darkness seems to apply more to the spiritual condition of the Lamanites than to any physical characteristic they may have had.

Ezra Taft Benson once told the Saints that The Book of Mormon can bring spiritual and intellectual unity to our lives. In two ways, he said, The Book of Mormon brings us to Christ. "First, it tells in a plain manner of Christ, and His gospel. It testifies of His divinity and the necessity for a Redeemer and the need of our putting trust in Him. It bears witness of the Fall, the Atonement, and the first principles of the gospel, including our need of a broken heart, a contrite spirit, and spiritual rebirth. It proclaims we must endure to the end in righteousness and live the moral life of a Saint. Second, The Book of Mormon exposes the enemies of Christ. It confounds false doctrines and contentions. It fortifies the humble followers of Christ against the evil designs, strategies, and doctrines of the devil, in our day." (C.R., 4/1975).

As the Lord told Joseph: "There are many things engraven upon the plates of Nephi which do throw greater views upon my gospel; therefore, it is wisdom in me that you should translate this first part of the engravings of Nephi (the Small Plates of Nephi)." (V. 45).

"My holy prophets," the Savior declared, "yea, and also my disciples, desired in their prayers" that these things "should come forth unto this people. (V. 46). "This was their faith," said the Lord, "that my gospel, which I gave unto them that they might preach in their days, might come unto their brethren the Lamanites, and also all that had become Lamanites because of their dissensions." (V. 48).

As Brigham Young said: "Though our children are begotten in righteousness, and brought forth in holiness, they must be tried and tempted, for they are agents before our Father, the same as you or I." (J.D., 3:51). It is inevitable that some will stumble over hidden obstacles as they make their way along the path leading to the Tree of Life.

Even among members of the church, unbelief results in spiritual sclerosis, or a hardening of the heart. As a result, some will not remain faithful to their covenants in times of trial. They become "a separate people as to their faith." (Mosiah 26:4). They become cultural Lamanites. They commit sins that require repentance, but they cannot muster the faith necessary to call upon God, Who has created a portal, a Stargate, as it were, leading to forgiveness. Therefore, they end up in a tailspin, spiraling downward in a sustained stall from which it becomes increasingly difficult to regain control.

Even though such people are identifiable by their faithlessness, they mingle socially with members of the church, and exert influence over them. Consequently, those who commit such sins must be "admonished by the church." (Mosiah 26:6). As Alma the Younger exhorted: "Come ye out from the wicked, and be ye separate, and touch not their unclean things." (Alma 5:57). The situation is not so different today.

Nevertheless, The Book of Mormon waits to bless the lives of any and all who will read it and accept its teachings. The ancients left "a blessing upon this land in their prayers, that whosoever should believe in His gospel in this land might have eternal life. Yea, that it might be free unto all of whatsoever nation, kindred, tongue, or people they may be." (V. 50-51).

Thus, The Book of Mormon is a blueprint for survival for those living in the Last Days. It articulates a policy guaranteed to make God's people free from satanic influences, as well as from all foreign nations under his evil control. "Behold, this is a choice land, and whatsoever nation shall possess it shall be free from bondage, and from captivity, and from all other nations under heaven if they will but serve the God of the land, who is Jesus Christ." (Ether 2:12).

"And now, behold, according to their faith in their prayers will I," the Lord, "bring this part of my gospel to the knowledge of my people." (V. 52). It is particularly important that He do this, because "we live in a day and in a world full of doubts and confusion, where people do not know what to believe, where tensions are high, where the pace is frantic and progress in terms of righteousness is not a popular goal. Violence and crudity are everyday patterns all around us. What a blessing it is to know there is a haven, a place of rest from the turmoil of the world. The prophets and the Savior have called upon us to enter into the rest of the Lord, where life has purpose and direction, and where priesthood power is possible." ("Gospel Doctrine Manual," p. 79). "Therefore, whosoever belongeth to my church need not fear," the Lord reassured Joseph, "for such shall inherit the kingdom of heaven." (V. 55).

"But it is they who do not fear me, neither keep my commandments but build up churches unto themselves to get gain, yea, and all those that do wickedly and build up the kingdom of the devil - yea, verily, verily, I say unto you, that it is they that I will disturb, and cause to tremble and shake to the center." (V. 56, see 1 Nephi 2:14, & 17:55).

There are, after all, "save two churches only; the one is the church of the Lamb of God, and the other is the church of the devil; wherefore, whoso belongeth not to the church of the Lamb of God belongeth to that great church, which is the mother of abominations; and she is the whore of all the earth." (1 Nephi 14:10, see 2 Nephi 9:37, & 2 Nephi 10:16).

It is a characteristic of the Last Days that society is becoming increasingly polarized. On the one hand is the kingdom of God, and on the other is the kingdom of the devil. "East is east, and west is west, and never the twain shall meet." (Rudyard Kipling). Satan's kingdom is typified as the whore of the earth in the sense that it is a corrupt or idolatrous community. It was Wycliffe (in 1302) and Tyndall (in 1530) who first applied this epithet to the church of Rome, but we should not specifically do so. From our perspective, we can see that "the church of the devil" is any organization, society, or system of beliefs that leads men away from Christ or hinders or prevents them from accepting the gospel.

That the "whore" is powerful today is attested in 1 Nephi 14:11, where we learn that she "sat upon many waters." Revelation 17:5 teaches us that "the waters... are peoples, and multitudes, and nations, and tongues." Her "dominion" is the power, control, and influence of government.

Zion will ultimately be redeemed from the "whore of the earth" by the power of the priesthood. "The role of Israel as the depositary of true religion and the freeing of mankind from the idolatry which obstructs its salvation is almost self-evident. As Isaiah envisioned, there can be no hope for our redemption unless we conquer self-deification. We must abandon the worship of our own creations, and liberate ourselves from our lust for power, avarice, domination, and the cult of the state. There can be no redemption until we recognize our moral obligations as transcendent and divine. No form of government, no level of material well-being, will save us. We will be redeemed only when towers fall, and Jerusalem triumphs over Babylon. What is at stake, finally, is not only intelligence, but also feeling. We have to change our hearts. Salvation, the prophets tell us, is preconditioned by repentance. The redeeming act of God waits upon our initiative." (Abba Eban, "My People: The Story of The Jews," p. 59-60).

In D&C Section 29:12, we find the only instance in the Doctrine & Covenants where the term 'great and abominable church' is employed, although it is used twelve times in The Book of Mormon, in 1 Nephi 4:3, 9, 15, & 17, 1 Nephi 13:6, 8, 26 & 28, 1 Nephi 22:13 & 14, 2 Nephi 6:12, & 2 Nephi 28:18. That is enough, however, to entrench the phrase in our lexicon. Nephi was given, in vision, a broad view of the state of the world in the Last Days, and clearly saw "the great persecutor of the church, the apostate, the whore, even Babylon, that maketh all nations to drink of her cup, in whose hearts the enemy, even Satan, sitteth to reign." (D&C 86:3).

For Christ is "the light which shineth in darkness, and the darkness comprehendeth it not." (V. 58). The Savior was physically lifted up upon the cross, but He was also figuratively lifted up as a light to the world, as the great Teacher and Exemplar, and spiritually lifted up to heaven as a glorified God. As a result, He has tremendous power to draw us to Him. It is for these purposes that He was lifted up. (See 3 Nephi 27:15).

Christ is "the law, and the light. Look unto (Him), and endure to the end, and ye shall live; for unto him that endureth to the end, will (He) give eternal life." (3 Nephi 15:9). All things have become new in Christ. Moroni ushered in the restoration of the New and Everlasting Covenant, the Fulness of the Law of Christ.

Christ was lifted up for all of us. It is He who said: "Other sheep have I which are not of this fold.... And I will show unto this people that I had other sheep, and that they were a branch of the house of Jacob." (V. 59-60). He revealed to His twelve Nephite disciples that He had never told their brethren at Jerusalem of their existence, or that of the Ten Tribes, who had been "led away out of the land." (3 Nephi 15:15, see 2 Nephi 20:21, & Alma 7:10). He had only told them "that other sheep I have which are not of this fold; them also I must bring, and they shall hear my voice; and there shall be one fold, and one shepherd." (3 Nephi 15:17).

Jesus had been commanded by the Father to reveal no more to Israel. This was "because of stiffneckedness and unbelief." (3 Nephi 15:18). Had they been given more insight into their brethren in the New World, they would probably not have understood it anyway. As Joseph Smith said: "As far as we degenerate from God, we descend to the devil and lose knowledge." ("Teachings," p. 217). His counsel applies equally to all of Heavenly Father's children.

Most Christians today believe the "other sheep" mentioned by the Savior refer to the Gentiles, who would at some subsequent day receive the gospel. But The Book of Mormon makes very clear that this is not the case. The Savior explained: "And verily I say unto you, that ye are they of whom I said: Other sheep I have which are not of this fold; them also I must bring, and they shall hear my voice; and there shall be one fold, and one shepherd."

He continued: "And they understood me not, for they supposed it had been the Gentiles; for they understood not that the Gentiles should be converted through their preaching. And they understood me not that I said they shall hear my voice; and they understood me not that the Gentiles should not at any time hear my voice - that I should not manifest myself unto them save it were by the Holy Ghost. But behold, ye have both heard my voice, and seen me; and ye are my sheep, and ye are numbered among those whom the Father hath given me." (3 Nephi 15:21-24).

It is ordained that the Gentile nations of the earth are to receive the gospel, and the elect among them are to be converted by the power of the Holy Ghost. Peter, who brought the gospel to the Gentiles, said: "On the Gentiles also was poured out the gift of the Holy Ghost." (Acts 10:45). The gifts of the Spirit are sufficient to carry us along the path leading to eternal life, but the special gift of the Word was given to Israel in both the Old and the New World. As Peter said: "Of a truth I perceive that God is no respecter of persons: But in every nation he that feareth him, and worketh righteousness, is accepted with him." (Acts 10:34-36).

All shall learn "the true points" of the doctrine of Christ, in order that the gospel might be established, and that contention might be diminished. (V. 62-63). For "Satan doth stir up the hearts of the people to contention concerning the points of my doctrine: and in these things they do err, for they do wrest the scriptures and do not understand them." (V. 63). It is a typical strategy of false teachers to lead the people astray by attacking the fundamental doctrines of the church. They do this by wresting the scriptures.

The Oxford English Dictionary defines 'to wrest' as "to turn away from true or proper signification. To twist or pervert. To misinterpret. To misapply. To turn from the right application." When self-appointed prophets and teachers wrest the scriptures, and especially when they twist their meaning to their own material advantage, we can be sure that the welfare of Zion is not the focus of their concern.

Stephen Robinson very forthrightly addressed this issue. He wrote: "Time and again, the Latter-day Saints are denied the privilege of defining and interpreting their own doctrines. Quite frequently a Latter-day Saint attempting to explain the tenets of his or her faith to non-Mormons will be interrupted by some self-styled expert who says, 'No, that's not what you believe; this is what you believe.'

There generally follows a recital of some hocus-pocus that is certainly not taught by the L.D.S. church. The resulting fictions generally fall into one of three categories: outright fabrications, distortions of genuine L.D.S. doctrines into unrecognizable forms, or the representation of anomalies within the L.D.S. tradition as mainline or official L.D.S. teachings." ("Are Mormons Christians?" "The Exclusion by Misrepresentation," p. 9-10).

Even church members who have been called to preach the gospel risk falling into transgression in consequence of a shallow understanding of principles and doctrines. As Alma had declared to the inhabitants of Ammonihah, "Behold, the scriptures are before you; if ye will wrest them it shall be to your own destruction." (Alma 13:20). Picking apart the scriptures can distort the doctrines into meaningless fragments without any coherent connection.

In 1820, the Lord characterized such individuals as those who "draw near to me with their lips, but (whose) hearts are far from me. They teach for doctrines the commandments of men, having a form of godliness, but they deny the power thereof." (J.S.H. 2:19). They are all form and no substance, because they do not have anything to contribute to our welfare. The advertising executives of Madison Avenue, and not the Holy Ghost, are the driving force and power which propels their message. As a result, they often meet with success among those who have 'itching ears.' The great appeal of so-called 'Psychic Hotlines,' that began to be promoted on television in the 1990s, is a good example.

The true doctrine of Christ, however, is this: "Whosoever repenteth and cometh unto me," said the Lord, "the same is my church. Whosoever declareth more or less than this, the same is not of me, but is against me; therefore he is not of my church." (V. 67-68). Since the day the church was established, on April 6, 1830, this doctrine has not changed.

Simply stated, this doctrine is that all who have faith in Jesus Christ, and truly repent of their sins, entering into a baptismal covenant with the Lord, will receive the Holy Ghost. This third member of the Godhead will then direct their path, showing them the things they must do to achieve salvation. (See 3 Nephi 11:31-40, 27:8-22, & Moses 6:48-68). "For the gate by which ye should enter is repentance and baptism by water; and then cometh a remission of your sins by fire and by the Holy Ghost." (2 Nephi 31:17). This puts us on the "strait and narrow path that leads to eternal life." (2 Nephi 31:18).

Then, we must "press forward" with complete dedication and "steadfastness," or confidence and a firm determination in Christ, "having a perfect brightness of hope," or perfect faith, and "a love of God and of all men," or charity. If we do this, "feasting upon the word of Christ," or receiving strength and nourishment from the scriptures, and endure to the end in righteousness, we "shall have eternal life," that is the greatest gift of the gifts of God. (2 Nephi 31:20). This is our on-going opportunity and responsibility.

Nephi stated this doctrine in simple language that was difficult to be misinterpreted. "This is the way," he said, "and there is none other way nor name given under heaven whereby man can be saved in the kingdom of God.

And now, behold, this is the doctrine of Christ, and the only and true doctrine of the Father, and of the Son, and of the Holy Ghost, which is one God, without end." (2 Nephi 31:21, see D&C 20:28).

This doctrine is properly the gospel of the Father as well as of the Son and the Holy Ghost, because these three distinct members of the Godhead are One, in complete unity, love, and purpose. Moses taught how all three members of the Godhead work together to provide the opportunity for us to have immortality and eternal life. "For by the water ye keep the commandment; by the Spirit ye are justified, and by the blood ye are sanctified." (Moses 6:60).

Christ is the Author of Salvation (Hebrews 5:9), but the Plan was introduced to His spirit children by Heavenly Father. (2 Nephi 9:13). By the spirit of revelation, the Holy Ghost testifies of Christ and of the Father's Plan. (D&C 8:2-3). Working in perfect harmony, the three members of the Godhead promote the doctrine of Christ with one shared goal: to bring us to the waters of baptism.

As the gate revealing the path leading to the Celestial Kingdom swings open to admit the penitent faithful, the words of King Benjamin ring in our ears: "And now, because of the covenant which ye have made ye shall be called the children of Christ, his sons, and his daughters; for behold, this day he hath spiritually begotten you; for ye say that your hearts are changed through faith in his name; therefore, ye are born of him and have become his sons and his daughters." (Mosiah 5:7).

So critically important to our eternal welfare is the decision to enter the waters of baptism, that Benjamin further counseled: "And under this head ye are made free, and there is no other head whereby ye can be made free. There is no other name given whereby salvation cometh; therefore, I would that ye should take upon you the name of Christ, all you that have entered into the covenant with God that ye should be obedient unto the end of your lives." (Mosiah 5:8).

The doctrine of Christ speaks to our spirits, for every gospel principle carries within it a witness that it is true. (See Neal Maxwell, C.R., 4/1991). "The Lord giveth light unto the understanding;" taught Nephi, "for he speaketh unto men according to their language, unto their understanding." (2 Nephi 31:3). The language of the spirit is universal, and when we have the Holy Ghost to illuminate our minds, we enjoy spiritual fluency. Such familiarity open up vistas of eternal proportion.

The word of the Lord has been validated in every whit: "Whosoever is of my church, and endureth of my church to the end, him will I establish upon my rock, and the gates of hell shall not prevail against them." (V. 69). Those who endure to the end in righteousness may lay claim to the promise of the Lord, who "will disperse the powers of darkness from before you, and cause the heavens to shake for your good, and his name's glory." (D&C 21:6).

The doors to the so-called spirit prison of the unjust (see "Doctrines of the Gospel Student Manual, (2000), p. 87–89, D&C 76:73, 88:97-102, Alma 40:11-14, & Moses 7:57) will no longer loom large, and our confidence shall "wax strong in the presence of God; and the doctrine of the priesthood shall distill upon (our) soul as the dews from heaven. The Holy Ghost shall be (our) constant companion, and (our) scepter an unchanging scepter of righteousness and truth; and (our)dominion shall be an everlasting dominion, and without compulsory means it shall flow unto (us) forever and ever." (D&C 121:45-46).

# Section 11

## (Received prior to the organization
## of the church).

This is a "revelation given through Joseph Smith the Prophet to his brother Hyrum Smith. The "History of The Church suggests that this revelation was received after the restoration of the Aaronic Priesthood, sometime late in the month of May, 1829." (Superscript).

Following his and Oliver Cowdery's receipt of the Aaronic Priesthood and their baptism, Joseph wrote:: "Our minds being now enlightened, we began to have the scriptures laid open to our understandings, and the true meaning and intention of their more mysterious passages revealed unto us in a manner which we never could attain to previously, nor ever before had thought of." (J.S.H. 1:74).

"A great and marvelous work is about to come forth among the children of men." (V. 1). The Restoration ushered in a new era of understanding of gospel principles. Thousands of years earlier, an angel had shown to Nephi a vision that in the Last Days, "these last records, which thou hast seen among the Gentiles, shall establish the truth of the first." (1 Nephi 13:40).

In other words, the Gentiles would be instruments in bringing forth a great body of scripture, other books, which would stand as witnesses of the Bible. These include not only The Book of Mormon, but also the Doctrine and Covenants, the Pearl of Great Price, the Joseph Smith Translation of the Bible, and even various apocryphal works.

The words of Christ were to be made known in The Book of Mormon, as well as in the Bible, "wherefore they both shall be established in one." (1 Nephi 13:41). This verse is reminiscent of the prophecy of Ezekiel, wherein he wrote: "Moreover, thou son of man, take thee one stick, and write upon it, For Judah, and for the children of Israel his companions: then take another stick, and write upon it, For Joseph, the stick of Ephraim, and for all the house of Israel his companions. And join them one to another into one stick; and they shall become one in thine hand." (Ezekiel 37:16-17).

And so, "that which shall be written (in the Bible and Book of Mormon) shall grow together, unto the confounding of false doctrines and laying down of contentions, and establishing peace among the fruit of thy loins, and bringing them to the knowledge of my covenants, saith the Lord." (2 Nephi 3:12).

This restoration of earth shaking proportion began with the humble petition of one young boy in a Sacred Grove. Of that event, Christ said: "Wherefore, I the Lord, knowing the calamity which should come upon the inhabitants of the earth, called my servant Joseph Smith, Jun., and spake unto him from heaven, and gave him commandments. ...That faith also might increase in the earth; that mine everlasting covenant might be established." (D&C 1:17, 21-22).

Thus, the gospel began to be "proclaimed by the weak and the simple unto the ends of the world, and before kings and rulers." (D&C 1:23). This is a time that includes a fulness of those gospel principles and ordinances that have been taught in all other dispensations. That is one of the reasons why it is called "the dispensation of the fulness of times."

Secondly, it dispenses greater blessings to more people than any other dispensation, for its work involves not only the living, but the dead, as well. "Behold, I will send you Elijah the prophet," promised Malachi, "before the coming of the great and dreadful day of the Lord. And he shall turn the heart of the father to the children, and the heart of the children to their fathers." (Malachi 4:5-6).

Isaiah also foresaw that, in the Last Days, a new dispensation of gospel knowledge would be necessary. "Forasmuch as this people draw near unto me with their mouth, and with their lips do honor me, but have removed their hearts far from me, and their fear towards me is taught by the precepts of men. Therefore, I will proceed to do a marvelous work among this people, yea, a marvelous work and a wonder." (Isaiah 29:13-14).

The marvelous work to which Isaiah referred includes The Book of Mormon, the restoration of the church and priesthood authority, temple ordinances, and latter-day prophets on the earth. It is indeed the restoration of all things, culminating once again in the establishment of Zion, which "shall flourish, and the glory of the Lord shall be upon her." (D&C 64:41).

"Behold, I am God; give heed to my word, which is quick and powerful, sharper than a two-edged sword, to the dividing asunder of both joints and marrow." (V. 2). The word of the Lord is 'quick," which, in a biblical sense, means 'to be alive or living;' therefore, to be quickened by the spirit is to be spiritually alive. God's word is 'powerful,' as well, or is a source of energy. The word of God, like a sword, separates truth from error, and strikes terror into the hearts of the wicked when delivered by the voice of the priesthood. It "is the legitimate rule of God whether in the heavens or on the earth, and it is the only legitimate power that has a right to rule upon the earth; and when the will of God is done on earth as it is in the heavens, no other power will bear rule." (John Taylor, J.D., 5:187).

It was in this sense that the Savior warned His disciples: "Think not that I am come to send peace on earth. I came not to send peace, but a sword." (Matthew 10:34). John recorded: "There was a division among the people because of him." (John 7:43). J. Reuben Clark, Jr. taught: "The peace He proclaimed was the peace of everlasting righteousness which is the eternal enemy of sin. Righteousness is peace wherever it abides. Sin in itself is war wherever it is found." (C.R., 4/1939).

"Behold, the field is white already to harvest; therefore, whoso desireth to reap let him thrust in his sickle with his might, and reap while the day lasts, that he may treasure up for his soul everlasting salvation in the kingdom of God." (V. 3). The field is the earth, and it is white, or pure, in the sense that there are living upon its face those who have been spiritually prepared to receive the glad tidings of the Restoration.

Missionaries will commence the work of gathering the Covenant People of the Lord "among all nations, kindreds, tongues, and people." (2 Nephi 30:8). In 1982, missionaries were actively proselyting in fewer than half the nations of the earth. The church has a long way to go, although great progress is being made. Between 1830 and 1970, The Book of Mormon had been translated into 25 languages. In the next 11 years, there were an additional 25 language translations. As of 2015, The Book of Mormon has been translated, at least in part, into 110 languages. The Church Translation Services Department, that was created in 1965 to accelerate the process, has a daunting task before it, but is doing a marvelous job.

The Lord's work among all nations includes technology that will aid in the process of teaching the gospel, and in administering the ordinances of salvation throughout the world. When these remarkable innovations invoke wonder and amazement, we should remember from Whom they have come, and for what purpose they have been given.

"And with righteousness shall the Lord God judge the poor, and reprove with equity for the meek of the earth. And he shall smite the earth with the rod of his mouth; and with the breath of his lips shall he slay the wicked." (2 Nephi 21:4 & 2 Nephi 30:9). The "rod" is a symbol of the power of the priesthood. The Lord has revealed His battle plan for the Last Days, when He will engage in mortal combat the forces of Babylon, whose soldiers will be taken captive and suffer spiritual death if they fail to heed the liberating call to repentance.

By the power of the priesthood and the word of God, His army of missionaries will smite the earth and defeat the wicked. As Alma found, "the preaching of the word had a great tendency to lead the people to do that which was just - yea, it had more powerful effect upon the minds of the people than the sword, or anything else." (Alma 31:5).

The battle lines during the war in heaven were drawn according to contrasting ideologies. (See 2 Nephi 29:3). The weapons used were the words that powerfully articulated opposing positions. That Satan was persuasive is attested by the fact that he drew a third part of the heavenly host to his point of view. In the Last Days, the combatants are once again forming into diametrically opposed camps with increasingly polarized ideologies. "For the time speedily cometh that the Lord God shall cause a great division among the people." (2 Nephi 30:10 see 1 Nephi 22:19).

"Yea, whosoever will thrust in his sickle and reap, the same is called of God." (V. 4). When we completely pattern our lives after the divine model, we earn the right to speak in the name of the Lord. Bruce McConkie composed a statement of belief that is still carried by many of the missionaries of The Church of Jesus Christ of Latter-day Saints. He wrote: "I am called of God. My authority is above that of the kings of the earth. By revelation I have been selected as a personal representative of the Lord, Jesus Christ. He is my master and He has chosen me to represent Him, to stand in His place, to say and do what He Himself would do if he personally were administering among the very people to whom He has sent me. My voice is His voice and my acts are His acts, my words are His words and my doctrine His doctrine, for I am His agent. My commission is to do what He wants done, to say what He wants said, to be a living modern witness in word and in deed of the divinity of His great and marvelous latter day work, and he that receiveth me receiveth Him, while he that rejects me rejects Him that sent me. How great is my calling!" ("My Missionary Commission").

"Therefore, if ye will ask of me you shall receive; if you will knock it shall be opened unto you." (V. 5). Nephi counseled his own people to pray, for the same reasons. He had perceived that they were having difficulty accepting the doctrine of Christ, because they were not exercising faith sufficient to pray. He equated the acquisition of the knowledge and qualities necessary for salvation with the ability and willingness to approach the Lord in prayer. "If ye would hearken unto the

Spirit which teacheth a man to pray," he wrote, "ye would know that ye must pray; for the evil spirit teacheth not a man to pray, but teacheth him that he must not pray. But behold, I say unto you that ye must pray always, and not faint; that ye must not perform any thing unto the Lord save in the first place ye shall pray unto the Father in the name of Christ, that he will consecrate thy performance unto thee, that thy performance may be for the welfare of thy soul." (2 Nephi 32:8-9).

Long ago, the Psalmist wrote: "Evening, and morning, and at noon, will I pray, and cry aloud: and he shall hear my voice." (Psalms 55:17). In the Garden of Gethsemane, the Savior counseled Peter: "Watch and pray, that ye enter not into temptation: the spirit indeed is willing, but the flesh is weak." (Matthew 26:41). To his brethren, Nephi provided the additional insight that it is the evil one who teaches that we must not pray. It is the practice of the church to consistently pray to God for His assistance; for regular reinforcement against encroachments by Satan and the tendency to be carnal, sensual, and devilish.

Brigham Young once observed that it does not matter if we feel like praying or not; we should nevertheless pray. He said if we waited until we felt like praying, there would not be much prayer in this world. (See D.B.Y., p. 44).

One of David O. McKay's favorite poems reads: "The builder who first bridged Niagara's gorge, before he swung his cable, shore to shore, sent out across the gulf his venturing kite, bearing a slender cord for unseen hands to grasp upon the further cliff and draw a greater cord, and then a greater yet; 'Til at last across the chasm swung The Cable - then the mighty bridge in air! So may we send our little timid thoughts, across the void, out to God's reaching hands. Send our love, and faith, to thread the deep, thought after thought, until the little cord, and we, are anchored to the Infinite! " (Edwin Markham).

"Keep my commandments, and seek to bring forth and establish the cause of Zion." (V. 6). Whereas priestcraft results in affliction, apostasy, contention, and persecution, the service of the faithful brings peace, prosperity, and unity. Most important to righteous stewards are the quality of their service, and not their position within the church, or the recognition by others of their worthy deeds.

"Seek not for riches, but for wisdom, and behold, the mysteries of God shall be unfolded unto you, and then shall ye be made rich." (V. 7). To understand spiritual things, we must have the discerning guidance of the Holy Ghost. Those who receive the missionaries are taught by the Spirit, and when they are confirmed as members of the church they receive the special gift of the Holy Ghost, in an ordinance of the priesthood.

One of His purposes is to guide the faithful from the covenant waters of baptism, along the strait and narrow path leading to other ordinances that are necessary for them to obtain eternal life. This is one reason why members of the church receive the Holy Ghost shortly after their baptism.

"He that will not harden his heart, to him is given the greater portion of the word, until it is given unto him to know the mysteries of God until he know them in full." (Alma 12:10, see Mosiah 2:9, & D&C 88:67). All may have access to the mysteries of God, that are the saving principles of the gospel of Jesus Christ. (See Alma 29:8, & 3 Nephi 26:9-10).

When individuals harden their hearts to the truth, however, "to them is given the lesser portion of the word until they know nothing concerning his mysteries, and then they are taken captive by the devil, and led by his will down to destruction. Now this is what is meant by the chains of hell." (Alma 12:11).

The terrible thing about hardening our hearts is that our understanding of "the word" is withheld, which leaves us vulnerable to the devil's influence. The scriptures identify the consequences of sin in very plain language. The effect of sin on those who have been taught the principles of the gospel in plainness is that the guidance of the Spirit is withdrawn, and they are left alone to grope in darkness.

Guilt causes them to shrink from church activity, and in the absence of the Spirit, sinners have no claim on blessings, prosperity, or preservation. Tragically, those individuals, feeling uncomfortable in proximity to spiritual experiences, withdraw to lifestyles devoid of such associations. Thus begins a downward spiral that gains momentum as sinful practices, more easily committed, become entrenched.

Even worse, those who do this, "the same cometh out in open rebellion against God." (Mosiah 2:37). "Thus saith the Lord concerning all those who know my power, and have been made partakers thereof, and suffered themselves through the power of the devil to be overcome, and to deny the truth and defy my power. They are they who are the sons of perdition." (D&C 76:31-32).

In contrast to these benighted souls, Hyrum was reassured: "You shall be the means of doing much good in this generation." (V. 8). In the Kingdom of God, it is not ability, or inability, but availability that is important when His servants are called to the work. Brigham Young once declared: "I never count the cost of anything. I just find out what the Lord wants me to do, and I do it." It is this kind of total commitment and dedication that establishes the church.

When Joan of Arc was carried to the stake in circumstances reminiscent of the fate that befell the Prophet Abinadi, she was given the opportunity to obtain her freedom by denying her beliefs. Instead, she made this statement: "I know this now. Every man gives his life for what he believes. Every woman gives her life for what she believes. Sometimes people believe in little or nothing, and so they give their lives for little or nothing. One life is all we have, and we live it as we believe in living it, and then it is gone. But to surrender what you are and live without belief is more terrible than dying, even more terrible than dying young." (B.Y.U. "Speeches of The Year," 1975, p. 428). Resolutely, then, she faced death, still true to her faith and her beliefs. Her final acts on earth were consistent with her convictions. It is this quality of total commitment and dedication that establishes the church.

In the early years of the Restoration, with the spirit of religious revivalism burning brightly among the people, Joseph Smith's younger brother Hyrum sought diligently to establish the church. His efforts are carried on today by those to whom the torch has been passed. At that time, he was counseled: "Say nothing but repentance unto this generation." (V. 9).

Perhaps our Father in Heaven wants us to accept His Son and His gospel because He is anxious for us to avoid the "weeping and gnashing of teeth" that accompany the recognition that our "days of probation are past; (when we) have procrastinated the day of (our) salvation until it is everlastingly too late, and (our) destruction is made sure." (J.S.M. 1:54, & Helaman 13:38).

If we seek "all the days of (our) lives for that which (we) cannot obtain, and...have sought for happiness in doing iniquity, which thing is contrary to the nature of that righteousness which is in our great and Eternal Head," we must ultimately face the consequences. (Helaman 13:38). It is then, in the most difficult circumstances of repentance imaginable, that the necessary reform must be initiated and the uttermost farthing paid.

How much better it would have been to have listened to the prophets. "And in the days of your poverty ye shall cry unto the Lord; and in vain shall ye cry, for your desolation is already come upon you, and your destruction is made sure; and then shall ye weep and howl in that day, saith the Lord of Hosts. And then shall ye lament, and say: O that I had repented, and had not killed the prophets, and stoned them, and cast them out. Yea, in that day ye shall say: ...O that we had repented in the day that the word of the Lord came unto us." (Helaman 13:32-36).

"Behold, thou hast a gift," the Lord told Hyrum. (V. 10). He had a tender, sympathetic heart and a merciful spirit. "Blessed is my servant Hyrum Smith; for I, the Lord, love him because of the integrity of his heart and because he loveth that which is right before me, saith the Lord." (D&C 124:15). The Lord had a larger purpose in building faith and other divine qualities in Hyrum Smith. It was "that the residue of men (might) have faith in Christ, that the Holy Ghost (might) have place in their hearts." (Moroni 7:32)

"It is I that speak; behold, I am the light which shineth in darkness, and by my power I give these words unto thee." (V. 11). On one occasion, the Lord told Joseph Smith that "this generation shall have my word through you." (D&C 5:10). On another, He said: "And I, Jesus Christ, your Lord and your God, have spoken it. These words are not of men nor of man, but of me; wherefore, you shall testify they are of me and not of man; For it is my voice which speaketh them unto you; for they are given by my Spirit unto you, and by my power you can read them one to another; and save it were by my power you could not have them; Wherefore, you can testify that you have heard my voice, and know my words." (D&C 18:33-36).

When we read the words of The Doctrine and Covenants, or of The Book of Mormon, we are hearing the voice of the Lord, as well as reading His words, if we do so by the Spirit. The Savior said, "Learn of me, and listen to my words; walk in the meekness of my Spirit, and you shall have peace in me." (D&C 19:23). Referring to the Lord's anointed, the Lord said: "And whatsoever they shall speak when moved upon by the Holy Ghost shall be scripture, shall be the will of the Lord, shall be the mind of the Lord, shall be the word of the Lord, shall be the voice of the Lord, and the power of God unto salvation." (D&C 68:4).

"Put your trust in that Spirit which leadeth to do good - yea, to do justly, to walk humbly, to judge righteously; and this is my Spirit." (V. 12). "A man being a servant of the devil cannot follow Christ; and if he follow Christ he cannot be a servant of the devil. One cannot have it both ways. Double mindedness creates instability and spiritual schizophrenia." ("Doctrinal Commentary on The Book of Mormon," 4:334).

Mormon revealed the simple test by which we might gauge the worth of all things. He said: "That which is of God inviteth and enticeth to do good continually; wherefore, every thing which inviteth and enticeth to do good, and to love God, and to serve him, is inspired of God." (Moroni 7:13). Because the advertising executives of Madison Avenue do an excellent job of confusing the issue, Moroni cautioned: "Wherefore, take heed, my beloved brethren, that ye do not judge that which is evil to be of God, or that which is good and of God to be of the devil." (Moroni 7:14).

There are no shades of grey for those who have received the ordinances of the

Priesthood of God. Members of the church have not only the Light of Christ, but their minds are also illuminated by the greater light and knowledge given by the Holy Ghost. "For behold, my brethren, it is given unto you to judge, that ye may know good from evil; and the way to judge is as plain, that ye may know with a perfect knowledge, as the daylight is from the dark night." (Moroni 7:15).

"The Spirit of Christ is given to every man, that he may know good from evil; wherefore, I show unto you the way to judge; for every thing which inviteth to do good, and to persuade to believe in Christ, is sent forth by the power and gift of Christ; wherefore ye may know with a perfect knowledge it is of God." (Moroni 7:16, see John 1:19). This is the Light of Christ, that gives order even to the universe. (See D&C 88:6-13).

"My Spirit...shall enlighten your mind (and) fill your soul with joy." (V. 13). When spiritually prepared individuals approach a gospel principle, the mysteries of God that are related to its understanding and application may be unfolded to their view. The scriptures encourage us to find wisdom and great treasures of knowledge, even hidden treasures; they suggest the need to search for those pearls that may not be readily discernible after only a cursory glance. The language of the Spirit is universal, and when we have the Holy Ghost to illuminate our minds, we enjoy spiritual fluency. Such familiarity opens up vistas of eternal proportion.

With that blessing, however, comes accountability. "And all they who receive the oracles of God, let them beware how they hold them lest they are accounted as a light thing, and are brought under condemnation thereby, and stumble and fall when the storms descend, and the winds blow, and the rains descend, and beat upon their houses." (D&C 90:5). If we have access to the revelations, but do not take them seriously, we will not be able to withstand the fiery darts of the adversary, let alone the obstacles to our progress that life regularly throws in our path.

"By this shall you know all things whatsoever you desire of me, which are pertaining unto things of righteousness, in faith believing in me that you shall receive." (V. 14). Jacob explained that "no man knoweth of (God's) ways, save it be revealed unto him." (Jacob 4:8). This verse echoes the teaching of John Taylor, who said: "No matter what ability and talent a man may possess, all must come under this rule if they wish to know the Father and the Son. If knowledge of them is not obtained through revelation it cannot be obtained at all." ("The Gospel Kingdom," p. 112). The light and knowledge we receive of God is given by a process called "revelation." This basic principle requires little definition, because it speaks to our hearts and our souls.

"You need not suppose that you are called to preach until you are called." (V. 15).

Teaching is the main function of the priesthood. "This is the order after which I am called, yea, to preach unto my beloved brethren, yea, and every one that dwelleth in the land." (Alma 5:49). Alma did not define his responsibilities only in terms of what he could do to reclaim those who had been previously baptized. He also understood that his covenant of baptism and the Oath and Covenant of the Melchizedek Priesthood required him to stand as a witness of God to those who were not yet members of the church, who lived among the Saints in the Land of Zarahemla.

Alma later reiterated that preaching the gospel is the responsibility of those who bear the priesthood of God. "This is the order after which I am called, yea, to preach unto my beloved brethren, yea, and every one that dwelleth in the land." (Alma 5:9). He did not make a distinction between member and non-member. Rather, he felt that it was his duty to teach the gospel to all, and his message was the same, that all "must repent and be born again." (Alma 5:49).

"Wait a little longer, until you shall have my word, my rock, my church, and my gospel, that you may know of a surety my doctrine." (V. 16). The only way that we may know for certain is by entering into gospel covenants after uniting ourselves with the church of Jesus Christ. When we recognize that it is the Savior Who stands at the head of His church and directs its affairs by revelation to His authorized priesthood servants, we have moved from faith, through conversion, and on to testimony. We avail ourselves of the ordinances of salvation and exaltation. Through this process of the Plan, all are welcome to participate fully in these gospel ordinances.

The invitation is: "Come unto Christ." (Moroni 10:32). All that the Lord requires is "the hearts of the children of men." (D&C 64:22). Truly, He is "no respecter of persons." (D&C 1:35). Spirituality, or holiness is not an office or a calling, but is simply living in harmony with the principles and ordinances of the gospel of Jesus Christ.

A central reason for the organization of the church was to make possible the kind of priesthood directed teaching of which Alma and the Sons of Mosiah were such fine examples. The goal of such teaching was to introduce to the elect the principles of the gospel, the ordinances of the priesthood, the covenants of God, and instruction that empowers the Saints to keep their promises. When we learn how to do so, we take our places among the citizens of a Zion society.

In the Last Days, a unique house of learning has been established and is maintained by the power of the priesthood. It is in this house that we learn to make covenants that orient us to the Celestial Kingdom. Increasingly, this house is being made available to the world's population. "The temple is the place where we get our bearings on the universe." (Hugh Nibley, "On The Timely & Timeless"). It is where we can "put on the whole armor of God." (Ephesians 6:11). The key of the mysteries of the kingdom is revealed to us in the temple, because the key of the knowledge of God is personified by the endowment of spiritual and priesthood power that is bestowed there.

It is in this sense that "power in the priesthood" is vested in all those who receive their endowment in the temple. "And this greater priesthood administereth the gospel and holdeth the key of the mysteries of the kingdom, even the key of the knowledge of God. Therefore, in the ordinances thereof, the power of godliness is manifest." (D&C 84:19-20). Because Heavenly Father desires that all his children possess this power, He has always commanded His people to build temples. (D&C 124:39). It is in the temples of the Lord that His people internalize His doctrine with a certainty and and surety that the world can neither provide nor understand.

"Cleave unto me with all your heart, that you may assist in bringing to light those things of which has been spoken - yea, the translation of my work; be patient until you shall accomplish it." (V. 19). In fact, Hyrum did just that, and the Book of Mormon translation was completed in just six weeks, between April 7, 1829, and the first week of June, 1829.

"Behold, this is your work, to keep my commandments, yea, with all your might, mind and strength." (V. 21). A child who had been raised in the home of faithful parents who had taught all their youngsters the principles of the gospel was asked what he wanted to be when he grew up. His answer was articulated in just one word: "Obedient."

The Savior's statement was equally clear: "Not every one that saith unto me, Lord, Lord, shall enter into the kingdom of heaven, but he that doeth the will of my Father which is in heaven." (Matthew 7:21). He continued: "If a man will do his will, he shall know of the doctrine, whether it be of God, or whether I speak of myself." (John 7:17).

"Seek not to declare my word, but first seek to obtain my word, and then shall your tongue be loosed; then, if you desire, you shall have my Spirit and my word, yea, the power of God unto the convincing of men." (V. 21). Deficiencies in our knowledge of basic gospel principles can be traced back to our superficial familiarity with the scriptures.

Our lack of understanding can contribute to transgression, that underscores the need for sustained and meaningful gospel scholarship. Perspiration, soul-sweat, and "brain sweat," as B.H. Roberts called it, precede inspiration. Once enlightened by the Holy Ghost, we are prepared to understand gospel principles that are mysteries to the world because they can only be spiritually discerned.

Alma taught: "There are many mysteries which are kept, that no one knoweth them save God himself." (Alma 40:3, see Alma 37:11). Therefore, we should not be impatient to gain mastery of that which is apparently beyond our comprehension, or that which is unnecessary for us to have at this stage of our intellectual or spiritual development.

Nevertheless, bathed in the stunning clarity of the missionary message, those who are taught the gospel stare in wide-eyed wonder at the beautiful simplicity of the tapestry of principles that make up the Plan of Salvation. This is in sharp contrast to the slit-eyed skepticism with which the unrepentant and hard-hearted greet the truth. As Alma said of the influence of Heavenly Father on his Lamanite converts: "He changed their hearts and they awoke unto God. Behold, they were in the midst of darkness; nevertheless, their souls were illuminated by the light of the everlasting word." (Alma 5:7).

"But now hold your peace; study my word which hath (and which shall) come forth among the children of men." (V. 22). When our lives conform to the pattern established by the Savior, and the scales of darkness fall away, the eyes of our spiritual understanding are opened, that we may see clearly, and discern between good and evil. Our ears hear the word of the Lord, and we increasingly understand otherwise inaudible whisperings, as spiritual fluency swells our hearts with the pure love of Christ, and as we lose ourselves in compassionate service.

Hyrum Smith was one of the best men ever to grace the earth. If his desire to labor in the kingdom was initially refused because he first needed to study the word of the Lord, then how much more need have we to labor in the traces, and to prepare to be ready when our own time comes to have the spirit of revelation?

Our preparation includes building upon the rock of Christ, that He revealed "is my gospel." (V. 24). As the spark of faith, struck off the Divine Anvil of God, ignites the flame of resolve within us, we develop the "power to do whatsoever thing is expedient" or right to do, under the circumstances. That thing, said the Savior, is to "repent all ye ends of the earth, and come unto me, and be baptized in my name, and have (more) faith in me, that ye may be saved." (Words of Mormon 1:34). This is the fruits of faith, that is, to be saved in the Celestial Kingdom of God. It is the very reason for the ministry of Jesus Christ and His servants among the children of men.

"Deny not the spirit of revelation, nor the spirit of prophecy, for wo unto him that denieth these things." (V. 25). As Paul taught, the key to gospel knowledge is personal revelation, and "let him be accursed who preaches any other gospel." (Galatians 1:8-12). "That which is of God is light; and he that receiveth light, and continueth in God, receiveth more light: and that light groweth brighter and brighter until the perfect day." (D&C 50:24).

The testimony of Jesus is the spirit of prophecy. (See Revelation 19:10). Every member of the church may receive a personal witness of the divinity of the Savior. The spirit of prophecy is the revealed word of God that has been ratified by the Holy Ghost. Every member of the church who bears testimony of the principles of the gospel has experienced personal revelation and the spirit of prophecy. Therefore, testimony may stand independently without qualification or corroboration by any other external proof. We need never apologize when we bear our testimony, because its expression is a tangible manifestation of the unimpeachable witness of the Holy Ghost.

"Behold, I am Jesus Christ, the Son of God. I am the life and the light of the world." (V. 28). Christ is the Life of the world. He said: "I am the resurrection and the life; he that believeth in me, though he were dead, yet shall he live. And whosoever liveth and believeth in me shall never die." (John 11:25-26). "God so loved the world, that He gave his Only Begotten Son, that whosoever believeth in Him should not perish, but have everlasting life." (John 3:16, see 3 Nephi 27:13-14).

Christ is the Light of the world. "I said to the man who stood at the gate of the year, Give me a light, that I may tread safely into the unknown. And he replied, Go out into the darkness, and put your hand in the hand of God. That shall be to you better than a light, and safer than the known way." (Minnie Haskins, "A Dialogue Between a Man, and the Keeper of The Gate of The Year").

"As many as receive me, to them will I give power to become the sons of God." (V. 30). These are my towering examples who, over the years, have been my mystical mentors, my sensible chaperones, my spiritual guides, my surrogate saviors, my compassionate critics, and everything in between. They are my avatars, manifestations of deity in bodily forms, my na'vi, the visionaries, who communicate with God on a level to which I can only aspire, and my tsaddik, whom I esteem as intuitive interpreters of biblical law and scripture. They are my divine teachers incarnate.

They have shown me the way, stretched my mind, reinforced my faith, strengthened my testimony, lifted my spirits, helped me to discover my wings, provided of their means, given immaterial support, emboldened me with words of encouragement, cheered me on with wise counsel, taught me humility, been there to steady me, soothed my troubled soul, stepped in to nurture me, led me to fountains of living water, wet my parched lips with inspired counsel, bound up my wounds, offered listening ears, and extended open arms. They have taught me to find the silk purse in every sow's ear and the silver lining in every cloud. When I have been given a lemon, they have shown me how to find the recipe for lemonade.

From their positive influence, I have learned that there is so much good in the worst of us, and so much bad in the best of us, that it hardly behooves any of us to talk about the rest of us. I have done my best to keep tempests confined to the teapots where they belong, and to put the confusion of the world in perspective. I have tried to retain the joyful anticipation of the optimistic little boy, who, when faced with the daunting task of shoveling up an enormous pile of manure in a horse stall near his home, enthusiastically set about his task with the exclamation: "There's got to be a pony in there, somewhere!"

I think of my friends, family, and mentors each time I read "Lays of Ancient Rome," by Thomas Babbington Mccaulay: "Then out spake brave Horatius, the Captain of the Gate: 'To every man upon this earth, death cometh soon or late. And how can man die better, than by facing fearful odds, for the ashes of his fathers, and the temples of his gods?" (Stanza 27).

# Section 12

## (Received prior to the organization
## of the church).

"At Joseph Knight's request the Prophet inquired of the Lord and received the revelation." (Superscript).

A great and marvelous work is about to come forth among the children of men." (V. 1). In the Last Days, God will perform a work of unprecedented importance and scale among the people, and will remember the Abrahamic Covenant made to their forefathers. "I shall proceed to do a marvelous work among them, that I may remember my covenants which I have made unto the children of men, that I may set my hand again the second time to recover my people, which are of the house of Israel." (2 Nephi 29:1). All who qualify by the Lord's own standards, will once again receive the blessings and ordinances associated with the Covenant. These include baptism, which is a covenant of salvation, the companionship of the Holy Ghost, which is a covenant of justification, the Sacrament, which is a covenant of sanctification, and celestial marriage, which is a covenant of exaltation. These blessings also include an inheritance in the various lands of the Covenant. Through the power of the Covenant, scattered Israel will be gathered a second time, and God will also remember the promises made to the Nephites of old, as His words "hiss forth unto the ends of the earth." (2 Nephi 29:2).

But at the same time, many will deny the reality and necessity of the Covenant, even though Paul taught: "If ye be Christ's, then are ye Abraham's seed, and heirs according to the promise." (Galatians 3:29). Some lack faith in the universal application of the Covenant, while others do not understand how easy God has made it for true believers to join with Israel through a process called adoption. Many have closed their minds to the possibility that He has always had an interest in His scattered people. In response to the bold declaration that The Book of Mormon is another testament of Jesus Christ, such individuals will cry: "A Bible! A Bible! We have got a Bible and there cannot be any more Bible." (2 Nephi 29:3). With that cry of protest, these same people deny the power of God, do not feel the need to receive more instruction from Him, and rebel against light and truth. (See 2 Nephi 28:26-28). But He has declared: "I am God; give heed to my word, which is quick and powerful, sharper than a two-edged sword, to the dividing asunder of both joints and marrow." (V. 2). His word will not only separate light from darkness, and truth from error, but also the righteous from the wicked.

Truman Madsen compared the word of God to the currents that are "part of the flowing fountain of the church. If we do not drink," he said, "if we die of thirst while only inches from the fountain, the fault comes down to us. For the free, full, flowing, living water is there." ("Christ & The Inner Life," p. 31). When the Spirit touches us, we yearn for the opportunity to find expression for the wonderful feelings that well up inside us. We desire to be baptized and to enter the fold of the Good Shepherd. is our yearning to put to death the old, sinful person, the font being symbolic of the grave. But there is a dual symbolism in baptism, as it also represents the rebirth of a new, spiritual person. Gospel principles, clearly understood, define both good and evil, righteousness and wickedness, and put light and darkness in their proper perspective. It is no wonder that angels now bide their time with swords raised, as they await the command to bring judgment upon a wicked world.

"Behold, the field is white already to harvest; therefore, whoso desireth to reap let him thrust in his sickle with his might, and reap while the day lasts, that he may treasure up for his soul everlasting salvation in the kingdom of God." (V. 3). Ammon metaphorically described the harvest to illustrate for his brethren how thousands of wicked Lamanites had been gathered through their missionary efforts. "Behold, the field was ripe," he said, "and blessed are ye, for ye did thrust in the sickle, and did reap with your might, yea, all the day long did ye labor; and behold the number of your sheaves!" (Alma 26:5).

A fulness of joy comes in the resurrection (see D&C 93:33), but missionary work can point us toward the same quality of happiness. (See D&C 93:20). The Savior told the Three Nephite Disciples, whose desire was to tarry: "And for this cause ye shall have fulness of joy; and ye shall sit down in the kingdom of my Father; yea, your joy shall be full." (3 Nephi 28:10). There is no mistaking how important missionary work is to the successful execution of the Plan, or in the eyes of the Savior.

The continuing focus of attention on their less fortunate brethren by those enlisted in the missionary army of Jesus Christ will eventually bring them into complete harmony with the attributes of their Father in Heaven, whose concern is for the eternal welfare of all of His children. "And ye shall be even as I am, and I am even as the Father, and the Father and I are one," said the Savior. (3 Nephi 28:10).

Helaman had exhorted his sons: "It is upon the rock of our Redeemer, who is Christ, the Son of God, that ye must build your foundation." (Helaman 5:12). Those who follow His counsel will not be blown away and tumble down to misery and a gulf of endless wo by the "mighty winds" of the devil, which represent the sectarian philosophies and false theories of men that are continually raking the face of the earth. (Helaman 5:12).

"Yea, whosoever will thrust in his sickle and reap, the same is called of God." (V. 4). Bruce R. McConkie composed a statement of belief that is carried by many of the missionaries of The Church of Jesus Christ of Latter-day Saints. He wrote: "I am called of God. My authority is above that of the kings of the earth. By revelation I have been selected as a personal representative of the Lord, Jesus Christ. He is my master and He has chosen me to represent Him, to stand in His place, to say and do what He Himself would do if he personally were administering among the very people to whom He has sent me. My voice is His voice and my acts are His acts, my words are His words and my doctrine His doctrine, for I am His agent. My commission is to do what He wants done, to say what He wants said, to be a living modern witness in word and in deed of the divinity of His great and marvelous latter day work, and he that receiveth me receiveth Him, while he that rejects me rejects Him that sent me. How great is my calling!" ("My Missionary Commission").

"Therefore, if ye will ask of me you shall receive; if you will knock it shall be opened unto you." (V. 5). There are three frameworks within which we may develop saving faith in the doctrine of Christ: First, the scriptures, secondly, the inspired words of the prophet and teachers, and thirdly, the promptings of the Holy Ghost. The impressions of the Spirit and testimony by the power of the Holy Ghost are perhaps even more important than the scriptures and the pronouncements of the prophets.

In fact, "many have worshipped scripture (alone) with such exaggerated zeal that they (have) lost contact with the giver of the word and thus betrayed him with the kiss of false devotion. In their professed reverence for that which God had spoken in the past, they denied him the right to continue to speak. They lose themselves in the smoke of their own offerings. The life-giving force of the ancient Saints (is) not the echo of the past, as it was found in scriptural records, or in someone else's revelation; it (is) in the voice of (continuing) personal revelation." (Joseph F. McConkie, "Studies in Scripture," 1:80).

It is a terrible thing when we throw up barriers to the Spirit, and value as nothing the revealed written word of God. "But behold, there are many that harden their hearts against the Holy Spirit, that it hath no place in them; wherefore, they cast many things away which are written and esteem them as things of naught." (2 Nephi 33:2).

"For the things which some men esteem to be of great worth, both to the body and soul, others set at naught and trample under their feet. Yea, even the very God of Israel do men trample under their feet; I say, trample under their feet but I would speak in other words - they set him at naught, and hearken not to the voice of his counsels." (1 Nephi 19:7).

"Now, as you have asked, behold, I say unto you, keep my commandments, and seek to bring forth and establish the cause of Zion." (V. 6). This is general counsel to all who would ask: "What can I do to further the cause of truth?"

In response to escalating wickedness in the Land of Zarahemla, Nephi had taken "it upon himself to preach the word of God all the remainder of his days, and his brother Lehi also, all the remainder of his days." (Helaman 5:4). The ministry of Nephi and Lehi was destined to be one of the most powerful in the Book of Mormon historical record. Their experiences reflect their understanding that the Lord's servants do not preach and teach only to make people's lives better. They do so in order that baptisms might be performed by the authority of the priesthood, thus unlocking for the children of God the gateway leading to the Celestial Kingdom. The conduct of the lives of Nephi and Lehi illustrates the principle that individual spiritual growth precedes collective numerical growth. It was to be so in the restored church in the Last Days, as well.

To Joseph Smith, the Lord explained: "If you keep not my commandments, the love of the Father shall not continue with you, therefore you shall walk in darkness." (D&C 95:12). The Apostle John's message clarifies that same principle. He wrote: "Love not the world, neither the things that are in the world. If any man loves the world, the love of the Father is not in him." (1 John 2:15).

"No man can serve two masters," explained the Savior, "for either he will hate the one, and love the other; or else he will hold to the one, and despise the other. Ye cannot serve God and mammon. Therefore I say unto you, Take no thought for your life, what ye shall eat, or what ye shall drink; nor yet for your body, what ye shall put on. Is not the life more than meat, and the body than raiment?" (Matthew 6:24-25).

"Behold, I speak unto you, and also to all those who have desires to bring forth and establish this work." (V. 7). This helps to explain why the introductory statements in this revelation are so similar to the blessings given to Oliver Cowdery (D&C 6), Hyrum Smith (D&C 11), Joseph Knight, Sr. (D&C 12), and David Whitmer (D& 14). "So much depends upon our willingness to make up our minds," Spencer W. Kimball said, "that present levels of performance are not acceptable, either to ourselves or to the Lord. In saying that, I am not calling for flashy, temporary differences in our performance levels, but for a quiet resolve to lengthen our stride." ("Church News," 3/22/1975).

When President Kimball urged members of the church to lengthen their stride, he knew that the exertion would cause discomfort, as it tested their limits of endurance and stretched their spiritual muscles. But in doing so, they would be strengthened. Christ urged those in bondage to do the same thing, to go the second mile, doubling their stride. "The second mile is a gift of spiritual independence that removes the veil of insensitivity from a destiny." (Richard L. Gunn, "A Search for Sensitivity and Spirit," p. 197).

"And no one can assist in this work except he shall be humble and full of love, having faith, hope, and charity, being temperate in all things." (V. 8). The Lord declared: "We will prove them herewith, to see if they will do all things whatsoever the Lord their God shall command them." In other words, conditions and limitations were imposed upon their exercise of free will, so that they would be able to continue to progress. It was necessary that our first parents use their agency appropriately, in order to develop the qualities of divine nobility. Within the bounds and conditions established by loving Parents who honored the parameters of the Plan, the objective was that "they who keep their second estate (should) have glory added upon their heads for ever and ever." (Abraham 3:25-26).

When we engage our agency, we automatically limit our options. If we choose the better alternative, we automatically have made a decision not to choose less attractive consequences. Heavenly Father gives us commandments in order to help us to choose the better part, to allow us to grow through our exercise of agency, that we might approach our potential. We are best able to do that when we participate in His program of missionary work that is critical to the successful execution of the Plan.

Missionaries face one formidable obstacle, however, and that is the standard of the world, that "seeing is believing." But seeing is not only irrelevant to the acquisition of faith, it is often the wrong message that is being presented. The example of the advertising executives of Madison Avenue testifies that this is true. Harold B. Lee taught: "You must learn to walk to the edge of the light, and then a few steps into the darkness; then the light will appear and show the way before you." (Quoted by Boyd K. Packer, "What is Faith?" p. 42). This is the way faith is developed and strengthened.

Hope in Christ is to have the assurance of peace, that the direction of our lives is on course, and that the Lord is pleased with our efforts. As Mormon said, hope is born of faith. "Behold, I say unto you that ye shall have hope through the atonement of Christ and the power of his resurrection, to be raised up unto life eternal, and this because of your faith in him according to the promise." (Moroni 7:41). Hope is not trust in some wildly improbable promise, nor is it a high stakes gamble. It is the inevitable result of well-founded faith, when we are meek and lowly of heart, and are in complete control of our desires and emotions.

Charity follows the qualities of faith and hope, and is the supreme characteristic of faithful disciples. Mormon taught that if we are "meek and lowly in heart, and confess by the power of the Holy Ghost that Jesus is the Christ," with a sure hope born of faith, we "must needs have charity." (Moroni 7:44).

Neal A. Maxwell may have been thinking about temperance, when he wrote: "Freedom wisely used to interact with the principles of the gospel of Jesus Christ, far from producing drabness and uniformity in disciples, produces not only more significant individuals but more interesting individuals. There is something about the gospel that makes personality more luxuriant, whereas sin robs us of our individuality." ("Ensign," 9/98). When we are temperate in our behavior, we are able to see more clearly and more accurately through the refreshing eye of faith.

"Behold, I am the light and the life of the world, that speak these words." (V. 9). Joseph Smith wrote: "There are but a very few beings in the world who understand rightly the nature of God (and if we) do not understand the character of God (we) do not comprehend (our)selves." ("Teachings," p. 343). Ammon joined the ranks of the truly converted in the Last Days, when he declared: God "is my life and my light, my joy and my salvation, and my redemption from everlasting wo." (Alma 26:35).

It has never been more important to bring up our children in light and truth. The light of which we speak is any influence that draws His children to Jesus Christ, and truth is any belief that is in harmony with gospel principles. Charles Dickens wrote of Victorian England: "It was the best of times; It was the worst of times." ("A Tale of Two Cities," 1859). Because it is so even today, the Lord has given inspired counsel: "In consequence of evils and designs which do and will exist in the hearts of conspiring men in the last days, I have warned you, and forewarn you, by giving unto you this word of wisdom" or the fullness of the gospel, "by revelation." (D&C

89:4). Today, more than ever before, we need the Wisdom of Solomon to negotiate the minefields of mortality, and to avoid the potholes that we will surely encounter along the way on the path of progress.

David O. McKay observed that from the time a child is born until about their eighth birthday (which just happens to be the age of accountability), we teach the principles of the gospel. From their baptism until about the age of 16, we train our youth in the application of these principles with the goal of ingraining within them the habits of provident living. After their 16$^{th}$ birthday, by and large, we can only trust them to walk in the way of the Lord.

And so, we introduce our children to the Word. We "begin by teaching at the cradle-side." (Joseph Fielding Smith, Jr., C.R., 10/1948). We weave gospel principles into family activities, as our children commit the 13 Articles of Faith to memory and to lifestyle, before their baptism. We find priesthood purposes in activities that are oriented toward conversion to the gospel of Jesus Christ, living its teachings, serving faithfully in callings and dedicating ourselves to the responsibilities entrusted to us, giving meaningful service, living worthily to receive priesthood blessings and temple ordinances, preparing to serve honorable full-time missions, obtaining as much education as possible, preparing for and entering into temple marriage, and giving proper respect to others.

We surround ourselves with uplifting art, good music and literature, and other wholesome influences. We avoid indulging in the transient temptation of telestial toys, and we develop the discipline to focus on celestial sureties rather than temporal trinkets.

When we pass beyond the veil, we will leave with our loved ones a legacy of both tangible and intangible remembrances. We will leave them with our testimonies. We will leave them with gratitude for the privilege and blessing to have been knit together as an eternal family unit, which is the basic building block of our mansions above in the Celestial Kingdom of God.

# Section 13

## (Received from an angel, prior to the organization of the church).

"An extract from Joseph Smith's history, recounting the ordination of the Prophet and Oliver Cowdery to the Aaronic Priesthood near Harmony, Pennsylvania, May 15, 1829. The ordination was done by the hands of an angel who announced himself as John, the same that is called John the Baptist, in the New Testament. The angel explained that he was acting under the direction of Peter, James, and John, the ancient Apostles, who held the keys of the higher priesthood, which was called the Priesthood of Melchizedek. The promise was given to Joseph and Oliver that in due time this higher priesthood would be conferred upon them." (Superscript).

Those who anciently held the priesthood were called as a result of divine revelation given to their file leaders, and were ordained according to a holy ordinance. (See Alma 13:8). This revelation is a confirmation of that order: "Upon you my fellow servants," declared John The Baptist, "in the name of Messiah, I confer the Priesthood of Aaron, which holds the keys of the ministering of angels, and of the gospel of repentance, and of baptism by immersion for the remission of sins; and this shall never be taken again from the earth, until (see below) the sons of Levi do offer again an offering unto the Lord in righteousness." (D&C 13:1).

Laying his hands upon the heads of Joseph Smith and Oliver Cowdery, who knelt before him, John pronounced the words of the ordinance: "Upon you my fellow servants,"in the name of Messiah, I confer the Priesthood of Aaron."

John was a legal administrator whose words and acts were binding on earth and in heaven, and those who listened to him were obligated, at the peril of their salvation, to believe his words and heed his counsel. We do not know who sent John to baptize in the wilderness. (John 1:33). But we know that he came with power and authority. (D&C 84:28).

We do not know when John received the Aaronic Priesthood, but obviously, it came to him after his own baptism, at whatever age was then proper, and before he was sent by one whom he does not name to preach repentance and baptize with water. When he visited Joseph Smith and Oliver Cowdery by the banks of the Susquehanna River on May 15, 1829, "he acted under the direction of Peter, James and John, who held the keys of the Priesthood of Melchizedek." (J.S.H. 1:72).

The priesthood authority by which baptism has always been performed is "the only legitimate authority on the earth." (John Taylor, J.D., 5:157). During his apostolic ministry, Paul had prophesied of the coming apostasy and consequent loss of that priesthood authority. He wrote to the Thessalonian Saints: "Be not soon shaken in mind, or be troubled, neither by spirit, nor by word, nor by letter as from us, as that the day of Christ is at hand. Let no man deceive you by any means: for that day shall not come, except there come a falling away first." (2 Thessalonians 2:2-3).

A glimpse of the falling away referred to by Paul was provided by the early church historian Eusebius, in the third century A.D.. He wrote: "A change came over us. We yielded to pride and sloth. We yielded to mutual envy and abuse. We warred upon ourselves as occasion offered, and we used the weapons and the spears of words. Leaders fought with leaders, and laity formed factions against laity. Unspeakable hypocrisy and dissimulation traveled to the farthest limits of evil." ("The Essential Eusebius," p. 177).

Such contention persisted through the early nineteenth century, when Joseph Smith reported that "a scene of great confusion and bad feeling ensued - priest contending against priest, and convert against convert; so that all their good feelings one for another, if they ever had any, were entirely lost in a strife of words and a contest about opinions." (J.S.H. 1:6).

Thomas Jefferson declared of his day: "The religion builders have so distorted and deformed the doctrines of Jesus, so muffled them in mysticisms, fancies and falsehoods, have caricatured them into forms so inconceivable, as to shock reasonable thinkers. Happy in the prospect of a restoration of primitive Christianity, I must leave to younger persons to encounter and lop off the false branches which have been engrafted into it by the mythologists of the middle and modern ages." ("Jefferson's Complete Works," 7:210 & 257).

A leader of the Reformation in America, Roger Williams, wrote: "There is no regularly constituted church on earth, nor any person authorized to administer any church ordinance; nor can there be until new apostles are sent by the Great Head of the church, for Whose Coming I am seeking." (Quoted by William Cullen Bryant, "Picturesque America," p. 502). It was John the Baptist who initiated the restoration of that authority when he laid his hands upon the heads of Joseph Smith and Oliver Cowdery.

In April 1829, in preparation for the visit of John, Christ had given Joseph Smith the specific words that he was to employ in the baptismal prayer: "Having been commissioned of Jesus Christ, I baptize you in the name of the Father, and of the Son and of the Holy Ghost. Amen." (D&C 20:73).

John explained to Joseph and Oliver that the Aaronic Priesthood held "the keys of the ministering of angels." The scriptures teach that ministering angels may be any of the following: 1) Pre-earth existent spirits (Revelation 12:7, & D&C 130:5), 2) Translated beings (J.S.T. Genesis 14:26-36, & "Teachings," p. 170), 3) Spirits of just men made perfect, awaiting the resurrection (D&C 76:66-69), 4) Resurrected beings (D&C 129), or 5) Righteous mortal men (Genesis 19, & J.S.T. Genesis 19). All of the above have assisted at one time or another in the work of the kingdom, in a variety of ways, as occasion permitted, or as they were directed to do so by their file leaders.

"The gospel of repentance" spoken of by John is a preparatory gospel. The Aaronic priesthood holds the key of "the preparatory gospel; which gospel is the gospel of repentance and of baptism, and the remission of sins, and the law of carnal commandments." (D&C 84:26-27).

Repentance is essential since "the first condition of happiness is a clear conscience." (David O. McKay). As Abraham said so long ago: "Finding there was greater happiness and peace and rest for me, I sought for the blessings of the fathers" through the ordinances of the gospel. (Abraham 1:1). Before a wound can heal, it has to be clean. The Savior provided the way through faith on His name, repentance because of His Sacrifice, and forgiveness because the Atonement satisfied the demands of Justice. (See Moses 6:60).

"Mercy claimeth the penitent, and mercy cometh because of the Atonement; and the Atonement bringeth to pass the resurrection of the dead; and the resurrection of the dead bringeth back men into the presence of God. For behold, justice exerciseth all _his_ demands, and also mercy claimeth all which is _her_ own; and thus, none but the truly penitent are saved." (Alma 42:23-24, underlining mine).

As we live in harmony with the principles of the preparatory gospel, we are unerringly guided to do that which is right. "Every individual that lives according to the laws that the Lord has given to His people, and has received the blessings that He has in store for the faithful, should be able to know the things of God from the things which are not of God, the light from the darkness, that which comes from heaven and that which comes from somewhere else. This is the satisfaction and the consolation that the Latter-day Saints enjoy by living their religion. This is the knowledge which every one who thus lives possesses." (Brigham Young, D.B.Y., p. 35).

There is a great deal more involved in gaining salvation than in the initial expression of faith, or even in the act of baptism for admission into the church. We must never procrastinate the day of our repentance. If we do so for even a moment, we put our souls in jeopardy because we become subject to the spirit and influence of the devil.

Joseph and Oliver learned that "baptism by immersion for the remission of sins" is an earthly ordinance that must be performed by mortal men having proper authority. The Savior taught that immersion in water was the correct procedure, baptism being symbolic of the burial of Christ. (3 Nephi 11:23). Joseph Smith said the repentant "were baptized after the manner of his burial, being buried in the water in his name, and this according to the commandment which he has given - That by keeping the commandments they might be washed and cleansed from all their sins." (D&C 76:51-52). "Consequently, the baptismal font was (conceived to be, in the minds of the penitent faithful,) a similitude of the grave." (D&C 128:13). As Paul wrote: "Therefore we are buried with him by baptism into death: that like as Christ was raised up from the dead by the glory of the Father, even so we also should walk in newness of life. For if we have been planted together in the likeness of his death, we shall be also in the likeness of his resurrection." (Romans 6:4).

During the apostolic ministry there was no disputation among the Saints regarding the doctrine of Christ. But after the Apostles had been martyred, and their priesthood authority died with them, confusion arose in the congregations concerning the simplest policies, procedures, and doctrines of the kingdom, and there was no enlightened solution to the problem. Apostasy resulted, that was only abolished by the direct latter-day intervention of Heavenly Father and His Son Jesus Christ. (See J.S.H. 1:16-20).

Baptism serves at least nine purposes: 1) We are baptized to demonstrate our obedience, and 2) to follow in the footsteps of the Savior. 3) We are baptized to fulfill all righteousness. 4) Baptism allows us to receive a remission of our sins if we have reached the age of accountability. 5) Baptism enables us to gain admission to the Lord's church, "the only true and living church upon the face of the whole earth" with which He is pleased. (D&C 1:31). 6) Baptism provides us with the opportunity to be personally sanctified through fire and the Holy Ghost. 7) It is outwardly symbolic of our re-birth, as we pass through a portal in the similitude of the grave. 8) It is the gateway ordinance leading to the blessings reserved for the faithful that are found in the other ordinances of the gospel, and 9) it sets us squarely on the path that leads to the Celestial Kingdom of God.

Even in the days of the patriarchs, there was confusion among the ancients concerning the proper administration of the ordinance. "And it came to pass, that Abram fell on his face, and called upon the name of the Lord. And God talked with him, saying, My people have gone astray from my precepts, and have not kept mine ordinances, which I gave unto their fathers. And they have not observed mine anointing, and the burial, or baptism wherewith I commanded them; but have turned from the commandment, and taken unto themselves the washing of children, and the blood of sprinkling; And have said that the blood of the righteous Abel was shed for sins; and have not known wherein they are accountable before me." (J.S.T. Genesis 17:3-7).

In Book of Mormon times, Mormon considered the procedural dispute regarding baptism to be of such magnitude that immediately upon learning of it, he went and "inquired of the Lord concerning the matter." (Moroni 8:7). The ecclesiastical counsel that he then gave came by direct revelation from the Lord, "by the power of the Holy Ghost." (Moroni 8:7). The reason that a correct understanding of baptism is essential is that it is a foundation ordinance that lies at the very heart of the gospel of Jesus Christ.

As the Savior taught the Nephites: "This is the gospel which I have given unto you — that I came into the world to do the will of my Father, because my Father sent me. And my Father sent me that I might be lifted up upon the cross; and after that I had been lifted up upon the cross, that I might draw all men unto me. ...And it shall come to pass, that whoso repenteth and is baptized in my name shall be filled. (3 Nephi 27:13-20).

It is critically important that the ordinance admitting supplicants into the fold of Christ be carried out according to His specific and pointed instruction, for there is "one Lord, one faith, one baptism." (Ephesians 4:5). "Except a man be born of water and of the Spirit," declared the Savior, "he cannot enter into the kingdom of God." (John 3:5).

Because God is a party to every gospel covenant, those who make sacred promises with Him at the waters of baptism will be visited "with fire and with the Holy Ghost." (3 Nephi 11:36). Fire and smoke have always been symbolic of the presence of the Lord and the glory of God. They are frequently used to depict the glory of celestial realms. In the language of Joseph Smith: "God Almighty Himself dwells in eternal fire. Our God is a consuming fire." ("Teachings," p. 367, see Deuteronomy 4:24, & Hebrews 12:24). The Spirit of God is lie a burning fire.

One of the responsibilities of the Holy Ghost is to bear the most sacred witness of the validity of every gospel ordinance. Because there can be no greater witness, with the baptism of fire and the unimpeachable witness of the Holy Ghost, the Atonement is complete, Mercy satisfies Justice, and the penitent faithful receive a remission of sins in a symbolic rite of purification. (See 2 Nephi 31:17).

Stephen Robinson wrote: "Faith and repentance lead us to the strait gate of baptism. Those who pass through this gate, will obtain a remission of sins, gain membership in the church, and open the door leading to personal sanctification through repentance and receipt of the Holy Ghost. We may then find ourselves on the path of eternal progression leading to the Celestial Kingdom. The way is strait and narrow. The gospel standard is undeviating, with no room for rationalization or compromise." ("Ensign," 6/2001).

The authority restored by John will "never be taken again from the earth until..." (V. 1). "Until" is used in this phrase in a continuing sense; for example, "God be with you until we meet again." In the footnote to J.S.H. 1:71, "Oliver Cowdery describes these events thus: "What joy filled our hearts, and with what surprise we must have bowed...when we received under his hand the Holy Priesthood as he said, 'Upon you my fellow-servants, in the name of Messiah, I confer this Priesthood and this authority, which shall remain upon earth, that the Sons of Levi may yet offer an offering unto the Lord in righteousness."

"...the sons of Levi do offer again an offering unto the Lord in righteousness." (V. 1). The sons of Levi are "the sons of Moses and also the sons of Aaron (who) shall offer an acceptable offering and sacrifice in the house of the Lord." (D&C 84:31). Joseph taught that "the sons of Moses and of Aaron shall be filled with the glory of the Lord, upon Mount Zion in the Lord's house, whose sons are ye, and also many whom I have called and sent forth to build up my church. For whoso is faithful unto the obtaining these two priesthoods of which I have spoken, and the magnifying their calling, are sanctified by the Spirit unto the renewing of their bodies." All who are faithful and obtain these two priesthoods "become the sons of Moses and of Aaron, and the seed of Abraham, and the church and kingdom, and the elect of God." (D&C 84:32-34).

It is ordained that the Gentile nations of the earth are to receive the gospel, and the elect among them are to be converted by the power of the Holy Ghost. Peter, who first brought the gospel to the Gentiles, wrote: On them "also was poured out the gift of the Holy Ghost." (Acts 10:45). These gifts of the Spirit are sufficient to carry us along the path leading to eternal life, and so the Word was given to Israel in both the Old and the New World. As Peter said: "Of a truth I perceive that God is no respecter of persons: But in every nation, he that feareth him, and worketh righteousness, is accepted with him." (Acts 10:34-35).

By obedience to the covenant, we who have been born again through baptism make "an offering to the Lord in righteousness." (V. 1). We are valiant in the testimony of Jesus, and make our offering on the altar of faith. We "take the Lord's side on every issue. We think what He thinks, believe what He believes, say what He would say, and do what He would do." (Bruce R. McConkie, C.R., 10/1974). Fulfilling the requirements of our stewardship, or magnifying our calling, means to build it up in dignity and importance, to make it honorable and commendable in the eyes of all, to enlarge and strengthen it, to simply perform the service that pertains to it. John Taylor taught: "If you do not magnify your calling, God will hold you responsible for those whom you might have saved had you done your duty." (J.D., 20:23).

Even after the appearance of the resurrected Lord to the Apostles, Peter resumed his former occupation, and announced to the others, "I go a fishing." (John 21:3). When the Savior appeared on the shore, and after He had instructed the Apostles, he said to Peter: "Follow me." (John 21:19). We are assured by the accounts of Peter's subsequent ministry that he did just that. The dawning of recognition came to him that he was "elect according to the foreknowledge of God the Father, through sanctification of the Spirit, unto obedience and sprinkling of the blood of Jesus Christ." (1 Peter 1:2). He obtained "precious faith," and became a partaker "of the divine nature." (2 Peter 1:1 & 4).

The principles of true conversion point us in the direction of a clear recognition of iniquity, and then to a deep godly sorrow for our sins. Next comes inescapable suffering and torment that stimulates an appeal to the Savior, together with our awakening understanding of the power of the Atonement. From Him comes forgiveness, spiritual enlightenment, and great joy. This motivates us to a lifestyle of righteousness and service. Because of the Atonement, all have equal opportunity before the Lord. All "may have the privilege, living or dead, of accepting the conditions of the great Plan of Redemption provided by the Father, through the Son, before the world was." (John Taylor, "Mediation and Atonement," p. 181).

All those who have reached the age of accountability have the light of Christ to give them a foundation of understanding of what is good and what is evil. (2 Nephi 9:25-26). As Parley P. Pratt declared: "I have received the Holy Anointing and I can never rest until the last enemy is conquered, death destroyed, and truth reigns triumphant." ("Deseret News," 4/30/1853).

# Section 14
## (Received prior to the organization of the church).

"A great and marvelous work is about to come forth among the children of men." (V. 1). Nephi had foreseen that the Lord would raise up nations who would scatter Israel. But then a marvelous work would take place, beginning at a hill called Cumorah. It would be of worth "not only unto the Gentiles but unto all the house of Israel, unto the making known of the covenants of the Father of heaven unto Abraham, saying: In thy seed shall all the kindreds of the earth be blessed." (1 Nephi 22:9).

The Children of the Covenant would be despised of all nations, cast out of their promised land of inheritance, and characterized by a hiss and a by-word for two millennia, but they would ultimately become the agents through whom the Lord would bless all nations.

"Behold, I am God; give heed to my word, which is quick and powerful, sharper than a two-edged sword, to the dividing asunder of both joints and marrow." (V. 2). The word of God penetrates to the innermost parts. Hugh B. Brown said: "Sometimes during solitude I hear truth spoken with clarity and freshness; uncolored and untranslated it speaks from within myself in a language original but inarticulate, heard only with the soul."

Joseph Smith taught: "The word of Jehovah has such an influence over the human mind that it is convincing without other testimony. Faith cometh by hearing." (Willard Richards, "Joseph Smith's Diary"). At times, so completely thrilled are those who hear the voice of God, and so penetrating is the message of gladness, that words can not be articulated to convey the impressions thus received.

"Behold, the field is white already to harvest; therefore, whoso desireth to reap let him thrust in his sickle with his might, and reap while the day lasts, that he may treasure up for his soul everlasting salvation in the kingdom of God." (V. 3). A similar missionary harvest had taken place in the Land of Zarahemla, that had moved Mormon to observe: "The Lord is merciful unto all who will, in the sincerity of their hearts, call upon his holy name," and "the gate of heaven is open unto all, even to those who will believe on the name of Jesus Christ, who is the Son of God." (Helaman 3:26-27).

Mormon knew from experience that the word would "lead the man of Christ" through the valley of the shadow of death to "the right hand of God in the kingdom of heaven." (Helaman 3:29). He hoped that the examples of the great missionaries, recorded on the plates from which The Book of Mormon was later translated, would provide positive role models for readers living in strikingly similar circumstances in the Last Days.

"Yea, whosoever will thrust in his sickle and reap, the same is called of God." (V. 4). We must not rest on our laurels, or pause for too long in one place, when we need to be moving onward and upward. Eternal progression is a path, not a point. In New Testament times, there was to be no "Book of the Resolutions of the Apostles," but only the "Book of the Acts of the Apostles." Good intentions may be noble, but achievement is the hallmark of progress. Harold B. Lee was fond of quoting the anonymous author who declared: "Work without vision is drudgery, and vision without work is dreamery, but work with vision is destiny!"

Spencer W. Kimball told the Saints: "We have paused on some plateaus long enough. Let us resume our journey forward and upward. Let us quietly end our reluctance to reach out to others, whether in our own families, wards, or neighborhoods. We have been diverted, at times, from fundamentals on which we must now focus in order to move forward as a person or as a people." (C.R., 4/1979). "Therefore, if ye will ask of me you shall receive; if you will knock it shall be opened unto you." (V. 5). James taught: "The effectual fervent prayer of a righteous man availeth much." (James 5:16). We may not pray with eloquence, but we need to do it with fervor. Two examples illustrate the point.

Elaine Cannon related the following story. She said that in her ward fast meeting a young woman stood up under great difficulty, the first time she had been able to do so since her husband had passed away. They hadn't been married very long before he fell terminally ill. She said that in the last stages, he was suffering beyond belief, and she was really desperate. She knelt by the side of his bed, and cried out to the Lord as only a woman can do, full of anxiety, full of demands, pleading, almost scolding the Lord to hear her and answer her prayers and help her husband, to heal him. She was near hysteria.

Then she felt a touch on her shoulder, and it was her husband trying to calm her.

He said to her, "Just pray that I may be able to sleep through the night." As she spoke in that fast meeting, she said, "That sweet sustaining lesson taught me that you don't ask for the whole world, you don't demand that your will be done, you just pray that you can meet the challenges of the day. And that lesson from my husband just before he died has helped me to sleep through the night, too."

The second illustration comes from the life of Enzio Busche. While still a young man, and before joining the church, he found himself lying in a hospital bed, near death. He asked a nun: "Is the Catholic Church the true Church of Christ?" The nun hesitatingly replied, "My church is not the church you are seeking. Mine is a church of tradition." He asked, "How many churches are there?" and she said there were at least 700 in the world. He thought, "That's not so bad. If I get out of this hospital I'll investigate one a month until I find the true Church of Christ."

He recovered from his illness, and began to investigate the churches. But after many months, he and his wife despaired of ever finding Christ's true church. They cried unto the Lord "until the ceiling shook." Two days later, Latter-day Saint missionaries knocked on their door, and the rest is history. (Notes from a Fireside Address, Washington Spokane North Stake, 10/18/1980).

"Seek to bring forth and establish my Zion." (V. 6). In the Last Days, "more are the children of the desolate than the children of the married wife." (3 Nephi 22:1). In other words, there shall be a great gathering of Israel from among the Gentile nations, and those who enter the fold shall outnumber those who had previously found their way into the church and had been bound by covenant to Christ.

"Enlarge the place of thy tent," urged Isaiah, "and let them stretch forth the curtains of thy habitations; spare not, lengthen thy cords and strengthen thy stakes." (3 Nephi 22:2). That is to say, make room for the new Children of the Covenant, who will flock to the gospel standard, as the gathering of Israel gains momentum. "For Zion must increase in beauty, and in holiness; her borders must be enlarged; her stakes must be strengthened; yea, verily I say unto you, Zion must arise and put on her beautiful garments." (D&C 82:14).

"And, if you keep my commandments and endure to the end you shall have eternal life, which gift is the greatest of all the gifts of God." (V. 7). The real tragedy in life is not that we set our sights too high, and then fail to achieve our goals. Rather, it is that we aim too low, easily reaching our objectives, but accomplishing little, having nothing to show for our consistently timid efforts. We should never accept mediocrity in our lives; instead our behavior should be in harmony with the nature of God, Who dwells in the peace and harmony of the

Celestial Kingdom, and Whose work and glory is to bring to pass our immortality and eternal life. (See Moses 1:39).

What He has, He could easily give to us, if He chose to do so. But we would likely squander our unmerited inheritance, failing to recognize its value. Instead, God has chosen to provide a mortal experience where we can learn to be what He is. In this way, we will earn our reward. We will still be saved by His grace, but only after all we can do.

"And blessed are all they who do hunger and thirst after righteousness, for they shall be filled with the Holy Ghost." (3 Nephi 12:6). Nephi taught: "If ye shall press forward" with complete dedication, "feasting upon the word of Christ" or receiving physical and spiritual strength and nourishment, "and endure to the end" with continuing responsibility and accountability, "behold, thus saith the Father: Ye shall have eternal life," which is the greatest of His gifts. (2 Nephi 31:20).

Although endurance is often thought of in negative terms, as in "enduring pain" or "enduring persecution," endurance can ultimately be positive and pleasant. However, there is always a performance cost associated with this characteristic. Spiritual fitness, or endurance, does not come without effort. Nowhere are we led to believe that a testimony of the gospel and its exalting principles comes as an unearned gift. Rather, we read such things as: "Behold, you have not understood; you have supposed that I would give it unto you, when you took no thought save it was to ask me. But, behold, I say unto you, that you must study it out in your mind." (D&C 9:7-8).

Lorenzo Snow declared: "It is impossible to advance in the principles of truth, to increase in heavenly knowledge, except we exercise our reasoning faculties and exert ourselves." (J.D., 18:48). Agency is not free. It is purchased at a substantial price.

If we desire a testimony of family home evening, we must understand and obey the laws of the gospel associated with that principle. "For all who will have a blessing at my hands shall abide the law which was appointed for that blessing, and the conditions thereof, as were instituted from before the foundation of the world." (D&C 132:5). If we want to know that The Book of Mormon is the word of God, we must read with a desire to receive a witness. If we want to know that obedience to the gospel Plan is the path to happiness, we need to try the virtue of the word of God.

The Lord said: "Seek not for riches, but for wisdom; and, behold, the mysteries of God shall be unfolded unto you, and then shall you be made rich. Behold, he that hath eternal life is rich." (D&C 11:7). The mysteries of God are those truths that can only be known by revelation from the Holy Ghost. When we "hunger and thirst after righteousness," the doctrine of the priesthood will distill upon our souls as the dews from heaven, and the Holy Ghost will be our constant companion. (D&C 121:45-46). In fact, David Whitmer, to whom this revelation was addressed, was not able to abide by these conditions of faith, nor was he able to endure to the end in righteousness, and he was excommunicated from the church, on April 13, 1838.

Nevertheless, he was told in this revelation, received almost 9 years earlier: "It shall come to pass, that if you shall ask the Father in my name, in faith believing, you shall receive the Holy Ghost, which giveth utterance, that you may stand as a witness of the things of which you shall both hear and see, and also that you may declare repentance unto this generation." (V. 8). This blessing is significantly different than that given to the others, in Section 6 to Oliver Cowdery, Section 11 to Hyrum Smith, and Section 12 to Joseph Knight, Sr..

The Lord told the Three Witnesses: "You must rely upon my word, which if you do with full purpose of heart, you shall have a view of the plates, and also of the breastplate, the sword of Laban, the Urim and Thummim...and the miraculous directors.... And it is by your faith that you shall obtain a view of them.... And after that you have obtained faith, and have seen them with your eyes, you shall testify of them, by the power of God." (D&C 17:1-3). It has been proven millions of times that the real power of their witness, and that of those who have followed them, comes from the Holy Ghost.

"Behold, I am Jesus Christ, the Son of the living God, who created the heavens and the earth, a light which cannot be hid in darkness." (V. 9). In this verse and in The Book of Mormon, are found the clearest declarations in scripture that Jesus Christ is the Creator, Who acted under the direction of the Father by divine investiture of authority to form the earth. The Book of Mormon declarations read: "Behold, I am Jesus Christ the Son of God, I created the heavens and the earth, and all things that in them are. I was with the Father from the beginning. I am in the Father, and the Father in me; and in me hath the Father glorified his name." (3 Nephi 9:15). In the First Book of Nephi, with the simple statement of fact, "I am he," the Lord testified that it was He who, before time began, "laid the foundation of the earth, and (whose) right hand hath spanned the heavens" in both time and space. (1 Nephi 20:12-13).

His mighty works include the Pillars of Creation, elephant trunks of interstellar gas and dust in the Eagle Nebula, some 6,500 - 7,000 light years from Earth, and everything else in the universe. In an 1857 sermon by London pastor Charles Haddon Spurgeon titled "The Condescension of Christ," Spurgeon used the phrase to convey not only the physical world but also the force that keeps it all together, emanating from the divine: "And now wonder, ye angels," Spurgeon says of the birth of Christ, "the Infinite has become an infant; he, upon whose shoulders the universe doth hang, suckles at his mother's breast. He who created all things, and bears up the pillars of creation."

To those Nephites who listened to His voice in the midst of the darkness then enveloping the land, the words of Christ must have been powerful indeed, as He declared: "I am the light and the life of the world." (3 Nephi 9:18). The darkness of apostasy was no less enveloping in the early summer of 1829, when David Whitmer was given the same knowledge.

"Wherefore, I must bring forth the fulness of my gospel from the Gentiles unto the house of Israel." (V. 10). Jesus gave to His Nephite disciples the first principles and ordinances of the gospel, that was His only and true doctrine. D&C 20:8-10 declares that The Book of Mormon contains "the fulness of the gospel of Jesus Christ to the Gentiles and to the Jews also." This "has reference to the principles of salvation, by which we attain the glory of the Celestial Kingdom." (Joseph Fielding Smith, Jr.).

The gospel is "the good news" about Christ, His Kingdom, and salvation that only comes through Him. The church has the gospel, but the rest of the news is bad. The good news that Jesus gave to His disciples was that He came into the world to do the will of the Father, to be the Savior of the world, to accomplish the Plan of Redemption for mankind through His Infinite and Eternal Atonement. "For God so loved the world, that he gave his only begotten Son, that whosoever believeth in him should not perish, but have everlasting life." (John 3:16). Christ, Who was the lamb slain from the foundation of the world, became the Author of the Plan of Salvation by divine investiture of authority.

In this revelation, the Lord addressed David Whitmer, Jr. by name, and said: "Thou art called to assist; which thing if ye do, and are faithful, ye shall be blessed both spiritually and temporally, and great shall be your reward." (V. 11). He emphasized that "whoso remembereth these sayings of mine and doeth them, him will I raise up at the last day." (3 Nephi 15:1).

The disciples of Christ follow Him because they love Him. However, "there is a law irrevocably decreed in heaven before the foundation of this world, upon which all blessings are predicated. And when we obtain any blessing from God, it is by obedience to that law upon which it is predicated. (D&C 130:20-21).

Therefore, obedience to each specific commandment is always accompanied by an associated blessing. These rewards for obedience are sometimes temporal but are always spiritual. Now and then, the eternal immutability of that grand law is recognized, but in general, it is not. With a greater appreciation of the Plan of Salvation and an understanding of the nature of God, it becomes possible to see more clearly what the Lord meant, when He said: "I am bound when ye do what I say; but when ye do not what I say, ye have no promise." (D&C 82:10).

Brigham Young once declared: "There is no man who ever made a sacrifice on the earth for the kingdom of heaven, except the Savior. I would not give the ashes of a rye straw for that man who feels that he is making sacrifices for God. We are doing this for our own happiness, welfare, and exaltation, and for nobody else's. What we do, we do for the salvation of the inhabitants of the earth, not for the salvation of the heavens, the angels, or God." (J.D., 16:15).

There are really two dimensions to this statement by President Young. At first we are struck with the reality that much of what we do in this life we do for ourselves. As our altruistic sensitivities predominate, however, we will also labor in behalf of others and begin to lose ourselves in service. Then, when we really catch the vision and develop an eternal perspective, we will give ourselves to the Savior, yielding our agency to Him because of our implicit trust in His goodness. The gospel teaches that God holds Himself accountable to law, even as He expects us to be. He has set the perfect example of obedience. His expectations for David Whitmer, Jr. were no less demanding. Nor are they for us.

# Section 15
## (Received prior to the organization of the church).

This section and Section 16 have exactly the same wording. Evidently, the blessings given to John and Peter Whitmer were to be identical. Unfortunately, both Whitmer brothers were to personally discover that the enticements of the Adversary all too easily lead Father's children into conceptual cul de sacs, doctrinal dead ends, and irrelevant roundabouts from which there is no exit except retreat. His cunning caresses entice the weak to plunge into a perceived freedom that is really a freefall from God's favor into a bottomless pit of misery. In a perverted, twisted way, "the devil seeks that all men might be miserable like himself." (2 Nephi 2:27).

The Saints in the Last Days must avoid embracing "idea-gods" that rivet their attention, consume their energies, and demand their devotion. Sitting with the engine idling in neutral or wasting time in telestial traffic jams can damage our capacity and desire to move forward.

We all need the traction provided by listening "to the words of Jesus Christ, (our) Lord and (our) Redeemer." (V. 1). We believe in Christ. We belong to The Church of Jesus Christ of Latter-day Saints. The Book of Mormon is Another Testament of Jesus Christ. We are Saints of the Most High God!

We speak and testify of His ante-mortal existence, and His foreordination to be the Redeemer of the world. The scriptures reveal His relationship with the Father, and illustrate His divine investiture of authority. His appearances to His servants throughout history were many. The Book of Mormon, particularly, explains His condescension in taking a mortal body. Thus, we can better understand His temptations, and the power, might, dominion, and authority that typified His experience on the earth.

In His baptism, He demonstrated by example the way for all to follow. In His ministry, He taught the truths of the gospel in simplicity. In the Garden of Gethsemane, He demonstrated His strength and compassion. The crucifixion, then, was only an apostrophe; His death but a pause that would allow us to re-focus attention on His resurrection and ascension into heaven.

When He comes again, it will be in the clouds. He will be accompanied by the Church of the Firstborn, and His Second Coming will usher in His millennial reign. For a thousand years, His gospel will penetrate every soul and burn brightly in every bosom.

He is our Advocate with the Father, the Bread of Life, the Cornerstone of our creation, and the foundation of our existence. He is the Creator of worlds without number, and the Deliverer of the Covenant to all the children of the Father.

He is Emmanuel: truly, God is with us. The Firstborn of the spirit children of the Father, He is perfect in every detail. He is the Good Shepherd, and the Judge of both the quick and the dead. As Lord, King, and Jehovah, He has all power to act as Mediator, the Messenger of the Covenant.

The Lamb of God, He is the Messiah, the Anointed One, the anticipated Redeemer of all mankind. He is our Rock, and our Savior, the Only Begotten Son of God in the flesh. He is the Son of Man of Holiness, and will be the Second Comforter to those who trust completely in His holy name.

"For behold, I speak unto you with sharpness and with power, for mine arm is over all the earth." (V. 2). The Lord makes "bare his arm in the eyes of the nations," in a demonstration of His omnipotence. (2 Nephi 24:19). By comparison, the kings of Idumea and of spiritual Babylon, although once rulers of world-wide empires, today and forever have no monuments or tombs of any kind to memorialize their achievements.

They are as Ozymandias, of whom Shelley wrote: "I met a traveler from an antique land who said: Two vast and trunkless legs of stone stand in the desert. Near them, on the sand half sunk, a shattered visage lies, whose frown and wrinkled lip and sneer of cold command tell that its sculptor well those passions read, which yet survive. Stamped on these lifeless things, the hand that mocks them and the heart that fed; and on the pedestal these words appear: 'My name is Ozymandias, King of Kings; Look on my works, ye mighty, and despair!' Nothing beside remains. Round the decay of that colossal wreck, boundless and bare, the lone and level sand stretched far away." ("Ozymandias").

"And I will tell you that which no man knoweth save me and thee alone." (V. 3). Both Whitmer brothers had experiences similar to that of Oliver Cowdery, when they received knowledge from God that was known only to Him and them. (See D&C 6:6).

"For many times you have desired of me to know that which would be of the most worth unto you.... And now, behold, I say unto you, that the thing which will be of the most worth unto you will be to declare repentance unto this people, that you may bring souls unto me, that you may rest with them in the kingdom of my Father." (V. 4 & 6). "Behold, this is my doctrine, whosoever repenteth and cometh unto me, the same is my church." (D&C 10:67, see D&C 6:19, & 11:9).

Without our required repentance, the Spirit withdraws so that we no longer enjoy the fruits of faith or the gifts of the Holy Ghost. Without direction from Heavenly Father, we are left to face our demons alone, and to fight our own battles without His divine assistance. Consequently, the unalterable "judgments of God...stare (us) in the face." (Helaman 4:23). This was the fate of the Nephites just before Christ came to the Americas. "They saw that they had become weak, like unto their brethren, the Lamanites, and that the Spirit of the Lord did no more preserve them; yea, it had withdrawn from them because the Spirit of the Lord doth not dwell in unholy temples. Therefore, the Lord did cease to preserve them by his miraculous and matchless power, for they had fallen into a state of unbelief and awful wickedness." (Helaman 4:24-25).

This observation is more than an editorial comment. It is a clarion call to those living in the Last Days to learn from the mistakes of the Nephites, and to turn to the Lord for the protection so vital in these perilous times. The past is prologue. The Book of Mormon is no mere recitation of history, and no detached chronicle of a people distant from our time and circumstances. It is critical that we understand the forces that have always acted upon individuals and societies, and will forever continue to do so. Every prophet in former and latter days has stressed the same message: "If ye keep (the) commandments, ye shall prosper in the land, but if ye keep not (the) commandments, ye shall be cut off from His presence." (Alma 37:13).

# Section 16

(Received prior to the organization
of the church).

This section and Section 15 have exactly the same wording.

"Listen to the words of Jesus Christ, your Lord and your Redeemer." (V. 1). The Lord is our Redeemer. "With his stripes (or bruises) we are healed." He made possible our redemption. Even though all have transgressed the law, He has quietly borne our sins. Even during the mockery of His trial, He maintained a dignified silence. By oppression and a miscarriage of justice, His life was taken, and now "who shall declare his generation," or, in a very special sense, who shall be His posterity? (Isaiah 53:5-8).

He is the rudder of our ship, guiding us past unseen rocks and reefs. He is our helm, holding steady when winds of adversity blow. He is our telltale, alerting us to impending storms. He is our keel, helping us to move against the current and the wind. He is our mainsheet, holding firmly with just enough pressure to prevent us from capsizing when we are dangerously heeled over. He is our safety-line, providing security when our footing is unsure and the foaming sea is streaming across our deck. He is our compass, showing us the way, especially when the course is unclear. He is our chart, warning us of hidden dangers. He is our barometer, alerting us to impending storms. He is our lookout, standing as our sentinel when we are distracted by trivial concerns. He holds the line that trails in our wake, offering safety even when we fall overboard. He is the wind that fills our sails, giving us just enough of a gentle nudge to keep us moving along the pathway that leads to our eternal home.

With His sacrifice, made to satisfy the demands of Justice that required punishment as the consequence of the violation of eternal law, the way was opened for us to be born again and to become His spiritual posterity. In the so-called Spirit Prison, the doors swung open even as His body lay in the borrowed tomb of Joseph of Arimathea. (See "Doctrines of the Gospel Student Manual, (2000), p. 87–89, D&C 76:73, 88:97-102, Alma 40:11-14, & Moses 7:57). On the earth, to the extent that we will partake of the fruit of the Tree of Life, which is eternal life, the purposes of the Lord will be accomplished.

The Lord triumphed through His suffering, and He shall see His efforts bear fruit. Because of His affliction, His disciples are eager to carry the message of salvation to many. The Father has seen to it that His Son's suffering satisfies the requirements of the Law of Justice, that all who repent may be saved as a result of the merciful Atonement.

"For behold, I speak unto you with sharpness and with power, for mine arm is over all the earth." (V. 2). Isaiah asked "To whom is the arm of the Lord revealed?" (Isaiah 53:1). His answer was to no-one, for the Jews did not believe in Christ, His mighty works notwithstanding, and the world remained ignorant of His power. "But though he had done so many miracles before them," wrote the Apostle John, "yet they believed not on him; that the saying of Esaias the prophet might be fulfilled, which he spake, Lord, who hath believed our report? and to whom hath the arm of the Lord been revealed?" (John 12:37-38).

So it was that Christ brought new life to a spiritually dead world, although He appeared as other men, and humbly avoided the limelight. He was "despised and rejected of men," and many who witnessed the events of His ministry assumed that He suffered because He had done wrong. But, through His infinite and eternal Atonement, "he has borne our griefs, and carried our sorrows." (Isaiah 53:4).

"And I will tell you that which no man knoweth, save me and thee alone." (V. 3). "In the armory of thought we forge the weapons by which we destroy ourselves," said Spencer W. Kimball. "We also fashion the tools with which we builds for ourselves heavenly mansions of joy and strength and peace. Between these two extremes are all grades of character, and we are their maker. We are the master of thought, the shaper of condition, environment, and of destiny." ("The Miracle of Forgiveness," p. 103).

"Circumstance does not make us. It reveals us to ourselves, because as the master of our thoughts, we are the maker of ourselves, the shaper and author of our environment. We imagine that thought can be kept secret, but it cannot. It rapidly crystallizes into habit, and solidifies into circumstance." (James Allen, "As a Man Thinketh," Chapter 2).

"For many times, you have desired of me to know that which would be of the most worth unto you.... And now, behold, I say unto you, that the thing which will be of the most worth unto you will be to declare repentance unto this people, that you may bring souls unto me, that you may rest with them in the kingdom of my Father." (V. 4 & 6).

The Plan whereby we might be brought to a condition of repentance was "prepared from the foundation of the world." (Alma 42:26). John Taylor taught: "To the Son is given the power of the resurrection, the power of the redemption, the power of salvation, the power to enact laws for the carrying out and accomplishment of the design. Hence, life and immortality are brought to light, the gospel is introduced, and He becomes the Author of eternal life and exaltation." ("Mediation and Atonement," p. 171-172).

The only payment required for the gift of salvation is "the heart and a willing mind." (D&C 64:34). The only things that we must give up are our sins. (See Alma 22:18). Thus, Alma counseled his son Corianton to "only let your sins trouble you, with that trouble which shall bring you down unto repentance." (Alma 42:29).

The first step in that process is the turning point at which the guilty party consciously recognizes his sin. Secondly, one must cease excusing himself in sin. "O my son, I desire that ye should deny the justice of God no more. Do not endeavor to excuse yourself in the least point because of your sins, by denying the justice of God; but do let the justice of God, and his mercy, and his long-suffering have full sway in your heart; and let it bring you down to the dust in humility." (Alma 42:30).

Just as the Lord called Peter Whitmer to his missionary labors, so did Alma call his son Corianton: "And now, O my son, ye are called of God to preach the word unto this people. And now, my son, go thy way, declare the word with truth and soberness, that thou mayest bring souls unto repentance, that the great plan of mercy may have claim upon them." (Alma 42:31).

Corianton was faithful to his father's counsel. Seventeen years later, Mormon recorded that Shiblon "was a just man, and he did walk uprightly before God; and he did observe to do good continually, to keep the commandments of the Lord his God; and also did his brother (Corianton)." (Alma 63:2). Unfortunately, John and Peter Whitmer were not as strong as the sons of Alma.

# Section 17
## (Received prior to the organization
## of the church).

"Oliver Cowdery, David Whitmer, and Martin Harris were moved upon by an inspired desire to be the three special witnesses. The Prophet inquired of the Lord, and this revelation was given in answer, through the Urim and Thummim." (Superscript).

Verse 1 is a bold promise, made through a 23 year old prophet. Had the promise not been fulfilled, Joseph Smith might have been exposed as a fraud. "Behold, I say unto you, that you must rely upon my word, which if you do with full purpose of heart, you shall have a view of the plates, and also of the breastplate, the sword of Laban, (and) the Urim and Thummim....and the miraculous directors which were given to Lehi while in the wilderness." (V. 1).

Anciently, the plates, breastplate, sword, Liahona, and Urim and Thummim were examples of emblems, types, and national treasures that a ruler was required to possess to validate the legitimacy of his power. Royal orbs, spheres of the firmament, crystal balls, and the like have survived in religious art and folklore, although they are stylized almost beyond recognition, and understanding of the underlying power associated with them has been completely lost. These relics from the past provided a substantial foundation of physical evidence for the special witnesses to establish the validity of the Latter-day work of the Restoration.

What were the Urim and Thummim? The words are translated as "Lights and Perfections." (See D&C 130:6-9, Omni 1:20-2, Mosiah 8:13-19, 28:11-20, & Alma 37:21-26). Lucy Mack Smith said that they "consisted of two smooth three-cornered diamonds, set in glass, and the glasses were set in silver bows, which were connected with each other in much the same way as old fashioned spectacles, only much larger." ("Reminiscences of The Prophet Joseph Smith," p. 24). It is this published statement by the Prophet's mother that may have given rise to the comment by the historian Henry Steele Commager that Joseph Smith used "magic spectacles" to search for buried treasure. The "Wayne Sentinel," published in Palmyra, New

York, reported on February 16, 1825 that "we could name, if we pleased, at least five hundred respectable men who do in the simplicity and sincerity of their hearts believe that immense treasures lie concealed upon our green mountains, many of whom have been for a number of years industriously and perseveringly engaged in digging it up." In our day and age, men and women, and even boys and girls, would use their smart phones and Google Earth to assist them in their search for hidden treasures. We even have a name for it: "Geocaching."

But in Joseph Smith's day, such fervor notwithstanding, it is likely that the Urim and Thummim that passed into his hands was the Jaredite relic that Mosiah had possessed. (See Omni 1:20-21, & Mosiah 8:13). In his history, it is recorded that "there were two stones in silver bows - and these stones, fastened to a breastplate, constituted what is called the Urim and Thummim - deposited with the plates; and the possession and use of these stones were what constituted seers in ancient or former times." (J.S.H. 1:35).

The ball or director was the "Liahona," which possibly means "To Jehovah is light." (See Alma 37:38). The Liahona has been ridiculed by latter day critics of The Book of Mormon, but of all the symbols of royal authority, it is probably the most authentic. "Liahona" is clearly an "Old World" word from the forgotten language of the fathers, that had to be interpreted as "compass" for present day readers. "Compass" refers to a pair of things in motion, the nature of that motion being a circle. This fits the description given by Nephi of the Liahona as "a round ball of curious workmanship; and it was of fine brass. And within the ball were two spindles; and the one pointed the way whither we should go into the wilderness." (1 Nephi 16:10).

That the Liahona is an object lesson for us is made evident by Alma's comment to his son "that these things are not without a shadow, for as our fathers were slothful to give heed to the compass (now these things were temporal) they did not prosper; even so it is with things which are spiritual." (Alma 37:43, see v. 44-45).

The Liahona only worked according to faith. Alma characterized its operation as a miracle, but he went to great lengths to explain the principles by which it functioned. Religion itself becomes magical when the power by which things operate is transferred from God to the objects themselves. Alma pointedly wanted to avoid misinterpretation of the power by which the Liahona operated.

"And it is by your faith that you shall obtain a view of them, even by that faith which was had by the prophets of old." (V. 2). What was lacking in the Christian world in Joseph Smith's day was saving faith in Jesus Christ and in the principles of His gospel. Even the Bible had become a magical book in the eyes of many, conveying power and knowledge without the aid of revelation. Over the centuries, the priesthood itself had acquired the status of an office that automatically bestowed power and grace, regardless of the spiritual or moral qualifications of its possessor. The stories from the records translated by Joseph Smith help to bring our understanding of the eternal principles of the Plan of Salvation into perspective. Thus, we should neither be incredulous when reading them, nor should we fall into the trap of accepting them on blind faith. We need to tenaciously hold tightly to our faith, even as did the prophets of old. We need a testimony of individual principles of the gospel more than ever. For example: "It must needs be that the Gentiles be convinced also that Jesus is the Christ, the Eternal God." (2 Nephi 26:12). This is why members and missionaries of the Church of Jesus Christ testify publicly of their beliefs, because the world lacks both saving faith in the Savior, and a testimony of the truths interwoven throughout the restored gospel, that were brought to light by the prophet Joseph Smith.

"And after that you have obtained faith, and have seen them with your eyes, you shall testify of them, by the power of God." (V. 3). Our faith in Christ, "is not a leap in the dark. It is, instead, trust in what the spirit learned aeons ago and religious recognition is just that; re-cognition, a re-knowing." (Truman Madsen, "The Truth, The Way, The Life: B.H. Roberts' Masterwork," B.Y.U. Studies, 15:3, p. 263). "Intelligence cleaveth unto intelligence, truth embraceth truth, (and) light cleaveth unto light." (D&C 88:40). Testimony is a manifestation of the power of God Himself.

The testimony of Oliver Cowdery: "Before God and man I dare not deny what I have said, and what my testimony contains as written and printed on the front page of the Book of Mormon. May it please your honor and gentlemen of the jury, this I say, I saw the angel and heard his voice - how can I deny it? It happened in the daytime when the sun was shining brightly in the firmament; not at night when I was asleep. The glorious messenger from heaven, dressed in white, standing above the ground, in a glory that I have never seen anything to compare with - the sun is insignificant in comparison - told us if we denied that testimony there is no forgiveness in this life or in the world to come. Now how can I deny it? I dare not; I will not."

The last testimony of David Whitmer: "The record of the Nephites is true... You have heard me bear my testimony on my death bed." (Recorded January 22, 1888, three days before his death).

The last testimony of Martin Harris: "Yes, I did see the plates on which the Book of Mormon was written. I did see the angel. I did hear the voice of God, and I do know that Joseph Smith is a prophet of God, holding the keys of the Holy Priesthood." (Recorded July 20, 1875, 10 days after his death in Clarkston, Cache County, Utah).

Oliver Cowdery also gave an account of his receipt of the Aaronic Priesthood, under the hands of John the Baptist, on May 15, 1829. "On a sudden, as from the midst of eternity, the voice of the Redeemer spake peace to us, while the veil was parted and the angel of God came down clothed with glory, and delivered the anxiously looked for message, and the keys of the gospel of repentance. What joy! What wonder! What amazement! While the world was racked and distracted, while millions were groping as the blind for the wall, and while all men were resting upon uncertainty, as a general mass, our eyes beheld, our ears heard, as in the 'blaze of day'; yes, more, above the glitter of the May sunbeam, which then shed its brilliancy over the face of nature!" ("Messenger & Advocate," V. 1, p. 14-16, October 1834).

"And this you shall do that my servant Joseph Smith, Jun., may not be destroyed, that I may bring about my righteous purposes unto the children of men in this work." (V. 4). In his last hours of mortality, Joseph Smith was able to declare: "I have a conscience void of offense towards God, and towards all men." (D&C 135:5). He gave us all the confidence to walk in the valley of the shadow of death, and yet to fear no evil. "Life actually has no significance except as a preparation for the ultimate goal of death," wrote Carl Jung. "In Christianity, the meaning of existence is consummated in its end." ("Collected Works of C.G. Jung," V. 8, p. 804).

For Latter-day Saints, "one of the greatest contributions of Joseph Smith was his knowledge of what is to come after death. He did much to clarify our understanding of heaven, and to make it seem worth working for." ("My Religion and Me" Lesson Manual). Truly, he was able to perform a righteous work among the children of men.

To those who would be special witnesses, the Lord said: "Ye shall testify that you have seen (the relics), even as my servant Joseph Smith, Jun., has seen them; for it is by my power that he has seen them, and it is because he had faith." (V. 5). Joseph recalled how an angel had exhorted the Three Witnesses: "These plates have been revealed by the power of God. The translation which you have seen of them is correct, and I command you to bear record of what you now see and hear." (H.C., 1:54-55).

The Lord Himself testified of the divine mission of Joseph Smith and of the truthfulness of The Book of Mormon: "And he has translated the book, even that part which I have commanded him, and as your Lord and your God liveth it is true." (V. 6). This constitutes an ancient Hebrew oath. As Paul wrote to the Hebrews: "Because he could swear by no greater, he sware by himself." (Hebrews 6:13). There is no other book on earth that has been validated by the Lord Himself.

Wherefore, you have received the same power, and the same faith, and the same gift like unto him." (V. 7). We may be filled with the Spirit just as food nourishes our physical bodies. Authority comes by the laying on of hands, but power in the ministry is exercised on condition of our personal righteousness or worthiness. "For without this no man can see the face of God, even the Father, and live." (D&C 84:20-22).

"And if you do these last commandments of mine, which I have given you, the gates of hell shall not prevail against you; for my grace is sufficient for you, and you shall be lifted up at the last day." (V. 8). "No matter how good we have tried to be, we are unable in and of ourselves to receive redemption from our sins by any act of our own. It is (only) by the grace of Jesus Christ that we are saved." (Joseph Fielding Smith, Jr., "Doctrines of Salvation," 2:309, see 2 Nephi 25:23).

We learn in The Book of Mormon how Jacob urged us to "reconcile" ourselves to God's will. (2 Nephi 10:24). "Reconciliation" restores friendly relations after an estrangement. 2 Nephi 31:12-21 discusses the steps of our reconciliation with God, and stresses that it is only through His grace that we are saved. (See 2 Nephi 10:24).

In the same sermon, Jacob explained how grace operates. We are raised from physical death by the power of the Resurrection, and from spiritual death by the power of the Atonement. Grace is granted to us proportionately as we conform to the standards of personal righteousness that are part of the gospel Plan. Thus, we are commanded to "grow in grace" (D&C 50:40), until we are sanctified and justified "thru the grace of our Lord and Savior Jesus Christ." (D&C 20:30-32). Grace is an attribute of perfection possessed by Deity, and consists of His love, mercy, and condescension toward all of His children. (See D&C 66:12, 84:102, & 93:6-20). It consists of the gifts and power of God by which we may be brought to perfection.

When we have a true understanding of grace, the scriptures make a lot more sense. For example: "For by grace are ye saved, through faith; and that not of yourselves: it is the gift of God." (Ephesians 2:8). Some Christian denominations distort the understanding of grace and teach that we are saved by God's good pleasure, without any individual effort whatsoever, other than a confession of faith. But as Nephi made clear: "We know that it is by grace that we are saved, after all we can do." (2 Nephi 25:23). And what we can do is primarily to repent on a regular basis.

"And I, Jesus Christ, your Lord and your God, have spoken it unto you, that I might bring about my righteous purposes unto the children of men." (V. 9). The Lord explained that He came into the world "to do the will, both of the Father and of the Son - of the Father because of me, and of the Son because of my flesh." (3 Nephi 1:14). In other words, the Savior was the Firstborn spiritual child of Heavenly Father, to Whom was given the responsibility to bring to pass the spiritual rebirth of all of mankind. Christ is the Father of our spiritual regeneration, with the power, by divine investiture of authority, to carry out that responsibility by coming to earth as the Savior and Redeemer of the world.

# Section 18

(Received prior to the organization
of the church).

"When the Aaronic Priesthood was conferred, the bestowal of the Melchizedek Priesthood was promised. In response to supplication for knowledge on the matter, the Lord gave this revelation" in June, 1829. (Superscript).

"I have manifested unto you, by my Spirit in many instances, that the things which you have written are true; wherefore you know that they are true." (V. 2). On October 1, 1834, Oliver Cowdery wrote in the "Messenger and Advocate:" I shall not attempt to paint for you the feelings of this heart, nor the majestic beauty and glory which surrounded us on this occasion (when we received the Aaronic Priesthood), but you will believe me when I say, that earth, nor men, with the eloquence of time, cannot begin to clothe language in as interesting and sublime a manner as this holy personage. No; nor has this earth power to give the joy, to bestow the peace, or comprehend the wisdom which was contained in each sentence as they were delivered by the power of the Holy Spirit!

One touch with the finger of his love, yes, one ray of glory from the upper world, or one word from the mouth of the Savior, from the bosom of eternity, strikes (the deception of man) into insignificance and blots it forever from the mind. The assurance that we were in the presence of an angel, the certainty that we heard the voice of Jesus, and the truth as if flowed from a pure personage, dictated by the will of God, is to me past description, and I shall ever look upon this expression of the Savior's goodness with wonder and thanksgiving while I am permitted to tarry; and in those mansions where perfection dwells and sin never comes, I hope to adore in that day which shall never cease." (J.S.H. 1:71).

"For in them are all things written concerning the foundation of my church, my gospel, and my rock." (V. 3). The Church of Jesus Christ consists of assembled believers and disciples who have taken upon themselves His name and covenanted to be obedient to His gospel. It was defined by the Lord Himself, Who said: "And this is my gospel: repentance and baptism by water, and then cometh the baptism of fire and the Holy Ghost, even the comforter, which showeth all things, and teacheth the peaceable things of the kingdom." (D&C 39:6). A portion of Joseph's instruction by the Spirit included the identification of the "rock" in verse 3. In His teachings, the Lord had said: " Upon this rock I will build my church, and the gates of hell shall not prevail against it." (Matthew 16:18). "What rock?" asked Joseph Smith. He answered unequivocally and definitively: "The rock of revelation." (H.C., 5:258).

"Wherefore, if you shall build up my church, upon my rock, the gates of hell shall not prevail against you." (V. 5). The gates of hell mark the entrance to the so-called spirit prison of the unjust. (See "Doctrines of the Gospel Student Manual, (2000), p. 87–89. & D&C 88:97-102). Nephi prayed: "May the gates of hell be shut continually before me, because that my heart is broken and my spirit is contrite." (2 Nephi 4:32).

As he indicated, the way to barricade those doors is to offer to the Lord the required sacrifice, which is to "be broken down with deep sorrow for sin, to be humbly and thoroughly penitent, and to have attained sincere and purposeful repentance." (Bruce R. McConkie, "Mormon Doctrine," p. 161).

The Lord offers his Atoning Sacrifice to such individuals. This sacrifice satisfies the requirement of repentance before the ordinance of baptism for the remission of sins is performed, and before partaking of the Sacrament following baptism. (See D&C 20:37). In addition, we must be contrite, or "bruised in heart, sorrow, or affliction of mind for some fault or injury done. It is penitence for sin." ("Oxford English Dictionary.").

"Behold, the world is ripening in iniquity; and it must needs be that the children of men are stirred up unto repentance, both the Gentiles and also the house of Israel." (V. 6). When people are "fully ripe in iniquity" they no longer have the capacity or desire for repentance. Fullness and ripeness identify that state when the process has reached an end and righteous judgment becomes inevitable. Without the protective influence of our Heavenly Father, we become vulnerable to the lethal storms of sin sweeping the face of the earth, that have been initiated by the destroyer, whose suffocating winds threaten to suck the life sustaining marrow from our bones.

Spencer W. Kimball taught: "It is true that the great principle of repentance is always available, but for the wicked and rebellious there are serious reservations to this statement. For instance, sin is intensely habit forming, and sometimes moves men to the tragic point of no return. Without repentance, there can be no forgiveness, and without forgiveness all the blessings of eternity hang in jeopardy. As the transgressor moves deeper and deeper in his sin, and the error is entrenched more deeply and the will to change is weakened, it becomes increasingly near hopeless, and he skids down and down until either he does not want to climb back, or he has lost the power to do so." ("The Miracle of Forgiveness," p. 117).

In spite of the wickedness and abominations of the world in the Last Days, the Lord still offers unconditional forgiveness predicated upon repentance. Because of the Atonement, and because of the acceptable sacrifice by repentant souls that consists of a broken heart and a contrite spirit, God is able to extend Mercy without jeopardizing the demands of Justice. Those who take advantage of His offer satisfy His ultimate purpose, which is to bring about our immortality and eternal life. (See Moses 1:39).

"And now, Oliver Cowdery, I speak unto you, and also unto David Whitmer." (V. 9). Brigham Young taught that Joseph Smith, Oliver Cowdery, and David Whitmer were the first Apostles of this dispensation. (J.D., 6:320). To these, according to Heber C. Kimball, Martin Harris was later added. (J.D., 6:29). These men were instructed to find and ordain 12 others who would constitute the Quorum of The Twelve. (V. 37).

"Remember the worth of souls is great in the sight of God." (V. 10). The devil scores a major victory when we succumb to his temptations, for "the destruction of the soul is the destruction of the greatest thing that has ever been created." (Joseph Fielding Smith, Jr., "Doctrines of Salvation," 1:314).

"For, behold, the Lord your Redeemer suffered death in the flesh; wherefore he suffered the pain of all men, that all men might repent and come unto him." (V. 11). Moroni wrote that it was important for the members to rely solely "upon the merits of Christ, who was the author and the finisher of their faith." (Moroni 7:4, see Hebrews 5:9 & 12:2). In reality, it is God the Father Who is the Author of the Plan of Salvation. But God the Son, by divine investiture of authority, executed the Plan when He accepted the role of Redeemer, as "the lamb slain from the foundation of the world." (Revelation 13:8).

"And he hath risen again from the dead, that he might bring all men unto him, on condition of repentance." (V. 13). "Behold, the resurrection of Christ redeemeth mankind, yea, even all mankind, and bringeth them back into the presence of the Lord" to the end that the Judgment might take place. (Helaman 14:17). Then, those who have repented while in the probationary state of mortality will stand before the judgment bar of Christ and will be redeemed by the power of the Atonement from the second, spiritual death.

That is to say, the repentant will be allowed to come into the presence of God, because the Atonement of Christ has paid the price that is demanded by Justice for their sins. All others who are unrepentant, and thus without mercy, will be cut off pertaining to righteousness. Having temporarily been brought into the presence of the Lord, they will not be able to endure His Holiness, because they remain filthy.

Therefore, the prophets have always cried: "Repent ye, repent ye, lest by knowing these things and not doing them ye shall suffer yourselves to come under condemnation, and ye are brought down unto the second death." (Helaman 14:19).

"And how great is his joy in the soul that repenteth!" (V. 13). Justice demands that "all things shall be restored to their proper order, every thing to its natural frame, raised to endless happiness to inherit the kingdom of God, or to endless misery to inherit the kingdom of the devil." (Alma 41:4).

Therefore, the mortal mission of the Savior was to "redeem those who will be baptized unto repentance, through faith on his name." (Alma 9:27). The Atonement is for those who enter into the covenants and have faith to repent. The saving faith that is required is like a screw that is slowly being turned in a solid piece of wood. Initially, a little tap from above may be required before the screw can stand independently and upright, balanced somewhat precariously on the surface of the wood, now ready and eager to fulfill its purpose.

If the wood seems impenetrable, or is particularly hard, a little basic ground work might be necessary, such as pre-drilling a small guide hole. Then, the screw may be oriented in the direction it should take before it is turned into the wood, and it may be gently pressed into place, by the screwdriver that is poised above its head. The little screw, if it were self-aware, would know, at this point, what was shortly coming. If it could, it would probably brace itself for the gentle pressure coming from above, as the weight of the screwdriver, and more particularly the driving force behind it, was brought to bear on its head. The screw might initially think that it was accomplishing little; turning only in circles, as it were.

But, depending upon the resistance encountered, the screw would twist and turn deeper and deeper into the wood. The Master Craftsman who is in charge of all woodworking projects might direct that the screw be soaped, to make it easier to turn with less friction. Or, He might want to have an apprentice drill a larger guide hole that would more easily accommodate the screw. On the other hand, He might want to leave everything well-enough alone, in order to allow the expenditure of energy required to set the screw in place to be commensurate with the feelings of satisfaction and reward that could only come upon the successful completion of a project that had been well-executed.

Sometimes, there are only 4 or 5 threads on the shaft of a screw; but more frequently there are many more that are designed to address the requirements of the blueprint defining the task at hand. At times, turning a screw with many threads might seem tedious, and an impending sense of fatigue might overpower the muscles of the hand or wrist. But perseverance will insure that the joints will be tight. In any woodworking project, weakness when initially setting a screw can only result in loud squeaks and instability later on, after hard and sustained use has taken its toll. Projects that have been shoddily thrown together, will not stand the test of time.

But properly executed, with each turn, and with each expenditure of energy, the anchor will become more sure. Even after only a few twists, although the screw has not yet been driven all the way in, it will not come out or wiggle loose without the application of an equal and opposite force, or an even greater force than that which had been required to set it, in the first place.

As the screw is driven further and further into the wood, its reason for being will become self-evident. Something as simply designed as a wood screw can serve a multitude of purposes. It can hold a coat hook in place so that the garments of the priesthood may be appropriately cared for, or it can orient in its proper position a treasured family photo that has been hung in a place of honor on the wall.

By bonding two separate and distinct pieces of wood together, a well-placed screw can transform them into something quite different from the raw materials, that is simply beautiful, such as an altar. It can secure the rod from which a veil may be hung. It can hold together a truss that has been designed to bear the weight of the statue of the angel Moroni.

When that little screw has been driven all the way in, so that its head is flush with the surface of the material that is being stabilized, it might blend in so well that it is hardly noticeable. Sometimes, the best screw does its job without ever being consciously recognized. Little feet running toward the Bishop across the floor at church will not trip on it, even as approving adult eyes look right past it.

Most screws are very inexpensive, but they provide solid anchors, and properly driven in place may remain there for years, with the need for only periodic maintenance inspections. An occasional turn with a screwdriver may be all that is necessary to confirm that everything remains as it should be.

With the anchor sure, just as is the case with well-driven faith, the screw, together with the energy that had been required to set it in place will not be wasted; it is not dead. The screw serves an on-going, sustaining purpose, but the energy that had been expended to accomplish the initial task at hand will no longer be required to maintain the integrity of the screw. Kinetic energy of motion has been transformed to the potential energy of position, and so it can be profitably directed elsewhere. But the end product of the expenditure of energy that had been necessary to drive the screw remains, just as the result of the expenditure of faith remain as a testament to good works.

One might legitimately ask what would have happened if the screw had been left in its original packaging? What if it had never been utilized in its foreordained manner? We can look to the scripture that asks those who fear man more than they fear God, if it is true that faith without works is dead, being alone. The question begs our answer, and then it demands that we head straight to God's hardware store to pick up a few essentials.

It helps to have in our toolboxes enough compartments to maintain a healthy collection of wood screws. If we find ourselves engaged in a project that needs a specific screw to complete the job, we will know exactly where to go to select the right one. Rarely will we find ourselves at a standstill because we don't have the right fasteners, or the proper tools, for the job.

We want our faith to be like the screw in this illustration. As we build a foundation, we want it to be sturdy. We want to be worthy of our hire. We are reminded that we "are little children and...cannot bear all things now; (and that we) must grow in grace and in the knowledge of the truth." (D&C 50:40). "For the word of the Lord is truth, and whatsoever is truth is light, and whatsoever is light is Spirit, even the Spirit of Jesus Christ. And the Spirit giveth light to every man that cometh into the world; and the Spirit enlighteneth every man through the world, that hearkeneth to the voice of the Spirit." (D&C 84:45-46).

Initially, our budding faith is to believe what we do not see, and the reward of our faith is to see what we believe; to see what is real. We realize that some things have to be believed to be seen. Even so, belief is only our mental assent to the actuality of a tangible object or the truth related to an intangible principle, without the moral element of responsibility that we call faith. Someone once said that duct tape is like the Force. It has a light side and a dark side, and it holds the universe together. That may not be entirely accurate. It may be that faith is the screw that holds it all together.

We see our faith as evidence that the gospel Plan is working. It provides us with the opportunity to benefit from the Law of Mercy, that the demands of the Law of Justice might be satisfied through the Atonement for sin by the Savior of the world.

"Happiness is the object and design of our existence and will be the end thereof," taught Joseph Smith, "if we pursue the path that leads to it; and this path is virtue, uprightness, faithfulness, holiness, and keeping all the commandments of God." ("Teachings," p. 255). But God will always grant to His children agency to choose their own path, "for behold, they are their own judges, whether to do good or do evil." (Alma 41:7).

We can choose our own actions, but we cannot choose to escape the consequences of those actions. "The decrees of God are unalterable; therefore, the way is prepared that whosoever will may walk therein and be saved." (Alma 41:8). But we cannot hope to "be restored from sin to happiness." For "wickedness never was happiness." (Alma 41:10). Samuel the Lamanite said of the wicked inhabitants of the land of Zarahemla: "Ye have sought all the days of your lives for that which ye could not obtain; and ye have sought for happiness in doing iniquity, which thing is contrary to the nature of that righteousness which is in our great and Eternal Head." (Helaman 13:38).

Moroni taught; 'Despair cometh because of iniquity." (Moroni 10:22). Every law has both a blessing and a punishment affixed to it. When the law is obeyed, a blessing is given that results in happiness, or joy. Disobedience activates punishment that results in unhappiness, or misery. Despair is the feeling of hopelessness that accompanies disobedience.

As Alma explained: "All men that are in a state of nature, or I would say, in a carnal state, are in the gall of bitterness and in the bonds of iniquity; they are without God in the world, and they have gone contrary to the nature of God; therefore, they are in a state contrary to the nature of happiness." (Alma 41:11). The Savior taught that if we lack vision, and build "upon the works of men, or upon the works of the devil, verily I say unto you they have joy in their works for a season, and by and by the end cometh, and they are hewn down and cast into the fire, from whence there is no return." (3 Nephi 27:11).

As we read the words of Alma, we begin to understand that "the meaning of the word restoration is to bring back again evil for evil, or carnal for carnal, or devilish for devilish, good for that which is good; righteous for that which is righteous; just for that which is just; (and) merciful for that which is merciful." (Alma 41:13).

Sometimes, it is very difficult to tell just what brings us happiness. Both poverty and wealth have failed miserably. Neither fame nor anonymity holds the key. Neither sickness nor health seems to have the ability. Both principalities and the absence of worldly influence are inadequate. Neither beauty nor the beast has the advantage.

Sometimes, we forget that when we pray for rain, and our prayers are answered, we are going to also have to deal with some mud. "The dark threads are as needful in the weaver's skillful hand as the threads of gold and silver, in the pattern he has planned." (Benjamin Malachi Franklin). We can never hope to understand the answers we receive, if we continue to ask the wrong questions. Life has no coherence, and is in fact, a cruel joke, without the spiritual symmetry and balance that we enjoy by adhering to the Lord's fitness program.

"And if it so be that you should labor all your days in crying repentance unto this people, and bring, save it be one soul unto me, how great shall be your joy with him in the kingdom of my Father!" (V. 15). The fundamental truth concerning the message of salvation is that, in a broad sense, it is of personal relevance to both the deliverer and recipient, for "that which ye do send out shall return unto you again." (Alma 41:15).

"Behold, you have my gospel before you, and my rock, and my salvation." (V. 17). It is not enough to call our organization the Church of Christ. It must also properly administer the ordinances of the true gospel. Caricatures of the true church are quite popular with those who seek form without substance, the steak without the sizzle, and who enjoy the relative ease of putting forth minimal effort in organizations that make no demands for personal sacrifice. These types of churches "multiply exceedingly because of iniquity, and because of the power of Satan." (4 Nephi 1:28). Satan's intent, after all, is to lead us very "carefully down to hell." (2 Nephi 28:21).

Other churches seem to go out of their way to "persecute the true church of Christ." (4 Nephi 1:29). Those who have apostatized from the truth harden their hearts, and even seek to kill the servants of God, their miracles notwithstanding. (4 Nephi 1:21). As the Savior told Joseph Smith: "Faith cometh not by signs, but signs follow those that believe." (D&C 63:9).

"Ask the Father in my name, in faith believing that you shall receive, and you shall have the Holy Ghost, which manifesteth all things which are expedient unto the children of men." (V. 18). The process by which faith is developed is one of testing. The Lord gives certain principles, and by obedience to them, blessings and power follow. But we have no proof of that promise until we act on the basis of trust. Then comes confirmation of the reality, but only after we act in faith. That is why James taught: "Faith, if it hath not works, is dead, being alone." (James 2:17).

When we understand this process, we can see why sign seeking is condemned. Those who demand outward evidence of the power of God as a condition for belief seeks to circumvent the process by which faith is developed. They wants proof without price. As with the adulterer, they seek the result without accepting the responsibility.

"And if you have not faith, hope, and charity, you can do nothing." (V. 19). The various gifts of the Spirit allow us to grow in stature. As we do so, we become more and more like our Heavenly Father. It becomes a realistic goal to follow the counsel of the Savior, Who commanded: "I would that ye should be perfect, even as I, or your Father who is in heaven is perfect." (3 Nephi 12:48, see Matthew 5:48). God is not jealous of His perfection, but glories in the possibility that His children who obey Him and endure to the end might become like Him. (See Moses 1:39).

"If ye by the grace of God are perfect in Christ, and deny not his power, then are ye sanctified in Christ by the grace of God, through the shedding of the blood of Christ, which is in the covenant of the Father unto the remission of your sins, that ye become holy, without spot." (Moroni 10:33).

It would be difficult to state more succinctly, yet more powerfully, the essence of the gospel of Jesus Christ, than in this one verse. All that Moroni had written builds to this climax. If we open our hearts to the gospel of Jesus Christ, we can become holy, without spot. "Holy," after all, is one of the name-titles of the Savior Himself, Who was as a lamb without spot, or blemish. (See 1 Peter 1:19, & Hebrews 9:14)

"Contend against no church, save it be the church of the devil." (V. 20). One of the principal points of vulnerability of those with weak character is that they are particularly susceptible to the darkening of their minds by the spirit of contention. If they allow this influence into their hearts and homes, they open the door to Satan's missionaries, beckoning them to enter as invited guests, to teach them the principles of perdition upon their very own hearthstones. Love is an effective counter-measure to this spirit because it is alien to Satan. Therefore, when love is found in the home and in society, Satan and his disciples uncomfortably slink away to knock on more promising doors.

"I love everybody, even though some people make mistakes," said five year old Kathryn Hudson. "Where did you learn that?" she was asked. "In Church?" "No.

When I was up in Heaven. Heavenly Father told me that." She learned very early in life that the best way to counter those who would negatively influence her, would be to make friends out of them.

Relationships between individuals and societies can work for both good and for evil. "When we sow a thought, we reap an act," taught Spencer W. Kimball. "When we sow an act, we reap a habit. When we sow a habit, we reap a character. When we sow a character, we reap an eternal destiny." Our fate then, is ultimately in our own hands. The judgment will be eminently fair, because the creation of our own heaven or hell can be traced back to the sum-total of our thoughts, acts, and habits; these are the things that define our character.

However, we are to contend against all evil. (1 Nephi 14:10). "The church of the devil is his kingdom, the sphere of his influence, and the whole of his area of power. It, and the great and abominable church, identify all organizations of whatever name or nature that are designed to take us on a course that leads away from God, and thus from salvation in His kingdom." (Bruce R. McConkie, "Mormon Doctrine," p. 137-138).

Satan's fiefdom is called by various names: Babylon, the Church of The Devil, the Great and Abominable Church, and the Mother of Harlots. In reality, "there are save two churches only. The one is the Church of the Lamb of God; the other is the church of the Devil." (1 Nephi 14:10).

In D&C Section 29:12, we find the only instance in the Doctrine & Covenants where the term 'great and abominable church' is employed, although it is used twelve times in The Book of Mormon, in 1 Nephi 4:3, 9, 15, & 17, 1 Nephi 13:6, 8, 26 & 28, 1 Nephi 22:13 & 14, 2 Nephi 6:12, & 2 Nephi 28:18. That is enough, however, to entrench the phrase in our lexicon. Nephi was given, in vision, a broad view of the state of the world in the Last Days, and clearly saw "the great persecutor of the church, the apostate, the whore, even Babylon, that maketh all nations to drink of her cup, in whose hearts the enemy, even Satan, sitteth to reign." (D&C 86:3).

"Behold, Jesus Christ is the name which is given of the Father, and there is none other name given whereby man can be saved." (V. 23). King Benjamin made a statement of equally profound doctrinal certainty, when he declared: "There shall be no other name given nor any other way nor means whereby salvation can come unto the children of men, only in and through the name of Christ." (Mosiah 3:17).

The Law of Justice made the Atonement of Jesus Christ necessary, while the Law of Mercy made it possible. The two laws are in complete harmony, with Mercy introducing the possibility of vicarious payment for the required punishment in consequence of laws that have been transgressed. Intriguingly, Alma seemed to treat mercy and justice as counterpoints, if not outright opposites, in the grand scheme of the Plan of Salvation. He explained to his son: "Mercy claimeth the penitent, and mercy cometh because of the Atonement; and the Atonement bringeth to pass the resurrection of the dead; and the resurrection of the dead bringeth back men into the presence of God. For behold, justice exerciseth all his demands, and also mercy claimeth all which is her own; and thus, none but the truly penitent are saved." (Alma 42:23-24, underlining mine). This scripture brings to mind Lehi's hokmah, or truism, that there must needs be opposition in all things. Apparently, this includes foundation principles of the Plan, as well as gender assignment that makes those principles easier to comprehend. It is possible that Alma consciously used the natural differences between men and women to intentionally illustrate, against the backdrop of masculinity and femininity, the unique individuality of Justice on the one hand, and Mercy on the other.

Next, in this section, the Lord identified the need for twelve special witnesses. A Council of Twelve had been appointed by Moses (Numbers 1:1-16), that consisted of one representative from each tribe in Israel. They had, to a large extent, responsibility to provide leadership among the people. They are called "Princes in Israel," from "Princeps - one who takes the first place, a leader." There were also Councils of the Twelve at the time of Christ on both hemispheres. Today, the Twelve are again called to "go into all the world to preach (the) gospel unto every creature." (V. 28).

The Lord told Joseph Smith: "To some, it is given by the Holy Ghost to know that Jesus Christ is the Son of God, and that he was crucified for the sins of the world. To others, it is given to believe on their words, that they also might have eternal life if they continue faithful." (D&C 46:13-14). This would equally apply to non-members who listen to the General Authorities of the church bear testimony. "And by doing so, the Lord God prepareth the way that the residue of men may have faith in Christ, that the Holy Ghost may have place in their hearts." (Words of Mormon 1:32).

Consequently, the Twelve Apostles today declare with boldness their witness of the truth, that faith might be developed in the hearts of those who hear their testimony. Hence the following representative sampling from the Council of the Twelve: "I know that God lives, for as in the words of my predecessor, John Taylor, I have seen Him." (Spencer W. Kimball). "I know of the divinity of the Lord Jesus Christ, for it has been revealed to me in a most interesting, complete, and beautiful way." (L. Tom Perry).

Elder Perry also said: "I leave you with that special witness which is mine to bear, for I have witnessed it with my own eyes, and heard it with my own ears." The last testimony of Bruce R. McConkie concluded with these words: "I shall feel the nail marks in his hands and in his feet and shall wet his feet with my tears. But I shall not know any better then than I know now that he is God's Almighty Son, that he is our Savior and Redeemer, and that salvation comes in and through his atoning blood and in no other way." ("Ensign," 6/1975).).

"Take upon you the name of Christ, and speak the truth in soberness." (V. 21). Covenants are binding contracts, and since God is a party to every gospel covenant, they must come through revelation. No person enters into such covenants except on the basis of direct revelation from God. It follows that, since its organization on April 6, 1830, the only ones who can legally enter into covenants are members of the church of Jesus Christ!

Just as we are known by the name of our mortal parents, so too are we called by the name of Christ in a familial way. We are Christ's children in the sense that He united our bodies and spirits through the Resurrection: "For this day He hath spiritually begotten you," explained Benjamin. (Mosiah 5:7). There is a special family relationship reserved for the faithful that is in addition to the reality that we are all spirit children of our Father.

Those who enter into the Covenant "are born of him." (Mosiah 5:7). A "Born Again Christian" is one who is in a covenant relationship with the Lord, and since only members of Christ's true church can do that through the administration of a priesthood whose authority is recognized, it follows that the only real Born Again Christians are Latter-day Saints! (See Mosiah 27:25, Alma 5:14, & 7:14, then Mosiah 15:10-11, Alma 22:15, & 36:24).

As the Lord revealed to Joseph Smith, the "greater priesthood administereth the gospel and holdeth the key of the mysteries of the kingdom, even the key of the knowledge of God. Therefore, in the ordinances thereof, the power of godliness is manifest. And without the ordinances thereof, and the authority of the priesthood, the power of godliness is not manifest unto men in the flesh." (D&C 84:19-21).

"And as many as repent and are baptized in my name, which is Jesus Christ, and endure to the end, the same shall be saved." (V. 22). Keeping the covenants we have made with God puts us beyond the power of the adversary, for obedience gives us the priesthood and spiritual power necessary to overcome evil and obtain exaltation.

The Prophet Joseph Smith said that salvation consists of our being placed beyond the power of our enemies, meaning the enemies of our progression, such as dishonesty, greediness, lying, immorality, and other vices. (Sermon delivered at the Nauvoo temple site on May 21, 1843. Sources: Joseph Smith diary (Willard Richards), Howard and Martha Jane Knowlton Coray Notebook, Franklin D. Richards "Scriptural Items," and James Burgess Notebook. See "Teachings," p. 297-298). "For by doing these things (entering into covenants) the gates of hell shall not prevail against you; yea, and the Lord God will disperse the powers of darkness from before you, and cause the heavens to shake for thy good, and His name's glory." (D&C 21:6).

Only by making covenants with God and Christ can we break the bands of death, and are we made free. "There is no other name given whereby salvation cometh," said Benjamin; "therefore, I would that ye should take upon you the name of Christ, all you that have entered into the covenant with God." (Mosiah 5:8). Is it any wonder that The Church of Jesus Christ of Latter-day Saints is a missionary oriented church, and that the Savior Himself proclaims that it "is the only true and living church upon the face of the whole earth, with which I, the Lord, am well pleased?" (D&C 1:30).

No other church has the authority of the priesthood, that is necessary to bind and ratify the covenants we make with God. The reality of the apostasy and the subsequent restoration of priesthood authority are well documented in the scriptures and in the history of the church. No other organization has the power to break the death grip of Satan, who would drag our souls down to hell in an instant, if he were given free reign to do so.

"Behold, Jesus Christ is the name which is given of the Father, and there is none other name given whereby man can be saved. Wherefore, all men must take upon them the name which is given of the Father, for in that name shall they be called at the last day." (V. 23-24). The Nephite Saints had always been clearly taught to Whom they should look for salvation. Jacob recorded: "For this intent have we written these things, that they may know that we knew of Christ, and we had a hope of his glory many hundred years before his coming; and not only we ourselves had a hope of his glory, but also all the holy prophets which were before us." (Jacob 4:4). Nephi said: "We talk of Christ, we rejoice in Christ, we preach of Christ, we prophesy of Christ, and we write according to our prophecies, that our children may know to what source they may look for a remission of their sins." (2 Nephi 25:26).

The attitude of the subjects of King Benjamin following his discourse was the same as that of true believers 50 years later. At that time, many "took upon them, gladly, the name of Christ, or Christians, as they were called, because of their belief in Christ who should come." (Alma 46:15). They recognized the source of the only legitimate authority on earth with the power to sanctify them so that they could be brought into the presence of God.

In fulfillment of Benjamin's promise, they were no longer "the people of Zarahemla" or "the people of Nephi," but "Christians." He who took upon himself the name of Christ would be found "at the right hand of God, for he (would) know the name by which he (was) called; for he (should) be called by the name of Christ." (Mosiah 5:9). As the Savior said: "My sheep hear my voice, and I know them, and they follow me. " (John 10:27).

Benjamin pointed out that those who would not take upon themselves the name of Christ would find themselves in His disfavor, for their misplaced fealty would be manifest. "Whosoever shall not take upon him the name of Christ," Benjamin declared, "must be called by some other name; therefore, he findeth himself on the left hand of God." (Mosiah 5:10).

Alma asked: "If ye will not hearken unto the voice of the good shepherd, to the name by which ye are called, behold, ye are not the sheep of the good shepherd. And now if ye are not the sheep of the good shepherd, of what fold are ye? Behold, I say unto you, that the devil is your shepherd, and ye are of his fold; and now, who can deny this? ...Whosoever bringeth forth evil works, the same becometh a child of the devil, for he hearkeneth unto his voice, and doth follow him." (Alma 5:38-41).

Benjamin also warned that through transgression the name of Christ would be blotted out of the heart. When this occurs, one no longer feels like a Christian, or more pointedly, a Latter-day Saint. (Mosiah 5:11). After all, the heart is the repository of feeling.

The invitation to deny the cares of the world and respond to a more noble calling, to come unto Christ, is extended by every missionary to those who are pure in heart. However, the discipline required to follow the Royal Law is alien to the natural man. "Urging self-restraints on hedonists is like asking Dracula to avoid hanging around the blood bank." (Neal Maxwell, C.R., 4/1995). But Christians know that it is only the redeeming blood of Jesus Christ that sanctifies the soul.

It is important to both hear and know "the name by which (Christ) shall call you." (Mosiah 5:12). Many hear, yet do not comprehend, "for how knoweth a man the master whom he has not served, and who is a stranger to him, and is far from the thoughts and intents of his heart?" (Matthew 7:23).

Baptism alone does not assure us of eternal life. We also need to be "steadfast and immovable, always abounding in good works." (Mosiah 5:15). We need to be sealed by the ratifying power of the Holy Spirit of Promise, which is the Holy Ghost. (See D&C 88:3-4). Our calling and election is made sure only after the Lord has fully proven us. Then, when we receive "the other Comforter," Christ will appear to us and personally teach us the visions of eternity.

"There are others who are called to declare my gospel.... yea, even twelve; and the Twelve shall be my disciples, and they shall take upon them my name; and the Twelve are they who shall desire to take upon them my name with full purpose of heart.... They are called to go into all the world to preach my gospel unto every creature. And they are they who are ordained of me to baptize in my name." (V. 26-29).

As the spark of faith struck off the Divine Anvil of God ignites the flame of resolve within our hearts, we develop the "power to do whatsoever thing is expedient" or right to do, under the circumstances. That thing, said the Savior, is to "Repent all ye ends of the earth, and come unto me, and be baptized in my name, and have (more) faith in me, that ye may be saved." (Moroni 7:34). This is the fruits of faith, that is, to be saved in the Celestial Kingdom of God. It is the very reason for the ministry of the Twelve among the children of men.

"And now I speak unto you, the Twelve - Behold, my grace is sufficient for you; you must walk uprightly before me and sin not. And, behold, you are they who are ordained of me to ordain priests and teachers; to declare my gospel, according to the power of the Holy Ghost which is in you, and according to the callings and gifts of God unto men." (V. 31-32). It is the duty of the Twelve to "preach the gospel of Christ unto all the people upon the face of the land." (3 Nephi 28:23). Since the organization of the church, these special witnesses, with only a few exceptions, have been true to their covenants, and have worked tirelessly to preach the gospel.

As a body, these men have so completely internalized the principles of the gospel that the conduct of their lives is beyond reproach, and is in complete harmony with the Law of Heaven. "There (are) no contentions and disputations among them, and every man...deal(s) justly one with another." (4 Nephi 1:2)

Through repentance, they are made free from the bondage of sin, and qualify by worthiness to enjoy the blessings reserved for the obedient. The characteristics of the Zion society they work to create are simply the results of a spiritual transformation in the lives of the people, that comes about as they live the celestial law of the Lord.

These Apostles of Jesus Christ work all manner of miracles because the power of the priesthood finds expression as the fruits of their faith. The Lord prospers them exceedingly in the land. Those whom they influence enjoy the blessings of the priesthood, according to the multitude of the promises that the Lord has made unto them. They grow up within the secure embrace of the covenants of the temple that bind families together forever.

The Twelve, and those within the sphere of their influence, no longer walk after the manner of the world, copying its lifestyle and mimicking its customs, but they "walk after the commandments which they (have) received from their Lord and their God." (4 Nephi 1:12). They enjoy the blessings of the fulness of the gospel.

If the world would heed the message of these special witnesses of Christ, there would be no more contention in the land, because of the love of God that would dwell in the hearts of the people. The Lord would call his people Zion, because they would be of one heart and one mind, and dwell in righteousness. (See Moses 7:18).

What kind of power would there be in Zion? There would be the power to "break mountains, to divide the seas, to dry up waters, to turn them out of their course; to put a defiance the armies of nations, to divide the earth, to break every band, (and) to stand in the presence of God." (J.S.T., Genesis 14:30-31). Complete unity would exist among the people. There would be "no envyings, nor strifes, nor tumults, nor whoredoms, nor lyings, nor murders, nor any manner of lasciviousness." (4 Nephi 1:16-17).

They would seek to unify the people, knowing that the whole is truly greater than the sum of its parts. We can take an analogy from simple mechanics: One two-by-four, eight feet long and standing on end, will support a weight of 615 pounds. Two of these, standing together, will support a weight of 2,400 pounds! With such unity, "surely there could not be a happier people among all the people who had been created by the hand of God." (4 Nephi 1:16). "They (would be) in one, the children of Christ, and heirs to the kingdom of God." (4 Nephi 1:17).

It is the mission of the Twelve to seek out the elect, and to invite them to "come out of the world and to leave the loneliness and estrangement of a fallen creation and enter the realm of divine experience, to forsake the orphanage of spiritual alienation, and be received into the family and household of the Lord Jesus Christ. They are invited to leave the ranks of the nameless, and take upon them the blessed name of Jesus Christ. They are invited to become Christians. Through their Master, they are invited to become, in time, joint heirs to all that the Father has." ("Doctrinal Commentary on The Book of Mormon," 4:202).

Those who heed the message of the Twelve are often blessed to live abundantly, and then to go to enjoy the paradise of God. There they enter into God's Rest, to find joy in the Spirit World, where they are free from the cares of this telestial world. There they prepare themselves to experience the resurrection, thereafter to enter into the presence of the Lord, in His kingdom.

Although counsel in this section was specifically given to the Twelve, it is generally applicable to all Latter-day Saints: "These words are not of men, nor of man, but of me; wherefore, you shall testify they are of me and not of man. For it is my voice which speaketh them unto you; for they are given by my Spirit unto you, and by my power you can read them one to another; and save it were by my power you could not have them. Wherefore, you can testify that you have heard my voice, and know my words." (V. 34-36). As S. Dilworth Young put it: "When I read a verse in the Doctrine & Covenants, I am hearing the voice of the Lord, as well as reading His words, if I hear by the Spirit." (C.R., 4/1963).

By the power of the priesthood and the word of God, His army of missionaries will smite the earth and completely neutralize the influence of the wicked in the Last Days. As Alma found, "the preaching of the word had a great tendency to lead the people to do that which was just - yea, it had more powerful effect upon the minds of the people than the sword, or anything else." (Alma 31:5).

The battle lines during the war in heaven were drawn according to contrasting ideologies. The weapons used were words that powerfully articulated opposing positions. That Satan was persuasive is attested by the fact that he drew a third part of the heavenly host to his point of view. In the Last Days, the combatants are once again forming into diametrically opposed camps with increasingly polarized ideologies.

"For the time speedily cometh that the Lord God shall cause a great division among the people." (2 Nephi 30:10). We should remember how enticingly Satan beckons us with his soothing words. With deceit and deception, he tries to ensnare us. But the word of God is "quick," or living, in a biblical sense. It is "powerful," or a source of life and energy; it is "sharper than a two-edged sword, to the dividing asunder of both joints and marrow." It penetrates to our innermost parts. "Therefore, give heed unto (his) words." (D&C 6:2).

"And now, behold, I give unto you, Oliver Cowdery, and also unto David Whitmer, that you shall search out the Twelve." (V. 37). This search culminated in Kirtland, Ohio, on February 14, 1835, when 12 special witnesses were called by the first witnesses of the Restoration.

"For all men must repent and be baptized, and not only men, but women, and children who have arrived at the years of accountability." (V. 42). "Little children also have eternal life." (Mosiah 15:25). They are "redeemed from the foundation of the world through (the) Only Begotten." (D&C 29:46). "All children who die before they arrive at the years of accountability are saved in the Celestial Kingdom of heaven." (D&C 137:10).

In other words, provision for their exaltation was made at the Grand Council in Heaven, even before the world was. "Little children cannot (or need not) repent; wherefore, it is awful wickedness to deny the pure mercies of God unto them, for they are all alive in him because of his mercy." (Moroni 8:19).

As children advance in years, however, they "become accountable." This suggests that with maturity, children gradually assume complete responsibility for their actions. "Heaven lies about us in our infancy," wrote William Wordsworth. "Shades of the prison house begin to close upon the growing boy, but he beholds the light and whence it flows. He sees it in his joy. The youth, who daily farther from the east must travel, still is nature's priest, and by the vision splendid, is on his way attended. At length, the man perceives it die away, and fade into the light of common day." ("Ode: Intimations of Immortality").

"Since "children shall be baptized for the remission of their sins when eight years old," it seems that this is the age of accountability. (D&C 68:27). J.S.T. Genesis 17:11 reads: "And I will establish a covenant of circumcision with thee, and it shall be my covenant between me and thee, and thy seed after thee, in their generations; that thou mayest know for ever that children are not accountable before me until they are eight years old."

The practice of infant baptism in the various sects in the last days, and the differences of opinion regarding the correct method of baptism in Joseph Smith's day, in particular, made the restoration of the gospel administered by the true church even more necessary. It is critically important that the ordinance that would admit applicants into the fold of Christ be carried out according to His explicit instruction, for there is "one Lord, one faith, (and) one baptism." (Ephesians 4:5). "Except a man be born of water and of the Spirit," declared the Savior, "he cannot enter into the kingdom of God." (John 3:5).

Mormon had a correct understanding of the mission of the Redeemer, and knew that the Savior had come "into the world not to call the righteous but sinners to repentance. The whole need no physician," he taught, "but they that are sick; wherefore little children are whole, for they are not capable of committing sin."

(Moroni 8:8). Therefore, he said, "it is solemn mockery before God, that ye should baptize little children," because to do so denies the power of the Atonement. (Moroni 8:9).

The doctrine of infant baptism is an implicit denial that Jesus Christ atoned for the "original sin" of Adam, and it neutralizes the concept of individual accountability. It asks us to believe that little children who die without baptism cannot enter heaven. But the simple fact is that the Atonement did redeem them from the Fall. It is true that children are capable of actions that are inconsistent with obedience to gospel principles, but they are not counted against them as sins. Children are not culpable.

Rather, Mormon wrote: "This thing shall ye teach - repentance and baptism unto those who are accountable and capable of committing sin; yea, teach parents that they must repent and be baptized, and humble themselves as their little children, and they shall all be saved with their little children." (Moroni 8:10). Then, for added emphasis, he declared: "Little children need no repentance, neither baptism. Behold, baptism is unto repentance to the fulfilling the commandments unto the remission of sins. But little children are alive in Christ, even from the foundation of the world." (Moroni 8:11-12).

It was an integral part of the Plan of Salvation, ordained in the Grand Council in heaven before the world was, that little children who died before the age of accountability would be saved in the Celestial Kingdom by the far reach of the power of the Infinite Atonement. "If not so, God is a partial God, and also a changeable God, and a respecter of persons; for how many little children have died without baptism!" Those who labor under the burden of a belief in infant baptism are "in the gall of bitterness," for how could a just and loving Father in Heaven consign so many of His innocent children to an eternal fate that, on their own merits, they did not deserve? (Moroni 8:14).

Such unenlightened individuals are "in the bonds of iniquity" in the sense that they must experience despair, or a sense of hopelessness regarding their little ones who have died without baptism. (Moroni 8:14). "Despair cometh because of iniquity," because when sin clouds vision, unrepentant sinners can see no way out of their miserable situations. (Moroni 10:22). Apostate teachings leave no alternative but to suggest that "if little children could not be saved without baptism, these must have gone to an endless hell." (Moroni 8:13).

Mormon would have us recognize the doctrine of infant baptism for the damnable heresy that it is. Those who persist in this practice "must go down to hell." (Moroni 8:14). "For awful is the wickedness to suppose that God saveth one child because of baptism, and the other must perish because he hath no baptism. We be unto them that shall pervert the ways of the Lord after this manner, for (after they understand the role of accountability, its effects on the fall of Adam, and the necessity of the Savior's redemption) they shall perish except they repent." (Moroni 8:15-16).

Whereas those who teach the doctrine of infant baptism believe that those children who die without the ordinance will go to hell, the truth is that "they (the professors of the doctrine, are the ones who) are in danger of death, hell, and an endless torment." (Moroni 8:21). Mormon knew that he was speaking boldly, but God had commanded him to do so. Our eternal welfare depends upon our correct understanding of this doctrine. (Moroni 8:21).

"And by your hands I will work a marvelous work among the children of men, unto the convincing of many of their sins, that they may come unto repentance, and that they may come unto the kingdom of my Father." (V. 44). The essential ingredient of saving faith is to first believe in the Son of God. This, in itself, is a marvelous thing in our day of rational thinking and secular humanism.
Every discussion of faith, however, must distinguish it from the caricatures so widely and energetically promoted by those who have no faith. It is not credulity. It is not believing things you know are not so. It is not a formula to get the world to do your bidding. It is not an expression of the cynicism and pessimism so cleverly glamorized by the media. Faith inspires confidence that life is a school of discipline whose Author and Teacher is God.

Truth is at the very foundation of faith. Heavenly Father will not cause us to have faith in that which is false. Justifiable faith is faith with sufficient evidence. It is faith in action, supported by good works that are ratified by the Holy Ghost. It is faith of such quality that at the Bar of Justice, the Holy Ghost will stand beside us and legitimately demand that the power of the Atonement raise us to a resurrection of glory and eternal life.

Heavenly Father does not expect us to exercise faith in those things for which there is insufficient evidence. The key to liberation from enslavement to apostate religious dogma is our testimony of the Son of God, that is a gift of the Spirit.

Many who lived before the mortal ministry of the Savior had such faith that they received the Second Comforter, the personal ministry of Jesus Christ, and "they truly saw with their eyes the things which they had beheld with an eye of faith, and they were glad." (Ether 12:19). While Moroni taught: "If there be no faith among the children of men, God can do no miracle among them" (Ether 12:12), he explained that the opposite is also true. Our faith in God may become so great, that He cannot "be kept without the veil." (Ether 12:21). When we reach that point in our spiritual development, "the veil shall be rent," and we shall know the truth of the Lord's promise: "You shall see me and know that I am." (D&C 67:10).

# Section 19

## (Received prior to the organization of the church).

Section 19 is a revelatory commandment. "In his history, the Prophet introduced it as a commandment of God and not of man, to Martin Harris" who was still tormented by doubt to the extent that it became sinful." (Superscript). Skepticism has its legitimate purpose, insofar as it prompts investigation, but to doubt in the face of overwhelming evidence is perversity. The gospel is as much the sum of "Thou shalt" commandments, including "Thou shalt believe," as it is "Thou shalt not" commandments, including "Thou shalt not doubt."

The composite principles of the Plan of Salvation invite us to make constructive decisions, and take affirmative action. When we adopt its lifestyle, we see the wisdom in Alma's counsel to the Zoramites: "Plant the word in your hearts...and then may God grant unto you that your burdens may be light, through the joy of his Son." Alma could have been speaking to Martin Harris, when he concluded: "And even all this can ye do, if ye will." (Alma 33:23). Certainly, Martin Harris had agency, but once the Lord had spoken, the debate was over. It was time for Martin Harris to act.

The revelation opens with a definitive declaration that the Savior is the beginning and the end, or "alpha and omega" (the first and last letters of the Greek alphabet), that He is the Anointed One, or "Christ the Lord," and that He is "the Redeemer of the world." (V. 1). Elsewhere in the Doctrine & Covenants, Jesus Christ reconfirmed that He exists in the present tense; He is "the Great I AM, Alpha and Omega, the beginning and the end, the same which looked upon the wide expanse of eternity, and all the seraphic hosts of heaven, before the world was made." (D&C 38:1-2). He is the Creator and Ruler of this world, and the God of this earth. (See below).

Less than a year after this revelation was given in the summer of 1829, the Lord again testified that Joseph Smith was given "power from on high, by the means which were before(hand) prepared, to translate The Book of Mormon; which contains a record of a fallen people, and the fulness of the gospel of Jesus Christ to the Gentiles and to the Jews also; which was given by inspiration and is confirmed to others by the ministering of angels, and is declared unto the world by them - Proving to the world" these three critically important truths: (1) "that the holy scriptures are true, and (2) that God does inspire men and call them to his holy work in this age and generation, as well as in generations of old; (3) thereby showing that he is the same God yesterday, today, and forever." (D&C 20:8-12).

Something wonderful surrounds our testimonies of the living Prophet, Seer, and Revelator of The Church of Jesus Christ of Latter-day Saints. Over 150 years ago, John Greenleaf Whittier said of "these modern prophets, I discovered, as I think, the great secret of their success in making converts. They speak to a common feeling; they minister to a universal want. They speak a language of hope and promise to the weak, weary hearts, tossed and troubled, who have wandered from sect to sect, seeking in vain for the primal manifestations of the divine power." (Quoted in "A Mormon Conventicle," p. 461, and in "Howitt's Journal in the Millennial Star," 1848, p. 302-3).

Joseph Smith taught us how to live in harmony with God's Plan, he showed us how to prepare the way for the Lord's return, and he gave us the tools to establish His kingdom on the earth. "The greatest event that has ever occurred in the world since the resurrection of the Son of God from the tomb and his ascension on high," declared Joseph F. Smith, "was the coming of the Father and of the Son to that boy Joseph Smith, to prepare the way for the laying of the foundation of his kingdom." ("Deseret Evening News," 7/14/1917).

Joseph Smith showed us how to be happy. He had a knack for seeing the eternal principle of agency in a light that was distinct from that of his contemporaries. He recognized that the exercise of free will does entail risk, because the element of failure is real and is always just one decision away, but he learned by experience that it is the only way that we may justify our claim to unspeakable joy in our Father's kingdom. He provided repetitive opportunities for us to recommit ourselves to our covenants of obedience to tried and true principles. At the same time, he revealed the laws pertaining to happiness that will qualify us to receive the blessings tied to obedience. With words of encouragement, he continually nurtured our spiritual well-being and inner peace. "Happiness (after all) is the object and design of our existence, " he taught, "and will be the end thereof, if we pursue the path that leads to it, and this path is virtue, uprightness, faithfulness, holiness, and keeping all the commandments of God." ("Teachings," p. 255).

He established a legacy of prophetic guidance that continues to this day. He nurtured our testimony of the office of the President of The Church of Jesus Christ of Latter-day Saints. He helped us to understand that "the most important prophet, so far as we are concerned, is the one who is living in our day and age. Every generation has need of (counsel) from the living prophet. Therefore, the most crucial reading and pondering which (we can) do is of the latest inspired words from the Lord's mouthpiece." (Ezra Taft Benson, President of the Quorum of The Twelve Apostles).

Our living prophet not only shares our perspective, but he also sees through the clarifying and purifying lens of eternity. He blesses our lives in many ways by nurturing our understanding of the Plan of Salvation. The veil that has been drawn over our eyes, preventing us from seeing eternity with an unimpeded view, is nearly transparent to our prophet. Joseph Smith explained as a statement of fact: "Could you gaze into heaven five minutes, you would know more than you would by reading all that has ever been written on the subject." (H.C. 6:50). Asked how he could govern so many people, he replied: "I teach them correct principles, and they govern themselves." (John Taylor, "The Organization of the Church," "Millennial Star," 11/15/1851, p. 339). His understanding of the Plan of Salvation allowed him to teach the body of known truth, to clarify truth that had been heretofore hidden from the world, and to reveal new truth. "Truly, the Prophet Joseph Smith "was a prism of the Lord Jesus Christ." (Truman Madsen, ("Defender of The Faith," p. 93).

One of his greatest contributions was sharing with the world his knowledge of what is to come after death. He clarified our understanding of heaven, taught that it was an attainable goal, and by example encouraged those around him. He created desire in the hearts of millions to follow the difficult road to Gethsemane. What he did validated the promises made by the Father to each of us, that the struggles of mortality would be worth every effort, and that we would look back on our experiences in appreciation for the personal growth and development that grew out of our struggles. But he always emphasized that only if the drama is played out within the context of the gospel, according to the rules established by the Plan of Salvation, will the anticipated blessings come. There is no other way.

Christ is the ruler of this world and the God of the earth, "retaining all power, even to the destroying of Satan and his works at the end of the world." (V. 2). The end of the world is the end of unrighteousness, or of worldliness as we know it, and this will be brought about by "the destruction of the wicked." (Joseph Smith Matthew 1:4)

"No power on earth or hell can overthrow or defeat that which God has decreed," declared Joseph Fielding Smith, Jr. "Every plan of the adversary will fail, for the Lord knows the secret thoughts of men, and sees the future with a vision clear and perfect, even as though it were in the past." ("Church History and Modern Revelation," 1:26). "O how great the holiness of our God!" cried Jacob. "For he knoweth all things, and there is not anything save he knows it." (2 Nephi 9:20). "Else He would cease to be God, and man could not have faith in him." (Joseph Fielding Smith, Jr., "Doctrines of Salvation," 1:7-10).

Because faithful Saints hold to the rod of iron, "no unhallowed hand can stop the work from progressing; persecutions may rage, mobs may combine, armies may assemble, calumny may defame, but the truth of God will go forth boldly, nobly, and independent, until it has penetrated every continent, visited every clime, swept every country, and sounded in every ear, 'til the purposes of God shall be accomplished and the Great Jehovah shall say 'The work is done.'" (Joseph Smith, in "The Wentworth Letter," H.C., 4:540).

Telestial turf, on the other hand, is Satan's home ground, and when we venture onto it, we risk losing our way. For such individuals, "the gates of hell are...open to receive them." (3 Nephi 18:13). The quicksand of secular humanism lies beneath an inviting sod that may be disguised as Astroturf, but that is really a quicksand of false ideology patiently waiting to suck the unwary into the unstable underworld of the Adversary.

Verses 4-12 continue the important doctrinal instruction regarding the character of God. "And surely every man must repent or suffer, for I, God, am endless. Wherefore, I revoke not the judgments which I shall pass, but woes shall go forth, weeping, wailing and gnashing of teeth, yea, to those who are found on my left hand." (V. 4-6).

Jesus Christ "created the heavens and the earth." (D&C 14:9). In the Doctrine & Covenants, and in The Book of Mormon, are found the clearest declarations in scripture that Jesus Christ is the Creator, Who acted under the direction of the Father by divine investiture of authority to form the earth. The Book of Mormon declarations read: "Behold, I am Jesus Christ the Son of God, I created the heavens and the earth, and all things that in them are. I was with the Father from the beginning. I am in the Father, and the Father in me; and in me hath the Father glorified his name." (3 Nephi 9:15). In the First Book of Nephi, with the simple statement of fact, "I am he," the Lord testified that it was He who, before time began, "laid the foundation of the earth, and (whose) right hand hath spanned the heavens" in both time and space. (1 Nephi 20:12-13). The right hand is a symbol of righteousness, and of the power that comes through obedience to law. This is why it is appropriate to use it when making covenants and performing and receiving ordinances.

Addressing the Lord's characterization of "endless torment," in verses 4 - 6, James

E. Talmage concluded: "Souls that attain to salvation and eternal life shall have glory added upon their heads forever and ever. But the thought of never-ending punishment (or endless torment) as the fate of all who die in their sins is repugnant, and rightly so.

As reward for righteous living is to be proportionate to desserts, so punishment for sin must be graded according to the offense. The purpose of punishment is disciplinary, reformatory, and in support of justice. God's mercy is as truly manifest in the suffering which He allows, as in the joy of salvation which He bestows." Once again, we see the opposition in all things that permeates the provisions of the Plan.

"As to the duration of punishment, we may take assurance that it shall be measured to the individual in just accordance with the sum of his iniquity. That every sentence for sin must be interminable (or endless) is as directly opposed to a rational conception of justice as it is contradictory to the revealed Word of God. It was mercifully foreordained that even the prisoners thronging the pit should in due time be visited (See Isaiah 24:21-22), and be offered means of amelioration. (See Isaiah 42:7)." Equal but opposite forces are at play, here.

"True, the scriptures speak of endless punishment (or endless torment) and depict everlasting burnings, eternal damnation, and suffering incident to unquenchable fire, as features of the Judgment reserved for the wicked. But none of these awful possibilities are anywhere in scripture declared to be the unending (or endless) fate of the individual sinner." For that would undermine the balance and symmetry of the Plan.

"Blessing or punishment ordained of God is eternal, for He is eternal, and eternal are all His ways. His is a system of endless and eternal punishment, for it will always exist as the place or condition provided for the rebellious and disobedient, but the penalty as visited upon the individual will terminate when, through repentance, the necessary reform has been effected and the uttermost farthing paid." Thus, is preserved the equity between Justice and Mercy.

"Even to hell there is an exit as well as an entrance; and when sentence has been served, commuted perhaps by repentance and its attendant works, the prison doors shall open and the penitent captive be afforded opportunity to comply with the law which he aforetime violated. But the prison remains, and the eternal (or endless) decree prescribing punishment for the offender stands unrepealed. So it is even with the penal institutions established by man." ("The Vitality of Mormonism," p. 264-265). Thus, the eternal nature of the Plan is preserved.

"Again, it is written eternal damnation; wherefore it is more express than other scriptures, that it might work upon the hearts of the children of men, altogether for my name's glory." (V. 7). The Christian world in Joseph Smith's day had lost its way. It no longer enjoyed an appreciation of the relationship between God and mankind, and its knowledge of His character was perverted by a distorted understanding of the Plan for His children. Even well-meaning Christians wrested the scriptures, and believed that "eternal damnation" meant that the duration of the penalty would be forever.

But as B.H. Roberts, suggested, in the eternities to come, "environment will correspond to nature, with always the possibility present of improving both the environment and nature, until a fulness of joy is attained." ("Joseph Smith the Prophet-Teacher," p. 27-28). With this understanding, we can see more clearly that the Plan is perfect, and why we sang together and shouted for joy when it was presented to us. (See Job 38:4 & 7).

J. Reuben Clark, Jr. reasoned: "I am not a strict constructionist, believing that we seal our eternal progress by what we do here. It is my belief that God will save all His children that He can; and while, if we live unrighteously here, we shall not go to the other side in the same status, so to speak, as those who live righteously; nevertheless, the unrighteous will have their chance, and in the eons of the eternities that are to follow, they, too, may climb to the destinies to which they who are righteous and serve God, have climbed." ("Church News," 3/23/1960). This sounds suspiciously like a validation of the concept of progression between kingdoms of glory.

Wherefore, I will explain unto you this mystery, for it is meet unto you to know even as mine apostles. For, behold, the mystery of godliness, how great it is!" (V. 8 & 10). When we read Alma's counsel to his son Corianton, we realize that "there are many mysteries which are kept, that no one knoweth them save God himself." (V. 3, see Alma 37:11). Therefore, we should not be impatient or anxious to gain intellectual or spiritual mastery of that which is apparently beyond our comprehension, or that is unnecessary for us to have at the present stage of our development. The time will surely come when, with spiritual maturity, we will better appreciate those principles that are presently mysterious and incomprehensible to us in our spiritually uninitiated and immature state. Perhaps only then, we will better appreciate how great the gospel really is.

For, behold, I am endless, and the punishment which is given from my hand is endless punishment, for Endless is my name. Wherefore - Eternal punishment is God's punishment. Endless punishment is God's punishment." (V. 10-12). Is there a hell? Yes. (D&C 76:84-85). It is the spirit world. Yes. (Alma 40:11-14). But "to hell there is an exit as well as an entrance. It is a place prepared for the teaching and disciplining of those who failed to learn here on earth what they should and could have. No man will be kept in hell longer than is necessary to bring him to a fitness for something better." (James E. Talmage, C.R., 4/1930, see Moses 1:39).

Our Heavenly Father loves all of His children, and He does not want any of them to suffer endlessly, or forever. "Therefore," the Lord said, "I command you to repent - repent, lest I smite you by the rod of my mouth." (V. 15). When Jesus Christ reproves the world for its sins, it is in the hope that its inhabitants will be "awakened to a remembrance of their duty." (Alma 4:3, see Hebrews 12:6, D&C 95:1 & 121:43). The purpose of chastisement is to bring sinners to repentance. God wants all of His children to grasp the horns of sanctuary and rely upon the Atonement of His Son, rather than upon their own energies, intellect, or abilities, so that they might more easily qualify for eternal life. Christ is the Mediator of the Covenant, and the bargaining chips He uses when dealing with Justice are our purposeful repentance and His Atonement. It is in this context that we work out our "salvation with fear and trembling" before the Lord. (Philippians 2:12). It is a joint process in which we are mutually engaged. It works to our benefit because we are saved in the Celestial Kingdom, and it works to His benefit because it consummates His work and glory, which is to bring about our immortality and eternal life. (See Moses 1:39).

Neal Maxwell said that in "the Last Days, discipleship will be lived in crescendo." The actions of each individual member of the church, cleansed from the blood and sins of this generation, will swell the chorus of voices shouting "Hallelujah," and significantly hasten the millennial reign of the Lord. B.H. Roberts once said that "the Latter-day Saints are the white hot sparks struck off the Divine Anvil of God," destined to kindle a fire that will burn brightly to purify and celestialize the earth, so that it might receive its rightful King.

"For behold, I, God, have suffered these things for all, that they might not suffer if they would repent; But if they would not repent they must suffer, even as I." (V. 16-17). The Atonement was infinite; it was for all of our sins past, present, and future. (See Alma 41:6). But those who do not take advantage of the Atonement through repentance must atone for their own sins, before the final judgment. (See Alma 40:14). This is why the Lord has so consistently instructed His servants to preach nothing but repentance. "The great misery of departed spirits in the world of spirits (in hell) is to know that they have come short of the glory that others enjoy and that they might have enjoyed themselves," had they repented. (Joseph Smith, H.C., 5:425). Therefore, the Lord reiterated: "I command you again to repent." (V. 20).

"I command you that you preach naught but repentance." (V. 21). Repentance is all that ever needs to be taught. It means to stop doing things that are wrong, and to start doing what is right. Has God broken the bands of death and the chains of hell? The answer is an absolute and unequivocal 'Yes!' God is the Master of all circumstances. Every provision of the Plan had been carefully thought out before its implementation, so that it would harmonize perfectly with its companion principles. Truly, God's work and glory is to bring about the immortality and eternal life of all His children, while preserving free will and addressing the effects of the violation of law. (See Moses 1:39).

On what condition, then, are we saved? On what grounds do we have hope of salvation? It is the Atonement that establishes the firm foundation. Any other conditions are only corollaries to the Atonement, as well as to its supportive covenants made possible by Christ's sacrifice.

How is it that we have been loosed from the bands of death, and the chains of hell? It is because the Lamb slain from the foundation of the world is the Author of Salvation and the Savior of the world. His sacrifice is central to the Plan of Salvation, and made our repentance possible.

"For (the world) cannot bear meat now, but milk they must receive." (V. 22). Joseph Smith said: "As far as we degenerate from God, we descend to the devil and lose knowledge, and without knowledge we cannot be saved." ("Teachings," p. 217). It was important in the days of the infancy of the restored church that the Saints focus their attention on the first principles and ordinances of the gospel. The necessity of maintaining that focus is equally important today.

"Learn of me," said the Lord, "and listen to my words; walk in the meekness of my Spirit, and you shall have peace in me." (V. 23). Satan is at the root of contention. "His is the power of delusion, confusion, strife, bitterness, and class distinctions, and not one of peace and righteousness." (Joseph Fielding Smith, Jr., "Doctrines of Salvation," 3:315). Therefore, the world's definition of peace is remarkably superficial: often-times peace is only equated with the lack of bloodshed or of opposing combatants who are actively seeking each others lives.

The Lord's definition is quite different. "His peace is not the peace of the world of ease, of luxury, idleness, absence of turmoil and strife, but the peace born of the righteous life, the peace that lifts the soul, that day by day brings us closer to the home of Eternal Peace, the dwelling place of our Father." (J. Reuben Clark, Jr.).

"I am Jesus Christ; I came by the will of the Father, and I do his will." (V. 24). Latter-day Saints understand that there is a physical and spiritual rapport between the

Father and the Son, and between Them and true believers. Through this rapport, that is effected by the Holy Ghost, they become "one" in the spiritual sense.

"This unity is a Type of completeness. The mind of any one member of the Godhead is the mind of the others. Seeing, as each of them does, with the eye of perfection, they understand alike, guided by the same principles of unerring justice and equity." (James E. Talmage, "Articles of Faith," p. 41). The Priesthood facilitates this unity by administering gospel ordinances, allowing God's children to be organized into eternal family units as they enter into the patriarchal order of celestial marriage. In the temple, the unification of the Saints is consummated. It is there that we learn the principles of temporal and spiritual government, and in sacred assemblies covenant to consecrate our time and talents to the church and kingdom, and to lend our efforts to the preparation of the earth for the coming millennial reign of Jesus Christ.

The fulness of the gospel is contained in The Book of Mormon, and the Lord was anxious in March 1830, when this revelation was given, to have the book published. Therefore, he commanded Martin Harris to freely impart of his means "to the printing of The Book of Mormon, which contains the truth and the word of God." (V. 26). Nephi urged us to "hearken unto these words" (2 Nephi 33:10) precisely because "The Book of Mormon is the keystone of our religion." (Joseph Smith, H.C., 4:46). "Take away The Book of Mormon and the revelations, and where is our religion? We have none." (Joseph Smith, "Teachings," p. 71). Christ has the power to demonstrate that The Book of Mormon contains His words. He has the power to dispense knowledge. Indeed, He has power over all things. With great glory, He will reveal The Book of Mormon to His serious disciples.

The Lord explained to Martin Harris that soon, The Book of Mormon would "go to the Jew, of whom the Lamanites are a remnant." (V. 27). In the time of Lehi, all of the inhabitants of the house of Israel were known as Jews, and so, in The Book of Mormon, the term 'Jew' generally refers to those of any of the tribes of Israel. However, the People of Zarahemla were the only Book of Mormon group who were actually of the tribe of Judah, or "Jews." (See Omni 1:14-19, Mosiah 25:2 & Helaman 8:21).

"And again, I command thee that thou shalt pray vocally as well as in thy heart; yea, before the world as well as in secret, in public as well as in private." (V. 28). Living without prayer is a form of atheism because it takes no cognizance of God. Those who have difficulty with the doctrine of Christ often have not exercised faith sufficient to pray. "If ye would hearken unto the Spirit which teacheth a man to pray," Nephi wrote, "ye would know that ye must pray; for the evil spirit teacheth not a man to pray, but teacheth him that he must not pray. But behold, I say unto you that ye must pray always, and not faint; that ye must not perform any thing unto the Lord save in the first place ye shall pray unto the Father in the name of Christ, that he will consecrate thy performance unto thee, that thy performance may be for the welfare of thy soul." (2 Nephi 32:8-9).

Long ago, the Psalmist wrote: "Evening, and morning, and at noon, will I pray, and cry aloud, and he shall hear my voice." (Psalms 55:17). In the Garden of Gethsemane, the Savior counseled Peter: "Watch and pray, that ye enter not into temptation. The spirit indeed is willing, but the flesh is weak." (Matthew 26:41). Brigham Young once observed that it does not matter if we feel like praying or not; we should nevertheless pray. He said if we waited until we felt like praying, there would not be much prayer in this world. (See D.B.Y., p. 44). The practice in the church of consistent and even repetitive prayer makes sense, since its members need regular reinforcement against encroachments by Satan, and the tendency to be carnal, sensual, and devilish.

To his brethren, Nephi provided the additional insight that it is the evil one who teaches that we must not pray. With this knowledge, the practice in the church of consistent and even repetitive prayer makes sense, since its members need regular reinforcement against encroachments by Satan, and the tendency to be carnal, sensual, and devilish.

David O. McKay enjoyed quoting Edwin Markham, one of his favorite poets: "The builder who first bridged Niagara's gorge, before he swung his cable, shore to shore, sent out across the gulf his venturing kite, bearing a slender cord for unseen hands to grasp upon the further cliff and draw a greater cord, and then a greater yet; 'til at last across the chasm swung The Cable - then the mighty bridge in air! So may we send our little timid thoughts, across the void, out to God's reaching hands. Send our love, and faith, to thread the deep, thought after thought, until the little cord, and we, are anchored to the Infinite!"

"And thou shalt declare glad tidings, yea, publish it upon the mountains, and upon every high place, and among every people that thou shalt be permitted to see." (V. 29). Today, the Latter-day Saints are under the same obligation. (See D&C 18:9-10). "After all that has been said," declared Joseph Smith, "the greatest and most important duty is to preach the gospel." (Joseph Smith, "Teachings," p. 113).

A key to missionary success is scripture mastery. The Saints recognize God's word as a personal message, and accept it as an individually crafted blueprint for their everyday behavior and pattern for the direction their lives should take. When converts are snatched "from (their) awful, sinful, and polluted state" they are redeemed from the chains of hell. (Alma 26:17). They gain scriptural literacy as they learn to listen to the voice of the Spirit.

Ammon, one of the Sons of Mosiah, explained a most significant principle of missionary work: "He that repenteth and exerciseth faith," he said, "and bringeth forth good works, and prayeth continually without ceasing - unto such it is given to know the mysteries of God; yea, unto such it shall be given to reveal things which never have been revealed; yea, and it shall be given unto such to bring thousands of souls to repentance.' (Alma 26:22).

Nephi reported how Isaiah foresaw the Last Days, when the Lord would "lift up an ensign to the nations from far," or would raise the gospel standard, which would "hiss unto them from the end of the earth," after the manner of the electronic media, and summon them from afar. They would respond to that call, and "come with speed swiftly; none shall be weary nor stumble among them." They would come to Zion with such haste that before they would have had time to be tired, they would have arrived at their destination. "None shall slumber nor sleep; neither shall the girdle of their loins be loosed, nor the latchet of their shoes be broken." During their travels, they would have required neither sleep nor even a change of clothing.

Isaiah further described the sparking and flashing of "their horses' hoofs," and the great noise the wheeled vehicles that he envisioned would make. He wrote that those who would respond to the call would bring many converts to Zion. "They shall roar like young lions...and lay hold of the prey, and shall carry away safe." In the day of Israel's restoration, the gospel would go forth amid general conditions of destruction and apostasy raging upon the face of the earth. "And in that day...behold, darkness and sorrow, and the light is darkened in the heavens thereof." (2 Nephi 15:26-30).

"And of tenets (or doctrine) thou shalt not talk, but thou shalt declare repentance and faith on the Savior, and remission of sins by baptism, and by fire, yea, even the Holy Ghost. Behold, this is a great and the last commandment which I shall give unto you concerning this matter." (V. 31-32). The Savior did not want Martin Harris, or others who were called to the ministry, to dwell on the more difficult doctrines of the kingdom, that could only be discerned by those who were more spiritually mature. Rather, He wanted an emphasis to be placed only upon the first principles and ordinances of the gospel. Simply stated, these codify the doctrine of Christ, which is that all who have faith in Jesus Christ, and truly repent of their sins, entering into a baptismal covenant with the Lord, will receive the Holy Ghost. This third member of the Godhead will then direct that person, revealing the path that must be followed to achieve salvation.

The doctrine of Christ speaks to our spirits, for every gospel principle carries within it a witness that it is true. "The Lord giveth light unto the understanding," taught Nephi, "for he speaketh unto men according to their language, unto their understanding." (2 Nephi 31:3). The language of the spirit is universal, and when we have the Holy Ghost to illuminate our minds, we enjoy spiritual fluency. Such familiarity then opens up vistas of eternal proportion.

"And misery thou shalt receive, if thou wilt slight these counsels, yea, even the destruction of thyself and property." (V. 33). A knowledge of the gospel would not come to Martin Harris automatically, as a fringe benefit of maintaining body temperature. Effort would be required, even though he had already made significant progress along the uncomfortable road to which the Savior had directed him. Now, he was beginning to understand that it had grown too late to turn back, or even to falter in his steps. He realized that he must yield his agency to the Lord upon the altar of faith. But he also learned that blessings follow obedience and that the inevitable result of his submission to the Lord's will would be a magnificent outpouring of the Spirit.

The Savior taught an important principle, when He said: "No man can serve two masters; for either he will hate the one and love the other, or else he will hold to the one and despise the other. Ye cannot serve God and Mammon." (Matthew 6:24). A house divided against itself cannot stand. Neither the church nor its members can homogenize their principles so that they become popular with the world, for then all hell would want to join them. The Saints cannot hold membership in both the Church of God and the Great and Abominable Church of the Devil. They cannot live in Zion, but enjoy a summer home in Babylon. They cannot journey through Idumea, stopping along the way to sample its pleasures.

In D&C Section 29:12, we find the only instance in the Doctrine & Covenants where the term 'great and abominable church' is employed, although it is used twelve times in The Book of Mormon, in 1 Nephi 4:3, 9, 15, & 17, 1 Nephi 13:6, 8, 26 & 28, 1 Nephi 22:13 & 14, 2 Nephi 6:12, & 2 Nephi 28:18. That is enough, however, to entrench the phrase in our lexicon. Nephi was given, in vision, a broad view of the state of the world in the Last Days, and clearly saw "the great persecutor of the church, the apostate, the whore, even Babylon, that maketh all nations to drink of her cup, in whose hearts the enemy, even Satan, sitteth to reign." (D&C 86:3).

There is a fundamental instability associated with those who attempt to walk the line between righteousness and wickedness. Eternally damaging consequences are the result, because they are faced with a conundrum of cosmic proportion. Agency was preserved as the crown jewel of mortality in order to avoid this dilemma. We are free to choose, but choose we must. We are free to follow one lifestyle or another, but not both. That desire runs counter to the laws of nature and is fatally flawed. Those who pursue that path travel down a one-way road that leads inevitably to a personality precipice. Disciples of Christ do not have the option to walk "in (their) own way, and after the image of (their) own god, whose image is in the likeness of the world, and whose substance is that of an idol." (D&C 1:16).

Those who have consecrated their time, talents, energy, and their very lives to the kingdom of God, have long since "crossed over Jordan." They stand with Joshua, who declared: "Choose you this day whom ye will serve; whether the gods which your fathers served that were on the other side of the flood, or the gods of the Amorites, in whose land ye dwell: but as for me and my house, we will serve the Lord." (Joshua 24:15).

This has been the pattern since the foundation of the world. "And thus the gospel began to be preached, from the beginning, being declared by holy angels sent forth from the presence of God, and by his own voice, and by the gift of the Holy Ghost. And thus all things were confirmed unto Adam, by an holy ordinance, and the gospel preached, and a decree sent forth, that it should be in the world, until the end thereof." (Moses 5:58-59).

"Pay the debt thou hast contracted with the printer. Release thyself from bondage." (V. 35). Bondage obligates us to the whims of others, and puts our fate in their hands. "Our stand for freedom is a most basic part of our religion. This stand helped us get to this earth, and our reaction to freedom in this life will have eternal consequences. We have many duties, but we have no excuse that can compensate for our loss of liberty." (Ezra Taft Benson, C.R., 10/1966).

In this vein, Joseph Smith exhorted the Saints: "Brethren, shall we not go on in so great a cause? Go forward and not backward. Courage, brethren; and on, on to the victory! Let your hearts rejoice, and be exceedingly glad. Let the earth break forth into singing." (D&C 128:22). "Speak freely to all," the Lord told Martin Harris. "Yea, preach, exhort, declare the truth, even with a loud voice, with a sound of rejoicing, crying - Hosanna (Save Now), hosanna (Grant us Salvation), blessed be the name of the Lord God!" (V. 37).

"Pray always, and I will pour out my Spirit upon you, and great shall be your blessing." (V. 38). Mormon urged: "Pray unto the Father with all the energy of heart, that ye may be filled with this love, which he hath bestowed upon all who are true followers of his son Jesus Christ; that ye may become the sons of God; that when he shall appear we shall be like him, for we shall see him as he is; that we may have this hope; that we may be purified even as he is pure." (Moroni 7:48).

The sturdiest plants that bear the best fruit are those that have deep roots in good soil. The rich loam of prayer can help to nourish our gospel roots. Part of the blessing we receive when we develop a relationship with God through prayer is a solid foundation of gospel principles upon which we may blossom as creative individuals, and at the same time stand out as champions on the Lord's team. "Happiness" after all, "is the object and design of our existence, and will be the end thereof, if we pursue the path that leads to it, and this path is virtue, uprightness, faithfulness, holiness, and keeping all the commandments of God." (Joseph Smith, "Teachings," p. 255).

"Canst thou read this without rejoicing and lifting up thy heart for gladness? Or canst thou run about longer as a bind guide? Or canst thou be humble and meek, and conduct thyself wisely before me?" (V. 39-41). The Lord said that we should seek "for wisdom; and, behold, the mysteries of God shall be unfolded unto (us), and then shall (we) shall be made rich. Behold, he that hath eternal life is rich." (D&C 11:7).

The mysteries of God are those truths that can only be known by revelation from the Holy Ghost. When we "hunger and thirst after righteousness," the doctrine of the priesthood will distill upon our souls as the dews from heaven, and the Spirit will be our constant companion. (See D&C 121:45-46).

In the concluding verse of this revelation, the Lord explained to Martin Harris that the world was about to emerge from a long dark night of apostasy into the brilliant sunshine of the latter-day Restoration. The marvelous work would include The Book of Mormon, the restoration of the church and of priesthood authority, the temple ordinances, and prophetic direction. It is indeed the restoration of all things, and will only culminate in the establishment, once again, of Zion upon the earth.

In short, the Spirit would have surely borne witness to Martin Harris that "Zion shall flourish, and the glory of the Lord shall be upon her." (D&C 64:41). How could Martin Harris, or anyone else for that matter, understand these things without rejoicing and lifting up their hearts for gladness?

# Section 20
## (Instructions in 1830 to the newly organized church in New York, received by inspiration).

This was the first revelation to be formally sustained by the church membership. It is a "revelation on Church Organization and Government, given through Joseph Smith the Prophet, April 1830." (Superscript). During the first decade of the church, it was known as the Articles and Covenants of the Church of Christ.

During the first conference of the church, held on June 9, 1830, the complete Articles and Covenants were read by Joseph Smith as one of the first items of business. By unanimous vote, they were accepted by the congregation, and thus became the first revelation during this dispensation to be canonized. They later became D&C Section 20, that was the first revelation to be printed on the first page of the first newspaper of the church, the "Evening and Morning Star." (1:1, 6/1832). Since that time, the administrative affairs of the church have been conducted in accordance with this section. In subsequent conferences, the Articles and Covenants were customarily read so that the Saints could be familiarized with the policies and procedures they were to follow.

These verses begin the careful scriptural documentation of the basic organizational structure of the Church of Christ. The fact that the Lord went to the trouble to give this revelation in the first place attests to the necessity of a formal church organization among the people. "These ordinances are not empty, passive rituals; rather, they bind the individual to receive the promises and blessings of the gospel by means of a covenant of action between himself and the Lord." ("Doctrinal Commentary on The Book of Mormon," 4:319). This instruction reveals the nature of Jesus Christ, and illustrates that His church is founded on unchanging principles, and that the requirements for obtaining salvation are the same for all.

Much of that which Joseph Smith received from the Lord and from heavenly messengers before April, 6, 1830, pertained to the organization of the church. "Preceding his record of this revelation, the Prophet wrote: "We obtained of him (Jesus Christ) the following, by the spirit of prophecy and revelation." (Superscript).

Section 20 illustrates the principles taught in Section 67 of the Doctrine & Covenants, that was received some time later, in November 1831. The superscript to that revelation tells us: "Joseph Smith's history records that after the revelation known as Section 1 had been received, some conversation was had concerning the language used in the revelations. The present revelation followed." "Now, seek ye out of the Book of Commandments, even the least that is among them, and appoint him that is the most wise among you; Or, if there be any among you that shall make one like unto it, then ye are justified in saying that ye do not know that they are true; But if ye cannot make one like unto it, ye are under condemnation if ye do not bear record that they are true. (D&C 67:6-8).

These revelations were given in the language of the Prophet Joseph Smith, and included his communicative imperfections. Nevertheless, they were received under the powerful influence of the Holy Ghost. "And whatsoever they shall speak when moved upon by the Holy Ghost shall be scripture, shall be the will of the Lord, shall be the mind of the Lord, shall be the word of the Lord, shall be the voice of the Lord, and the power of God unto salvation." (D&C 68:4).

The revelation that we now know as Section 20 not only gave Joseph Smith much valuable doctrinal information, but it also identified the precise day when the church should be organized, it "being one thousand eight hundred and thirty years since the coming of our Lord and Savior Jesus Christ in the flesh, (the church) being regularly organized and established agreeable to the laws of our country, by the will and the commandments of God, in the fourth month, and on the sixth day of the month which is called April," in the year 1830. (V. 1).

It wasn't until April 26, 1838 that the Lord unequivocally revealed: "For thus shall my church be called in the last days, even The Church of Jesus Christ of Latter-day Saints." (D&C 115:4). Before this revelation, the church had been variously called the Church of Christ, the Church of Jesus Christ, the Church of God, and The Church of The Latter-day Saints. Even today, these misnomers persist and it is sometimes erroneously called the Mormon Church, or the L.D.S. Church.

James E. Talmage stated: "We believe that Jesus Christ was born in Bethlehem of Judea, April 6, B.C. 1." ("Jesus The Christ," p. 102-104). Harold B. Lee also stated: "April 6 (is) the anniversary of the birth of the Savior." (C.R., 4/1973). It is possible, although there is no proof, that April 6 also commemorates the date of His Resurrection.

Joseph Smith "was called of God, and ordained an apostle of Jesus Christ, to be the first elder of this church." (V. 2). Oliver Cowdery was "also called of God, an apostle of Jesus Christ, to be the second elder of this church, and ordained under his hand." (V. 3). Joseph Smith was ordained to the office of High Priest, on June 3, 1831, and Oliver Cowdery, on August 28, 1831. Nevertheless, after they both had knelt in the presence of heavenly messengers and received the priesthood, they became Apostles or special witnesses for Christ, even before the organization of the church, or any office within the priesthood had been conferred upon any man in this generation.

All this was done "according to the grace of our Lord and Savior Jesus Christ, to whom be all glory." (V. 4). Grace is an attribute of perfection possessed by Deity and consists of His love, mercy, and condescension toward His children. (See D&C 66:12, 84:102, and especially 93:6-20). Grace consists of the gifts and power of God by which we may be brought to perfection.

Jacob explained in 2 Nephi 10:25 how the grace of God operates. We are raised from physical death by the power of the Resurrection, and from spiritual death by the power of the Atonement. Grace is granted unto us proportionately as we conform to the standards of personal righteousness that are part of the gospel Plan. Thus, the Saints are commanded to "grow in grace" (D&C 50:40), until they are sanctified and justified "thru the grace of our Lord and Savior Jesus Christ." (D&C 20:30-32). This is why Nephi declared that we are saved by grace "after all we can do," and this is why repentance is so important. (2 Nephi 25:23). When the day of repentance is past, so is the day of grace. (See Mormon 2:15).

It is most remarkable that our opportunity for happiness is a gift from God. Brigham Young rightly observed: "There is no man who ever made a sacrifice on this earth for the kingdom of heaven except the Savior. I would not give the ashes of a rye straw for that man who feels he is making sacrifices for God. We are doing this for our own happiness, welfare, and exaltation, and for nobody else's. What we do, we do for the salvation of the inhabitants of the earth, not for the salvation of the heavens, the angels, or God." (J.D., 16:114). All the glory associated with the Plan of Happiness resides in Christ, the Author of Salvation.

Even as he struggled to grasp the responsibilities associated with his apostolic calling, Joseph "was again entangled in the vanities of the world; but after repenting, and humbling himself sincerely, through faith, God ministered unto him by an holy angel, whose countenance was as lightning, and whose garments were pure and white above all other whiteness." (V. 6).

An appeal to vanity is Satan's way of turning our minds against the Plan of Salvation. "I" and "Mine" are usually accompanied by an unbended knee. Neal

Maxwell wrote: "To the humble, the simpleness and the easiness of the way are glad realities; to the crowded, ego filled minds of proud men, the sudden burst of light from a spiritual sunrise is irritating rather than awesome, and causes them to blink rather than to stare in reverent awe." ("That My Family Should Partake," p. 82).

This holy angel who ministered to Joseph was Moroni, who gave him "commandments which inspired him; and gave him power from on high, by the means which were before prepared, to translate The Book of Mormon." (V. 7-8). Moroni had earlier explained to Joseph: "Wherever the sound (of the marvelous work) shall go, it shall cause the ears of men to tingle, and wherever it shall be proclaimed, the pure in heart shall rejoice, while those who draw near to God with their mouths, and honor him with their lips, while their hearts are far from him, will seek its overthrow, and the destruction of those by whose hands it is carried. Therefore, marvel not if your name is made a derision, and had as a by-word among such, if you are the instrument in bringing it, by the gift of God, to the knowledge of the people." ("Joseph Smith & The Restoration," p. 14).

The translation and publication of The Book of Mormon was essential to the Restoration, for it "contains a record of a fallen people, and the fulness of the gospel of Jesus Christ to the Gentiles and to the Jews also." (V. 9). The Book of Mormon is a record of God's dealings with a people who had the fulness of the gospel, meaning 'an abundance' or 'sufficient for the purposes intended.'

In the Last Days, the children of the covenant will receive the gospel message. When speaking of Israel, most people think of the Jews, and when referring to the Gathering of Israel, they have in mind the return of the Jews to the land of Jerusalem. It should be remembered, however, that the Jews represent but one of the twelve tribes of the house of Israel. "For lo," said the Lord Jehovah, "I will sift the house of Israel among all nations." (Amos 9:9).

Isaiah foresaw the Gathering, that the house of Israel would return from the seven known countries of his day, "from Assyria, and from Egypt, and from Pathros (or upper Egypt), and from Cush (or Ethiopia), and from Elam (east of Babylonia), and from Hamath (Northern Syria), and from the isles of the sea (the rest of the world)." (Isaiah 11:11).

The Lord would "set up an ensign for the nations" as a homing beacon. (Isaiah 11:12). This "ensign" is the church in the Last Days. The Lord explained to Joseph Smith: "I have sent mine everlasting covenant into the world, to be a light to the world, and to be a standard for my people, and for the Gentiles to seek to it, and to be a messenger before my face to prepare the way before me." (D&C 45:9).

There will be two general components associated with the gathering. First, there are the "outcasts of Israel" and secondly, "the dispersed of Judah." (2 Nephi 21:2). These might refer distinctly to the Ten Tribes, and to Judah, respectively.

When the gathering takes place, the jealousy of Ephraim and the Ten Tribes of the Northern Kingdom will have disappeared, and they will no longer envy the Kingdom of Judah. In fact, it will be Ephraim who will bring to Judah the message of the Restored Gospel.

Thus, Ephraim and Judah will gather to the lands of their inheritance. "They shall fly upon the shoulders of the Philistines towards the west; they shall spoil them of the east together; they shall lay their hand upon Edom and Moab; and the children of Ammon shall obey them." (2 Nephi 21:14). In other words, they shall settle on the lands of the Gentiles to the west (Gaza), and on the lands of their ancient enemies to the east, which is now modern Jordan. This could also include that land now known as "The West Bank" or "The Occupied Territories," or as the State of Israel prefers to call it, "Judea and Samaria."

The final gathering of Israel in the Last Days will prepare her for her celestial destiny. In the Last Days, the Gentiles are to have the gospel preached to them first, and then the Jews will have their turn. "Graft in the branches," Zenos prophesied. "Begin at the last that they may be first, and that the first may be last, and dig about the trees, both old and young, the first and the last; and the last and the first, that all may be nourished once again for the last time." (Jacob 5:63).

The imagery is graphic: "Wherefore, dig about them, and prune them, and dung them once more, for the last time." (Jacob 5:64). To "dung" a plant, or to spread manure around its base, is symbolic of nourishing gathered Israel with the Restored Gospel. This will cause it to grow, and to increase in righteousness.

The roots and the top branches grafted into the tree should be "equal in strength." (Jacob 5:66). As such, they will be nourished with the word of the Lord, as they receive "line upon line, (and) precept upon precept." (D&C 98:12). Gathered Israel and the Gentiles will grow together in the knowledge of the Lord. It will not be as it was formerly, when the branches grew faster than the strength of the roots could bear. The natural branches, or Blood Israel, that had grown wild, will be grafted back in to the natural tree, in a spiritual rebirth.

Joseph received the Book of Mormon record "by inspiration, and (it was) confirmed to others by the ministering of angels, and is declared unto the world by them." (V. 10). The Lord always utilizes the Law of Witnesses. "In the mouth of as many witnesses as seemeth him good will he establish his word." (V. 14). Joseph Smith uncovered pearls of wisdom within the translation, that served as a personal message from Moroni concerning the plates and the Three Witnesses. That ancient prophet wrote: "And in the mouth of three witnesses shall these things be established; and the testimony of three, and this work, in the which shall be shown forth the power of God and also his word, of which the Father, and the Son, and the Holy Ghost bear record - and all this shall stand as a testimony against the world at the last day." (Ether 5:4).

It was the opinion of Joseph Fielding Smith, Jr. that "the Lord does not intend that The Book of Mormon, at least at the present time, shall be proved true by any archaeological findings. The Book of Mormon is itself a witness of its truth." ("Answers to Gospel Questions," 2:196). The Book of Mormon is in good company; by comparison, archaeological correlation with biblical scriptures has not created significant faith among Christians, in general. However, for those who already possess faith, pilgrimages to the Holy Land or to the lands of The Book of Mormon, for that matter, may strengthen existing religious conviction.

It was only when engaged in the work of translation, that Joseph Smith learned that there were to be special witnesses of the work he was performing. "The book shall be hid from the eyes of the world, that the eyes of none shall behold it save it be that three witnesses shall behold it, by the power of God, besides him to whom the book shall be delivered; and they shall testify to the truth of the book and the things therein. And there is none other which shall view it, save it be a few according to the will of God, to bear testimony of his word unto the children of men." (2 Nephi 27:12-13).

Ultimately, there would be eleven special witnesses in all. To three of these, God Himself declared that the plates were a true record, and an angel showed them the plates, as well. Eight of the eleven witnesses, including all three to whom God had spoken, eventually left the restored church and were either excommunicated or disfellowshipped for conduct unbecoming members, but none ever denied his testimony.

"Critics of The Book of Mormon often remark sarcastically that it is a great pity that the golden plates have disappeared, since they would conveniently prove Joseph Smith's story. Of course, they would do nothing of the sort. The presence of the plates would only prove that there were plates, and no more. It would not prove that Nephites had written them, or that an angel had brought them, or that they had been translated by the gift and power of God, and we can be sure that scholars would quarrel about the writing on them for generations without coming to any agreement, exactly as they have done with the Bible. If Joseph Smith had retained possession of the plates following his translation, it would have had a very disruptive effect on the progress of the Restoration, and it would have proven nothing.

On the other hand, a far more impressive claim is put forth when the whole work is given to the world in what is claimed to be a divinely inspired translation. In this case, any cause or pretext for disagreement and speculation about the text is reduced to an absolute minimum. It is a text for all the world to read and understand, and (as a gift of God) it is far more miraculous than any gold plates would be." (High Nibley, "An Approach to The Book of Mormon," p. 17-18).

The Lord will not indulge the prurient interest of those who only want theological titillation to satisfy their wicked and adulterous curiosity. To sum it up, Heavenly Father is more interested in converting than in convincing, more concerned with faith than fault-finding, more involved in pure and undefiled religion than in cold and hard rationalism, drawn more to testimony than to those who trash His word, more impressed with meekness than with murmuring, and finds humility rather than hubris more effective in building character. He is less impressed by those who let intellect do for intelligence.

Embracing the glad message qualifies recipients for the greatest of rewards. For "those who receive it in faith," the Lord promised, "and work righteousness, shall receive a crown of eternal life." (V. 14). In a way, each of us is told: "Work our your own salvation with fear and trembling" before the Lord. (Mormon 9:27).

In fact, our works are necessary, but insufficient, and in the truest sense, we cannot work out our own salvation by ourselves. But when our works become His works, they are empowered and motivated from the High Priest of our profession, and the miracle of salvation by the grace of God is achieved. (See Philippians 2:12-13).

The Atonement makes possible our redemption from sin. "Therefore, blessed are they who will repent and hearken unto the voice of the Lord their God; for these are they that shall be saved in the Celestial Kingdom of God. And may God grant, in his great fulness, that men might be brought unto repentance and good works, that they might be restored unto grace for grace, according to their works." (Helaman 12:24).

Ultimately, we must all come to the realization that "there is a God in heaven, who is infinite and eternal, from everlasting to everlasting the same unchangeable God, the framer of heaven and earth, and all things which are in them." (V. 17). The clearest declaration in all scripture that Jesus Christ is the Creator, Who acted under the direction of the Father by divine investiture of authority to form the earth, is given in the Doctrine & Covenants and in The Book of Mormon. In 3 Nephi 9:15, we read:: "Behold, I am Jesus Christ the Son of God, I created the heavens and the earth, and all things that in them are. I was with the Father from the beginning. I am in the Father, and the Father in me; and in me hath the Father glorified his name." In the First Book of Nephi, with the simple statement of fact, "I am he," the Lord testified that it was He who, before time began, "laid the foundation of the earth, and (whose) right hand hath spanned the heavens" in both time and space. (1 Nephi 20:12-13).

"He created man, male and female, after his own image and in his own likeness." (V. 18). When we receive the image of the Lord in our countenances, our faces reflect the Light of Christ. The mighty change in our hearts transforms the inner vessel. The world seeks change from the outside, and fails miserably. The gospel works from the inside, and succeeds brilliantly. We are thus created to reach our potential in both the image and likeness of God our Father.

In our Dispensation, B.H. Roberts "wrote repeatedly that without the renewing insights of modern revelation, no official creed or statement of faith, and no high-sounding abstractions of the philosophers really answered the question: 'Why did God create man?' For him the gloriously emancipating truth was that the self-existence of God is paralleled by the uncreate spark in the spirit of man, and that God transmitted to his sons and daughters the highest potential in the universe - his likeness." (Truman Madsen, "Defender of The Faith," p. 192).

Steven Robinson taught: "The Latter-day Saints teach that God the Father is an anthropomorphic being - that is, He has a tangible body. "The Father has a body of flesh and bones as tangible as man's; the Son also; but the Holy Ghost has not a body of flesh and bones, but is a personage of Spirit. Were it not so, the Holy Ghost could not dwell in us." (D&C 130:22). Some critics of the church have argued that belief in an anthropomorphic Deity represents a departure from biblical teaching, since the Bible teaches very clearly that "God is a Spirit, and they that worship him must worship him in spirit and in truth." (John 4:24).

Latter-day Saints agree that God the Father is spirit in the highest sense of the word, but they deny that this limits him to incorporeality. God is a spirit in the person of the Holy Ghost, but in the person of the Son, God has a tangible body. On the grounds of modern revelation, Latter-day Saints believe that God the

Father also has a tangible body, but they grant that this cannot be proved or disproved from the Bible alone. If conceiving of God in anthropomorphic terms, as the Latter-day Saints do, excludes one from being a Christian, then most Christians, both ancient and modern, must also be excluded, for most are guilty in some degree of conceiving of God in anthropomorphic biblical terms rather than in the abstract terms of philosophical theology. Moreover, since the Bible itself describes God in anthropomorphic language, even if such descriptions are understood merely as helpful symbolism or allegory, it cannot be seriously argued that perceiving God in anthropomorphic terms is an un-Christian practice." ("Are Mormons Christians? The Doctrinal Exclusion: Trinity and The Nature of God").

Members of the church generally understand this concept, if only abstractly. One thing is for sure: "The natural man receiveth not the things of the Spirit of God: for they are foolishness unto him: neither can he know them, because they are spiritually discerned." (1 Corinthians 2:14).

The great messages of the Restoration include the declaration that Elohim is our Heavenly Father. We were born of Him as His spirit children. We acquired His spiritual qualities and characteristics and were raised by Him to spiritual maturity, until we could progress no more. As spirit children, there were some laws that pertain only to mortality that we were denied the opportunity to obey, and so there were some blessings that were unavailable to us.

Therefore, we left His presence to follow our star and to fulfill a mission on earth. Even now, living on foreign soil, we are yet His spirit sons and daughters who enjoy a measure of His divine nature. If we continue to develop His characteristics during this period of probation, we will eventually become as He is. We will assume both His image and likeness. The Spirit bears witness that these things are true.

Our earthly fathers have given us mortal life, and, in general, we have inherited their qualities and characteristics that relate to mortality. We bear their names, and reflect their nature. If they have been honorable, we may choose to emulate them, and become as they are.

Jesus Christ gave every child of God immortality, or life beyond the grave, through the Resurrection. In this sense, He is a Father to all the family of our Heavenly Father. Through the sanctifying influence of His Atonement, we may all be spiritually reborn as well. Thus, He becomes the Father of all who follow His example, and subordinate their will to His. We may likewise inherit His nature.

Through the process of this rebirth, we acquire the distinctive characteristics of Christ and become His sons and daughters. By the covenant of baptism we take upon ourselves a new name, which is His name, and by our obedience to the principles of the gospel, we enjoy the companionship of the Holy Ghost. This spiritual rebirth permits a mighty change in our nature, so that we may become as He is. We incorporate His likeness into our very being.

It is for this reason that God "gave unto them commandments that they should love and serve him, the only living and true God, and that he should be the only being whom they should worship." (V. 19). One of the greatest sins that we can commit, and one of the greatest expressions of dishonor to God, is that of ingratitude. Gratitude is deeper than thanks. Appreciation is the beginning of gratitude and may consist merely of words, but gratitude is shown in action. It is independent of circumstances, penetrating to the deepest undercurrents of life because it is founded upon our Maker. We show our gratitude to God by our obedience to His commandments.

These verses clear up the controversies that have always existed relating to the basic goodness versus the inherent evil nature of man, for it is here revealed that it was only because of "the transgression of these holy laws (that we) became sensual and devilish." (V. 20). The natural man refers to the state to which we have fallen through disobedience to God's commandments. The brother of Jared realized that "because of the fall, our natures have become evil continually." (Ether 3:2). He recognized the necessity of being born again. It is not a question of development or of maturation, but rather of generation.

One of the most emotional, miraculous, and awe-inspiring events of mortality is birth; it would be difficult to more dramatically conceptualize in metaphor the process of kindling the divine spark, of awakening the divine potential, or of igniting the spirit lying dormant within the God in embryo, than to say that we must be born again in order to inherit eternal life. Truly, as Henri Bergson declared, "the universe is a machine for the making of Gods." (Truman Madsen, "Eternal Man," p. 18, see Henri Bergson, "Two Sources of Morality and Religion," p. 306).

The arduous process of our spiritual rebirth can be likened to a primer on midwifery. When we feel the urge to push the Lord's agenda, the Spirit can be our labor coach, providing us with just the right amount of encouragement to successfully deliver our witness of the Savior without being overbearing.

"Wherefore, the Almighty God gave his Only Begotten Son." (V. 21). We acknowledge the Fall of Adam, but it can only be correctly understood if, in the same breath, we emphasize the transcendent event of all time, which was the Atonement of Christ. "To teach Atonement without teaching Fall is to relegate Jesus to no more than a guide, a great teacher, a coach, or an inspiring cheerleader." ("Doctrinal Commentary on The Book of Mormon," 4:272). The Fall made possible our opportunity to be born again, and gives vitality to God's mission statement, which is to bring to pass our immortality and eternal life. (See Moses 1:39). As Lehi taught: "Adam fell that men might be; and men are, that they might have joy." (2 Nephi 2:25).

The Savior "suffered temptations, but gave no heed unto them" because He so powerfully had the Spirit with Him. (V. 22). The sibling rivalry between Lucifer and Jesus Christ was first manifest during the War in Heaven, that was fought with intensity and single-minded purpose by combatants on both sides. The battles were not waged with guns and bombs; the struggle was between two contrasting and diametrically opposed, irreconcilable ideologies.

One would give the spirit children of our Heavenly Father the opportunity to exercise moral agency, or free will during a mortal probation, while the other would compel, or require, obedience. One ideology was the Plan of Salvation, whose Author was our Father in Heaven. The other ideology embraced a counterfeit, bogus, and inoperable plan, conjured up by he "who was a liar from the beginning," even he who has been called "the father of lies." (2 Nephi 2:18, & Moses 4:4). Obedience to one of the ideologies promised life and light, while the brutal reality of the other could deliver only death and darkness. The conflict in the premortal existence was, in fact, the quintessential life or death struggle, and a third part of the combatants were eternal casualties.

That we fought on the side of the Firstborn is attested by our physical presence here in mortality. We have kept our first estate, have been "added upon," and now on the earth we find that we are being tested further, to see if we will do, in faith, all things whatsoever the Lord God will command us. And we who keep our second estate shall have glory added upon our heads for ever and ever. (See Abraham 3:25-26).

Central, then, to Satan's battle plan in the pre-mortal existence was the clever utilization of ideology intended to conflict with the stability and harmony of the Plan of Salvation that had been proposed by Heavenly Father. After 6,000 years of temporal existence, the war still rages, with Satan continuing to rely upon the proven tactic of false ideology. He enlists in his army those who are only professors of religion, who are easily conscripted into his service to "teach for doctrines the commandments of men" mingled with scripture. (J.S.H. 1:19).

Satan's strategy has always focused on thwarting our progression. At times, he will "rage in the hearts of the children of men, and stir them up to anger against that which is good. And others will he pacify, and lull them away into carnal security, and thus the devil cheateth their souls, and leadeth them away carefully down to hell. And behold, others he flattereth away, and telleth them there is no hell, and thus he whispereth in their ears until he grasps them with his awful chains from whence there is no deliverance." (2 Nephi 28:20-22). He is the master of disguise, which explains how he is able to lead them so easily "by the neck with a flaxen cord, until he bindeth them with his strong cords forever." (2 Nephi 26:22).

The Lord "was crucified, died, and rose again the third day; and ascended into heaven, to sit down" in a favorable, or preferred, position, "on the right hand of the Father, to reign with almighty power according to the will of the Father." (V. 23-24). The gospel principle of resurrection is a mystery that is kept from the world because it can only be spiritually discerned. It is difficult to understand for even the spiritually mature and scripturally literate among us. However, the latter-day revelations clarify many principles of the gospel, including that of resurrection.

The Book of Mormon clearly teaches that the purpose of the Fall was to give us the opportunity to come to the earth in order to prepare for a resurrection. "And we see that death comes upon mankind...which is the temporal death; nevertheless there was a space granted unto man in which he might repent; therefore this life became a probationary state; a time to prepare to meet God; a time to prepare for that endless state which has been spoken of by us, which is after the resurrection of the dead." (Alma 12:24).Through the Atonement, we would be raised in that resurrection, clothed in the kinds of bodies needed to dwell in eternity in various degrees of glory.

The Plan of Salvation is the Plan of Redemption, the Plan of Mercy, and the Plan of Happiness, because it makes possible the resurrection of otherwise imperfect mortals to eternal lives of glory. "Now, if it had not been for the plan of redemption, which was laid from the foundation of the world, there could have been no resurrection of the dead; but there was a plan of redemption laid, which shall bring to pass the resurrection of the dead." (Alma 12:25).

"As many as would believe and be baptized in his holy name, and endure in faith to the end, should be saved." (V. 25). When the word and the will of the Lord came to the Saints through Brigham Young in Winter Quarters, it was: "Let him that is ignorant learn wisdom by humbling himself and calling upon the Lord his God, that his eyes may be opened that he may see, and his ears opened that he may hear. For my Spirit is sent forth into the world to enlighten the humble and contrite." (D&C 136:32-33). A merciful God has given His children additional scripture to be a companion to the Bible, to illuminate its more mysterious principles and doctrines, and to testify independently that Jesus is the Christ, the Savior of the World.

These scriptures can be put to the test in very simple, uncomplicated ways. The pattern of the world is to scrutinize from every rational angle, to form committees charged with the responsibility to analyze data, compile reports, develop hypotheses and paradigms, search for compromise, reach consensus, homogenize suppositions, and finally publish conclusions.

"But "O that cunning plan of the evil one! O the vainness, and the frailties, and the foolishness of men! When they are learned they think they are wise, and they hearken not unto the counsel of God, for they set it aside, supposing they know of themselves, wherefore, their wisdom is foolishness and it profiteth them not. And they shall perish. But to be learned is good if they hearken unto the counsels of God." (2 Nephi 9:29-30).

For the spiritual education of the faithful, all the prophets have testified of Christ, and many signs and wonders have been given. Types and shadows have been raised up in similitude of the Only Begotten. God has been generous to all those who have eyes to see, and ears to hear. He has manifested Himself "not only (to) those who believed after he came in the meridian of time, in the flesh, but (also to) all those from the beginning, even as many as were before he came, who believed in the words of the holy prophets, who spake as they were inspired by the gift of the Holy Ghost, who truly testified of him in all things." (V. 26).

All these "should have eternal life, as well as those who should come after, who should believe in the gifts and callings of God by the Holy Ghost, which beareth record of the Father and of the Son." (V. 27). In the Last Days, those who are spiritually deaf and blind through no fault of their own will have the gospel preached to them. The wicked and disobedient who grope about in the shadows cast by Spiritual Babylon will be overcome. There will be a great outpouring of the Spirit, that all might "come to understanding, and they that murmured shall learn doctrine." (2 Nephi 27:35). Visualizing that day, the prophet Joel wrote: "And it shall come to pass afterward, that I will pour out my spirit upon all flesh, and your sons and your daughters shall prophesy, your old men shall dream dreams, your young men shall see vision." (Joel 2:28).

Orson Pratt declared: "Every principle of the doctrine of Christ is set forth in such great plainness that it is impossible for any two persons to form different ideas in relation to it after reading The Book of Mormon." (J.D. 15:189). But those who reject prophesy in our time will find that The Book of Mormon remains a sealed book that it is beyond the reach of their limited understanding. As Jacob taught: "The things of the wise and the prudent shall be hid from them forever." (2 Nephi 9:43).

The reality is that the "Father, Son, and Holy Ghost are one God, infinite and eternal, without end." (V. 28). There is one unified Godhead that presides over us. For mankind, there is no other God. "There be gods many, and lords many, but to us, there is but one God, the Father, of whom are all things, and we in him, and one Lord Jesus Christ, by whom are all things, and we by him." (1 Corinthians 7:5-6).

God the Father knows all things, "being from everlasting to everlasting." (Moroni 7:22). He is eternal, and His influence extends from a land before time when we were uncreated intelligence, through our pre-mortal spiritual development, on into mortality, and finally to our reunion with Him in the resurrection. From our perspective, God has always existed and His unchangeable attributes define His flawless character. He is the perfect model for our behavior; so likewise is His Son Jesus Christ, who in every quality is One with the Father. This is why Mormon taught that "in Christ there should come every good thing." (Moroni 7:22).

That simple fact explains why "all men must repent and believe on the name of Jesus Christ, and worship the Father on his name to the end, or they cannot be saved in the kingdom of God." (V. 29). "And we know that justification through the grace of our Lord and Savior Jesus Christ is just and true." (2 Nephi 16:30). "For by the water ye keep the commandment; by the Spirit ye are justified, and by the blood ye are sanctified." (Moses 6:61). We keep the commandment of God when we submit to baptism by water. We are then justified, or the validity of the ordinance is ratified, and we are purged of the effects of sin when we submit to the second baptism by the laying on of hands to receive the Holy Ghost. We are sanctified through the atoning sacrifice of Christ, and redeemed from the Fall.

The Atonement of Christ took into account the reality that we would yield in varying degrees to carnality, sensuality and devilish enticements. But the gospel of Jesus Christ, that is at the foundation of the Plan of Salvation, provides a way for us to learn from our mistakes and to rely upon the sacrifice of the Savior, putting us in a position to be justified by the Spirit. Miracle of miracles: We may yet be found worthy to enter into God's rest even after we have been bruised and battered by our experiences in the telestial world! God's Plan is perfect, and has anticipated every exigency!

"And we know also, that sanctification through the grace of our Lord and Savior Jesus Christ is just and true, to all those who love and serve God with all their mights, minds, and strength." (V. 31). This measures the depth and breadth of commitment that we may make to the Lord and His work. Possibly the most significant difference that accounts for the superiority of obedience to the principles of the Plan of Salvation over any other possible lifestyle choice is the process whereby the gospel of Jesus Christ can be internalized by His disciples, in a phenomenon that is called sanctification by the Spirit.

When the gospel drives the law into our inward parts, and it is written upon our hearts, a mighty change is wrought, as we experience the process of sanctification. (See Jeremiah 31:33). Thus, the Savior commanded His church: "Sanctify yourselves that your minds become single to God, and the days will come that you shall see him; for he will unveil his face unto you." (D&C 88:68, see D&C 93:1).

A major purpose of the gospel is to provide those principles and ordinances that enable us to become sanctified so that we may be worthy to live once again in a state of holiness in the presence of our Heavenly Father. Through sanctification, the Saints are cleansed from the effects of sin; thus spiritually renewed, they stand prepared to pass through the veil to enter the presence of the Lord. We must first submit to His will, yield our hearts to Him, and be obedient to all of the teachings of His church. "Therefore, if ye do these things blessed are ye, for ye shall be lifted up at the last day." (3 Nephi 27:22).

"But there is a possibility that (we) may fall from grace," or from good standing in His sight, "and depart from the living God," our past service or righteousness, notwithstanding. (V. 32). This is partly because, in our day, Babylon has become firmly entrenched in the world. She is "the great whore that sitteth upon many waters, with whom the kings of the earth have committed fornication." (Revelation 17:1-2). To some extent, all have been unfaithful to our Righteous King, and have committed fornication with the whore, that has been defined as "a wicked, and idolatrous community."

One of the terrible consequences of the fascination of the world with Babylon is spiritual insensitivity. Isaiah foresaw the Last Days, when he wrote: "Stay yourselves, and wonder; cry ye out, and cry: they are drunken, but not with wine; they stagger, but not with strong drink. For the Lord hath poured out upon you the spirit of deep sleep, and hath closed your eyes: the prophets, and your rulers, and seers hath he covered. And the vision of all is become unto you as the words of a book that is sealed." (Isaiah 29:9-11).

"Therefore let the church take heed and pray always, lest they fall into temptation." (V. 33). Prayer is a way to exercise faith, and is a powerful antidote to the enticements of the devil. Joseph Fielding Smith, Jr. taught: "No man can retain the spirit of the Lord unless he prays." Paul wrote: "Pray without ceasing." (1 Thessalonians 5:17). But "after ye have done all these things, if ye turn away the needy, and the naked, and visit not the sick and afflicted, and impart of your substance, if ye have, to those who stand in need, behold your prayer is vain and availeth you nothing, and ye are as hypocrites who do deny the faith. (Alma 34:28).

What could be more natural than the simple statement expressed in the 9th Article of Faith: "We believe all that God has revealed, all that He does now reveal, and we believe that He will yet reveal many great and important things pertaining to the Kingdom of God." The world needs is a listening ear, for there is no revelation where there is no student.

There are many who deny themselves the blessings of heaven simply because they do not ask for them. The Savior explained how anxious Heavenly Father is to grant the righteous requests of His children. Comparing His benevolence to that of our earthly fathers, the Savior declared: "How much more shall your Father who is in heaven give good things to them that ask him?" (3 Nephi 14:11).

"And we know that these things are true and according to the revelations of John, neither adding to, nor diminishing from the prophecy of his book, the holy scriptures, or the revelations of God which shall come hereafter by the gift and power of the Holy Ghost, the voice of God, or the ministering of angels." (V. 35).

John the Revelator closed the Apocalypse by stating: "And if any man shall take away from the words of the book of this prophecy, God shall take away his part out of the book of life." (Revelation 22:19). Moses had similarly written: "Ye shall not add unto the word which I command you, neither shall ye diminish ought from it." (Deuteronomy 4:2). In fact, the "great and abominable church, which is most abominable above all other churches, (has) taken away from the gospel of the Lamb many parts which are plain and most precious; and also many covenants of the Lord have they taken away." (1 Nephi 13:26). The consequence of their removal is that "an exceedingly great many do stumble, yea, insomuch that Satan hath great power over them." (1 Nephi 13:29).

In D&C Section 29:12, we find the only instance in the Doctrine & Covenants where the term 'great and abominable church' is employed, although it is used twelve times in The Book of Mormon, in 1 Nephi 4:3, 9, 15, & 17, 1 Nephi 13:6, 8, 26 & 28, 1 Nephi 22:13 & 14, 2 Nephi 6:12, & 2 Nephi 28:18. That is enough, however, to entrench the phrase in our lexicon. Nephi was given, in vision, a broad view of the state of the world in the Last Days, and clearly saw "the great persecutor of the church, the apostate, the whore, even Babylon, that maketh all nations to drink of her cup, in whose hearts the enemy, even Satan, sitteth to reign." (D&C 86:3).

Additional scripture is important because it "shall establish the truth of the first, which are of the twelve apostles of the Lamb, and shall make known the plain and precious things which have been taken away from them, and shall make known to all kindreds, tongues, and people, that the Lamb of God is the Son of the Eternal Father, and the Savior of the world; and that all men must come unto him, or they cannot be saved." (1 Nephi 13:40).

In spite of these revelations that have come by the gift and power of the Holy Ghost, the voice of God, or by the ministering angels, many of the Gentiles shall say: A Bible! A Bible! We have got a Bible, and there cannot be any more Bible." (2 Nephi 29:3). But God is interested in other nations, besides the Jews: "Know ye not that there are more nations than one? Know ye not that I, the Lord your God, have created all men, and that I remember those who are upon the isles of the sea; and that I rule in the heavens above and in the earth beneath; and I bring forth my word unto the children of men, yea, even upon all the nations of the earth?" (2 Nephi 29:7).

These other scriptures serve as a second witness of Christ. "Know ye not that the testimony of two nations is a witness unto you that I am God, that I remember one nation like unto another. Wherefore, I speak the same words unto one nation like unto another. And when the two nations shall run together the testimony of these two nations shall run together also." (2 Nephi 29:8).

The vast body of scripture is the basis upon which God shall judge the world. "For I command all men, both in the east and in the west, and in the north, and in the south, and in the islands of the sea, that they shall write the words which I speak unto them; for out of the books which shall be written I will judge the world, every man according to their works, according to that which is written." (2 Nephi 29:11).

There are also other books of revelation that have been sealed, in general due to the iniquity of the people, because they have not been sufficiently spiritually prepared to receive revelation from God. The Lord told His prophet Daniel: "Shut up the words, and seal the book, even unto the time of the end." (Daniel 12:4).

John saw God the Father on His holy throne in heaven, and described the scene: "And I saw in the right hand of him that sat on the throne a book written within and on the backside, sealed with seven seals. And I saw a strong angel proclaiming with a loud voice, Who is worthy to open the book, and to loose the seals thereof?

...And I wept much, because no man was found worthy to open and to read the book, neither to look thereon." (Revelation 5:1-4).

The record of John the Revelator is itself incomplete, but the Lord has promised: "If you are faithful you shall receive the fulness of the record of John." (D&C 93:18). Many things have been written that were "sealed up to come forth in their purity, according to the truth which is in the Lamb, in the...due time of the Lord, unto the house of Israel." (1 Nephi 14:26).

Those parts of The Book of Mormon that Joseph Smith was forbidden to translate "shall be kept in the book until the...due time of the Lord, that they may come forth; for behold, they reveal all things from the foundation of the world unto the end thereof." (2 Nephi 27:10). When the people prove themselves worthy and capable of accepting it, God will reveal to them the contents of these sealed scriptures.

For "the Lord God has spoken (these words), and honor, power and glory be rendered to his holy name." (V. 36). "And the day cometh that the words of the book which were sealed shall be read upon the house tops; and they shall be read by the power of Christ; and all things shall be revealed unto the children of men which ever have been among the children of men, and which ever will be even unto the end of the earth." (2 Nephi 27:11).

"All those who (1) humble themselves before God, and (2) desire to be baptized, and (3) come forth with broken hearts and contrite spirits, and (4) witness before the church that they have truly repented of all their sins, and (5) are willing to take upon them the name of Jesus Christ, (6) having a determination to serve him to the end, and (7) truly manifest by their works that they have received of the Spirit of Christ unto the remission of their sins, shall be received by baptism into his church." (V. 37).

When Joseph Smith received this revelation, he had recently finished the translation of The Book of Mormon. The qualifications for baptism that had been articulated by Mormon were fresh in his mind; that none had been "baptized save they brought forth fruit meet that they were worthy of it. Neither did they receive any unto baptism save they came forth with a broken heart and a contrite spirit, and witnessed unto the church that they truly repented of all their sins. And none were received unto baptism save they took upon them the name of Christ, having a determination to serve him to the end." (Moroni 6:1-3).

Those who approach the waters of baptism demonstrate a manifestation of deep sorrow for sin, a realization of their wrongdoing, a determination to right the wrongs committed, insofar as is possible, a desire to change their ways, and a sense of urgency to receive forgiveness in the cleansing waters.

The restored church is "a house of order...and not a house of confusion." (D&C 132:8). Therefore, the Lord said: "Now let every man learn his duty, and act in the office in which he is appointed, in all diligence." (D&C 107:99). The church has always required faithful service from the Lord's disciples, and the priesthood has always been a robe of responsibility, said Thomas S. Monson, and not a cloak of convenience, to those who bear it. ("Ensign," 8/2012).

Thus, the Lord gave the following instruction: "An apostle is an elder, and it is his calling to baptize; and to ordain other elders, priests, teachers, and deacons; and to administer bread and wine - the emblems of the flesh and blood of Christ - And to confirm those who are baptized into the church, by the laying on of hands for the baptism of fire and the Holy Ghost, according to the scriptures; And to teach, expound, exhort, baptize, and watch over the church; And to confirm the church by the laying on of the hands, and the giving of the Holy Ghost; and to take the lead of all meetings, (and) to conduct the meetings as they are led by the Holy Ghost, according to the commandments and revelations of God." (V. 38-45).

The Lord counseled His Nephite Apostles: "Therefore I say unto you, take no thought for your life, what ye shall eat, or what ye shall drink; nor yet for your body, what ye shall put on. Is not the life more than meat, and the body than raiment?" (3 Nephi 13:25, see Moroni 2:1). The ministry of the Twelve was to be a full time job. There were to be no anxieties or distractions associated with earning a livelihood.

The Lord would provide, as the next verses indicate. After all, He asked, does He not watch over the fowls of the air and His other creations? "Consider the lilies of the field how they grow; they toil not, neither do they spin; And yet I say unto you, that even Solomon, in all his glory, was not arrayed like one of these." (3 Nephi 13:28-29).

It is clear that the Lord intends that the government of the church is to be presided over by those holding the Melchizedek Priesthood, which "holds the right of presidency, and has power and authority over all the offices in the church in all ages of the world, to administer in spiritual things." (D&C 107:8).

"The power and authority of the higher, or Melchizedek, Priesthood is to hold the keys of all the spiritual blessings of the church - to have the privilege of receiving the mysteries of the kingdom of heaven, to have the heavens opened unto them, to commune with the general assembly and church of the Firstborn, and to enjoy the communion and presence of God the Father, and Jesus the mediator of the new covenant." (D&C 107:18-19).

It is equally clear that the Lord intends that the Aaronic Priesthood completes the government of the kingdom. "The power and authority of the lesser, or Aaronic Priesthood, is to hold the keys of the ministering of angels, and to administer in outward ordinances, the letter of the gospel, the baptism of repentance for the remission of sins, agreeable to the covenants and commandments." (D&C 107:20).

Power to bestow the Holy Ghost rests with the Melchizedek Priesthood. In a meeting with the Nephite Twelve, the Lord "touched with his hand the disciples whom he had chosen, one by one, even until he had touched them all, and spake unto them as he touched them. And the multitude heard not the words which he spake, therefore they did not bear record; but the disciples bare record that he gave them power to give the Holy Ghost." (3 Nephi 18:36).

Jesus called each by name, and taught them: "Ye shall call on the Father in my name, in mighty prayer; and after ye have done this ye shall have power." (Moroni 2:2). The power to confer the Holy Ghost had to be earned, and then retained, through continuing personal righteousness.

Joseph Smith emphasized: "Many are called, but few are chosen," and it is critical to "learn this one lesson - that the rights of the priesthood are inseparably connected with the powers of heaven, and that the powers of heaven cannot be controlled nor handled only upon the principles of righteousness." (D&C 121:34-36).

"The priest's duty is to preach, teach, expound, exhort, and baptize, and administer the sacrament, And visit the house of each member, and exhort them to pray vocally and in secret and attend to all family duties. And he may also ordain other priests, teachers, and deacons. And he is to take the lead of meetings when there is no elder present and in all these duties the priest is to assist the elder if occasion requires." (V. 46-52).

The priests are to preach the gospel, which involves introducing the principles, truth, and concepts pertaining to the Plan of Salvation. Afterward, they are to teach the principles, or bring them into focus, and illustrate them in meaningful ways. Then, the priests are to expound, or enlarge upon the principles, to expand the understanding of the listener. Next, the priests are to offer exhortation, to encourage disciples to want to incorporate the principles into their own lives; to foster ownership through personal witness or testimony, and to validate the worth of the principle.

When the commitment level is appropriate, the priests stand ready with authority to baptize. This ordinance is outward evidence of a personal commitment to obedience. It is the public manifestation of a personal covenant relationship made with God. It is an expression of trust, the ultimate voluntary surrender of agency to a higher power. It is the expression of "Thy will, and not my will, be done."

The waters of baptism invite the penitent, the humble, the meek, the poor in spirit, and the pure in heart. When Elisha directed Naaman to wash in the River Jordan seven times in order to be cured of his leprosy, this proud captain of the host of the King of Syria at first refused. But "his servant came near, and spake unto him, and said, My father, if the prophet had bid thee do some great thing, wouldest thou not have done it? How much rather then, when he saith to thee, Wash, and be clean? Then went he down, and dipped himself seven times in Jordan, according to the saying of the man of God: and his flesh came again like unto the flesh of a little child, and he was clean." (2 Kings 5:13-14).

"Strait is the gate, and narrow is the way, which leadeth unto life, and few there be that find it." (Matthew 7:14). When our hearts are set upon temporal things, our worldly focus drains us spiritually, until the things of God are no longer a part of our daily lives. How much better to "lay aside the things of this world, and seek for the things of a better." (D&C 25:10).

Priests may then administer the sacrament to worthy individuals who have been washed clean in the waters of baptism. The sacrament represents the mystical or spiritual transformation from a self-centered life to a Christ-centered life. It allows us to regularly recommit ourselves by ordinance, to internalize every truth, every principle, and every doctrine, and then to endure to the end, not in wickedness, but in righteousness.

It is "the teacher's duty is to watch over the church always, and be with and strengthen them; and see that there is no iniquity in the church, neither hardness with each other, neither lying, back-biting, nor evil speaking; and see that the church meet together often, and also see that all the members do their duty." (V. 53-55).

In the Nephite church, the names of new members "were taken, that they might be remembered and nourished by the good word of God, to keep them in the right way, to keep them continually watchful unto prayer." (Moroni 6:4). The home teaching organization is charged with the same responsibility to assist the membership in the restored church.

Paul wrote: "When for the time ye ought to be teachers, ye have need that one teach you again which be the first principles of the oracles of God; and are become such as have need of milk, and not of strong meat." (Hebrews 5:12). In other words, new members of the church should be taught the first principles and basic doctrines of the gospel, in order to strengthen their faith and develop their testimonies following conversion. At the same time, a question that should always be in the minds of those to whom this stewardship responsibility falls is: "Are we giving new members skim milk, or 2% milk, or are we giving them rich, whole, fresh, fortified milk?"

"And (the teacher is) to take the lead of meetings in the absence of the elder or priest - And is to be assisted always, in all his duties in the church, by the deacons, who are also "to warn, expound, exhort, and teach, and invite all to come unto Christ." (V. 56 -59). The four Satan-inspired influences that threaten to infect us are 1) hardness of the heart, 2) deafness of the ear, 3) blindness of the mind, and 4) stiffness of the neck. (See Jarom 1:4). When we take our priesthood responsibilities seriously enough to want to be the vessels through whom the Lord might pour a healing balm of Gilead over spiritual wounds, the world within the sphere of our influence will change perceptibly for the better.

"Every elder, priest, teacher, or deacon is to be ordained....by the power of the Holy Ghost." (V. 60). The Savior acknowledged the awesome power of this third member of the Godhead. (See John 14:16). In the Last Days, He has probably been responsible for more real conversions than in all other ages of the world combined. As Joseph Fielding Smith, Jr. declared: " The impressions on the soul that come from the Holy Ghost are far more significant than a vision. It is where spirit speaks to spirit, and the imprint upon the soul is far more difficult to erase." ("Improvement Era," 11/1966).

On another occasion, he wrote that because of the Holy Ghost, "there should be no laymen in The Church of Jesus Christ of Latter-day Saints. If there are any such, then they have neglected their responsibilities and obligations which the Lord has placed upon them." ("Melchizedek Priesthood Personal Study Guide," 1972-73, p. 190). In the Last Days, through the instrumentality of the Holy Ghost, "they shall teach no more every man his neighbor, and every man his brother, Saying, Know the Lord: for they shall all know me, from the least of them unto the greatest of them." (Jeremiah 31:34).

In our day, the Holy Ghost is being poured out in rich abundance. The Lord has promised: "God shall give unto you knowledge by his Holy Spirit, yea, by the unspeakable gift of the Holy Ghost, that has not been revealed since the world was, until now." This is a time when "nothing shall be withheld. ...All thrones and dominions, principalities and powers, shall be revealed. ...And also, if there be bounds set to the heavens or to the seas, or to the dry land, or to the sun, moon, or stars, (all this) shall be revealed in the days of the dispensation of the fulness of times." (D&C 121:26-31).

Worthy members of the church should strive to be the agents through whom this knowledge comes. The Prophet Joseph Smith wrote: "As the dews of Carmel, so shall the knowledge of God descend upon" the Latter-day Saints. (D&C 128:19). There is more to the gospel than obedience and covenants. The knowledge of God's active concern for His children, and the application of the principles of the gospel for their benefit is progress, too. "In one sense of the word, the keys of the kingdom...consist in the key of knowledge" that comes through the Holy Ghost. (D&C 128:14).

In the church today, there are many striking evidences of the sanctifying and unifying influence of the Holy Ghost. For example, in spite of the many translations of the scriptures used by members worldwide, there is remarkably little disagreement as to their meaning. In church organization and church government, ecclesiastical leaders enjoy virtual harmony in spite of cultural, social, political, and economic differences. The ordinances of the gospel, from baptism to the endowment in the temple, are universally understood and faithfully administered.

In order for the world-wide church to function smoothly, "the several elders composing this church of Christ are to meet in conference....from time to time... to do whatever church business is necessary." (V. 61-62). Every six months, Saints from all over the world gather at church headquarters to hear the word of the Lord from His authorized servants, as it falls from their mouths.

As Harold B. Lee once explained in his closing remarks at General Conference: "If you want to know what the Lord has for this people, I would admonish you to get and read the discourses that have been delivered at this conference, for what these brethren have spoken by the power of the Holy Ghost is the mind of the Lord, the will of the Lord, the word of the Lord, and the power of God unto salvation." (C.R., 4/1973).

David O. McKay taught that there are four principal purposes of conferences in the church. 1) To transact current church business. 2) To hear reports and general church statistics. 3) To approve "those names which (the Lord has) mentioned, or else disapprove of them." (D&C 124:144). The leaders are to receive their licenses... by vote of the church to which they belong, or from the conferences.... No person is to be ordained to any office in this church...without the vote of that church." (V. 63 & 65). "Every president of the high priesthood...bishop, high councilor, and high priest, is to be ordained by the direction of a high council or general conference." (V. 67). 4) To worship the Lord in sincerity and reverence, and to give and to receive encouragement, exhortation, and instruction. (C.R., 10/1938).

"The elders or priests are to have a sufficient time to expound all things concerning the church of Christ to their understanding, previous to their partaking of the sacrament and being confirmed by the laying on of the hands of the elders, so that all things may be done in order." (V. 68).

"The members shall manifest before the church, and also before the elders, by a godly walk and conversation, that they are worthy of the sacrament and other ordinances of the gospel, that there may be works and faith agreeable to the holy scriptures - walking in holiness before the Lord." (V. 69). "Not every one that saith unto me, Lord, Lord, shall enter into the kingdom of heaven; but he that doeth the will of my Father who is in heaven." (Matthew 7:21). This is particularly significant in light of the various "Born Again Christian" movements abroad in the land. Many claim that it is only necessary to "confess Christ," or to declare their faith in Him, in order to be saved. They miss the critical point the Savior made that we must do the will of the Father. The action verb "to do" implies more than just a weak effort; it demands active obedience over the long haul to the requirements established by God.

"Faith, if it hath not works, is dead, being alone." (James 2:17). There is no more power in faith that does not include works, than there is strength in food that is not eaten, or warmth in clothes that are not worn. The teachings on faith and works by Luther and the other Reformers who founded Protestantism are often misunderstood.

"By faith, Luther meant no merely intellectual assent to a proposition, but vital, personal self-committal to a practical belief. He heartily approved of good works; what he denied was their efficacy for salvation. 'Good works,' he said, 'do not make a good man. But a good man does good works.' And what makes a man good? Faith in God, and Christ." (Will Durant, "The Story of Civilization," "The Reformation," p. 374-375). This is consistent with the doctrine that we are saved by grace, after all that we can do.

"Every member of the church of Christ having children is to bring them unto the elders before the church, who are to lay their hands upon them in the name of Jesus Christ, and bless them in his name." (V. 70). This is an ordination of blessing, rather than of salvation. It is the practice of the church to include the naming of babies at this time, although this is not mandated by scripture.

"No one can be received into the church of Christ unless he has arrived unto the years of accountability before God, and is capable of repentance." (V. 71). Almost a year before this revelation was received, the Lord had taught Joseph Smith that "all men must repent and be baptized, and not only men, but women, and children who have arrived at the years of accountability." (D&C 18:42). Elsewhere in scripture, the age of accountability is established at 8 years. "And...children shall be baptized for the remission of their sins when eight years old, and receive the laying on of the hands." (D&C 68:27).

So that there would be no disputations among the Saints, the Savior told Joseph Smith that "baptism is to be administered in the following manner unto all those who repent - The person who is called of God and has authority from Jesus Christ to baptize, shall go down into the water with the person who has presented himself or herself for baptism, and shall say, calling him or her by name: Having been commissioned of Jesus Christ, I baptize you in the name of the Father, and of the Son, and of the Holy Ghost. Amen." (V. 73).

With priesthood authority, Peter had healed the lame beggar at the gate of the temple: "Then Peter said, Silver and gold have I none, but such as I have give I thee: In the name of Jesus Christ of Nazareth rise up and walk." (Acts 3:6). In the case of the baptismal prayer, however, the officiant invokes the names of all three members of the Godhead. This is equivalent to the words: "Thus saith the Lord," a phrase that is repeated at least 538 times in the scriptures.

Paul taught that there is "one Lord, one faith, (and) one baptism." (Ephesians 4:5). There was no disputation regarding the doctrine of Christ as long as the Apostles walked the earth. When they were martyred, however, and their priesthood authority died with them, confusion arose concerning the simplest policies and procedures of the church and the doctrines of the kingdom, and there was no enlightened solution to the problem. Apostasy resulted, that was only ended by the direct Latter-day intervention of Heavenly Father and His Son Jesus Christ.

There is a worthiness component to baptism, that is related to faith and repentance. Moroni wrote of the qualifications for baptism, that none were "baptized save they brought forth fruit meet that they were worthy of it." (Moroni 6:1). In other words, they demonstrated by their good works that the conduct of their lives had been brought into harmony with gospel principles. "Neither did they receive any unto baptism save they came forth with a broken heart and a contrite spirit, and witnessed unto the church that they truly repented of all their sins." (Moroni 6:2).

In other words, as our faith convicts us of our sins, it propels us forward on the path toward perfection by motivating us to good works. "And none were received unto baptism save they took upon them the name of Christ, having a determination to serve him to the end." (Moroni 6:3).

Our broken hearts are softened, and we become teachable so that we might receive the things of the Spirit. When we are "broken down with deep sorrow for sin, (we are) humble and thoroughly penitent, (and) have attained sincere and purposeful repentance." (Bruce R. McConkie, "Mormon Doctrine," p. 161).

Contrition is to be "bruised in heart, sorrow, or affliction of mind for some fault or injury done. It is penitence for sin." ("Oxford English Dictionary"). When we have contrite spirits, we are crushed or broken in spirit by a sense of sin, we are malleable and teachable, and we are brought to repentance. According to the abundant mercy of Jesus Christ, Who has begotten us again "unto a lively hope" by His resurrection from the dead, we recognize that the light at the end of the tunnel is not the headlamp of an approaching train, but a celestial beacon that has been fastened to the gates of heaven. (1 Peter 1:3). "Yea, thus we see that the gate of heaven is open unto all, even to those who will believe on the name of Jesus Christ, who is the Son of God." (Helaman 3:28). This gives a new meaning to the expression: "We'll leave the light on."

With that level of spiritual preparation, we are ready to ask, as did those on the Day of Pentecost: "What shall we do?" The answer is straightforward: "Repent and be baptized every one of you in the name of Jesus Christ for the remission of sins." (Acts 2:37-38). Wherever is found the authority of the Priesthood, there lies the power to receive repentant individuals unto baptism, that they might take upon themselves the name of Jesus Christ, having a determination to serve him to the end. Joseph Smith taught: "In the former ages of the world, before the Saviour came in the flesh, the Saints were baptized in the name of Jesus Christ to come, because there never was any other name whereby men could be saved." ("Teachings," p. 266).

Joseph Fielding Smith, Jr. taught: "Baptism for the remission of sins is an ordinance of the gospel which has been required of all who seek the Kingdom of God since the transgression of Adam." The Pseudepigraphic Book of Adam and Eve records how "Adam came to Jordan and he entered into the water and he plunged himself altogether into the flood, even to the hairs of his head, while he made supplication to God and sent up prayers to him." (Preston Robinson, "Christ's Eternal Gospel," p. 118-119).

There seems to have been pre-Christian baptism at Qumran, as well. From "The Manual of Discipline," of the Dead Sea Covenanters, we read: "His sin is forgiven him and in the humility of his soul he is for all the Laws of God; his flesh is cleansed shining bright in the waters of purification, even in the waters of baptism, and he shall be given a new name in due time to walk perfect in all the ways of God." (Hugh Nibley, "An Approach to The Book of Mormon," p. 149).

"El Maghtas," or "the place of baptism" on the Jordan River, is reputedly the site of Christ's own baptism. It is here that numerous pilgrims come each year on January 6 for the feast of Epiphany, to immerse their bodies in the sacred waters. (Emmanuel Dehan, "And The Walls Came Tumbling Down," p. 28-29). The Jordan River is the lowest body of fresh water upon the face of the earth. When Jesus was baptized there, He not only symbolically, but also physically, descended beneath us all.

Moroni taught that after the baptism of water, the penitent faithful only became members of the church when they had received the gift of the Holy Ghost. When they "were wrought upon and cleansed by the power of the Holy Ghost, they were numbered among the people of the church of Christ." (Moroni 6:4). The scriptures repeatedly speak of "the baptism of fire and the Holy Ghost" as inseparable ordinances of the gospel.

Joseph Smith taught: "You might as well baptize a bag of sand as a man if not done in view of the remission of sins and getting the Holy Ghost. Baptism by water is but half a baptism, and is good for nothing without the other half, that is, baptism of the Holy Ghost." ("Teachings," p. 314).

Nephi taught: "The gate by which ye should enter is repentance and baptism by water; and then cometh a remission of your sins by fire and by the Holy Ghost." (2 Nephi 31:17). The presence of the Holy Ghost purges out the effects of sin, and works in concert with the blood of Jesus to purify our tainted souls. Through the miracle of the Atonement, one more repentant sinner is thus added to the rolls of Christ's church.

"Then shall he immerse him or her in the water, and come forth again out of the water." (V. 74). The Savior also taught the Nephite Saints that immersion in water was the correct procedure. (3 Nephi 11:23). Baptism is symbolic of the burial of Christ. Joseph Smith said the repentant "were baptized after the manner of his burial, being buried in the water in his name, and this according to the commandment which he has given - That by keeping the commandments they might be washed and cleansed from all their sins." (D&C 76:51-52). "Consequently, the baptismal font was instituted as a similitude of the grave." (D&C 128:13).

As Paul wrote: "Therefore, we are buried with him by baptism into death: that like as Christ was raised up from the dead by the glory of the Father, even so we also should walk in newness of life. For if we have been planted together in the likeness of his death, we shall be also in the likeness of his resurrection." (Romans 6:4).

"It is expedient that the church meet together often to partake of bread and wine in the remembrance of the Lord Jesus." (V. 75). The Nephite church did so, that its members might "speak one with another concerning the welfare of their souls." (Moroni 6:5). These faithful Saints regularly reviewed and renewed their covenants with the Lord, in order to maintain their spiritual fitness and focus. Today, attendance at church is equally important to the welfare of our souls.

The Lord counseled Joseph Smith: "That thou mayest more fully keep thyself unspotted from the world, thou shalt go to the house of prayer and offer up thy sacraments upon my holy day. For verily this is a day appointed unto you to rest from your labors, and to pay thy devotions unto the Most High." (D&C 59:9-10). In his second epistle to Timothy, the Apostle Paul urged the faithful to strengthen each other. He wrote: "And the things that thou hast heard of me among many witnesses, the same commit thou to faithful men, who shall be able to teach others also." (2 Timothy 2:2).

Too often, though, our services are vulgar and profane, and demeaning to the character of those who would call themselves the Saints of the Most High God. John Taylor once declared: "I think it altogether out of place on such occasions to hear people talk about secular things." (J.D., 22:226). He was saying that in too many ways, we secularize sacred things. Unconsciously trivializing and tarnishing the celestial, we cheapen it and render it telestial.

The Gospel of Mark documents the administration of the Sacrament at the Lord's Last Supper: "And as they did eat, Jesus took bread, and blessed, and brake it, and gave to them, and said, Take, eat: this is my body. And he took the cup, and when he had given thanks, he gave it to them: and they all drank of it. And he said unto them, This is my blood of the new testament, which is shed for many. Verily I say unto you, I will drink no more of the fruit of the vine, until that day that I drink it new in the kingdom of God." (Mark 14:22-25).

The Joseph Smith Translation renders these verses from Mark as follows: "And as they did eat, Jesus took bread and blessed it, and brake, and gave to them, and said, Take it, and eat. Behold, this is for you to do in remembrance of my body; for as oft as ye do this ye will remember this hour that I was with you. And he took the cup, and when he had given thanks, he gave it to them; and they all drank of it. And he said unto them, This is in remembrance of my blood which is shed for many, and the new testament which I give unto you; for of me ye shall bear record unto all the world. And as oft as ye do this ordinance, ye will remember me in this hour that I was with you and drank with you of this cup, even the last time in my ministry. Verily I say unto you, Of this ye shall bear record; for I will no more drink of the fruit of the vine with you, until that day that I drink it new in the kingdom of God." (J.S.T. Mark 14:20-25).

The Gospel of Matthew renders the relevant verses as follows: "And as they were eating, Jesus took bread, and blessed it, and brake it, and gave it to the disciples, and said, Take, eat; this is my body. And he took the cup, and gave thanks, and gave it to them, saying, Drink ye all of it; For this is my blood of the new testament, which is shed for many for the remission of sins. But I say unto you, I will not drink henceforth of this fruit of the vine, until that day when I drink it new with you in my Father's kingdom." (Matthew 26:26-29).

The Joseph Smith Translation of the same verses from Matthew gives the following clarification: "And as they were eating, Jesus took bread and brake it, and blessed it, and gave to his disciples, and said, Take, eat; this is in remembrance of my body which I give a ransom for you. And he took the cup, and gave thanks, and gave it to them, saying, Drink ye all of it. For this is in remembrance of my blood of the new testament, which is shed for as many as shall believe on my name, for the remission of their sins. And I give unto you a commandment, that ye shall observe to do the things which ye have seen me do, and bear record of me even unto the end. But I say unto you, I will not drink henceforth of this fruit of the vine, until that day when I shall come and drink it new with you in my Father's kingdom." (J.S.T. Matthew 26:22-26).

The Joseph Smith Translation of these verses removes all doubt as to the meaning of these passages. It is in complete harmony with the words of the covenant as it is contained in this section (Section 20) of the Doctrine and Covenants and in The Book of Moroni chapters 4 & 5, that clearly teach that the emblems of the Sacrament are symbolic of Christ's sacrifice.

"And the elder or priest shall administer it; and after this manner shall he administer it - he shall kneel with the church and call upon the father in solemn prayer." (V. 76). The sacramental prayer is offered over emblems that represent the flesh and blood of Christ. Officiating at the table are elders or priests, who "kneel down with the church, and pray to the Father in the name of Christ." (Moroni 4:2). Some have wondered why the congregation today does not kneel during the sacramental prayers. The instruction given in the Doctrine and Covenants should be interpreted to mean that the priesthood bearers who administer the sacrament kneel "in the presence of the church." If it were necessary for the congregation to literally kneel with the officiant, the priesthood leaders of the church would have given that instruction. The body of the church participates in this ordinance of the gospel through the words of the prayer that are critical to the execution of the covenant.

"O God, the Eternal Father, we ask thee in the name of thy Son, Jesus Christ, to bless and sanctify this bread to the souls of all those who partake of it, that they may eat in remembrance of the body of thy Son, and witness unto thee, O God, the Eternal Father, that they are willing to take upon them the name of thy Son and always remember him and keep his commandments which he has given them; that they may always have his Spirit to be with them. Amen." (V. 77). The Sacrament conveys great power as Heavenly Father extends His blessings to His children. When we 'witness' before God as we participate in the ordinance, we covenant to take upon ourselves the name of Christ, remember Him, and keep His commandments. His part of the covenant is to grant us the Holy Ghost to help us to do our duty. As baptized members of the church, we receive the greater light of the Holy Ghost, because we have the responsibility to be true to our baptismal covenants. "For of him unto whom much is given much is required; and he who sins against the greater light shall receive the greater condemnation." (D&C 82:3).

When members of the church make a mistake, as they inevitably do, the Articles and Covenants of the Church provide the opportunity to recognize it, acknowledge it, right the wrong if possible, refrain from repeating it, receive forgiveness for the transgression, and then move on. Potential stumbling blocks thus become stepping stones, and mortality with all its potential pitfalls can become the vital growth experience it was designed to be. As Moroni wrote: "And as oft as they repented and sought forgiveness, with real intent, they were forgiven." (Moroni 6:8).

Without the Atonement, our mortal experiences would be nothing more than cruel jokes. None of us could measure up, no matter how hard we tried or how desperately we wanted to, and the demands of Justice would require that we stand condemned. Even the Savior said: "There is none good, but God." But then He qualified this harsh sounding judgment by continuing: "But if thou wilt enter into life, keep the commandments." (Matthew 19:17).

Since we will be judged by the law to which we have been responsible while on the earth, the requirement to account for our deeds at the Bar of Justice will vary. As the Savior said: "And that servant, which knew his lord's will, and prepared not himself, neither did according to his will, shall be beaten with many stripes. But he that knew not, and did commit things worthy of stripes, shall be beaten with few stripes. For unto whomsoever much is given, of him shall much be required." (Luke 12:47-48).

This may also explain why it is the practice of the church that only worthy members partake of the Sacrament. Of non-members it is not required, because only baptized individuals have promised to take upon themselves the name of Christ, always remember Him, and keep His commandments, so that they may have his Spirit to be with them, to strengthen them, and prompt them to keep on the strait and narrow path to which they have committed themselves by covenant.

"The manner of administering the wine - he shall take the cup also, and say: O God, the Eternal Father, we ask thee in the name of thy Son, Jesus Christ, to bless and sanctify this wine to the souls of all those who drink of it, that they may do it in remembrance of the blood of thy Son, which was shed for them; that they may witness unto thee, O God, the Eternal Father, that they do always remember him, that they may have his Spirit to be with them. Amen." (V. 78-79). The Sacramental Prayer received by Joseph Smith and recorded in this section of the Doctrine & Covenants is identical to that recorded by Moroni in the Book of Mormon. (See Moroni 5:2).

What was the nature of the wine used in ancient times? There is little doubt that Jesus and His disciples drank fermented wine, and not 'new wine' as so many Latter-day Saints would naively believe. There is nothing inherently wrong with drinking wine; the Word of Wisdom was only given "in consequence of the evils and designs which do and will exist in the hearts of conspiring men in the last days," who would subvert the drinking of spirits to suit the evil purposes of the adversary. (D&C 89:4).

In response to the wicked designs that existed in the hearts of his enemies, the Prophet Joseph Smith received a revelation in August, 1830, regarding the use of wine in the Sacrament. He wrote: "Early in the month of August Newel Knight and his wife paid us a visit at my place in Harmony, Pennsylvania; and as neither his wife nor mine had been as yet confirmed, it was proposed that we should confirm them, and partake together of the Sacrament, before he and his wife should leave us. In order to prepare for this I set out to procure some wine for the occasion, but had gone only a short distance when I was met by a heavenly messenger, and received the following revelation, the first four paragraphs of which were written at this time." (H.C., 1:106).

"Listen to the voice of Jesus Christ, your Lord, your God, and your Redeemer, whose word is quick and powerful. For, behold, I say unto you, that it mattereth not what ye shall eat or what ye shall drink when ye partake of the sacrament, if it so be that ye do it with an eye single to my glory - remembering unto the Father my body which was laid down for you, and my blood which was shed for the remission of your sins. Wherefore, a commandment I give unto you, that you shall not purchase wine neither strong drink of your enemies; Wherefore, you shall partake of none except it is made new among you; yea, in this my Father's kingdom which shall be built up on the earth." (D&C 27:1-4).

The revelation known as D&C 27, that is a companion to D&C 20, witnesses the simplicity of the ordinance of the Sacrament, emphasizing that it is does not matter what we drink, as long as we do it in sincerity, with an eye single to the glory of God. It is important to remember that wine is only symbolical of the redeeming blood of Christ. It does not become His blood through a mystical transformation, as many would believe.

The Catholic doctrine of transubstantiation is false. The emblems of the Sacrament, whether they be water or wine, bread or wafers, or anything else, help us to focus our attention where it belongs, which is on the Son of God and His sacrifice for us, and on the covenants we made with Him at the waters of baptism.

It should also be pointed out that the revelation known as Section 27 was given some two and a half years before The Word of Wisdom was received. The church did not adopt the practice of using water in place of wine because of the Word of Wisdom, although the two are loosely connected. In each case, intervention by the Lord was prompted by the evil designs of conspiring men who would go to any length to destroy the order of the church.

The Lord taught the Nephites: "Ye shall not suffer any one knowingly to partake of my flesh and blood unworthily, when ye shall minister it. For whoso eateth and drinketh my flesh and blood unworthily eateth and drinketh damnation to his soul; therefore if ye know that a man is unworthy to eat and drink of my flesh and blood ye shall forbid him." (3 Nephi 18:28-29).

These verses suggest that it is not the purpose of the Sacrament to obtain a remission of sins, but rather to recommit in a priesthood ordinance to the covenant of baptism, and to receive by covenant the Spirit of God so that we might more surely hold fast to the rod of iron. If the purpose of the Sacrament were to obtain a remission of sins, it would not be forbidden to those in greatest need.

The reason that those who partake without proper prior preparation, meaning repentance, drink damnation to their souls, is that their unworthy actions block the channels through which spiritual power flows. It is the consequent halt in progression that is damning to our souls. Conversely, this is why partaking of the Sacrament in worthiness conveys great power. Heavenly Father blessed us with the ordinance that we might approach Him by covenant, that His promises to us might be freely fulfilled.

Through Joseph Smith, He said: "Let thy bowels also be full of charity towards all men, and to the household of faith, and let virtue garnish thy thoughts unceasingly; then shall thy confidence wax strong in the presence of God; and the doctrine of the priesthood shall distill upon thy soul as the dews from heaven. The Holy Ghost shall be thy constant companion, and thy scepter an unchanging scepter of righteousness and truth; and thy dominion shall be an everlasting dominion, and without compulsory means it shall flow unto thee forever and ever." (D&C 121:45-46).

Melvin J. Ballard counseled that "the road to the Sacrament table is the path of safety for the Latter-day Saints." ("Sermons and Missionary Services of Melvin Joseph Ballard," pp. 147-57). We must recognize the truth in that statement, for Satan surely does. If he can convince us that the Sacrament is not essential to our spiritual well-being, or that it is foolish, or that our weekly participation in the ordinance is nothing more than vain repetition, or if we have lost our way and no longer experience the feeling of its powerful effect on us and of its importance to our spiritual well being, he will have won a major victory. Satan will attempt to pacify church members "and lull them away into carnal security, that they will say: All is well in Zion; yea, Zion prospereth, all is well - and thus the devil cheateth their souls, and leadeth them away carefully down to hell." (2 Nephi 28:21).

Satan tries to move us from white, through every subtle shade of grey, to black. He tries to make us believe we are gaining something, when we are really losing. Therefore, "any member of the church of Christ transgressing, or being overtaken in a fault, shall be dealt with as the scriptures direct." (V. 80).

Perhaps it is because it is easy to get out of focus, lose our grip on the rod of iron, and wander from obedience to our covenants, that Moroni recorded that the church was "strict to observe that there should be no iniquity among them." (Moroni 6:7). Perhaps <u>his</u> is lament was that, had it been more zealous, there would not have been apostasy in the church. Fanaticism and blind obedience have no place there, and agency ought to rule supreme among its guiding principles, but there is something to be said for strict orthodoxy among its members.

The government of the church is ruled by law, and the Savior is both its Author and Judge. But His is not the iron hand of tyranny, by any means. Only those who have not been born again feel restricted by the commandments, for they have not yet experienced the freedom that obedience to gospel principles can bring. For the obedient, the gospel is the perfect law of liberty. (See James 1:25). "Stand fast therefore in the liberty wherewith Christ hath made us free, and be not entangled again with the yoke of bondage" to sin. (Galatians 5:1). With the slate wiped clean, the Saints enjoy a calming serenity in their meetings, which are "conducted by the church after the manner of the workings of the Spirit, and by the power of the Holy Ghost; for as the power of the Holy Ghost (leads) them whether to preach, or to exhort, or to pray, or to supplicate, or to sing, even so it (is) done." (Moroni 6:9).

"The great objective of all our work is to build character and faith in the lives of those whom we serve." (Spencer W. Kimball, C.R., 4/1948). The power to convey gospel principles comes through the Spirit. It must reside in both the deliverer and the recipient of the word. This is the beauty of gospel instruction. It is an infallible method for disseminating information of eternal worth, but must not be mishandled or misrepresented. It is no wonder that the Savior warned: "Be ye clean that bear the vessels of the Lord." (D&C 38:42, see D&C 133:5, Isaiah 52:11, & 3 Nephi 20:41).

Of the occasion of the organization of the church, on April 6, 1830, the Prophet Joseph Smith later wrote: "After a happy time spent in witnessing and feeling for ourselves the powers and blessings of the Holy Ghost, through the grace of God bestowed upon us, we dismissed with the pleasing knowledge that we were now individually members of, and acknowledged of God, 'The Church of Jesus Christ.'" (H.C., 1:79). It must have been an exhilarating feeling! It is one that every member of the church today can feel with an equal intensity.

# Section 21

## (Instructions in 1830 to the newly organized church in New York, received by inspiration).

"This revelation was given at the organization of the church," April 6, 1830. (Superscript). Although the Melchizedek Priesthood had previously been conferred upon Joseph Smith and Oliver Cowdery, they were told to defer ordaining each other to the office of Elder within the priesthood, until the church had been formally organized. (H.C., 1:61). Now, with its foundations in place, by "the laying on of hands, Joseph...ordained Oliver an elder of the church; and Oliver similarly ordained Joseph." (Superscript).

"Behold, there shall be a record kept among you; and in it thou shalt be called a seer a translator, a prophet, an apostle of Jesus Christ, an elder of the church through the will of God the Father, and the grace of your Lord Jesus Christ." (V. 1).

A seer is an interpreter and clarifier of eternal truth; one who walks in the Lord's light with open eyes. (See Mosiah 8:13). "A seer is one who may see God, who may talk with God, who may receive personal instruction from God. Our prophet is a seer and a revelator. There must be someone to whom the people can turn and trust, who can speak for God. God must have someone on earth who can point the way and say: 'This is true.' God has given us a living seer and prophet (who) reveals personal testimony that Jesus is in very deed the Risen Savior, the Living God." (Theodore Burton, C.R., 10/61). A seer is literally a 'see-er,' one who has the right to use the Urim and Thummim.

By seers "shall all things be revealed." (Mosiah 8:17). Helen Keller once remarked: "There is one tragedy in life worse than to be born without sight, and that is to be born with sight, but without vision." Our loving Father has "provided a means that man, through faith, might work mighty miracles; therefore he becometh a great benefit to his fellow beings." (Mosiah 8:18). A seer can see the storm clouds before they appear on the horizon.

A translator is one who converts one written language into another, or one who gives a clearer meaning to a language, or one who preserves by revelation the thoughts and intent of an original writer. Joseph would soon commence his work of translation of the King James Version of the Bible. "Joseph himself called his work a translation. This is apparently the sense in which he understood the work he was doing with the Bible. Since, in part, he was effecting a restoration of lost meaning and material, and since the Bible did not originate in English, his work to some degree would amount to an inspired, or revelatory, translation into English of that which the ancient prophets and apostles had written in Hebrew, Aramaic, and/or Greek." (Robert J. Matthews, "A Plainer Translation - Joseph Smith's Translation of The Bible," p. xxx).

A prophet is a teacher of the body of truth, or of the gospel, revealed by the Lord, and under inspiration explained to the understanding of the people. The word "prophet" comes from the Greek 'prophetes,' which means 'inspired teacher.' "He that prophesieth," wrote Paul, "speaketh unto men to edification, and exhortation, and comfort." (1 Corinthians 14:3). Strictly speaking, by scriptural definition, "the testimony of Jesus Christ is the spirit of prophecy. (Revelation 19:10). In Old Testament times, Moses exclaimed: "Would God that all the Lord's people were prophets, and that the Lord would put his spirit upon them!" (Numbers 11:26-29). To that end, schools of prophets existed in Old Testament times, and provided the model for one that was started by Joseph Smith, in 1832. (See D&C 88:127).

Isaiah was a prophet of God, confirming to all Israel: "Behold, I have declared the former things from the beginning; and they went forth out of my mouth, and I showed them." (Isaiah 48:3). It is one thing to recount the dealings of God with man from the beginning. Those events that have come to pass which were prophesied long ago serve to confirm our faith and strengthen our testimony that God maintained an intimate relationship with His children.

It is quite another thing to witness the prophetic power of the servants of God, who reveal truths that have been hidden from the world. "New things do I declare," wrote Isaiah, and "before they spring forth I tell you of them." (Isaiah 42:9). I declare "the end from the beginning, and from ancient times the things that are not yet done, saying, My counsel shall stand, and I will do all my pleasure. Yea, I have spoken it, I will also bring it to pass; I have purposed it, I will also do it. Hearken unto me, ye stouthearted, that are far from righteousness." (Isaiah 46:10-11).

This counsel from Isaiah is appropriate to all ages, and so our reliance upon the word of the Lord has been reiterated in our day: "We believe all that God has revealed, all that He does now reveal, and we believe that He will yet reveal many great and important things pertaining to the Kingdom of God." (9th Article of Faith).

Continual spiritual guidance, known as revelation, is critical to vital religion, for it "cannot be maintained and preserved on the theory that God dealt with our human race only in the far past ages, and that the Bible is the only evidence we have that our God is a living, revealing, communicating God. If God ever spoke, He is still speaking. He is the great I Am, not the great He was." (Rufus Jones, "A Flash of Eternity," newspaper article).

The Lord wanted to make very clear to the church that had been restored to the earth on that very day, that Joseph Smith was His prophet. In ancient Israel, the Lord had repeatedly foretold events long before they came to pass, lest in the hardness and obstinacy of the people they should claim that it was their idols and images that were responsible. As Isaiah explained: "I showed them for fear lest thou shouldest say - Mine idol hath done them, and my graven image, and my molten image hath commanded them." (Isaiah 48:5).

Doctrine & Covenants Section 21 stands as a testimony against those who would take the credit for the fulfillment of prophecy. Speaking in the name of the Lord, Isaiah declared to an apostate world: "For mine own sake will I do this, for I will not suffer my name to be polluted, and I will not give my glory unto another." (Isaiah 48:11).

Satan is a skillful imitator, and as we become distracted from our mission, he can successfully distort our perception. "For there shall arise false Christs, and false prophets," warned Jesus, "and shall shew great signs and wonders; insomuch that, if it were possible, they shall deceive the very elect." (Matthew 24:24). When He taught this principle, the Savior did not say that He would leave His sheep without a Shepherd, or that there would be no-one to guide the people; He only made the distinction between true and false prophets.

An Apostle is "a special witness of the name of Christ in all the world - thus differing from other officers in the church in the duties of their calling." (D&C 107:23). Garden-variety members of the church, by virtue of the priesthood and the gift of the Holy Ghost, may be witnesses for Christ. But only Apostles hold the fulness of authority, keys, and priesthood to open the way to preach the gospel to every nation, kindred, tongue, and people. "And no man taketh this honour unto himself, but he that is called of God." (Hebrews 5:4).

As of 2017, there have been a total of 100 Apostles called to the work, since the church was organized. The Apostles currently serving in the church are:

Thomas S. Monson – year called: 1963 - 54 years of service
Russell M. Nelson – year called: 1984 - 33 years of service

Dallin H. Oaks – year called: 1984 - 33 years of service
M. Russell Ballard – year called: 1985 - 32 years of service
Robert D. Hales – year called: 1994 - 23 years of service
Jeffrey R. Holland – year called: 1994 - 23 years of service
Henry B. Eyring – year called: 1995 - 22 years of service
David A. Bednar – year called: 2004 - 13 years of service
Deiter F. Uchtdorf – year called: 2004 - 13 years of service
Quentin L. Cook – year called: 2007 - 10 years of service
D. Todd Christofferson – year called: 2008 - 9 years of service
Neil L. Anderson – year called: 2009 - 8 years of service
Ronald A. Rasband – year called: 2015 - 2 year of service
Gary E. Stevenson – year called: 2015 - 2 year of service
Dale G. Renlund – year called: 2015 - 2 year of service

The Lord told Joseph Smith: "To some it is given by the Holy Ghost to know that Jesus Christ is the Son of God, and that he was crucified for the sins of the world. To others it is given to believe on their words, that they also might have eternal life if they continue faithful." (D&C 46:13-14). "And by doing so, the Lord God prepareth the way that the residue of men may have faith in Christ, that the Holy Ghost may have place in their hearts." (Words of Mormon 1:32).

Consequently, as an Apostle of Jesus Christ, Joseph Smith was commissioned to declare with boldness his witness of the truth, that faith might be developed in the hearts of those who heard his testimony. His was a unique perspective. "I had actually seen a light," he said, "and in the midst of that light I saw two Personages, and they did in reality speak to me; and though I was hated and persecuted for saying that I had seen a vision, yet it was true...and who am I that I can withstand God. ...For I had seen a vision; I knew it, and I knew that God knew it, and I could not deny it, neither dared I do it." (J.S.H. 1:25).

Joseph also declared: "Could we read and comprehend all that has been written from the days of Adam, on the relation of man to God and angels in a future state, we should know very little about it. Reading the experience of others, or the revelation given to them, can never give us a comprehensive view of our condition and true relation to God. Knowledge of these things can only be obtained by experience through the ordinances of God set forth for that purpose. Could you gaze into heaven five minutes, you would know more that you would by reading all that has ever been written on the subject." (H.C., 6:50).

In his history, Joseph repeatedly stated that he had received instruction that the world was not yet prepared to receive: "And many other things did (the personage) say unto me, which I cannot write at this time." (J.S.H. 1:20). Moroni "quoted many other passages of scripture, and offered many explanations which cannot be mentioned here." (J.S.H. 1:41).

On one occasion, Joseph Smith lamented; "Would to God I could tell you what I know. But you would call it blasphemy, and there are men upon this stand who would want to take my life. If the church knew all of the commandments, one half they would reject through prejudice and ignorance." ("Joseph Smith & The Restoration," p. 522).

Elder is the general title used to address one who holds the Melchizedek Priesthood. "An individual who holds a share in the priesthood and continues faithful to his calling will secure to himself not only the privilege of receiving, but the knowledge how to receive the things of God, that he may know the mind of God continually; and he will be enabled to discern between right and wrong, between the things of God and the things that are not of God. And the priesthood, the spirit that is within him, will continue to increase until it becomes like a fountain of living water; until it is like the tree of life; until it is one continued source of intelligence and instruction to that individual." (Brigham Young, J.D., 3:192).

Joseph Smith was "inspired of the Holy Ghost to lay the foundation" of the church, "and to build it up unto the most holy faith." (V. 2). In the first decade of the nineteenth century, "men were following with bated breath the march of Napoleon and waiting with feverish impatience for news of the wars. And all the while in their homes babies were being born. But who could think about babies? Everybody was thinking about battles. (In that decade) there stole into the world a host of heroes: Gladstone was born in Liverpool; Tennyson at the Somersby Rectory; and Oliver Wendell Holmes in Massachusetts. Abraham Lincoln was born in Kentucky, and music was enriched by the arrival of Felix Mendelssohn in Hamburg." Joseph and Lucy Mack Smith welcomed the arrival of a son, and named him after his father and grandfather before him. "But nobody thought of babies; everybody was thinking of battles. Yet which of the battles mattered more than the babies? We fancy God can manage His word only with great battalions, when all the time, He is doing it with beautiful babies. When a wrong wants righting, or a truth wants preaching, or a continent wants discovering," or a religion wants restoration, "God sends a baby into the world to do it." (F.M. Bareham).

"When theologians are reeling and stumbling, when lips are pretending and hearts are wandering, and people are running to and fro, seeking the word of the Lord and cannot find it, when clouds of error need dissipating and spiritual darkness needs penetrating and heavens need opening, a little infant is born." (Spencer W. Kimball, C.R., 4/1960).

Abraham clearly taught that there are "intelligences that were organized before the world was, and among all these there were many of the noble and great ones; (And God said) these I will make my rulers." (Abraham 3:22-23). Joseph Smith, who commenced the work of restoration and lay the foundation, was in this company. Even before he received the plates from which The Book of Mormon was translated, he went to the Hill Cumorah "at the end of each year, and at each time (he) found the same messenger there, and received instruction and intelligence from him at each of (his) interviews, respecting what the Lord was going to do, and how and in what manner his kingdom was to be conducted in the last days." (J.S.H. 1:54).

Today it is our habit in the church "to think of the restoration of the gospel as a past event," wrote Bruce R. McConkie. "It is true that we have the fulness of the everlasting gospel in the sense that we have those doctrines, priesthoods, and keys which enable us to gain the fulness of reward in our Father's kingdom. But the restoration of the wondrous truths known to Adam, Enoch, Noah, and Abraham has scarcely commenced. The sealed portion of The Book of Mormon is yet to be translated. All things are not to be revealed anew until the Lord comes. The greatness of the era of restoration is yet ahead. We are now making a beginning, but the transcendent glories and wonders to be revealed are for the future. Much of what Isaiah, prophet of the restoration, has to say is yet to be fulfilled." ("10 Keys to Understanding Isaiah").

The "church was organized and established in the year of your Lord eighteen hundred and thirty, in the fourth month, and on the sixth day of the month which is called April." (V. 3). On that date, "Joseph Smith and others met at the Peter Whitmer home in Fayette, New York. During this momentous meeting, six brethren officially organized the church. The Lord also spoke through Joseph to the assembly, giving the revelation that is now D&C Section 21.

The Prophet said of this occasion: "After a happy time spent in witnessing and feeling for ourselves the powers and blessings of the Holy Ghost, through the grace of God bestowed upon us, we dismissed with the pleasing knowledge that we were now individually members of, and acknowledged of God, The Church of Jesus Christ." (H.C., 1:79).

Those who had joined with the church were admonished by the Lord: "Give heed unto all" of Joseph Smith's "words and commandments which he shall give unto you as he receiveth them. For his word ye shall receive, as if from mine own mouth." (V. 4-5). When the prophet of the Lord speaks when moved upon by the Holy Ghost, his words assume "the power of God unto salvation." (D&C 68:4).

Joseph Smith taught: "Wherever there is a righteous man on the earth unto whom God revealed His word and gave power and authority to administer in His name, and wherever there is a priest of God, a minister who has power and authority from God to administer in the ordnances of the gospel and officiate in the Priesthood of God, there is the Kingdom of God." (H.C., 5:256).

"For by doing these things," the Lord will bless us in three distinct ways. 1) "The gates of hell shall not prevail against you; yea, and 2) the Lord God will disperse the powers of darkness from before you, and 3) cause the heavens to shake for your good, and his name's glory." (V. 6). The gates of hell mark the entrance to the so-called spirit prison of the unjust, where the wicked go to await the day when they will come forth to participate in the second resurrection of the unjust. (See "Doctrines of the Gospel Student Manual, (2000), p. 87–89, D&C 76:73, 88:97-102, Alma 40:11-14, & Moses 7:57).

At the opening of every dispensation of the gospel, ever since Satan deceived the sons and daughters of Adam and Eve during the First Gospel Dispensation, he has made a frontal attack against the reintroduction of truth. At the beginning of the Mosaic Dispensation, "Satan came tempting him saying: Moses, son of man, worship me." (Moses 1:12). In the Meridian of Time, he attacked the Master Himself. (Luke 4:1-13). We learn from the Prophet Joseph Smith that Satan was also present and contested the opening of the Dispensation of The Fulness of Times. (See J.S.H. 1:15).

The power of darkness that he commands is the influence of bitterness, class-distinction, confusion, delusion, and strife, that blinds the mind and stirs up the wicked to anger. "The devil has done very well in his various projects of distorting the truth or using a little truth to color lies and deceive people in the world. There is only one clear, bright light of truth, but there is a many faceted flickering, dancing light show of deceptive error with many shades of darkness engulfing the world. It is difficult sometimes to pick out truth and identify it amid the various counterfeits for it." ("Gospel Doctrine Teacher's Manual").

"Young women of Scotland, life is before you," exhorted Helen Keller. "Two voices are calling you. One comes from the marsh of selfishness and force where success is won at any cost, and the other from the hilltops of justice and progress where even failure may ennoble. Two lights are on your horizon for you to choose. One is the fast-fading, will-o-the-wisp of power and materialism, the other the slowly rising sun of human brotherhood. Two laws stand today opposed, each demanding your allegiance. One is the law of death which daily invents new means of combat; this law obliges the nations to be ever at war. The other is the law of peace, of labour, of salvation, which strives to deliver man from the scourges which assail him. One looks only for violent conquest, the other for the relief of suffering humanity. Two ways lie open before you, one leading to a lower and yet lower plane of life, where are heard the weeping of the poor, the cries of little children, and the moans of pain, where manhood and womanhood shrivel, and possessions destroy the possessor; and the other leading to the highlands of the mind where are heard the glad shouts of humanity, and honest effort is rewarded with immortality." (Commencement Address to Queen Margaret College, Glasgow, Scotland, June 15, 1932, in "Helen Keller: Sightless but Seen; Deaf but Heard," p. 113).

Truman Madsen observed of those groping about in spiritual confusion: "In their efforts to clarify their consideration of Christ, they were often simply multiplying mirrors and studying angles, without increasing the light. The New Dispensation brought a flood of light that did not simply replace the darkness, but illuminated elements and principles, and their relationships, that heretofore had been only dimly perceived." ("B.H. Roberts, The Truth, The Way, The Life," p. 263).

Surely, the heavens will shake in defense of the righteous. Joseph Fielding Smith, Jr. declared: "No power on earth or hell can overthrow or defeat that which God has decreed. Every plan of the Adversary will fail; for the Lord knows the secret thoughts of men, and sees the future with a vision clear and perfect, even as though it were in the past." ("Church History and Modern Revelation," 1:26).

Joseph Smith explained to John Wentworth: "No unhallowed hand can stop the work from progressing. Persecutions may rage, mobs may combine, armies may assemble, calumny may defame, but the truth of God will go forth boldly, nobly, and independent, until it has penetrated every continent, visited every clime, swept every country, and sounded in every ear; till the purposes of God shall be accomplished, and the Great Jehovah shall say 'The work is done.'" (H.C., 4:540). "The truth is, that after the thousands of attacks, and scores of books that have been published, not one criticism has survived, and thousands have borne witness that the Lord has revealed to them the truth of this marvelous work." (Joseph Fielding Smith, Jr., "Church History and Modern Revelation," 1:218-29)

"To the Son is given the power of the resurrection, the power of the redemption, the power of salvation, and the power to enact laws for the carrying out and accomplishment of the design. Hence, life and immortality are brought to light, the gospel is introduced, and He becomes the Author of eternal life and exaltation." (John Taylor, "Mediation and Atonement," p. 171-172).

"For thus saith the Lord God," the Prophet Joseph Smith "have I inspired to move the cause of Zion in mighty power for good, and his diligence I know, and his prayers I have heard." (V. 7). Even though conditions in the world are degenerating and peace has been taken from the wicked, those in Zion shall enjoy the safety and security that only righteousness can guarantee, and there will be such an outpouring of the Spirit that "the earth shall be full of the knowledge of the Lord, as the waters cover the sea." (Isaiah 11:9).

B.H. Roberts had a great testimony of the Prophet, and "having gone word by word and line by line through his writings, and having read everything he could find on his life, he found Joseph Smith to be possessed of a deeper and richer comprehension of Christ than anyone he had read in the Christian tradition since the Apostles. Through all Roberts' buffetings and his intellectual probings, honing his own mind with the major figures in the history of Western thought, this conviction never diminished. And as his extensive knowledge of the alternatives increased, his convictions deepened: Joseph Smith told the truth. Joseph Smith was a prism of the Lord Jesus Christ." (Truman Madsen, "Defender of The Faith," p. 93).

"I will bless all those who labor in my vineyard with a mighty blessing," said the Lord, "and they shall believe on his words, which are given him through me by the Comforter." (V. 9). In our own decaying environment, the status of our hearts and minds will determine the final printout. As conditions in the world continue to deteriorate, blessings that follow obedience will not have a monetary cost, but instead, they will have a performance cost. The Lord said: "He that receiveth my law, and doeth it, the same is my disciple." (D&C 41:5).

Lorenzo Snow declared: "It is impossible to advance in the principles of truth, to increase in heavenly knowledge, except we exercise our reasoning faculties and exert ourselves." (J.D., 18:48). Agency is not free. It is purchased at a substantial price. If we desire a testimony, we must understand and obey the laws of the gospel associated with the principle in question. "For all who will have a blessing at my hands shall abide the law which was appointed for that blessing, and the conditions thereof, as were instituted from before the foundation of the world." (D&C 132:5). If we want to know that the Doctrine & Covenants, or The Book of Mormon, is the word of God, we must read with a desire to receive a witness. (See Moroni 10:4). If we want to know that obedience to the gospel Plan introduced by the church is the path to happiness, we need to try the virtue of the word of God. (See Alma 31:5). Therefore, "let us not be slothful because of the easiness of the way, for so was it with our fathers; for so was it prepared for them, that if they would look they might live; even so it is with us. The way is prepared, and if we will look, we may live forever." (Alma 37:46). The Plan of Salvation makes it that simple.

# Section 22
## (Instructions in 1830 to the newly organized church in New York, received by inspiration).

"This revelation was given to the church in consequence of some who had previously been baptized desiring to unite with the church without rebaptism." (Superscript). The first conference held in the church convened at the home of Peter Whitmer, on June 9, 1830. Those in attendance officially accepted this section and Section 20 as the "Articles and Covenants of the Church of Christ." ("Far West Record," p. 1-2). The leaders used these two sections as a General Handbook of Instructions, as it were, to help them as they engaged in the ongoing process of establishing the government of the church.

"Behold, I say unto you that all old covenants have I caused to be done away in this thing; and this is a New and an Everlasting Covenant, even that which was from the beginning." (V. 1). The New and Everlasting Covenant is the fulness of the Law of Christ. It is composed of all associations, bonds, connections, contracts, covenants, expectations, oaths, obligations, performances, rites, or vows, that are sealed upon members of the church by the Holy Spirit of Promise, or the Holy Ghost, under the authority of the President of the Church, who in their fulness, holds the keys to exercise priesthood powers. Those who conform their lives to every element of the New and Everlasting Covenant and follow the example of Christ in every whit, will have their calling and election made sure.

The violation of the New and Everlasting Covenant affects the entire body of the Saints. Joseph Fielding Smith, Jr. warned that "we should wake up to the realization that it is because of the breaking of covenants, especially the New and Everlasting Covenant, which is the fulness of the gospel as it has been revealed, that the world is to be consumed by fire and few men left. Since this punishment is to come at the time of the cleansing of the earth when Christ comes again, should not Latter-day Saints take heed unto themselves? We have been given the New and Everlasting Covenant, and many among us have broken it, and many are now breaking it; therefore all who are guilty of this offense will aid in bringing to pass the destruction in which they will find themselves swept from the earth when the great and dreadful day of the Lord shall come." ("New Era." 7/1972).

One of the best known teachings of the Jews is that when we alienate ourselves from God, all nature becomes our enemy. In the days of Enoch, because of the wickedness of the people, when he spoke the word of the Lord by the power of the priesthood, "the earth trembled, and the mountains fled, even according to his command; and the rivers of water were turned out of their course; and the roar of the lions was heard out of the wilderness." (Moses 7:13).

In the Last Days, "plagues shall go forth, and they shall not be taken from the earth" until the Lord has completed His work. (D&C 84:97). "And thus, with the sword and by bloodshed the inhabitants of the earth shall mourn; and with famine, and plague, and earthquake, and the thunder of heaven, and the fierce and vivid lightning also, shall the inhabitants of the earth be made to feel the wrath, and indignation, and chastening hand of an Almighty God, until the consumption decreed hath made a full end of all nations." (D&C 87:6). As Brigham Young declared, when people refuse the gospel, their "land will eventually become desolate, forlorn, and forsaken" as nature refuses her bounties. (J.D., 16:10).

The church had been organized in the month that this revelation was given. The Lord took this opportunity to emphasize to Joseph Smith that old covenants had been done away with, and he should now bring all his energies to bear on introducing the saving ordinances of the New and Everlasting Covenant to a world in need.

"Wherefore, although a man should be baptized an hundred times it availeth him nothing, for you cannot enter in at the strait gate by the law of Moses, neither by your dead works." (V. 2). Stephen Robinson wrote: "Faith and repentance lead us to the strait gate of baptism. Those who pass through this gate will obtain a remission of sins, gain membership in the church, and open the door leading to personal sanctification through repentance and receipt of the Holy Ghost. We may then find ourselves on the path of eternal progression leading to the Celestial Kingdom. The way is strait and narrow. The gospel standard is undeviating, with no room for rationalization or compromise. There is no latitude in God's declaration, when He said: 'For I the Lord cannot look upon sin with the least degree of allowance.' (D&C 1:31)."

In the church, "we believe that a man must be called of God, by prophecy, and by the laying on of hands by those who are in authority, to preach the gospel, and to administer in the ordinances thereof." (5th Article of Faith). Before we can hope to administer these ordinances, we must receive our errand from the Lord. As the Savior had explained to Hyrum Smith: "Behold, I command you that you need not suppose that you are called to preach until you are called." (D&C 11:15).

"No man is authorized to act in the name of the Lord, or to officiate in any ordinance unless he has been properly called. For this reason, the priesthood was restored and the church organized." Paul taught: "No man taketh this honour unto himself, but he that is called of God." (Hebrews 5:12). Therefore," said the Lord, "Let every man stand in his own office, and labor in his own calling, that the system may be kept perfect." (D&C 84:109-110).

When the Savior submitted to baptism, He demonstrated that our entrance into the church and kingdom is strait; that is to say, it is narrowly defined. There should be no discussion or variance of opinion regarding the prescribed way. He set the pattern, and then simply said "Come...follow me." (Matthew 19:21).

To the Nephites, the Savior taught these principles with unmistakable clarity. "And he said unto them: On this wise shall ye baptize; and there shall be no disputations among you." (3 Nephi 11:22). There followed explicit instruction to the priesthood leaders of the Nephite church regarding the manner of baptism. It is vitally important that the doctrine of Christ be clearly understood by the members of His church. "And there shall be no disputations among you," cautioned the Savior, "concerning the points of my doctrine." (3 Nephi 11:28). As Nephi asked: "Wherefore, my beloved brethren, can we follow Jesus save we shall be willing to keep the commandments of the Father? And the Father said: Repent ye, repent ye, and be baptized in the name of my Beloved Son." (V. 10-11).

Joseph Smith's contemporaries who questioned the need for re-baptism by those who held the authority of the priesthood in the restored church did not yet have a clear understanding that baptism serves at least nine purposes: 1) We are baptized to demonstrate our obedience, and 2) to follow in the footsteps of the Savior. 3) We are baptized to fulfill all righteousness. 4) Baptism allows us to receive a remission of our sins if we have reached the age of accountability. 5) Baptism enables us to gain admission to the Lord's church, "the only true and living church upon the face of the whole earth" with which the Lord is pleased. (D&C 1:31). 6) Baptism provides us with the opportunity to be personally sanctified through fire and the Holy Ghost. 7) It is outwardly symbolic as our re-birth, as we pass through a portal in the similitude of the grave. 8) It is the gateway ordinance leading to the blessings reserved for the faithful that are found in the other ordinances of the gospel, and 9) it sets us squarely on the path that leads to the Celestial Kingdom of God.

When the Saints grasped the concept that the purpose of their baptism was not to make their lives better, but rather to enable them to enter God's Rest, they were anxious to have the ordinance performed. The 'Rest of the Lord' is born of a settled conviction of the truths of the gospel in our minds. Since April 6, 1830, the invitation has been extended to all, to enter into God's Rest by internalizing celestial standards.

It is precisely "because of your dead works," said the Lord, "that I have caused this last covenant and this church to be built up unto me." (V. 3). Dead works have no power to save our souls. Benjamin taught that it is because of the covenant alone that the faithful are called the children of Christ. It is only when they submit to the ordinances of the gospel that their hearts are changed and they become the spiritual sons and daughters of Christ. (See Mosiah 5:7). The ordinance of baptism is the earthly expression of the spiritual reality that we have been born again.

There are three frameworks within which we may develop saving faith in the doctrine of Christ: first, the scriptures, secondly, the inspired words of the prophets and teachers, and thirdly, the promptings of the Holy Ghost. The impressions of the Spirit and testimony by the power of the Holy Ghost are perhaps even more important than the scriptures and the pronouncements of the prophets. In any event, the Church of Christ, that had so recently been organized, would provide the organizational matrix within which its members could develop faith unto salvation.

For those who would invite the Spirit to attend them, the experience would frequently be Pentecostal. The hearts of the people would be changed, and they would have no more disposition to do evil. Joseph Smith taught: "The nearer a man approaches perfection, the clearer are his views, and the greater his enjoyments, 'til he has overcome the evils of his life and lost every desire for sin." ("Teachings," p. 51). As they walked into the light, the scales of darkness would fall from the eyes of those who had embraced the gospel message.

"Wherefore, enter ye in at the gate, as I have commanded, and seek not to counsel your God." (V. 4). Baptism, properly administered, opens the portal to heaven in the sense that it puts us on the strait and narrow path leading to eternal life. It would be ludicrous for us to attempt in any way to counsel God, or to question His wisdom or judgment. He knows all things, "being from everlasting to everlasting." (Moroni 7:22). As far as we are concerned, God is in every sense perfect. We are completely helpless to alter the progress, or affect the outcome, of any of His activities. It was when Moses realized his utter dependence upon God that he exclaimed: "Now, for this cause I know that man is nothing, which thing I never had supposed." (Moses

1:10). When our faith convicts us of our sins, we recognize our utter dependence upon Him to redeem us from our fallen and hopeless state. The waters of baptism are like an infinity pool that opens onto a panorama of unlimited possibilities.

The fading light of day is the consequence of the corrosive nature of sin, the opposition in all things that is a necessary part of our mortal experience. In the absence of baptism, that is the lynchpin of the Plan of Salvation, all must be lost. Fortunately, the Lord reveals truth to those who are spiritually ready to understand it, and from the beginning, has provided a pathway that all might humble themselves as little children.

During the Creation, "God made two great lights; the greater light to rule the day, and the lesser light to rule the night. (Genesis 1:16, see also Moses 2:16, Abraham 3:5-6 & 4:16). It is illuminating to think of the greater light as the gift of the Holy Ghost, and the lesser light as the Light of Christ. The purpose of the Light of Christ would be to provide clarity, that all of Heavenly Father's children might be led to His doorstep, where the greater light of the Holy Ghost would be waiting to welcome them, as a beckoning lantern, through the portal of baptism of water, and of fire, into celestial glory.

# Section 23

(Instructions given in 1830 to the
newly organized church in New York).

This revelation was given in April, 1830, the same month that the church was organized. It did not take long for Satan to marshal his forces, as "mobs harassed church members, even destroying a dam the Saints had constructed so they could perform baptisms. Much of this persecution focused on the Prophet himself. He was arrested on false charges for causing an uproar by preaching about The Book of Mormon. He was tried and acquitted by a court, but immediately arrested again on the same charges and required to endure another lengthy court proceeding. New converts were threatened and reviled, but the church continued to grow. The revelations given at this time show the Lord's love and support of his servants as they struggled to build His kingdom." ("Doctrine & Covenants Class Member Study Guide," p. 7).

Oliver Cowdery was cautioned: "Beware of pride, lest thou shouldst enter into temptation." (V. 1). Early in their history, the Prophet Jacob gave his Nephite brethren the antidote for pride. The formula consisted of the Nephite version of the Golden Rule: "Think of your brethren like unto yourselves," and "before seeking for riches," seek the kingdom of God. (Jacob 2:17). This should be our number one priority.

Pride is a character crippling personality trait that can prevent us from reaching the kingdom. The Lord wanted Oliver Cowdery to be more than just a "professor" of religion. He could see Oliver's potential, that his "heart (could) be opened to preach the truth from henceforth and forever." (V. 2). Many individuals disqualify themselves, in large part because of pride, from obtaining the blessings associated with church membership. Pride is enmity toward our contemporaries, as well as toward God, and it can lead to all other transgressions. Ezra Taft Benson called it "the universal sin (which) limits or stops progression and adversely affects all of our relationships." (C.R., 4/1989).

It is pride that leads to the oppression of the poor, when we have a distorted sense of self-importance that is unjustified, unsupportable, and completely inaccurate. Pride can blind us to the recognition of our complete dependence upon God, to the ultimate equality of all of His children, and to our responsibility to act as His stewards in the service of our fellowmen.

Pride initiates a spiritual sclerosis, a hardening of the spiritual arteries, and a stagnation of our sensitivities. In our rigidity, we tend to make "a mock of that which (is) sacred; denying the spirit of prophecy and of revelation." (Helaman 4:12). When pride prevents us from relating to phenomena that we do not directly and physically experience, we die as to things of the spirit. Therefore, we are prone to attack whatever and whomever we cannot understand, including the humble followers of Christ and His teachings.

Our pride is manifest in selfishness, which is "much more than an ordinary problem because, as one of the seven deadly sins, it activates all of the others," such as envy, gluttony, greed, lust, sloth, and wrath. "It is the detonator in the breaking of the Ten Commandments. The selfish individual thus seeks to please not God, but himself. He will even break a covenant in order to satisfy an appetite." (Neal Maxwell, C.R., 10/1990).

People boasting in their own strength is a manifestation of pride that is so commonplace that it is almost overlooked. The treatment for this disease is: "Pour out your souls in your closets, and your secret places, and in your wilderness. Yea, and when you do not cry unto the Lord, let your hearts be full, drawn out in prayer continually." (Alma 34:26-27). The effectiveness of this treatment is profound, for those who pray to the Father continually are not likely to lose sight of their utter dependence on Him for both their temporal and spiritual welfare, nor will they forget from Whom both talents and blessings flow.

If we turn to the arm of flesh for security, we will not prosper for long. The best course, in such circumstances, is to immediately repent. We remember the example of the Nephites, for "no matter how wicked and ferocious and depraved the Lamanites might have been" observed Hugh Nibley, "no matter how much they outnumbered the Nephites, darkly closing in on all sides, no matter how insidiously they spied and intrigued and infiltrated and hatched their diabolical plots and breathed their bloody threats and pushed their formidable preparations for all out war, they were not the Nephite problem. They were merely kept there to remind the Nephites of their real problem, which was (the difficulty with which they managed) to walk uprightly before the Lord." ("Since Cumorah," p. 376).

The Nephites "saw that they had become weak, like unto their brethren, the

Lamanites, and that the Spirit of the Lord did no more preserve them; yea, it had withdrawn from them because the Spirit of the Lord doth not dwell in unholy temples. Therefore, the Lord did cease to preserve them by his miraculous and matchless power, for they had fallen into a state of unbelief and awful wickedness." (Helaman 4:24-25). This observation by Mormon is more than an editorial comment. It is a clarion call to those living in the Last Days to learn from the mistakes of the Nephites, and to turn to the Lord for the protection so vital in our own perilous times.

The past is prologue and The Book of Mormon is no mere recitation of history, and no detached chronicle of a people distant from our time and circumstances. It is critical that we understand the forces that have always acted upon societies, and will forever do so. Every prophet in both former and latter times has stressed the same message: "If ye keep (the) commandments, ye shall prosper in the land, but if ye keep not (the) commandments, ye shall be cut off from His presence." (Alma 37:13).

To Hyrum Smith, the Lord said: "Thy heart is opened, and thy tongue loosed. (V. 3). Those who have a pure heart and clean hands have the image of God engraven upon their countenances, that imply permanence. "Who shall ascend into the hill of the Lord," asked the Psalmist, "or who shall stand in his holy place: He that hath clean hands and a pure heart; who hath not lifted up his soul unto vanity, nor sworn deceitfully." (Psalms 24:4-5).

We become enemies to righteousness when we are carried away in pride and vanity, as evidenced by the wearing of costly apparel and setting our hearts upon the vain things of the world. These things have no lasting worth, and when they become the focus of our attention, we slide down a slippery slope toward the precipice of idol worship.

With his heart open and exposed to the influences of the Spirit, Hyrum Smith would avoid the pitfall of becoming "a one-dimensional man with a one-dimensional view of the world who would surely focus upon the cares of the world, yielding to the things of the moment." (Neal A. Maxwell, C.R., 10/1985). The gospel develops us completely and gives us a multidimensional view of existence that provides a much more accurate context in which we may exercise our agency. In this sense, the glory of God is intelligence, which is the ability to perceive both the physical and spiritual worlds around us, and engage in appropriate activities based on truth and founded on our realistic appreciation of both cause and effect.

The Savior introduced the doctrine of absolute equality within the church, recognizing that those who enjoy the benefits of membership do so because of the priesthood that makes available the ordinances of baptism and receipt of the Holy Ghost. Faith then matures unto salvation wherein we can "bring forth works which are meet for repentance." (Alma 5:54). Works that qualify us for repentance may include the ordinance of the Sacrament, and the ordinances associated with the temple. We cannot 'work' our way into heaven; it is completely beyond our power to do so. Instead, "it is by grace that we are saved, after all we can do." (2 Nephi 25:23).

"Thy calling," Hyrum was told, "is to exhortation, and to strengthen the church continually." (V. 3). Paul wrote: "When for the time ye ought to be teachers, ye have need that one teach you again which be the first principles of the oracles of God; and are become such as have need of milk, and not of strong meat." (Hebrews 5:12). In other words, new members of the church should be taught the first principles and basic doctrines of the gospel, in order to strengthen their faith and testimonies. The question that should always be in the minds of those to whom this stewardship responsibility falls is: "Are we giving our people skim milk, or 2% milk, or are we giving them rich, whole, fresh, fortified milk?"

We are on safe ground when the scriptures are the foundation of our teaching of key doctrine. Indeed, as Mormon observed of Alma's efforts: "And now, as the preaching of the word had a great tendency to lead the people to do that which was just; yea, it had had more powerful effect upon the minds of the people than the sword, or anything else which had happened unto them – therefore Alma though it was expedient that they should try the virtue of the word of God." (Alma 31:5).

After teaching key doctrine, it follows that we should extend an invitation to action, and finally describe promised blessings that are linked to obedience. As an example, let's look at the duty of the priest, and how the Lord has proposed that we train young men to teach key doctrine, extend an invitation to action, and describe promised blessings. Their duty is to "preach, teach, expound, exhort" and then to baptize and administer the sacrament. (D&C 20:46). The pertinent key doctrine is to preach and teach the first principles and ordinances of the Gospel, in that order; then to expound upon the principles taught, and extend an invitation to act upon the doctrine that has been presented. Finally, the duty of the priest is to extend an invitation to enjoy the promised blessings of obedience, namely baptism and the sacrament.

Alvin R. Dyer referred to invitations to action that necessarily follow the introduction of key doctrine, when he said: "We must not be caught in the bind of building a church and killing the articles of its faith, or permitting form to triumph over spirit. The Church and kingdom of God is built by the ardor and conviction of its members" to come unto Christ in tangible, meaningful, and purposeful ways.

Our teacher/mentors from the scriptures all taught key doctrine, extended calls to action, and described anticipated blessings in ways that made the effort seem worthwhile. Think of the heroes from The Book of Mormon like Nephi, Jacob, Benjamin, Abinadi, Alma, Mormon, Moroni, and those from the Bible, like Isaiah, Paul, Peter, James, and John, and latter-day heroes like Joseph Smith, Brigham Young and today's General Authorities.

"Wherefore thy duty is unto the church forever, and this because of thy family." (V. 3). The Lord was referring here to the fact that Hyrum Smith was to be the Patriarch to the Church, a calling he received on January 19, 1841. At that time, the Lord said: "Blessed is my servant Hyrum Smith; for I, the Lord, love him because of the integrity of his heart, and because he loveth that which is right before me." (D&C 124:15). At the same time, the Lord instructed Joseph Smith that his brother Hyrum should "take the office of Priesthood and Patriarch, which was appointed unto him by his father, by blessing and also by right. That from henceforth he shall hold the keys of the patriarchal blessings upon the heads of all my people, that whoever he blesses shall be blessed, and whoever he curses shall be cursed; that whatsoever he shall bind on hearth shall be bound in heaven; and whosoever he shall loose on earth shall be loosed in heaven. And from this time forth I appoint unto him that he may be a prophet, and a seer, and a revelator unto my church, as well as my servant Joseph; That he may act in concert also with my servant Joseph; and that he shall receive counsel from my servant Joseph, who shall show unto him the keys whereby he may ask and receive, and be crowned with the same blessing, and glory, and honor, and priesthood, and gifts of the priesthood, that once were put upon him that was my servant Oliver Cowdery; That my servant Hyrum may bear record of the things which I shall show unto him, that his name may be had in honorable remembrance from generation to generation, forever and ever." (D&C 124:91-95).

To Samuel Smith, the Lord said: "Thy calling is to exhortation, and to strengthen the church." (V. 3). At this time, Samuel was admonished to encourage the congregation of the faithful to want to incorporate the principles of the gospel into their own lives; to promote ownership through personal witness and testimony, and thus to validate the worth of the principles so taught. In doing so, Samuel would strengthen the resolve of the Saints to be obedient.

"Thou art not as yet called to preach before the world." (V. 4). Samuel was at this time just 23 years of age. He was one of the Eight Witnesses, and he would become the first missionary in this dispensation. Joseph Smith wrote: 'There are but a very few beings in the world who understand rightly the nature of God (and) if men do not understand the character of God they do not comprehend themselves." ("Teachings," p. 343). Samuel would soon join the ranks of the truly converted, and preach before the world with power and authority, declaring as did Ammon: God "is my life and my light, my joy and my salvation, and my redemption from everlasting wo." (Alma 26:35).

To the father of the Prophet, the Lord said: "Thy calling also is to exhortation, and to strengthen the church; and this is thy duty from henceforth and forever." (V. 5). Joseph Smith, Sr. was also ordained a Patriarch, which he claimed "by blessing and also by right." (D&C 124:91). "No man is authorized to act in the name of the Lord, or to officiate in any ordinance unless he has been properly called. For this reason, the priesthood was restored and the church organized." (Joseph Fielding Smith, Jr., "Church History and Modern Revelation," 1:57). As Paul taught: "No man taketh this honour unto himself, but he that is called of God." (Hebrews 5:12).

When Joseph Smith, Sr. was set apart to his calling in the church, the position became his. It didn't belong to anyone else, and no-one else had a right to it. If he had not done the job, it would not have been done. True, the Lord would have called another to maintain the integrity and organization of the church; nevertheless, positions in the church should be accepted with the intention to carry out the associated responsibilities as though our lives depend on it, as indeed they do.

It is amazing what can happen when we set our minds to a task. The secret of success is to accept positions without reservation and to magnify them with strong hearts. When we become church members, great benefits accrue to us, but when we get the spirit of the gospel into our bloodstream, that is when things really begin to happen. This burning zeal to serve God lifts us to greatness. It gives us authority over all our weaknesses, and over the defeats of life. Such was the case of Joseph Smith, Sr.

The Prophet's father knew that we are the children of Divinity who have within ourselves the seeds of greatness, for we have been endowed with the attributes of our Father. We are greater than we sometimes realize, and can call forth the powers of heaven through faithful activity. We can believe in, and fight for, the greatest truths and highest standards. Joseph Smith, Sr. knew that he was set apart because his was a work of eternal significance, carried out in partnership with his Creator. He was set apart by his convictions, enthusiasm, righteousness, and faith.

In other words, when he responded to an inspired call from the prophet and was set apart to carry out his assignment, when he earnestly sought the gifts necessary to succeed in the tasks at hand, and when he supported and sustained others in their callings, he became "a fellowcitizen with the Saints and with the household of God." (Ephesians 2:19). The system became perfect in the sight of the Lord Who headed the church, and to Whom he was ultimately accountable.

To Joseph Knight, the Lord said: "Take up your cross, in the which you must pray vocally before the world as well as in secret, and in your family, and among your friends, and in all places." (V. 6). "And now, for a man to take up his cross is to deny himself all ungodliness, and every worldly lust, and keep my commandments." (J.S.T. Matthew 16:25-26). Amazingly, Joseph Knight, Sr. was, at this time, not yet a member of the church, and so he enjoyed a unique blessing as the recipient of revelatory counsel provided by a prophet of the Lord. He was a Universalist with liberal views, and evidently found it hard to pray. But the Lord, Who is no respecter of persons, knew his heart, and therefore exhorted him: "Unite with the true church, and give your language to exhortation continually." (V. 7).

# Section 24
## (Instructions in 1830 to the newly organized church in New York).

"Though less than four months had elapsed since the church was organized, persecution had become intense, and the leaders had to seek safety in partial seclusion. The following three revelations were given at this time to strengthen, encourage, and instruct them." (Superscript to Section 24). When life's experiences bring us trials, if we are rooted deeply in gospel soil, maintaining an eternal perspective can ennoble even the most difficult moments. The physical discomforts we endure when we refuse to renounce our testimonies of the truth does not seem to be all that significant to God. His focus is ever on the preservation of the eternal life of our spirits.

Spencer W. Kimball taught: "If pain and sorrow and total punishment immediately followed the doing of evil, no soul would repeat a misdeed. If joy and peace and rewards were instantaneously given the doer of good, there could be no evil. All would do good, and not because of the rightness of doing good. There would be no test of strength, no development of character, no growth of powers, no agency, but only satanic controls. If all the sick were healed, if all the righteous were protected, and the wicked destroyed, the whole program of the Father would be annulled and the basic principle of the gospel, agency, would be ended." ("Faith Precedes The Miracle," p. 97-98).

It would be wrong to assume that the more righteous we are, the less adversity we must endure. The promise is that we will be blessed even though our blessing may be only the strength to endure. All suffer. The difference is that the wicked must suffer the consequences of sin, in addition to the suffering that is a part of the mortal experience. Marion G. Romney once said: "If we can bear our afflictions with understanding, faith, and courage, we shall be strengthened and comforted and spared the torment which accompanies the mistaken idea that all suffering comes as a chastisement for transgression." (C.R., 10/1964).

"Thou wast called and chosen to write The Book of Mormon." (V. 1). Envisioning the Last Days, Mormon wrote: "Ye need not any longer spurn at the doings of the Lord." (3 Nephi 29:4). To spurn something is to 'ignore scornfully, to refuse, or to trample.' For almost 200 years, the world has tried very hard to ignore, to trivialize, to ridicule, or to distain The Book of Mormon. But our latter day church leaders have echoed the prophecies of Mormon, and put great emphasis on the witness of Christ found throughout the pages of The Book of Mormon. They have cautioned that if church members neglect to gain a testimony of the principles and doctrines found within its pages, they are "placing their souls in jeopardy, and neglecting that which could give spiritual and intellectual unity to their lives." (Ezra Taft Benson, C.R., 4/1986).

President Benson's caution applies equally to those who are not members of the church. The world, quite simply, needs The Book of Mormon. It was "written to the Lamanites, who are a remnant of the house of Israel; and also to Jew and Gentile." ("Title Page to The Book of Mormon"). Why was it preserved for our day, and why was its publication worth such great personal sacrifice? It is because the world's people need, more than anything else in their lives, spiritual and intellectual unity.

"Where will you find another work remotely approaching The Book of Mormon in scope and daring? It appears suddenly out of nothing - not an accumulation of 25 years like the Koran, but a single staggering performance, bursting on a shocked and scandalized world like an explosion, the full-blown history of an ancient people, following them through all the trials, triumphs, and vicissitudes of a thousand years without a break, telling how a civilization originated, rose to momentary greatness, and passed away, giving due attention to every phase of civilized history in a densely compact and rapidly moving story that interweaves dozens of plots with an inexhaustible fertility of invention and an uncanny consistency that is never caught in a slip or a contradiction. As a sheer tour-de-force there is nothing like it." (Hugh Nibley, "Since Cumorah," p. 156-157).

"Magnify thine office. And thou shalt continue in calling upon God in my name, and writing the things which shall be given thee by the Comforter, and expounding all scriptures unto the church. And it shall be given thee in the very moment what thou shalt speak and write." (V. 2, 5 & 6). Joseph Smith said: "I thank God that I have got this old book (as he held up the Bible) but I thank him more for the gift of the Holy Ghost. I have got the oldest book in the world, but I (also) have the oldest book in my heart, even the gift of the Holy Ghost." ("Teachings," p. 349).

The Lord explained the process to Joseph by asking: "He that is ordained of me and sent forth to preach the word of truth by the Comforter, in the Spirit of truth, doth he preach it by the Spirit of truth or some other way? And if it be by some other way it is not of God. And again, he that receiveth the word of truth, doth he receive it by the Spirit of truth or some other way? If it be some other way it is not of God." (D&C 50:17-20).

As Paul taught, the key to gospel knowledge is personal revelation, and "let him be accursed who preaches any other gospel." (Galatians 1:8-12). "That which is of God is light; and he that receiveth light, and continueth in God, receiveth more light: and that light groweth brighter and brighter until the perfect day." (D&C 50:24).

"For thou shalt devote all thy service in Zion; and in this thou shalt have strength." (V. 7). Those who have no personal agenda to follow are less likely to lead others into unrighteousness. Rather, they are more easily oriented toward obedience. As King Benjamin declared: "When ye are in the service of your fellow beings, ye are only in the service of your God." (Mosiah 2:17).

The Creator does not generally intervene personally in our affairs, nor is He typically served directly. The Savior set the pattern when He declared: "Verily I say unto you, inasmuch as ye have done it unto one of the least of these my brethren, ye have done it unto me." (Matthew 25:40). We should all focus on what C.S. Lewis called "acts of quiet Christianity," which is charitable service for which there is no recognition, recompense, or thought of reciprocation.

"Be patient in afflictions, for thou shalt have many, but endure them, for, lo, I am with thee, even unto the end of thy days." (V. 8). "Ye need not suppose that ye can turn the right hand of the Lord unto the left." (3 Nephi 29:9). "What power shall stay the heavens? As well might man stretch forth his puny arm to stop the Missouri river in its decreed course, or to turn it upstream, as to hinder the Almighty from pouring down knowledge from heaven upon the heads of the Latter-day Saints." (D&C 121:33).

"Declare my gospel as with the voice of a trump." (V. 12). Trumpets were used anciently to sound the alarm and signal for battle, or to announce the coming of royalty. "Blow ye the trumpet in Zion, and sound an alarm in my holy mountain: let all the inhabitants of the land tremble: for the day of the Lord cometh." (Joel 2:1-2). It will be a day of thick darkness and gloominess for the wicked, when even the sun and the moon and the stars of heaven obey the voice of the Master. "For the stars of heaven and the constellations thereof shall not give their light; the sun shall be darkened in his going forth, and the moon shall not cause her light to shine." (Isaiah 13:10). The purpose of the day of the Lord is to "destroy the sinners thereof" out of the land. (Isaiah 13:9). They will be punished for arrogance, haughtiness, iniquity, and pride, and because they have failed to repent.

In that day, a righteous man will be "more precious than fine gold." (Isaiah 13:12). This might be because they are few in number, or it could be because the true value of righteousness will stand out in sharp contrast to the inconsequential treasures of the earth. Even the wealth of the Golden Wedge of Ophir is insignificant when compared to one righteous individual. (See Isaiah 13:12).

"Require not miracles, except I shall command you." (V. 13). "Yea, and wo unto him that shall say at that day, to get gain, that there can be no miracle wrought by Jesus Christ; for he that doeth this shall become like unto the son of perdition, for whom there was no mercy, according to the word of Christ!" (3 Nephi 29:7). It will be difficult for those who have lived a telestial existence in the Last Days to justify their actions before God, in light of the many signs He has provided as warnings. These wonders "are kingdoms, and any man who hath seen any or the least of these hath seen God moving in his majesty and power." (D&C 88:47). Earth, in fact, "is crammed with heaven, and every common bush with fire of God. But only those who see, take off their shoes. The rest stand around picking blackberries." (Elizabeth Barrett Browning).

"And in whatsoever place you shall enter and they receive you not in my name, ye shall leave a cursing instead of a blessing, by casting off the dust of your feet against them as a testimony, and cleansing your feet by the wayside." (V. 15). Cursing, as well as blessing, may be administered by the power and authority of the priesthood. The Lord told Joseph Smith that his brother Hyrum would hold such power in the priesthood, "that whoever he blesses shall be blessed, and whoever he curses shall be cursed." (D&C 124:93, see D&C 75:20). Those who have rejected the truth are on their own. "Behold, I sent you out to testify and warn the people, and it becometh every man who hath been warned to warn his neighbor. Therefore, they are left without excuse, and their sins are upon their own heads." (D&C 88:81-82).

"And it shall come to pass that whosoever shall lay their hands upon you by violence, ye shall command to be smitten in my name; and, behold, I will smite them according to your words, in mine own due time." (V. 16). Eight years after the receipt of this revelation, when Joseph was a prisoner in Liberty Jail, incarcerated for months on false charges, and subjected to the repeated verbal abuse of his guards, he was finally moved to stand and declare: 'Silence, ye fiends of the infernal pit. In the name of Jesus Christ, I rebuke you, and command you to be still. I will not live another minute and hear such language. Cease such talk, or your or I die this instant.'

"He ceased to speak. He stood erect in terrible majesty, chained, and without a weapon, calm, unruffled, and dignified as an angel. He looked down upon his quailing guards, whose knees smote together, and who, shrinking into a corner, or crouching at his feet, begged his pardon, and remained quiet until an exchange of guards.

I have seen ministers of justice," declared Parley P. Pratt, who was the witness to this scene, "clothed in ministerial robes and criminals arraigned before them, while life was suspended upon a breath in the courts of England. I have witnessed a Congress in solemn session to give laws to nations. I have tried to conceive of kings, of royal courts, of thrones and crowns, and of emperors assembled to decide the fate of kingdoms, but dignity and majesty have I seen but once, as it stood in chains, at midnight, in a dungeon, in an obscure village in Missouri." ("Autobiography," p. 210-211).

Jacob Bronowski wrote: "We are all afraid - for our confidence, for the future, for the world. That is the nature of the human imagination. Yet, every man, every civilization, has gone forward because of its engagement with what it has set itself to do. The personal commitment of a man to his skill, the intellectual and emotional commitment working together as one, has made the Ascent of Man." ("The Ascent of Man," p. 438).

The religious commitment of the servants of God casts our potential in a new light, and opens to our minds a profoundly deeper perspective. Someone once said of Joseph Smith: "One of his greatest contributions was his knowledge of what is to come after death. He did much to clarify our understanding of heaven, and to make it seem worth working for."

"For thou art called to prune my vineyard with a mighty pruning, yea, even for the last time." (V. 19). The vineyard is the world, and its pruning is equivalent to the call to repentance. The vineyard in the Last Days has been corrupted by the haughtiness and pride of the world, because people tend to raise themselves above the word of the Lord, and "look beyond the mark" that is Jesus Christ. (See Jacob 4:14).

It is also corrupted, unfortunately, because some members of the church pay no heed to the teachings of the gospel, but follow their own agenda, and redefine their standards on the shifting sands of expediency, rather than relying upon the unchangeable bedrock of Christ. It is because even church members sometimes exercise unrighteous dominion. It is because we sometimes try to bring the world into the gospel, rather than the gospel into the world. Section 24 of the Doctrine & Covenants was designed to instill comfort, cheer, and hope within the little flock of Saints who had been sent as "sheep in the midst of wolves," in circumstances that have seemed distant to our experience, but that are now increasingly, and more uncomfortably, familiar to us. (Matthew 10:16).

# Section 25
## (Instructions in 1830 to Emma Smith, and the newly organized church in New York).

"This revelation manifests the will of the Lord to Emma Smith, the Prophet's wife." (Superscript to Section 25). When this revelation was given, Emma was 26 years old, and had been married to Joseph for 3 years. "I have never seen a woman in my life," wrote her mother-in-law, "who would endure every species of fatigue, and hardship, from month to month, and from year to year, with that unflinching courage, zeal, and patience, which she has ever done; for I know that which she has had to endure. She has breasted the storms of persecution, and buffeted the rage of men and devils, which would have borne down almost any other woman." (Lucy Mack Smith, "History of Joseph Smith," p. 190).

"All those who receive my gospel are sons and daughters in my kingdom." (V. 1). King Benjamin told his people that because of their covenant with God, they would "be called the children of Christ, his sons and his daughters." (Mosiah 5:7). Just as we are known by the name of our mortal parents, so too are we called by the name of Christ in a familial way.

There is a special relationship reserved for the faithful that is in addition to the reality that we are all spirit children of our Father. "For this day He hath spiritually begotten you," explained Benjamin. (Mosiah 5:7). Those who enter into the Covenant are thus born of him. A "Born Again Christian" is one who is in a covenant relationship with the Lord.

We are also Christ's children in the sense that He united our body and spirit through the Resurrection and the Atonement. We are raised from physical death by the power of the Resurrection, and from spiritual death by the power of the Atonement. "Surely he hath borne our griefs and carried our sorrows." (Mosiah 14:4). He was "offered to bear the sins of many." (Hebrews 9:28).

We are born of God when He gives birth to our spiritual nature. We are born of Him when we are introduced to righteousness, bear hardship, and endure the refiner's fire. We are born of Him as we carry the testimony of Jesus in our hearts. We are born of Him as we witness the creation of a new heaven, and a new earth, and bear that witness to others. We are born of God at sacred altars in the House of the Lord.

God's reach extends to all of His children. His grace is granted unto us proportionately as we conform to the standards of personal righteousness that are part of His gospel plan. Thus, the Saints are commanded to "grow in grace" (D&C 50:40) until they are sanctified and justified "through the grace of our Lord and Savior Jesus Christ." (D&C 20:30-32).

"I am the resurrection and the life," declared the Savior. "He that believeth in me, though he were dead, yet shall he live." (John 11:25). Jacob understood these principles, when he said: "Wherefore, may God raise you from death by the power of the resurrection, and also from everlasting death by the power of the Atonement, that ye may be received into the eternal kingdom of God, that ye may praise him through grace divine." (2 Nephi 10:25).

Emma Smith was told: "Thou art an elect lady." (V. 3). The elect are chosen, or set apart, to a specific work in the kingdom. In 1842, Emma would become the first President of the Female Relief Society of Nauvoo. Today, the Relief Society has become one of the largest women's organizations in the world, with over 6 million members, and chapters in over 170 countries. But neither baptism nor position in the church or its auxiliaries would assure Emma, or anyone else for that matter, of eternal life. Members of the church and of the Relief Society need to be "steadfast and immovable, always abounding in good works." (Mosiah 5:15). "By their works ye shall know them, for if their works be good, then they are good also." (Moroni 7:5).

We all need to be sealed by the ratifying power of the Holy Spirit of Promise which is the Holy Ghost. (See D&C 88:3-4). Our calling and election is made sure only after the Lord has fully proven us. Then, when we receive "the other Comforter," Christ will appear and personally teach us the visions of eternity. (D&C 88:3-4).

Emma was counseled: "Murmur not because of the things which thou hast not seen, for they are withheld from thee and from the world." (V. 4). Before this revelation was given, Emma had been upset that she had not been chosen to be one of the Special Witnesses of The Book of Mormon. After all, she had been a scribe to her husband during his translation of the sacred text.

But her murmuring has been the subdued and continually repeated expression of indistinct or inarticulate complaint or grumbling, and she was flirting with serious danger. It is no trifling thing when the disobedient murmur against the teachings of the prophets. Murmuring by otherwise active members of the church can be detrimental not only to individuals, but also to families, wards, and stakes of Zion.

In a positive way, Emma was counseled: "The office of thy calling shall be for a comfort unto my servant, Joseph Smith, Jun., thy husband." (V. 5). The Lord knew that if Emma could remain faithful to her covenants, the blessings of the Patriarchal Priesthood could be hers to share with her husband in the mansions of their Father. That unity would later be facilitated by the administration of gospel ordinances in the temple, where God's children enter into the patriarchal order of celestial marriage, and are organized into eternal family units.

It is within the family that we learn to govern ourselves temporally and spiritually. It is within its context that we covenant to consecrate our time and talents to the church and kingdom, and to lend our efforts to the preparation of the earth for the millennial reign of Jesus Christ. What greater calling could Emma have had, than to assist her husband to honor his priesthood responsibilities, so that together they could enjoy the blessings reserved for the faithful?

"And thou shalt...be unto him for a scribe." (V. 6). "My belief is that the Book of Mormon is of divine authenticity," Emma later declared to her son. "I have not the slightest doubt of it. I am satisfied that no man could have dictated the writing of the manuscript unless he was inspired; for, when (I was) acting as his scribe, your father would dictate to me hour after hour; and when returning after meals, or after interruptions, he would at once begin where he had left off, without either seeing the manuscript or having any portion of it read to him. It would have been improbable that a learned man could do this; and, for one so...unlearned as he was, it was simply impossible." (Quoted by Victor Ludlow, in "Book of Mormon Companion.").

"And thou shalt be ordained under his hand to expound scriptures, and to exhort the church. For he shall lay his hands upon thee, and thou shalt receive the Holy Ghost, and thy time shall be given to writing, and to learning much." (V. 7-8). Only later in the church was the distinction made between "ordination" and "setting apart." In this instance, "ordained" should be construed to mean "set apart" as that term is presently understood.

Although Paul wrote: "Let your women keep silence in the churches: for it is not permitted unto them to speak. ...For it is a shame for women to speak in the church.," the J.S.T. renders the word "speak" as "rule," which significantly changes the meaning, and makes sense to Latter-day Saints who understand more clearly the principles associated with priesthood authority, the power of administration, and the power to preside. (1 Corinthians 14:34-35).

"Thou shalt lay aside the things of this world, and seek for the things of a better." (V. 10). Worldly behavior harmonizes with a lack of spiritual understanding, and so whatever comfort or pleasure is derived from wicked ways is destined to be short-lived. We can only conduct our lives in opposition to the laws of heaven for so long, before "critical mass" is reached.

At that point, a readjustment is required, bringing errant individuals back into harmony with nature. Sometimes the separation of the physical body from the spirit is required, so great has been the violation of law, and so entrenched is the unwillingness to change. In the end, the principle that Alma taught his son Corianton is always validated: "Wickedness never was happiness." (Alma 41:10).

"And it shall be given thee, also, to make a selection of sacred hymns, as it shall be given thee, which is pleasing unto me, to be had in my church." (V. 11). Its first edition, published in 1835, contained 90 hymns, and consisted of 120 pages. It included words only; there was no music. Similarly, the psalms of David, in the Book of Psalms that has been preserved in the Old Testament, were not set to music, either.

"For my soul delighteth in the song of the heart; yea, the song of the righteous is a prayer unto me." (V. 12). Prayer takes many forms, and may involve just one person or an entire congregation. One of the most beautiful manifestations of prayer is that which is found in lyrics that have been set to music. The structure of meetings in the church permits only a few individuals to take an active part, but one thing that everyone can do is participate in congregational hymns. When the songs of Zion are sung, the Spirit of God burns like a fire.

The song of the heart may be inaudible, but its melody can brighten our day and lighten our burdens just as effectively as would a choir of angels. As Hugh B. Brown said: "Sometimes during solitude I hear truth spoken with clarity and freshness; uncolored and untranslated it speaks from with myself in a language original but inarticulate heard only with the soul."

When filled with gratitude, our hearts can burst into song as did the angels in heaven at the birth of the Savior: "And suddenly there was with the angel a multitude of the heavenly host praising God, and saying, Glory to God in the highest, and on earth peace, good will toward men." (Luke 2:13-14).

The scriptures can bring understanding to the depths of our hearts, which then resonate with the harmony of truth: "Where wast thou when I laid the foundations of the earth? When the morning stars sang together, and all the sons of God shouted for joy?" (Job 38:4 & 7).

The testimonies of the prophets can stir the sensitive chords of our spirits as would a symphony. Bruce R. McConkie softly and yet with a powerful melodic rhythm bore his last testimony: "In a coming day," he said, "I shall feel the nail marks in his hands and in his feet and shall wet his feet with my tears. But I shall not know any better then than I know now that he is God's Almighty Son, that he is our Savior and Redeemer, and that salvation comes in and through his atoning blood and in no other way." ("Ensign," 6/1975).

"Continue in the spirit of meekness, and beware of pride." (V. 14). The meek are not weak, but are instead those who neither take nor give offense. When faced with the challenge of adversity, they become "Pro-Gospel" rather than "Anti-Enemy." The meek delight in the grace of God, for they understand what the Lord meant when He said: "If men come unto me I will show unto them their weakness. I give unto men weakness that they may be humble; and my grace is sufficient for all men that humble themselves before me; for if they humble themselves before me, and have faith in me, then will I make weak things become strong unto them." (Ether 12:27). Those who develop the quality of meekness will qualify to inherit the celestialized earth.

"Keep my commandments continually, and a crown of righteousness thou shalt receive. And except thou do this, where I am you cannot come. And verily, verily, I say unto you, that this is my voice unto all." (V. 15-16). Nephi taught: "If ye shall press forward" with complete dedication, "feasting upon the word of Christ" or receiving physical and spiritual strength and nourishment, "and endure to the end" with continuing responsibility and accountability, "behold, thus saith the Father: Ye shall have eternal life," which is the greatest of God's gifts. (2 Nephi 31:20).

# Section 26

## (Instructions given in 1830, to the newly organized church in New York).

"Let your time be devoted to the studying of the scriptures, and to preaching, and to confirming the church at Colesville." (V. 1). God's ways can only be understood by the spirit of revelation, and by prayerful study of His word. The scriptures are an excellent path to a testimony of Jesus, and the love of God and scripture study go hand in hand.

When the two verses of this revelation were given, the church had been organized for just over three months. The dream of the Reformer Roger Williams had been fulfilled. After carefully studying the various denominations of his day, he had written: "There is no regularly constituted church on earth, nor any person authorized to administer any church ordinance, nor can there be, until new apostles are sent by the Great Head of the church, for Whose Coming I am seeking." (Quoted by William Cullan Bryant, in "Picturesque America," p. 502).

And all things shall be done by common consent in the church, by much prayer and faith, for all things you shall receive by faith." (V. 2, see Mosiah 29:26). Common consent involves the recognition that the righteous exercise of agency allows us to progress to ultimate salvation, for "no man can preside in this church in any capacity without the consent of the people." (Joseph Fielding Smith, Jr., "Doctrines of Salvation," 3:123, see D&C 20:65).

Abraham Lincoln said that you can fool some of the people some of the time, and you can fool some of the people all of the time, but you cannot fool all of the people all of the time. King Mosiah put it another way: "It is not common that the voice of the people desireth anything contrary to that which is right; but it is common for the lesser part of the people to desire that which is not right; therefore this shall ye observe and make it your law - to do your business by the voice of the people." (Mosiah 29:26).

This is the value of a "democratic" system. Inherent in this law is a warning, however. If the voice of the people chooses iniquity, the Lord will visit them with great destruction. (See Mosiah 29:27). Today, we recognize "iniquity" as legalized abortion, prostitution, pornography, gambling, Sabbath-breaking, filth on television and in motion pictures, corruption in the music industry, dishonesty in the market place, violence in society, a homogenization of standards in the spoken and written word, and so on.

"The world," after all, "seeks not the Lord to establish his righteousness, but every man walketh in his own way and after the image of his own god, whose image is in the likeness of the world, and whose substance is that of an idol which waxeth old and shall perish in Babylon, even Babylon the Great, which shall fall." (D&C 1:16).

"Freedom," you see, "does not mean the freedom to exploit law in order to destroy it. It is not freedom which permits the Trojan Horse to be wheeled within the gates, and those within it to be heard in the name of tolerating a different point of view." (Taylor Caldwell, "Pillar of Iron," p. 511). "No people can maintain freedom unless their political institutions are founded upon faith in God and belief in the existence of moral law. God has endowed us with certain inalienable rights and no legislature and no majority, however great, may morally limit or destroy those." (Ezra Taft Benson, "The American Challenge"). "Democracy," in Churchill's marvelous words, "is indeed the worst form of government ever tried, with the exception, only, of all the others." (Speech in the House of Commons, 11/11/1947).

When a leader is sustained by the voice of the people, personal accountability prevails, and if they later commit sins and iniquities, they are answered upon their own heads. The scriptures reinforce this concept of individual responsibility. They stress equality among all the members of the church. These scriptures focus on the philosophies of agency, accountability, individual liberty, and independence within the context of the gospel.

The issue of "independence" is charged with special emotion for Americans. The word, however, occurs only once in the scriptures, (D&C 78:14), and in that context describes the church as a body, and has no reference to individuals. The church, moreover, can "stand independent above all creatures" only because it is entirely dependent upon the providence of God. As King Benjamin taught, when we serve God with our whole heart and soul, we are free from dependence upon any other being. Our indebtedness to God, however, is transferred by Him to the poor (in spirit?), and it is through them that He asks us to pay our debt to Him. Thus, is a Zion society created.

No other religion puts so much stress upon the worth of the individual. It is the ultimate value, and the church is the instrument for its development. The family is the highest expression within the church of individual life. It is the foundation for individual and collective happiness on earth, and is the basic building block of eternal life.

# Section 27
## (Instructions in 1830 to the newly organized church in New York, received from an angel).

"In preparation for a religious service at which the sacrament of bread and wine was to be administered, Joseph set out to procure wine for the occasion. He was met by a heavenly messenger and received this revelation, a portion of which was written at this time, and the remainder in the September following." As a result of the instruction given by the angel, "water is now used instead of wine in the sacramental services of the church." (Superscript).

"It mattereth not what ye shall eat or what ye shall drink when ye partake of the sacrament," instructed the angel, speaking by divine investiture of authority, "if it so be that ye do it with an eye single to my glory - remembering unto the Father my body which was laid down for you, and my blood which was shed for the remission of your sins." (V. 2). This revelation stresses the simplicity of the ordinance of the Sacrament, emphasizing that it does not matter what we drink, as long as we do it in sincerity with an eye single to the glory of God.

The important thing to remember is that during the Sacrament, the Spirit clears our minds, and impels us to see things unambiguously. In contrast, think of our preparation for the holidays, and the strings of lights that we often hang under the eaves of our homes. As we take them out of the boxes in which they have been stuffed the previous winter, and attempt to unravel them, we often realize that we are faced with a hopelessly tangled mess. We can compare that Gordian Knot of wires and bulbs with the cacophony of the "Christmas Lights of Confusion" that are so prevalent in the world today.

As we partake of the emblems of Christ, we understand that wine is only symbolical of the redeeming blood of Christ. It does not become His blood through a mystical transformation, as many would believe. The Catholic doctrine of transubstantiation is false. The emblems of the Sacrament, whether water or wine, only serve to focus our attention where it belongs: on the Son of God and His sacrifice for us, and on the covenant we have made with Him at the waters of baptism.

It should also be pointed out that this revelation was given some two and a half years before the revelation known as The Word of Wisdom was received. The church did not adopt the practice of using water in place of wine because of the Word of Wisdom, although the two are related. In each case, intervention by the Lord was prompted by the evil designs of conspiring men who would go to any length to destroy the order of the church.

It is the purpose of the Sacrament to recommit ourselves by priesthood ordinance to the covenant of baptism, and to receive the Spirit of God so that we might more surely hold fast to the rod of iron. If the purpose of the Sacrament were to obtain a remission of our sins, it would not be forbidden to those of us in greatest need.

The reason that those who partake without repentance drink damnation to their souls is that their lack of proper prior priesthood-directed preparation blocks the channels through which spiritual power flows. It is the consequent halt in progression that is damning to the individual.

Conversely, this is why partaking of the Sacrament in worthiness conveys great power to the penitent. Heavenly Father has blessed us with an ordinance specifically designed to allow us to approach Him, that we might reaffirm our baptismal covenant, and that His promises to us might be freely fulfilled.

Through Joseph Smith, He said: "Let thy bowels also be full of charity towards all men, and to the household of faith, and let virtue garnish thy thoughts unceasingly; then shall thy confidence wax strong in the presence of God; and the doctrine of the priesthood shall distill upon thy soul as the dews from heaven. The Holy Ghost shall be thy constant companion, and thy scepter an unchanging scepter of righteousness and truth; and thy dominion shall be an everlasting dominion, and without compulsory means it shall flow unto thee forever and ever." (D&C 121:45-46).

The covenants we make with God reflect His attributes. God is moral, so He gives us the Covenant of Chastity; He has charity, so He commands us to love Him and each other. God is disciplined, so He gives us the Law of Obedience; because He is a righteous steward, He gives us the Law of Consecration. Because He loves His less fortunate children, He gives us the Law of the Fast.

Because His is a perfected, resurrected body, He gives us the Word of Wisdom. Because He is omniscient, He gives us the commandment to seek knowledge. In consequence of the Gift of His Son, He gives us the Law of Sacrifice. Because He rested from His labors on the seventh day, He gives us the Law of the Sabbath. Because He is Holy, He has given us the ordinance of the Sacrament.

God is our Father, and He is perfect in every way. He could give us everything He has, but what He is, we must earn for ourselves, as we struggle to overcome adversity and gain self-mastery. "Spirituality," David O. McKay was fond of saying, "is the consciousness of victory over self, and of communion with the infinite." (C.R., 10/1969). Our sacramental covenant helps us to focus our efforts to become as He is. This is its purpose. If it were not possible to become as God is, it would be unnecessary to make covenants with Him. We only partake of the emblems of the Sacrament because we want to be like our Father in Heaven.

"You shall not purchase wine neither strong drink of your enemies; wherefore, you shall partake of none except it is made new among you." (V. 3-4). In response to the wicked and evil designs that existed in the hearts of his conspiring enemies, the Prophet Joseph Smith received this revelation, regarding the use of wine in the Sacrament.

He later wrote: "Early in the month of August (1830) Newel Knight and his wife paid us a visit at my place in Harmony, Pennsylvania; and as neither his wife nor mine had been as yet confirmed, it was proposed that we should confirm them, and partake together of the Sacrament, before he and his wife should leave us. In order to prepare for this I set out to procure some wine for the occasion, but had gone only a short distance when I was met by a heavenly messenger, and received the following revelation." (D&C 27).

What was the nature of the wine used in ancient times? There is little doubt that Jesus and His disciples drank fermented wine, and not 'new wine' as so many Latter-day Saints would naively believe. There is nothing inherently wrong with drinking wine; the Word of Wisdom was only given "in consequence of the evils and designs which do and will exist in the hearts of conspiring men in the last days," who would subvert the drinking of spirits to suit the wicked purposes of the adversary. (D&C 89:4). That this is occurring today is readily attested by even a cursory review of the media, where the consumption of alcoholic beverages is glorified almost beyond imagination.

After he delivered the word of the Lord to Joseph Smith, the angel indicated to him that he would enjoy the sweet companionship of many of those who had fulfilled assignments of great responsibility relative to the restoration of the gospel. Among these would be the angel "Moroni, whom I have sent unto you to reveal The Book of Mormon, containing the fulness of my everlasting gospel, to whom I have committed the keys of the record of the stick of Ephraim." (V. 5, see D&C 20:9 & 42:12).

As John the Revelator witnessed in vision: "And I saw another angel fly in the midst of heaven, having the everlasting gospel to preach unto them that dwell on the earth, and to every nation, kindred, tongue, and people, saying with a loud voice, Fear God, and give glory to him; for the hour of his judgment is come: and worship him that made heaven, and earth, and the sea, and the fountains of water." (Revelation 14:6-7).

Joseph would commune with Elias, to whom had been "committed the keys of bringing to pass the restoration of all things spoken by the mouth of all the holy prophets since the world began, concerning the last days." (V. 6). "The title 'Elias' has...been applied to many...for specific missions or restorative functions that they are to fulfill." ("Bible Dictionary," p. 663).

The keys that are referred to in this revelation relate to those that were necessary to re-establish the Abrahamic Covenant in The Dispensation of The Fulness of Times. It was Elias who appeared to Joseph Smith in the Kirtland Temple, on April 3, 1836, and restored the priesthood keys relating to "the dispensation of the gospel of Abraham." (D&C 110:12).

The angel also mentioned "John, the son of Zacharias, (whom) I have sent unto you...to ordain you unto the first priesthood." (V. 7-8). Laying his hands upon the heads of Joseph Smith and Oliver Cowdery, who knelt before him, John had pronounced the words of the ordinance: "Upon you my fellow servants, in the name of Messiah, I confer the Priesthood of Aaron." (D&C 13). John was a legal administrator whose words and acts were binding on earth and in heaven, and his hearers were obligated, at the peril of their salvation, to believe his words and heed his counsel.

Just who had sent John to baptize in the wilderness we do not know. (John 1:33). But we know that the ordinance was not unfamiliar to the Jews of the day. (See D&C 84:28). It is not clear when he received the Aaronic Priesthood, but obviously, it came to him after his own baptism, at whatever age was then proper, and before he was sent by one whom he does not name to preach repentance and baptize with water.

When he appeared to Joseph Smith and Oliver Cowdery on the banks of the Susquehanna River on May 15, 1829, "he acted under the direction of Peter, James and John, who held the keys of the Priesthood of Melchizedek." (J.S.H. 1:72). The priesthood authority they exercised is "the only legitimate authority on the earth," and Joseph and Oliver were similarly bound to follow his counsel. (John Taylor, J.D., 5:157).

The angel then referred to "Elijah, unto whom I have committed the keys of the power of turning the hearts of the fathers to the children, and the hearts of the children to the fathers, that the whole earth may not be smitten with a curse." (V. 9). Malachi's prophecy concerning these keys and covenants was fulfilled April 3, 1836, which, in that year, happened to coincide with the Passover.

During the Paschal service each year, the door in Jewish homes is opened, and a place is set at the table with a vacant chair. This is done in order to be ready to admit Elijah so that, as the forerunner of the Messiah, he might partake of the Passover Feast. When Elijah appeared to Joseph Smith in the Kirtland Temple, he declared: "The keys of this dispensation are committed into your hands; and by this ye may know that the great and dreadful day of the Lord is near, even at the door." (D&C 110:16).

Elijah explained that "the time has fully come, which was spoken by the mouth of Malachi - testifying that he (Elijah) should be sent, before the great and dreadful day of the Lord come - To turn the hearts of the fathers to the children, and the children to the fathers, lest the whole earth be smitten with a curse." (D&C 110:14-15).

Elijah, said Spencer W. Kimball, "held the keys of the authority to administer in all the ordinances of the priesthood, (and especially the sealing ordinances), and without this authority that is given, the ordinances could not be administered in righteousness." (See Joseph Fielding Smith, "Doctrines of Salvation," 2:113).

The day when the Lord comes will be at once great and dreadful. For the righteous, it is the joyous day when Christ will come in power and glory; for the disobedient, it is when He will take vengeance upon the wicked and cleanse the earth of all unrighteousness. The Doctrine & Covenants emphasizes the Covenant made anciently with Abraham, Isaac, and Jacob. Because of the priesthood keys that Elijah delivered to the Prophet Joseph Smith, the blessings associated with obedience would be available to the faithful Saints in the Last Days.

Many prophets had held similar keys, but the reason that Elijah was reserved for this mission was that he was the last prophet to hold the fulness of the power of the priesthood. If God had not sent him to deliver these keys to Joseph Smith, "the whole earth would (have been) utterly wasted at his coming." (D&C 2:3). The Plan of Salvation would have been thwarted, for there would have been no sealing power to eternally bind the faithful, by covenant, to the ordinances of the gospel.

A righteous people must be prepared to meet Christ, or literally the whole population of the earth will be wasted at the Second Coming. The sealing power rests with the Melchizedek Priesthood, that "administereth the gospel and holdeth the key of the mysteries of the kingdom, even the key of the knowledge of God. Therefore, in the ordinances thereof, the power of godliness is manifest. And without the ordinances thereof, and the authority of the priesthood, the power of godliness is not manifest unto men in the flesh, for without this no man can see the face of God, even the Father, and live." (D&C 84:19-22).

Even though the Jews have waited in vain for Elijah, the purposes of God will not be thwarted. "No power on earth or hell can overthrow or defeat that which God has decreed. Every plan of the adversary will fail, for the Lord knows the secret thoughts of men, and sees the future with a vision clear and perfect, even as though it were in the past." (Joseph Fielding Smith, Jr., "Church History and Modern Revelation," 1:26).

The angel then spoke of "Joseph and Jacob, and Isaac, and Abraham, your fathers, by whom the promises remain." (V. 10). The promises of the Abrahamic Covenant have been preserved for those in the Last Days, and are recorded in The Book of Abraham. "My name is Jehovah," the Savior explained, "and I know the end from the beginning; therefore my hand shall be over thee. And I will make of thee a great nation, and I will bless thee above measure, and make thy name great among all nations, and thou shalt be a blessing unto thy seed after thee, that in their hands they shall bear this ministry and Priesthood unto all nations."

The Savior continued: "And I will bless them through thy name; for as many as receive His gospel shall be called after thy name, and shall be accounted thy seed, and shall rise up and bless thee, as their father; And I will bless them that bless thee, and curse them that curse thee; and in thee (that is, in thy Priesthood) and in thy seed (that is, thy Priesthood), for I give unto thee a promise that this right shall continue in thee, and in thy seed after thee (that is to say, the literal seed, or the seed of the body) shall all the families of the earth be blessed, even with the blessings of the gospel, which are the blessings of salvation, even of life eternal." (Abraham 2:8-11).

The blessings of the Covenant include, but are not limited to, the priesthood, eternal marriage, and a land of inhabitance. The temple and the authority vested in the Melchizedek Priesthood make these blessings possible. "Those portions of the Abrahamic Covenant which pertain to personal exaltation and eternal increase are renewed with each member of the House of Israel who enters the order of celestial marriage. Through that order, the participating parties become inheritors of all the blessings of Abraham, Isaac, and Jacob. (Bruce R. McConkie, "Mormon Doctrine," p. 13-14).

The angel then identified "Michael, or Adam, the father of all, the prince of all, (and) the ancient of days." (V. 11, see D&C 138:38). Michael, "Who is like God," is mentioned several times in both the Old and the New Testaments. He is the Archangel. "Latter-day revelation informs us that Michael is Adam, the Ancient of Days, a prince and the patriarch of the human family." ("Bible Dictionary," p. 732).

Daniel saw the Last Days in vision, and wrote: "I beheld till the thrones were cast down, and the Ancient of days did sit, whose garment was white as snow, and the hair of his head like the pure wool: his throne was like the fiery flame, and his wheels as burning fire." And "the Ancient of days came, and judgment was given to the saints of the most High; and the time came that the saints possessed the kingdom." (Daniel 7:9 & 22).

Then the angel spoke of "Peter, and James, and John, whom I have sent unto you, by whom I have ordained you and confirmed you to be apostles, and especial witnesses of my name, and bear the keys of your ministry and of the same things which I revealed unto them; unto whom I have committed the keys of my kingdom. (V. 12).

Part of the knowledge Joseph Smith received from heavenly messengers pertained to the organization of the church. This was done between the time the Witnesses viewed the plates of the ancient record, on June 8, 1829, and April, 6, 1830. That instruction included ordination to the Aaronic and Melchizedek Priesthood by servants sent from the presence of God. As the Doctrine and Covenants clearly teaches: "There are, in the church, two priesthoods, namely, the Melchizedek and Aaronic, including the Levitical Priesthood." These comprise "two divisions or grand heads." (D&C 107:1 & 6).

It seems clear that the Lord intends that the government of the church is to be presided over by those holding the Melchizedek Priesthood, that "holds the right of presidency, and has power and authority over all the offices in the church in all ages of the world, to administer in spiritual things." (D&C 107:8). "The power and authority of the higher, or Melchizedek Priesthood is to hold the keys of all the spiritual blessings of the church - to have the privilege of receiving the mysteries of the kingdom of heaven, to have the heavens opened unto them, to commune with the general assembly and Church of the Firstborn, and to enjoy the communion and presence of God the Father, and Jesus the mediator of the new covenant." (D&C 107:18-19).

All these messengers had come for one purpose, which was to hasten the "dispensation of the gospel for the last times; and for the fulness of times." (V. 13). Our day is that time in which all things shall be fulfilled that have been spoken of since the world was made. (See D&C 128:20). In the Last Days, all these messengers have declared "their rights, their keys, their honors, their majesty and glory, and the power of their priesthood; giving line upon line, precept upon precept; here a little, and there a little; giving us consolation by holding forth that which is to come, confirming our hope!" (D&C 128:21, see D&C 98:12).

In this Dispensation, the Lord has promised that we shall "receive revelation upon revelation, knowledge upon knowledge, that we may know the peaceable things - that which bringeth joy, that which bringeth life eternal." (D&C 42:61). Such was the case following the baptisms of Joseph Smith and Oliver Cowdery, who "began to have the scriptures laid open to (their) understandings, and the true meaning and intention of their more mysterious passages revealed unto (them) in a manner which (they) never could attain to previously, nor ever before had thought of." (J.S.H. 1:74).

Finally, the angel said that in this great company would be "all those whom my Father hath given me out of the world." (V. 14). These are they who have fled from Babylon and from her worldly influences, who have embraced gospel principles instead of prostituting themselves by compromising their standards in the idolatrous communities of unbelievers.

Those who respond to the call to Zion "shall roar like young lions...and lay hold of the prey, and shall carry away safe." (Isaiah 5:29). In the day of Israel's restoration envisioned by Isaiah, the gospel would go forth in the midst of general conditions of destruction and apostasy raging upon the face of the earth. "And in that day... behold, darkness and sorrow, and the light is darkened in the heavens thereof." (Isaiah 5:30).

Those whom the Father has given to His Son shall also wear the beautiful garments of the Melchizedek Priesthood, "and the sons of Moses and of Aaron shall be filled with the glory of the Lord, upon Mount Zion in the Lord's house, whose sons ye are, and also many whom I have called and sent forth to build upon my church." (D&C 84:32, see D&C 76:576-58, cited below). So declared the Lord to Joseph Smith in "a revelation on priesthood" in September, 1832.

Paul wrote: "Wherefore take unto you the whole armour of God, that ye may be able to withstand in the evil day, and having done all, to stand. Stand therefore, having your loins girt about with truth, and having on the breastplate of righteousness; And your feet shod with the preparation of the gospel of peace; Above all, taking the shield of faith, wherewith ye shall be able to quench all the fiery darts of the wicked. And take the helmet of salvation, and the sword of the Spirit, which is the word of God." (Ephesians 6:13-17).

When we read these verses, we think of the symbolical clothing worn in the temple: "Wherefore, lift up your hearts and rejoice, and gird up your loins, and take upon you my whole armor, that ye may be able to withstand the evil day, having done all, that ye may be able to stand. Stand, therefore, having your loins girt about with truth, having on the breastplate of righteousness, and your feet shod with the preparation of the gospel of peace, which I have sent mine angels to commit unto you; Taking the shield of faith wherewith ye shall be able to quench all the fiery darts of the wicked; And take the helmet of salvation, and the sword of my Spirit, which I will pour out upon you, and my word which I reveal unto you, and be agreed as touching all the things whatsoever ye ask of me, and be faithful until I come," (V. 15-18, see D&C 29:12).

"And ye shall be caught up, that where I am ye shall be also." (V. 18). "And thus we saw the glory of the celestial," Joseph later wrote, "which excels in all things - where God, even the Father, reigns upon his throne forever and ever." (D&C 76:92). Those who dwell in His presence "are priests of the Most High, after the order of Melchizedek, which was after the order of Enoch, which was after the order of the Only Begotten Son. Wherefore, as it is written, they are gods, even the sons of God." (D&C 76:57-58). "These shall dwell in the presence of God and his Christ forever and ever. These are they whom he shall bring with him, when he shall come in the clouds of heaven to reign on the earth over his people." (D&C 76:62:63).

# Section 28

## (Instructions in 1830 to the newly organized church in New York).

Shortly after the organization of the church, some of the members became overzealous in their desire to receive revelation. "Hiram Page," who had joined the church on April 11, 1830, and who later became one of the Eight Witnesses of The Book of Mormon, "had a certain stone, and professed to be receiving revelations by its aid concerning the upbuilding of Zion and the order of the church. Several members had been deceived by these claims," particularly the Whitmer family, "and even Oliver Cowdery was wrongly influenced thereby." (Superscript).

Members of the church are distinguished by their zeal toward God and their fellow men. Those who are zealous attend to their duties and responsibilities with ardent feeling and with fervor. Overzealousness, however, is similar to religious fanaticism, and is a condition in which we lose sight of our objectives, and consequently redouble our efforts. This condition puts us in jeopardy of seduction by the devil, for when we walk in darkness, we often stumble over hidden obstacles that have been intentionally designed to bring us in subjection to powerful adversaries.

Oliver Cowdery had been "called of God, an apostle of Jesus Christ, to be the second elder of the church, and ordained" under the hand of Joseph Smith. (D&C 20:3). As such, the Lord told him: "It shall be given unto thee that thou shalt be heard by the church in all things whatsoever thou shalt teach them by the Comforter, concerning the revelations and commandments which I have given." (V. 1). Teaching is one of the main functions of the priesthood. "This is the order after which I am called," declared Alma, "yea, to preach unto my beloved brethren." (Alma 5:49).

Through gospel teaching directed by those who hold the priesthood, the church fulfills a vital role as it leads us to make decisions that set us squarely on the path of eternal progress. As we continue to make correct choices, we ultimately qualify for eternal life and God's Rest.

Gospel oriented instruction is particularly important because "we live in a day and in a world full of doubts and confusion, where people do not know what to believe, where tensions are high, where the pace is frantic and progress in terms of righteousness is not a popular goal. Violence and crudity are everyday patterns all around us. What a blessing it is to know there is a haven, a place of rest from the turmoil of the world. The prophets and the Savior have called upon us to enter into the rest of the Lord, where life has purpose and direction, and where priesthood power is possible." ("Gospel Doctrine Manual," p. 79).

The Lord wanted both Oliver and Joseph to raise their voices in exhortation, that the Saints might be obedient to the laws and ordinances of the gospel as they were being revealed to the young prophet. As the Savior told the Pharisees: "It is also written in your law, that the testimony of two men is true." (John 8:17). Whenever Christ or His messengers have ministered on the earth, "he left not himself without witness, in that he did good." (Acts 14:17).

Jeremiah implored the spiritually blind and deaf inhabitants of Jerusalem: "Hear now this, O foolish people, and without understanding; which have eyes, and see not; which have ears, and hear not." (Jeremiah 5:21). "For this people's heart is waxed gross," said the Savior, "and their ears are dull of hearing, and their eyes they have closed; lest at any time they should see with their eyes, and hear with their ears, and should understand with their heart, and should be converted, and I should heal them." (Matthew 13:15).

"Verily, verily, I say unto thee, no one shall be appointed to receive commandments and revelations in this church excepting my servant Joseph Smith, Jun., for he receiveth them even as Moses." (V. 2). "It is contrary to the economy of God for any member of the church to receive instructions for those in authority, higher than themselves.... But if anyone have a vision or a visitation from a heavenly messenger, it may be for his own benefit and instruction." (Joseph Smith, H.C., 1:338).

On one occasion, the Lord told Joseph Smith: "This generation shall have my word through you." (D&C 5:10). On another, He said: "And I, Jesus Christ, your Lord and your God, have spoken it. These words are not of men nor of man, but of me; wherefore, you shall testify they are of me and not of man; For it is my voice which speaketh them unto you; for they are given by my Spirit unto you, and by my power you can read them one to another; and save it were by my power you could not have them; Wherefore, you can testify that you have heard my voice, and know my words." (D&C 18:33-36).

When we read the words of The Doctrine and Covenants, or of The Book of Mormon, we are hearing the voice of the Lord, as well as reading His words, if we do so by the Spirit. The Savior said, "Learn of me, and listen to my words; walk in the meekness of my Spirit, and you shall have peace in me." (D&C 19:23). Referring to the Lord's anointed, the Lord said: "And whatsoever they shall speak when moved upon by the Holy Ghost shall be scripture, shall be the will of the Lord, shall be the mind of the Lord, shall be the word of the Lord, shall be the voice of the Lord, and the power of God unto salvation." (D&C 68:4).

In the early days of the church in Utah, "a young man with a well developed sense of humor managed the ward store. After preparing a special ink that could be read only after heat was applied, he wrote scriptural messages on a certain brown hen's eggs. Soon the ward gathered to see what the hen had to say about the latest gossip in town. When the young man's father, an Apostle, returned from Salt Lake City and observed the situation, he called a special priesthood meeting. To the assembled men, he explained that he had just visited Brigham Young, and had verified that God was still speaking to his prophet. The Lord, said the Apostle, had not yet resorted to the hind end of a chicken to convey messages to his people." (Leonard Arrington, "The Mormon Experience," p. 217).

"And thou shalt be obedient unto the things which I shall give unto him, even as Aaron, to declare faithfully the commandments and the revelations, with power and authority unto the church." (V. 3). Oliver was to be obedient to the Lord's admonition to feed His sheep. "Faith in the gospel is much like a living organism," taught John Widtsoe. "To be healthy and vigorous, it must be fed. If starved, it sickens, weakens, and may die. Loss of faith may always be traced to neglect, mistreatment, and sin. The food of faith is simple but imperative. Knowledge of the gospel must be maintained and increased by regular, continuous study. It is an erroneous assumption to think that knowledge of the gospel comes, as it were, with breathing, while to secure academic knowledge requires toil." ("Evidences and Reconciliation").

Knowledge of the gospel comes from a study of the scriptures and of the words spoken by the servants of God, for, as the Lord declared: "whether by mine own voice or by the voice of my servants, it is the same." (D&C 1:38). Spirituality is not an office or a calling, but is daily living the gospel of Jesus Christ. "God is mindful of every people, whatsoever land they may be in; yea, he numbereth his people, and his bowels of mercy are over all the earth." (Alma 26:37). "And he inviteth them all to come unto him and partake of his goodness; and he denieth none that come unto him, black and white, bond and free, male and female; and he remembereth the heathen; and all are alike unto God, both Jew and Gentile." (2 Nephi 26:33).

When the prophet of the Lord speaks when moved upon by the Holy Ghost, his words assume "the power of God unto salvation." (D&C 68:4). Joseph Smith taught: "Wherever there is a righteous man on the earth unto whom God revealed His word and gave power and authority to administer in His name, and wherever there is a priest of God, a minister who has power and authority from God to administer in the ordnances of the gospel and officiate in the Priesthood of God, there is the Kingdom of God." (H.C., 5:256).

"And if thou are led at any time by the Comforter to speak or teach, or at all times by the way of commandment unto the church, thou mayest do it. But thou shalt not write by way of commandment, but by wisdom." (V. 4-5). It is the solemn responsibility of only one man to stand pre-eminent and to hold the keys of authority and give the Lord's commandments to the church. But the light and knowledge that all may receive of God is given by the process of personal revelation. The principle is so basic that it almost requires no explanation, because it speaks to our souls. Because God has the power to speak to His children according to his will and pleasure, it is wisdom that they should take counsel from Him.

"And thou shalt not command him who is at thy head, and at the Head of the Church." (V. 6). Oliver was inclined to take issue with the Prophet in regard to matters of revelation. But the Savior wisely cautioned: "Except ye are one, ye are not mine." (D&C 38:27). In our day, it is necessary in our discipleship to give our attention and our loyalty to the prophet of the church, the First Presidency, and to the united voice of the brethren of the Council of The Twelve. To do less than this is to offend the Head of the church, Who is Jesus Christ. J. Reuben Clark, Jr. observed: "We do not lack a prophet; what we lack is a listening ear by the people and a determination to live as God has commanded." (C.R., 10/1948). Do we listen to the counsel of the brethren at General Conference? Do we read what they have written? Do we live in conformity to the principles of the gospel so that we might be entitled to have the guidance of the Spirit, so that we might recognize the truth of which it testifies?

A pillar of light that was above the brightness of the sun stood exactly over the head of young Joseph Smith in the Sacred Grove, and apparently in defiance of the laws of physics it descended gradually, until it enveloped him within its brilliance. Thus, he received "The Mantle of the Prophet," and it has rested upon every subsequent President of the Church. "For surely the Lord God will do nothing but he revealeth his secret to his servants the prophets." (Amos 3:7).

"For I have given him the keys of the mysteries, and the revelations which are sealed, until I shall appoint unto them another in his stead." (V. 7). This provision was made in September 1830, so that the church would know the order, even if Joseph Smith should fall. Later, after Joseph had been tested and proven, D&C 90 was given, that explained the bestowal of the keys of the kingdom on the First Presidency, and ultimately, on the Twelve. "Thou art blessed from henceforth that bear the keys of the kingdom given unto you," the Lord then revealed to Joseph. "Thy brethren (in the First Presidency of the Church) are accounted as equal with thee in holding the keys of this last kingdom." (D&C 90:2 & 6). These keys are the right of presidency; they are the power and authority to govern, and to direct all of the Lord's affairs on the earth. Those who hold them have power to govern and control the manner in which all others may serve in the priesthood." (Joseph Fielding Smith, Jr., C.R., 4/1972).

As members of the First Presidency, Sidney Rigdon and Frederick G. Williams were equal with Joseph Smith in the sense that, under his direction, they could perform the same priesthood functions that he could perform. However, counselors in the First Presidency then and now have no power to act independently. They must have the approval of the President of the Church.

"By their fruits ye shall know them," the Lord had instructed. (3 Nephi 14:20). Do these prophets, or teachers who speak in the name of the Lord, bless the lives of their people? Is their doctrine edifying and uplifting? Do they encourage a lifestyle that promotes chastity, morality, and fidelity to family values? Do they hold dear the sanctity of life and the rights of the unborn? Do they believe that moral agency is an eternal principle vital to the successful completion of our probation on earth? Do they believe in obeying, honoring, and sustaining the law of the land? Do they believe in being honest, true, chaste, benevolent, virtuous, and in doing good to all men? Do they believe all things, hope all things, have they endured many things and do they hope to be able to endure all things? If there is anything virtuous, lovely, or of good report or praiseworthy, do they seek after these things? (See Philippians 4:8, & the 13th Article of Faith).

It is vital that those who seek the Church of Christ recognize the fruits of faith, because "not every one that saith unto me, Lord, Lord, shall enter into the kingdom of heaven; but he that doeth the will of my Father which is in heaven." (Matthew 7:21). This is a particularly significant verse in light of the various "Born Again Christian" movements sweeping the land in our day. Many claim that it is only necessary to 'confess Christ,' or to declare faith in Him, in order to be saved. However, the action verb 'to do' implies more than effort; it demands active obedience to the performance requirements that have been established by Heavenly Father.

"Faith, if it hath not works, is dead, being alone." (James 2:17). There is no more power in faith that does not include works, than there is strength in food that is not eaten, or warmth in clothes that are not worn. The teachings on faith and works by Luther and the other Reformers who founded Protestantism are often misunderstood. "By faith, Luther meant no merely intellectual assent to a proposition, but vital, personal self-committal to a practical belief. He heartily approved of good works; what he denied was their efficacy for salvation. 'Good works,' he said, "do not make a good man. But a good man does good works.' And what makes a man good? Faith in God, and Christ." (Will Durant, "The Story of Civilization," "The Reformation," p. 374-375). This is consistent with the Latter-day Saint doctrine that we are saved by grace, after all that we can do.

God exists in the present tense; He is the Great I Am, and not the Great He Was. (Rufus Jones, "A Flash of Eternity," newspaper article). In the Doctrine & Covenants, the Lord testified that Joseph Smith was given "power from on high, by the means which were before prepared, to translate The Book of Mormon; which contains a record of a fallen people, and the fulness of the gospel of Jesus Christ to the Gentiles and to the Jews also; which was given by inspiration and is confirmed to others by the ministering of angels, and is declared unto the world by them - Proving to the world that the holy scriptures are true, and that God does inspire men and call them to his holy work in this age and generation, as well as in generations of old; Thereby showing that he is the same God yesterday, today, and forever." (D&C 20:8-12).

Something wonderful surrounds our testimonies of the living Prophet, Seer, and Revelator of The Church of Jesus Christ of Latter-day Saints. Not long after the restoration of the gospel, John Greenleaf Whittier said of "these modern prophets, I discovered, as I think, the great secret of their success in making converts. They speak to a common feeling; they minister to a universal want. They speak a language of hope and promise to the weak, weary hearts, tossed and troubled, who have wandered from sect to sect, seeking in vain for the primal manifestations of the divine power." (Quoted in "A Mormon Conventicle," p. 461, and in "Howitt's Journal in the Millennial Star," 1848, p. 302-3).

As He did anciently, the Savior has given the keys of the kingdom to each of the latter-day Apostles. However, only the President of the church, who is the senior living Apostle, and the President of the Quorum of The First Presidency, may use these keys (or authorize others to use them) on behalf of the entire church. The Lord explained: "I have appointed unto my servant Joseph to hold this power in the last days, and there is never but one on the earth at a time on whom this power and the keys of this priesthood are conferred." (D&C 132:7).

Frequently, we are asked to do small things by the prophet or other ecclesiastical authorities. "The way of the gospel is a simple way. Some of the requirements may appear to you as elementary and unnecessary. Do not spurn them. Humble yourselves and walk in obedience. I promise that the results that follow will be marvelous to behold and satisfying to experience." (Gordon B. Hinckley, C.R., 10/1976).

Today, some fear that latter-day Israel is helpless to stand against the evils of the world. But we remember the story of Elisha: "And when the servant of the man of God was risen early, and gone forth, behold, an host compassed the city both with horses and chariots. And his servant said unto him, Alas, my master! how shall we do? And he answered, Fear not: for they that be with us are more than they that be with them. And Elisha prayed, and said, Lord, I pray thee, open his eyes, that he may see. And the Lord opened the eyes of the young man; and he saw: and, behold, the mountain was full of horses and chariots of fire round about Elisha." (2 Kings 6:15-17). In our day, temple ordinances bless us with eyes that see clearly, and discern between truth and error.

As Dallin H. Oaks taught: "When I read this wonderful story as a boy, I always identified with the young servant of Elisha. I thought, If I am ever surrounded by the forces of evil while I am in the Lord's service, I hope He will open my eyes and give me faith to understand that when we are about His errand, those who are with us are always more powerful than those who oppose us." (C.R., 10/1992). The Lord promised Joseph Smith: "I will go before your face. I will be on your right hand and on your left, and my Spirit shall be in your hearts, and mine angels round about you, to bear you up." (D&C 84:87). The President of the church is a prophet of God. We sustain him and follow his counsel, for his power, the power of God, is greater than any other.

"Thou shalt have revelations, but write them not by way of commandment." (V. 8). "There is no shortage of revelation in this world. The problem is to tell that which is true revelation given of the Lord, from that which is spurious revelation, given of the adversary." (Chauncey Riddle, "The Pillars of Testimony"). The story is told of one of the elders who had written a long communication which he deemed to be very important, and who requested that Brother Joseph hear him read it. The Prophet commended his style in glowing terms, and remarked that the ideas were ingeniously advanced, In fact, Joseph had but one objection to it. "What is that?" the writer eagerly inquired, greatly elated that his production was considered so near perfect. The Prophet replied, "It is not true." (J. Reuben Clark, Jr., "Messages of the First Presidency," p. 235).

"No man knoweth where the city of Zion shall be built, but it shall be given hereafter. Behold, I say unto you that it shall be on the borders by the Lamanites."

(V. 9). The city of Zion is the New Jerusalem. "The kingdom of Zion is in very deed the kingdom of our God and His Christ." (D&C 105:32). The prophet Ether had seen in vision Zion, "the Jerusalem from whence Lehi should come, (and that) after it should be destroyed it should be built up again, a holy city unto the Lord; wherefore, it could not be a new Jerusalem for it had been in a time of old." He also saw that "a New Jerusalem should be built up upon this land" of America. (Ether 13:5-6). Here, the remnant of the House of Joseph would "build up a holy city unto the Lord, like unto the Jerusalem of old." (Ether 13:8). In this millennial New Jerusalem would reside those "whose garments are white through the blood of the Lamb; and they are they who are numbered among the remnant of the seed of Joseph, who were of the House of Israel. And then also cometh the Jerusalem of old; (or Zion), and the inhabitants thereof, blessed are they, for they have (also) been washed in the blood of the Lamb; and they are they who were scattered and gathered in from the four quarters of the earth, and from the north countries, and are partakers of the fulfilling of the covenant which God made with their father, Abraham." (Ether 13:10-11).

Satan had deceived Hyrum Page, and the "revelation" he had received was not from God. Consequently, in Section 28, Joseph Smith was instructed: "For, behold, these things have not been appointed unto him, neither shall anything be appointed unto any of this church contrary to the church covenants. (V. 12). The Savior warned against "false prophets, who come to you in sheep's clothing, but inwardly they are ravening wolves." (Matthew 7:15). Some enemies have used this scripture to attack the church, claiming that it speaks pointedly of the President and Prophet. This is quite an accusation, coming as it does from a people "who never had faith enough to call down one scrap of revelation from heaven, and for all they have now are indebted to the faith of another people who lived hundreds and thousands of years before them. Does it remain for them to say how much God has spoken and how much he has not spoken?" (Joseph Smith, H.C., 2:17-18).

Even if their claim were reasonable, where then are the true prophets referred to in Christ's warning? They must exist, for "Adam's revelation did not instruct Noah to build his ark; nor did Noah's revelation tell Lot to forsake Sodom; nor did either of these speak of the Exodus. These all had revelations for themselves, and so had Isaiah, Jeremiah, Peter, Paul, John, and Joseph Smith." (John Taylor, "Gospel Kingdom," p. 34). In fact, "all things must be done in order, and by common consent in the church, by the prayer of faith." (V. 13). Common consent involves the recognition that the righteous exercise of agency allows us to progress to ultimate salvation. "No man can preside in this church in any capacity without the consent of the people." (Joseph Fielding Smith, Jr., "Doctrines of Salvation," 3:123, see D&C 20:65).

Abraham Lincoln said that you can fool some of the people some of the time, and you can fool some of the people all of the time, but you cannot fool all of the people all of the time. King Mosiah put it another way: "It is not common that the voice of the people desireth anything contrary to that which is right; but it is common for the lesser part of the people to desire that which is not right; therefore this shall ye observe and make it your law - to do your business by the voice of the people." (Mosiah 29:26).

When a leader is sustained by the voice of the people, personal accountability prevails, and if they later commit sins and iniquities, they are answered upon their own heads. The scriptures reinforce this concept of individual responsibility. They stress equality among all the members of the church. These scriptures focus on the philosophies of agency, accountability, individual liberty, and independence that are stitched into the fabric of the gospel.

"And thou must open thy mouth at all times, declaring my gospel with the sound of rejoicing." (V. 16). Abraham Lincoln said: "To sin by silence, when words should be spoken, makes cowards of men." The foundation of the unique source of peace enjoyed by the Saints is to have the assurance of a complete and all-encompassing forgiveness for sins, though the power of the Savior's Atonement. Such is their cleansing, that they are able to stand and witness that they have been born of God. Their behavior reminds us of Parley P. Pratt, who declared "I have received the holy anointing, and I can never rest until the last enemy is conquered, death destroyed, and truth reigns triumphant." ("Deseret News," 4/30/1853).

# Section 29
## (Instructions in 1830 to the newly organized church in New York).

At the end of this revelation, Christ speaks in the name of the Father, by divine investiture of authority, but initially He commands us to "listen to the voice of Jesus Christ, your Redeemer, the Great I AM, whose arm of mercy hath atoned for your sins." (V. 1). Because of the Atonement, all have equal opportunity before the Lord. They "have the privilege, living or dead, of accepting the conditions of the great Plan of Redemption provided by the Father, through the Son, before the world was." (John Taylor, "Mediation and Atonement," p. 181).

But "wo" unto those who have the law, if they transgress. "Wo" is a condition of deep suffering from misfortune, affliction, grief or calamity. Our lives are days of probation, a time of testing, or of putting to the proof our declared values. "Repentance is (always available) unto them that are under condemnation and under the curse of a broken law." (Mormon 8:24).

The gospel was created and fashioned so that all who abide by its laws may have the opportunity to enter into God's Rest. Following their mortal probation, this will be nothing less than exaltation in His presence in the Celestial Kingdom. When we listen to the voice of our Savior, we are entitled to enjoy a perfect knowledge of the divinity of the work. This blessing includes rest from fear, doubt, apprehension of danger, the religious turmoil of the world, and from the vagaries of men. It is the peace that follows obedience to celestial principles.

Since no unclean thing can enter into His kingdom, a process of purification is necessary to prepare us for admittance into His presence. The blood shed by the Savior is the symbolical equivalent of this cleaning agent. Having revealed the key that unlocks the door to God's Rest in His kingdom, Jesus declared: "Now this is the commandment: Repent, all ye ends of the earth, and come unto me and be baptized in my name, that ye may be sanctified by the reception of the Holy Ghost, that ye may stand spotless before me at the last day. Verily, verily, I say unto you, this is my gospel." (3 Nephi 27:20-21).

A major purpose of the gospel is to provide those principles, ordinances, and covenants that enable us to become sanctified so that we may be worthy to live once again in a state of holiness. Sanctification is the process whereby we are cleansed from the effects of sin; thus spiritually renewed, we may stand prepared to enter the presence of the Lord. We must submit to His will, yield our hearts to Him, and be obedient to all of the teachings of His church. "Therefore, if ye do these things blessed are ye," said the Savior, "for ye shall be lifted up at the last day." (3 Nephi 27:22).

In order to accomplish this, the Lord's elect must be gathered. Those of Ephraim have been gathering since 1830, by virtue of their membership in The Church of Jesus Christ of Latter-day Saints. Our innate yearning to find our way home always leads "to the waters of baptism, where a covenant is made to take upon ourselves the name of Christ. It always embraces being numbered among His sheep by being an active member of His church." ("Doctrinal Commentary on The Book of Mormon," 3:420). Therefore, the Lord characterized Himself as one who would "gather his people, even as a hen gathereth her chickens under her wings, even as many as will hearken to (His) voice and humble themselves before (him), and call upon (Him) in mighty prayer." (V. 2).

There is also a gathering taking place among the tribes of the House of Israel, particularly those of Judah. Zenos prophesied that "when that day cometh" that Israel no longer turns her heart aside from the Master, "then will he remember the covenants which he made to their fathers. Yea, then will he remember the isles of the sea; yea, and all the people who are of the house of Israel." (1 Nephi 19:15-16). Zenos pointedly prophesied that Israel would be gathered from the four quarters of the earth.

At that day, "all the earth shall see the salvation of the Lord, saith the prophet; every nation, kindred, tongue and people shall be blessed." (1 Nephi 19:17). The members and missionaries of The Church of Jesus Christ of Latter-day Saints are commissioned to minister to a world in desperate need of salvation, and by priesthood authority and ordinance to provide all nations with the covenant blessings of Abraham.

The signs given in the New World at the death of Jesus Christ were a foreshadowing of the scourging of Israel because it had crucified its God, and because it had turned its heart aside, rejecting His power. Her outward obedience and commitment to the letter of the Law was not enough to insure her temporal and spiritual salvation. Israel's heart had to be in the right place as well. A change of heart was required, suggesting the necessity of a spiritual rebirth.

God takes no satisfaction in Israel's scourging, but lets nature take its course according to the Law of the Harvest. As Mormon wrote: "The judgments of God will overtake the wicked, and it is by the wicked that the wicked are punished; for it is the wicked that stir up the hearts of the children of men unto bloodshed." (Mormon 4:5).

"Because they turn(ed) their hearts aside," Israel was to become a "hiss and a byword, and (would) be hated among all nations." (1 Nephi 19:14). Nevertheless, the Lord would remember His covenant people. Mormon wrote: "Ye need not any longer hiss, nor spurn, nor make game of the Jews, nor any of the remnant of the house of Israel; for behold, the Lord remembereth his covenant unto them, and he will do unto them according to that which he hath sworn." (3 Nephi 29:8). It is important to understand that whenever The Book of Mormon speaks of "the remnant of the house of Israel" it is a reference to the descendants of Lehi. In this case, those in the Last Days are cautioned against prejudicial behavior of any kind that is directed toward those who are Jews, in the broadest sense of the word.

In 1921, Heber J. Grant declared: "By the authority of the Holy Priesthood of God that has again been restored to the earth, and by the ministration under the direction of the Prophet of God, Apostles of the Lord Jesus Christ have been to the Holy Land and have dedicated that country for the return of the Jews; and we believe that in the due time of the Lord they shall be in the favor of God again. And let no Latter-day Saint be guilty of taking any part in any crusade against these people." (C.R., 10/1921). Significantly, President Grant delivered this address just a decade before the institutional destruction of the Jews as a people was conceived by the National Socialist Party, in Nazi Germany.

At that time, the Latter-day State of Israel was still 27 years from reality. For centuries, it had lived only as a dream of the most devout Jews and ardent Zionists. For almost 2,000 years, there had been no homeland for the Jews. Israel existed only in the hearts and minds of the people, in scripture, and in prophecy.

But, in 1842, the Holy Land was dedicated by Orson Hyde for the return of the Jews, even though at that time there were less than 7,000 of the lineage of Jacob living in Palestine. Surely, it was the latter-day prophets of God, and the power of their priesthood authority, that facilitated the return of the Jews, and made possible the miracle that is the modern State of Israel.

Today, "every nation is the gathering place for its own people," instructed Bruce R. McConkie at an Area Conference of the church in South America. At the time of the Restoration, however, the church was commanded to literally go out from Babylon, and establish itself in the wilderness. The church headed west to the frontier, in the pattern of the Jaredites, the family of Lehi, the little flock of Alma, as well as of the pious community at Qumran.

"At this time, your sins are forgiven you; therefore, ye receive these things; but remember to sin no more, lest perils shall come upon you." (V. 3). This is a revelation that was specifically addressed to baptized members of the church, whose sins had been forgiven in those cleansing waters. The obedient have joy, are filled with the love of God, and are privileged to claim and retain a remission of their sins. This is important, because "when an individual refuses to comply with the further requirements of heaven, the sins he had formerly committed return upon his head and his former righteousness departs from him." (Brigham Young, J.D., 8:124).

Also, as the obedient grow in the knowledge of God, their potential to live together in peace and harmony increases. Their children benefit from their righteous example, and "walk in the ways of truth and soberness (and) love one another, and serve one another." (Mosiah 4:15).

"Ye are chosen out of the world to declare my gospel with the sound of rejoicing, as with the voice of a trump." (V. 4). Trumpets were used anciently as a sign a warning, to signal for battle, or to announce the coming of royalty. "Blow ye the trumpet in Zion, and sound an alarm in my holy mountain: let all the inhabitants of the land tremble: for the day of the Lord cometh." (Joel 2:1-2). The purpose of the day of the Lord is to "destroy the sinners thereof out of (the land)." (Isaiah 13:9). They will be punished for iniquity, arrogance, pride, and haughtiness, if they have failed to repent.

"This is our first interest as a church - to save and exalt the souls of the children of men." (Ezra Taft Benson, C.R., 4/1974). "Proclaim my gospel from land to land, and from city to city. Bear testimony in every place, unto every people." (D&C 66:5 & 7). "Go ye into all the world, and preach the gospel to every creature" and "unto every nation, and kindred, and tongue, and people." (Mark 66:5 & 7, & D&C 133:37). The scriptures attest that the Lord's church is a missionary church: "And thus the gospel began to be preached, from the beginning." (Moses 5:58).

Every member of the church needs to be a missionary, because many of Heavenly Father's children are blinded by false teachings and "are only kept from the truth because they know not where to find it." (D&C 112:12). Studies have found that 5% of the church membership prays for guidance in doing missionary work. Interestingly, about 5% of the members of the church report that they regularly have missionary experiences. Consequently, Spencer W. Kimball urged: "Make no small plans, for they have no magic to stir men's souls." (Attributed to Daniel Burnham).

Each of us can share the glad tidings by being a light to the world and by living in harmony with gospel principles. We can show kindness to others. We can demonstrate by our behavior the principles of the gospel to our friends. We can invite them into our homes. We can prepare our children to serve missions. We can pay our tithing and contribute to the missionary fund. We can assist others who are financially unable to support themselves on missions. We can do family history research and temple work to support the three-fold mission of the church. We can support ward activities that promote missionary work.

We can "serve him with all (our) heart, might, mind and strength, that (we) may stand blameless before God at the last day." (D&C 4:2). Because the Master requires that we be unreservedly committed to the work, He calls us to higher planes of spirituality and to commitments to selfless consecration of effort. He urges us to lose ourselves in service and to let our lights shine before others. In the process, we will lay up for ourselves "treasures in heaven, where neither moth nor rust doth corrupt, and where thieves do not break through nor steal." (3 Nephi 13:19-20).

We think of Mother Teresa of Calcutta, and the capacity of her heart, rather than the numerical value of her intellect. She echoed the words of St. Francis of Assisi, who said: "Preach the gospel at all times, and when necessary use words." Mother Teresa taught: "Give Jesus not only your hands to serve, but your heart to love. Pray with absolute trust in God's loving care for you. Let Him use you without consulting you. Let Jesus fill you with joy, that you may preach without preaching." ("Love: A Fruit Always in Season, Daily Meditations").

Our Father in Heaven could give us everything He has, but what He is we must earn for ourselves as we struggle to overcome adversity and gain self-mastery. There is a palpable sense of urgency, when it comes to missionary work, because it is within the eternal reach of every child of God to become as He is. We are engaged in the work, not to make their lives better, but to expose them to a Plan of Salvation that extends to all the blessings of heaven.

Isaiah envisioned that, in the Last Days, a righteous man will be "more precious than fine gold." (Isaiah 13:12). This might be because they will be few in number, or it could be because the true value of righteousness, when compared to the inconsequential treasures of the earth, will be made manifest. Even the wealth of the Golden Wedge of Ophir will be insignificant when compared to one righteous individual. (See Isaiah 13:12).

"I am in your midst, and am your advocate with the Father." (V. 5). Christ "advocateth the cause of the children of men," when by faith they receive the power to become the sons of God. These are they who will "cleave unto every good thing." (Moroni 7:28). During our mortal probation, even as the test is in progress, our repentance for the violation of the commandments is still possible. Mid-course corrections for error, improvement in the quality and direction of our lives, and the realignment of our baby steps toward eternal realities, describe our conscious efforts to find our way home to heaven. Frequent debriefings after particularly stressful episodes help us to re-focus our concentration on the brass ring.

"Whatsoever ye shall ask in faith, being united in prayer, according to my command, ye shall receive." (V. 6). Moroni exhorted us with specific counsel: "O then, despise not, and wonder not, but hearken unto the words of the Lord, and ask the Father in the name of Jesus for what things soever ye shall stand in need. Doubt not, but be believing, and begin as in times of old, and come unto the Lord with all your heart." (Mormon 9:27).

"Work out your own salvation," he said, "with fear and trembling" before the Lord. (Mormon 9:27). In fact, our works are necessary, but insufficient, and we cannot work out our own salvation. But when our works become His works, and are motivated from on high, they become empowered by our righteousness, and the miracle of salvation by the grace of God is achieved. (See Philippians 2:12-13).

Moroni knew the power of prayer. He cautioned us to be careful about the things for which we would pray. He had seen quite enough of the mockery of God among the Nephites, and so he counseled that we should "do all things in worthiness." (Mormon 9:29).

"And ye are called to bring to pass the gathering of mine elect; for mine elect hear my voice and harden not their hearts." (V. 7). The first phase of the gathering is taking place as the elect are gathered out of the world into the church and Kingdom of God. (See 1 Nephi 14:15). The second phase will take place as the elect are gathered into one place, the New Jerusalem. In the meantime, however, wherever the Saints may gather, they are armed with righteousness and great glory.

There are some people in the world, however, who take a fiendish delight in the lost hopes and broken dreams of struggling Saints in embryo, and revel in destroying their faith. These misguided individuals seem to be happiest when they mistakenly loudly proclaim that the prophets are wrong, but it is only because they think they have found a justification for their unrighteous behavior. They are enthusiastically ignorant, Their behavior is the ultimate expression of rationalization. With the desire to push their desires to the extreme, they stone the prophets, cast them out, and put them to death.

In all ages of the world, there have been "lyings sent forth among the people, by Satan, to harden their hearts to the intent that they might not believe in those signs and wonders which they had seen." (3 Nephi 1:22). Satan is the destroyer, and the source of unbelief, and it is his goal to quickly and effectively countermand every good desire and counteract every good deed in the world.

"Wherefore the decree hath gone forth from the Father that they shall be gathered in unto one place upon the face of this land, to prepare their hearts and be prepared in all things against the day when tribulation and desolation are sent forth upon the wicked." (V. 8). On April 3, 1836, in the Kirtland Temple, Moses restored the Keys of the Gathering of Israel. One hundred and thirty nine years later, Spencer W. Kimball declared: "The brighter day has dawned. The gathering is in progress. May the Lord bless us, as we become nursing fathers and mothers unto our (Israelite) brethren and hasten the fulfillment of the great promises made to them." (C.R., 10/1975).

The Lord has not forgotten His people, despite the fact that they have repeatedly forsaken Him. "For can a woman forget her sucking child, that she should not have compassion on the son of her womb?" (1 Nephi 21:15). The nail prints in the palms of His hands will be an awful token to Israel of His fulfillment of the Atonement Covenant, despite the phylacteries or frontlets that are even today worn by men and boys in Israel as constant reminders of the promised Messiah.

Israel shall yet inherit her former lands in great glory. "For thy waste and thy desolate places, and the land of thy destruction, shall even now be too narrow by reason of the inhabitants; and they that swallowed thee up shall be far away." (1 Nephi 21:19). In 1830, there were fewer than seven thousand Jews living in the Holy Land. In 1980, there were over three million, and in 2015, there were six million. (In the United States, in 2015, there were between five and seven million Jews). In 1830, only one in five hundred persons living in the Holy Land was a Jew. In 1980, one in five was a Jew. The prophecies are being fulfilled.

In the Last Days, not only latter-day Covenant Israel (The Church of Jesus Christ of Latter-day Saints) but also the Gentile nations of the earth shall assist in the gathering. "Thus saith the Lord God: Behold, I will lift up mine hand to the Gentiles, and set up my standard to the people; and they shall bring thy sons in their arms, and thy daughters shall be carried upon their shoulders." (1 Nephi 21:22). The ensign to which the people will look is the gospel standard. As the Lord told Joseph Smith: "And even so I have sent mine everlasting covenant into the world, to be a light to the world, and to be a standard for my people, and for the Gentiles to seek to it, and to be a messenger before my face to prepare the way before me." (D&C 45:9).

So thoroughly and convincingly will the Lord touch the hearts of the Gentile nations, that the Lord promised Israel through Isaiah that "kings shall be thy nursing fathers, and their queens thy nursing mothers; they shall bow down to thee with their face towards the earth, and lick up the dust of thy feet; and thou shalt know that I am the Lord." (1 Nephi 21:23, see Isaiah 49:23). When the governments of the earth bow down in humility to assist the efforts of Blood Israel in her gathering to the land of her inheritance, we should recognize it as a sign that the Lord is God.

At the same time, those who have persecuted and oppressed Israel will be punished. "For I will contend with him that contendeth with thee, and I will save thy children." (1 Nephi 21:25). "For the mighty God shall deliver his covenant people." (J.S.T. Isaiah 49:25). "And I will feed them that oppress thee with their own flesh; they shall be drunken with their own blood as with sweet wine; and all flesh shall know that I, the Lord, am thy Savior and thy Redeemer, the Mighty One of Jacob." (1 Nephi 21:25-26).

For the righteous, though, a way of deliverance has been prepared. "A prophet shall the Lord your God raise up," said the Lord to Moses. (1 Nephi 22:20). "This prophet of whom Moses spake was the Holy One of Israel." (1 Nephi 22:21). In consequence of His ministry, the righteous will not be confounded, or brought to ruin. Because they will listen to His counsel that is given by revelation to the Prophet and that is also found in the scriptures, they will not be destroyed. For their own safety, though, they will need to gather in the wards, stakes, and missions of the church. "And the time cometh speedily that the righteous must be led up as calves of the stall." (1 Nephi 22:24).

The gathering of the Saints to the stakes of Zion "may be for a defense, and for a refuge from the storm, and from wrath when it shall be poured out without mixture upon the whole earth." (D&C 115:6). Ezra Taft Benson taught that our church ecclesiastical units called stakes have "at least four purposes. One is to unify and perfect the members who live within their boundaries, by extending to them the church programs, the ordinances, and gospel instruction. (Secondly), the members of stakes are to be models, or standards, of righteousness. (Third), stakes are to be a defense. They do this as stake members unify under their local priesthood officers and consecrate themselves to do their duty and keep their covenants. (Fourth), stakes are a refuge from the storm to be poured out over the earth." ("Ensign," 1/1991).

"For the hour is nigh and the day soon at hand when the earth is ripe; and all the proud and they that do wickedly shall be as stubble; and I will burn them up, saith the Lord of Hosts, that wickedness shall not be upon the earth." (V. 9). This is not a figure of speech. Christ is a glorified, celestial Being, and His glory is comparable to that of the sun. (See D&C 76:70). Thus, His presence when He comes in His glory, will be as a consuming fire. In the best poetical expression of an oriental mind, the mountains will flow down before Him, the elements will melt with fervent heat, and the waters will boil. Even the sun will hide its face in shame. (See Isaiah 64:1-2).

Today, the fate of the wicked is inevitable; they are marked for destruction as surely as were the people of Ammonihah. "And thus, with the sword and by bloodshed the inhabitants of the earth shall mourn; and with famine, and plague, and earthquake, and the thunder of heaven, and the fierce and vivid lightning also, shall the inhabitants of the earth be made to feel the wrath, and indignation, and chastening hand of an Almighty God, until the consumption decreed hath made a full end of all nations." (D&C 87:6). The question remains: Who will repent before the great and dreadful day of the Lord? "O repent ye, repent ye!" urged Nephi. "Why will ye die?" he asked. "Turn ye, turn ye unto the Lord your God." (Helaman 7:17).

The Lord confirmed that His Hand will rule in the Last Days, and His people need not fear the vile threats and wicked oaths of the unrighteous. He promised: "I will make my people with whom the Father hath covenanted, yea, I will make thy horn iron, and I will make thy hoofs brass. And thou shalt beat in pieces many people; and I will consecrate their gain unto the Lord, and their substance unto the Lord of the whole earth. And behold, I am he who doeth it." (3 Nephi 20:19).

The wicked will be dealt with in a fair and equitable manner. The awful reality, though, is that they will have no refuge to which they may turn, and no horns of sanctuary to grasp, for they have no claim upon Mercy. "The sword of my justice shall hang over them at that day," warned the Lord, "and except they repent it shall fall upon them, saith the Father, yea, even upon all the nations of the Gentiles." (3 Nephi 20:20).

Even as the demands of Justice require the destruction of the wicked, the Lord declared: "It shall come to pass that I will establish my people, O house of Israel." (3 Nephi 20:21). He specifically addressed that remnant of Israel dwelling in the land of the Americas, saying: "This people will I establish in this land, unto the fulfilling of the covenant which I made with your father, Jacob; and it shall be a New Jerusalem. And the powers of heaven shall be in the midst of this people; yea, even I will be in the midst of you." (3 Nephi 20:22).

"For the hour is nigh, and that which was spoken by mine apostles must be fulfilled; for as they spoke, so shall it come to pass." (V. 10). Of the wicked, the Lord told the Nephites: "Thy graven images I will also cut off, and thy standing images out of the midst of thee, and thou shalt no more worship the works of thy hands." (3 Nephi 21:17). "And it shall come to pass that all lyings, and deceivings, and envyings, and strifes, and priestcrafts, and whoredoms, shall be done away." (3 Nephi 21:19).

"For I will reveal myself from heaven with power and great glory, with all the hosts thereof, and dwell in righteousness with men on earth a thousand years, and the wicked shall not stand." (V. 11). Nephi saw the dawning of the millennial day, when there would be "nothing which is secret save it shall be revealed; there is no work of darkness save it shall be made manifest in the light; and there is nothing which is sealed upon the earth save it shall be loosed." (2 Nephi 30:17).

John The Revelator foresaw the millennial day, as well, as an event already accomplished, when "an angel (came) down from heaven, having the key of the bottomless pit and a great chain in his hand. And he laid hold on the dragon, that old serpent, which is the Devil, and Satan, and bound him a thousand years, and cast him into the bottomless pit, and shut him up, and set a seal upon him, that he should deceive the nations no more, till the thousand years should be fulfilled; and after that he must be loosed a little season." (Revelation 20:1-3).

It is those who are of the kingdom of the devil who should fear. They are "all churches which are built up to get gain, and all those who are built up to become popular in the eyes of the world, and those who seek the lusts of the flesh, and the things of the world, and to do all manner of iniquity; yea, in fine, all those who belong to the kingdom of the devil are they who need fear, and tremble, and quake." (1 Nephi 22:23).

The institutions that represent the devil's kingdom stand in stark contrast to Lord's righteous government. The Church of Jesus Christ of Latter-day Saints represents itself as the Lord's church on the earth. "He owns it, for He organized it. It is His, for He gave himself for it. It is the sacred depository of His truth. It is His instrumentality for the perfecting of the Saints, as well as for the work of the ministry and the redemption of the dead. It is the Christ's church in all these respects, but it is an institution that belongs to the Saints.

It is their refuge from the confusion and religious doubt and pessimism of the world. It is their instructor in principle, doctrine, and righteousness. It is their guide in matters of faith and morals. They have a conjoint ownership in it with Jesus

Christ, which ownership is recognized in the latter part of the title. (B.H. Roberts, H.C., 3:23-24).

The covenant relationship between the Lord and His church, manifest in the ordinances of the gospel performed by His priesthood representatives, defines: "Latter-day Saint." Members of the church who are content to identify themselves as "Mormons, or their church as "the L.D.S. Church," demean the institution to which they pledge their allegiance." (B.H. Roberts, "Comprehensive History of the Church," 1:393).

"Mine apostles, the Twelve which were with me in my ministry at Jerusalem, shall stand at my right hand at the day of my coming in a pillar of fire, being clothed with robes of righteousness, with crowns upon their heads." (V. 12). This verse reminds us of the symbolical clothing worn in the temple: "Wherefore, lift up your hearts and rejoice, and gird up your loins, and take upon you my whole armor, that ye may be able to withstand the evil day, having done all, that ye may be able to stand. Stand, therefore, having your loins girt about with truth, having on the breastplate of righteousness, and your feet shod with the preparation of the gospel of peace, which I have sent mine angels to commit unto you; Taking the shield of faith wherewith ye shall be able to quench all the fiery darts of the wicked; And take the helmet of salvation, and the sword of my Spirit, which I will pour out upon you, and my word which I reveal unto you, and be agreed as touching all the things whatsoever ye ask of me, and be faithful until I come." (D&C 27:15-18).

The Lord said that Special Witnesses would come "in glory even as I am, to judge the whole House of Israel, even as many as have loved me and kept my commandments, and none else." (V. 12). "And with righteousness shall the Lord God judge the poor, and reprove with equity for the meek of the earth. And he shall smite the earth with the rod of his mouth; and with the breath of his lips shall he slay the wicked." (2 Nephi 21:4). In this case, the "rod" is a symbol of priesthood power. The Lord has revealed His battle plan for the Last Days, when He will engage His servants in mortal combat against the forces of Babylon, whose soldiers will die both temporally and spiritually.

His army of missionaries will smite the earth with the word of God and by the power of the priesthood figuratively slay the wicked. As Alma found, "the preaching of the word had a great tendency to lead the people to do that which was just - yea, it had more powerful effect upon the minds of the people than the sword, or anything else." (Alma 31:5).

At that time, "a trump shall sound both long and loud, even as upon Mount Sinai, and all the earth shall quake, and they shall come forth - yea, even the dead which died in me, to receive a crown of righteousness, and to be clothed upon, even as I am, to be with me, that we may be one." (V. 13). We shall continue to progress, as we regain the glory of our former home. "I have warmed both hands before the fire of life," wrote Sir William Murdock. "The rich spoils of memory are mine. Mine, too, are the precious things of today. The best of life is always further on. Its real lure is hidden from our eyes somewhere behind the hills of time." (Quoted by Barbara Smith, in "The Love That Never Faileth").

"And then shall the righteous shine forth in the Kingdom of God." (Alma 40:25). In contrast, those who have lost the capacity to repent, who have died "as to things pertaining to things of righteousness," whose countenances no longer reflect the Light of Christ, will "drink the dregs of a bitter cup." (Alma 40:26).

Ancient Jerusalem will be rebuilt, and will become a millennial city, from which the word of the Lord will go forth. A New Jerusalem, a New Zion, a City of God will be built upon the American continent. (See the 10th Article of Faith). The city of Enoch, the original Zion taken into heaven, shall return as a New Jerusalem to join with its namesake. (See Moses 7:13-21).

"Before this great day shall come the sun shall be darkened, and the moon shall be turned into blood, and the stars shall fall from heaven, and there shall be greater signs in heaven above and in the earth beneath," for those who watch for the Second Coming of the Lord. (V. 14). "And I heard a great voice out of the temple, saying to the seven angels, Go your ways, and pour out the vials of the wrath of God upon the earth." (Revelation 16:1). Of the Four Horsemen of the Apocalypse, perhaps the most fearsome is Death: "And I looked, and behold a pale horse: and his name that sat on him was Death, and Hell followed with him. And power was given unto them over the fourth part of the earth, to kill with sword, and with hunger, and with death, and with the beasts of the earth." Revelation 5:8).

Speaking of Moroni's second visit to him, on September 21, 1823, Joseph Smith wrote: "(Moroni) informed me of great judgments which were coming upon the earth, with great desolations by famine, sword and pestilence; and these grievous judgments would come on the earth in this generation." (H.C., 1:111). It will be a day of thick darkness and gloominess for the wicked, when even the sun and the moon and the stars of heaven will obey the voice of the Master, in a full-on retreat as the Light of Christ is withdrawn. "For the stars of heaven and the constellations thereof shall not give their light; the sun shall be darkened in his going forth, and the moon shall not cause her light to shine." (Isaiah 13:10).

It will be as it was in the years before the birth of the Savior in Bethlehem, when great signs were given "to the intent that there should be no cause for unbelief," and also "to the intent that whosoever (would) believe might be saved, and that whosoever (would) not believe, a righteous judgment might come upon them; and also if they (would be) condemned, they (would) bring upon themselves their own condemnation." (Helaman 14:18-19).

"And there shall be weeping and wailing among the hosts of men; and there shall be a great hailstorm sent forth to destroy the crops of the earth." (V. 15-16, see Revelation 11:19 & 16:21). Nephi assured his brethren that these judgments would come upon the children of men, "yea, even blood, and fire, and vapor of smoke must come; and it must needs be upon the face of this earth; and it cometh unto men according to the flesh if it so be that they will harden their hearts against the Holy One of Israel." (1 Nephi 22:18). As a result of faithlessness and nonconformity to the prescribed requirements of the Plan of Salvation, "all they who fight against Zion shall be cut off" from access to enlightenment by the Spirit. (1 Nephi 22:19).

"And it shall come to pass, because of the wickedness of the world, that I will take vengeance upon the wicked, for they will not repent; for the cup of mine indignation is full; for behold, my blood shall not cleanse them if they hear me not." (V. 17). It would be a disservice to mankind, rather than a virtue, to extend the benefits of the Atonement to the unrepentant wicked. To them, the Atonement can be of no effect, for Justice must be served in the absence of Mercy.

Justice and Mercy may be likened to solar radiation (Justice) and the atmosphere of the earth (Mercy). By and large, solar radiation is a good thing, but it has certain properties that can be harmful, even fatal, to life forms. For example, the ozone in the stratosphere surrounding the earth protects us from ultraviolet radiation from the sun, while allowing beneficial infrared radiation to warm the planet just enough to support life in all of its thriving varieties. If we abuse our stewardship by exposing our skin to the sun for too long, by failing to apply sunscreen, or by destroying the ozone layer through the careless abuse of our stewardship over the earth itself, we may ruin the very thing that has protected us from destruction since the dawn of creation. Just so, the failure of the wicked to apply the sunscreen of repentance will prevent Mercy from becoming the shield of protection that it was meant to be, from the unmitigated effects of the Law of Justice.

The cup of the wrath of God is full when people have become so wicked that they will not repent. In that case, the Law of Justice, without the intervention of Mercy, must take effect. When the scriptures characterize the wicked as having drunk out of the cup of the wrath of God, they are not just using poetical metaphor. Rather, they allude to the symbolism of water, which communicated a very powerful message to the minds of the ancients. The "Internal Water Ordeal" is mentioned several times in The Book of Mormon. (See 2 Nephi 8:17, & 3 Nephi 11:11). We may dismiss ordeals as superstitious indulgences, but there is a wealth of symbolism associated with water and with its power to save or to destroy. (See FARMS Report, "Ordeal by Water").

In any event, Mercy has no claim on the wicked because they have chosen to deny themselves the blessings of the Atonement. The figure of speech used in the scriptures that "their torment is as a lake of fire and brimstone," should not be taken literally. However, at the Judgment and immediately thereafter, the cheeks of such individuals will nevertheless burn with guilt, and they will have a bright recollection of their sins. It will surely be a very unpleasant experience, as they squirm about in the face of an awful avalanche of consequences that smothers any prospect of immediate deliverance.

"Wherefore, I the Lord God will send forth flies upon the face of the earth, which shall take hold of the inhabitants thereof, and shall eat their flesh, and shall cause maggots to come in upon them; and their tongues shall be stayed that they shall not utter against me; and their flesh shall fall from off their bones, and their eyes from their sockets. And it shall come to pass that the beasts of the forest and the fowls of the air shall devour them up." (V. 18-20). In the Last Days, as the Spirit is withdrawn, "there shall be heard of fires, and tempests, and vapors of smoke in foreign lands; and there shall also be heard of wars, rumors of wars, and earthquakes in divers places." (Mormon 8:29-30). These are conditions with which Moroni was intimately familiar. He knew that the wrath of God requires the destruction of the wicked, and that our day would be frighteningly similar to the last days of the Nephites. Perhaps it is because The Book of Mormon speaks to our common feeling that it is so convincing.

Albeit somewhat pessimistically, Robert Preston puts forth the argument that, "in a sense, the earth is mounting an immune response against the human species. It is beginning to react to the human parasite, the flooding infection of people, the dead spots of concrete all over the planet, the cancerous rot-outs in Europe, Japan, and the United States, thick with replicating primates, the colonies enlarging and spreading and threatening to shock the biosphere with mass extinctions. Perhaps the biosphere does not "like" the idea of five billion humans. Or it could also be said that the extreme amplification of the human race, which has occurred only in the past hundred years or so, has suddenly produced a very large quantity of meat, which is sitting everywhere in the biosphere and may not be able to defend itself against a life form that might want to consume it. Nature has interesting ways of balancing itself. The rain forest has its own defenses. The earth's immune system, so to speak, has recognized the presence of the human species and is starting to kick in. The earth is attempting to rid itself of an infection by the human parasite. Perhaps AIDS is the first step in a natural process of clearance.

I suspect that AIDS may not be Nature's pre-eminent display of power. Whether the human race can actually maintain a population of five billion or more without a crash with a hot virus remains an open question. The answer lies hidden in the labyrinth of tropical ecosystems. AIDS is the revenge of the rain forest. It may be only the beginning." ("The Hot Zone," p. 408-409).

"And the great and abominable church, which is the whore of all the earth, shall be cast down by devouring fire, according as it is spoken by the mouth of Ezekiel the prophet." (V. 21). This is the only instance in the Doctrine & Covenants where the term 'great and abominable church' is employed, although it is used twelve times in The Book of Mormon, in 1 Nephi 4:3, 9, 15, & 17, 1 Nephi 13:6, 8, 26 & 28, 1 Nephi 22:13 & 14, 2 Nephi 6:12, & 2 Nephi 28:18. That is enough to entrench the phrase in our lexicon. Nephi was given, in vision, a broad view of the state of the world in the Last Days. He clearly saw "the great persecutor of the church, the apostate, the whore, even Babylon, that maketh all nations to drink of her cup, in whose hearts the enemy, even Satan, sitteth to reign." (D&C 86:3).

Nephi wrote: "And it came to pass that I saw among the nations of the Gentiles the formation of a great church." (1 Nephi 13:4). This verse is an example of typesetting changes that were made in the 1981 English language edition of The Book of Mormon. Oliver Cowdery's original manuscript had read "formation," but the original typesetter misread that word as "foundation," which for 150 years was incorrectly perpetuated and incorporated into the text.

When we encounter the term "great and abominable church," we should be careful not to apply too much literal significance. We learn in The Book of Mormon that there are really only two churches. (See 1 Nephi 14:10). So, the great and abominable church does not refer specifically to one church of Christendom, although it has been common among members of the L.D.S. Church to label the Holy Catholic Church as such. To do so would be a technical error.

The Book of Mormon explains why the church of the devil is abominable. "For behold, they have taken away from the gospel of the Lamb many parts which are plain and most precious; and also many covenants of the Lord have they taken away." (1 Nephi 13:26). Sometimes unwittingly, and at other times knowingly, it has changed the covenant, effectively eliminating the Old Testament as a witness for Christ. This is abominable because it at least temporarily stops the progression of those caught in its snares, as it destroys our comprehension of the purpose of mortality in the great Plan of Salvation. With this in mind, the "Church News" reported that "the witness for Christ was the most important thing in that ancient record." (1/1966). Without the testimony of Christ, however, the Old Testament loses much of its purpose and power.

"And all this have they done that they might pervert the right ways of the Lord," wrote Nephi, "that they might blind the eyes and harden the hearts of the children of men." (1 Nephi 13:27). This prophecy has literally come to pass. The Old Testament might read like The Book of Mormon were it not for the loss of its plain and precious parts. Instead, "an exceedingly great many do stumble, yea, insomuch that Satan hath great power over them." (1 Nephi 13:29). These verses underscore the power of the word of God, found within the pages of The Book of Mormon, to help us to conduct ourselves righteously and to resist the temptations of the devil, and conversely, they warn that without the iron rod, wandering off into mists of darkness is a stark and real possibility.

Those whose allegiance is to the great and abominable church of the devil will literally and figuratively 'find' their souls in hell, or in the so-called spirit prison of the disobedient. (See "Doctrines of the Gospel Student Manual, (2000), p. 87–89. & D&C 88:97-102). "For behold, this is according to the captivity of the devil, and also according to the justice of God, upon all those who will work wickedness and abomination before him." (1 Nephi 14:4). Clearly, the captivity of the devil brings us into spiritual bondage and estrangement from God. If we deny the Atonement, mercy cannot prevail on our behalf, and we forfeit our claim to the cleansing effect of the blood of Christ. Justice must then prevail, requiring that our souls be led away "down to hell - yea, (to) that great pit which hath been digged for the destruction of men (and which) shall be filled by those who digged it, unto their utter destruction." (1 Nephi 14:3). Our progression will grind to a halt, because for us, the Plan of Salvation has become inoperative. In counterpoint, the power of the Atonement comes into sharp focus with the Lord's injunction that "whoso repenteth not, must perish." (1 Nephi 14:5).

Zion will ultimately be redeemed from the "whore of the earth" by the power of the priesthood held by Jesus Christ and delegated to His servants on earth. Doctrine & Covenants 1:9 teaches that the wrath of God is reserved for the wicked, and that its fulness requires their destruction. As we see this occurring in the world about us, we are witnessing a significant sign of the times. "And when the day cometh that the wrath of God is poured out upon the mother of harlots, which is the great and abominable church of all the earth, whose founder is the devil, then, at that day, the work of the Father shall commence, in preparing the way for the fulfilling of his covenants, which he hath made to his people who are of the house of Israel." (1 Nephi 14:17).

Of the church and kingdom of the devil, Nephi prophesied that "the blood of that great and abominable church, which is the whore of all the earth, shall turn upon their own heads; for they shall war among themselves, and the sword of their own hands shall fall upon their own heads, and they shall be drunken with their own blood." (1 Nephi 22:13). The wicked feel neither loyalty nor love for anything or anyone but themselves. They do not enjoy the blessings of unity and certainly not the peace that is the province of the righteous. Instead, the father of contention, who is Satan, perversely manipulates those who follow him, and he enjoy sitting back and watching the process of their self-destruction unfold before his eyes.

Ominously, the Lord has assured us that every nation that fights against Zion will be destroyed, as will the great and abominable church of the devil. In the Last Days, God will not allow the wicked to subvert the Plan of Salvation by destroying the righteous. He has promised that after the restoration of the gospel, the church organization that administers the ordinances of salvation will never again be taken from the earth. The government of the church in the Last Days will remain throughout the turbulent times ahead, to insure that the promises that God has made to His Covenant people will come to pass. His words will be fulfilled in every whit.

Although the righteous will be caught up in the turmoil, they will be preserved by the power of God, and so they need not fear. Mark E. Peterson declared: "In the midst of all these tribulations, God will send fire from heaven if necessary to destroy our enemies while we carry forward our work." The Master of the Universe will not permit Satan or his lieutenants to thwart His purposes, no matter how hard they might try to interfere. As a matter of fact, those who have "perverted the right ways of the Lord, yea, that great and abominable church, shall tumble to the dust and great shall be the fall of it." (1 Nephi 22:14).

They shall be as Ozymandias, of whom Shelley wrote: "I met a traveler from an antique land who said: Two vast and trunkless legs of stone stand in the desert. Near them, on the sand half sunk, a shattered visage lies, whose frown and wrinkled lip and sneer of cold command tell that its sculptor well those passions read, which yet survive. Stamped on these lifeless things, the hand that mocks them and the heart that fed; and on the pedestal these words appear: 'My name is Ozymandias, King of Kings; Look on my works, ye mighty, and despair!' Nothing beside remains.

Round the decay of that colossal wreck, boundless and bare, the lone and level sand stretched far away." ("Ozymandias").

The battle lines during the war in heaven were drawn according to contrasting ideologies. The weapons used were the words that powerfully articulated opposing positions. That Satan was persuasive is attested by the fact that he drew a third part of the heavenly host to his point of view.

In the Last Days, the combatants are once again forming into diametrically opposed camps with increasingly polarized ideologies. "For the time speedily cometh that the Lord God shall cause a great division among the people." (2 Nephi 30:10). We should remember how enticingly Satan beckons us with his soothing words. With deceit and deception, he tries to ensnare us. But the word of God is quick, or living, in a biblical sense. It is powerful, or a source of life and energy; sharper than a two-edged sword, to the dividing asunder of both joints and marrow, or penetrating to our innermost parts. Therefore, we should give heed to all His words.

When the Millennium commences, there will be a great outpouring of the Spirit, when "there is nothing which is secret, save it shall be revealed; there is no work of darkness save it shall be made manifest in the light; and there is nothing which is sealed upon the earth save it shall be loosed. (2 Nephi 30:17). In that day, "Satan shall have power over the hearts of the children of men no more, for a long time." (2 Nephi 30:18). Spencer W. Kimball declared of these verses: "Through our faithfulness, all that God has promised will be fulfilled." (C.R., 4/1980). Then, "when the thousand years are ended, and men again begin to deny their God, then will I spare the earth but for a little season." (V. 22). "And when the thousand years are expired, Satan shall be loosed out of his prison. And he shall go out to deceive the nations which are in the four quarters of the earth." (Revelation 20:7-8). But then, "Michael...shall gather together his armies, even the hosts of heaven. And the devil shall gather together his armies; even the hosts of hell, and shall come up to battle against Michael and his armies. And then cometh the battle of the great God; and the devil and his armies shall be cast away into their own place, that they shall not have power over the Saints any more at all. For Michael shall fight their battles, and shall overcome him who seeketh the throne of Him who sitteth upon the throne, even the Lamb." (D&C 88:112-115).

"And the end shall come, and the heaven and the earth shall be consumed and pass away, and there shall be a new heaven and a new earth." (V. 23). "For behold, saith the prophet, the time cometh speedily that Satan shall have no more power over the hearts of the children of men; for the day soon cometh that all the proud and they who do wickedly shall be as stubble; and the day cometh that they must be burned." (1 Nephi 22:15). This is the unalterable decree of God, Whose judgments are just. Indeed, in a tangible way, the unrepentant will realize that the Word of Christ is sharper than a two-edged sword.

"For all old things shall pass away, and all things shall become new, even the heaven and the earth, and all the fulness thereof, both men and beasts, the fowls of the air, and the fishes of the sea." (V. 24, see D&C 77:2). The Millennium will signal the commencement of a limitless New World Order.

"And I saw a great white throne," emblematic of purity and justice, "and (Christ) that sat on it, from whose face the earth and the heaven fled away, and there was found no place for them." (Revelation 20:11). Thus, is described the end of the earth as it has been known. There will be a new earth, even a terrestrial sphere. John "saw a new heaven and a new earth: for the first heaven and the first earth were passed away; and there was no more sea. And I John saw the holy city, new Jerusalem, coming down from God out of heaven, prepared as a bride adorned for her husband." (Revelation 21:1-2). It descended "out of heaven from God, having the glory of God: and her light was like unto a stone most precious, even like a jasper stone, clear as crystal." (Revelation 21:10). Perhaps Zion, the city of Enoch, was translated in part so that it could return at the millennial day to stand as a "type" of life and conditions on the terrestrial earth. During the Millennium, the building materials used in the construction of the New Jerusalem will be "pure gold, like unto clear glass," and their foundations will be "garnished with all manner of precious stones." (Revelation 21:18-19). It will be a city of such magnificence, that it is described relative only to the most valuable and desirable elements on earth.

"And not one hair, neither mote, shall be lost." (V. 25). This is an indication of the thoroughness of the judgments of God. A wonderful truth was taught when Alma declared: "The soul shall be restored to the body, and the body to the soul; yea, and every limb and joint shall be restored to its body; yea, even a hair of the head shall not be lost; but all things shall be restored to their proper and perfect frame." (Alma 40:23. Joseph Fielding Smith, Jr. shed more light on this principle when he indicated: "All deformities and imperfections will be removed, and the body will conform to the likeness of the spirit." ("Doctrines of Salvation," 2:289). Joseph F. Smith said: "From the day of the resurrection, the body will develop until it reaches the full measure of the stature of its spirit." ("Gospel Doctrine," p. 23).

"But...before the earth shall pass away, Michael, mine archangel, shall sound his trump, and then shall all the dead awake, for their graves shall be opened, and they shall come forth - yea, even all." (V. 26). "And I saw the dead, small and great, stand before God; and the books were opened: and another book was opened, which is the book of life: and the dead were judged out of those things which were written in the books, according to their works." (Revelation 20:12). Figuratively speaking, the record of our lives is transcribed in the sinews of our being. Literally speaking, there is a record kept in heaven of the names and righteous deeds of the faithful. We will be judged by our obedience to the principles, doctrines, ordinances, and covenants contained in the Standard Works that collectively contain the Law of the Lord.

When we are enlightened by the Holy Ghost, we will be prepared to understand the gospel principle of resurrection, that is a mystery kept from the world because it can only be spiritually discerned. "There are many mysteries which are kept, that no one knoweth them save God himself." (Alma 40:3, see Alma 37:11). Therefore, we should not be impatient to gain an intellectual or even a spiritual mastery of that which is apparently beyond our comprehension, or which is unnecessary for us to have at this stage of our development. Perhaps the mystery of resurrection is difficult for even the spiritually mature and scripturally literate to understand. Certainly, it was a difficult doctrine even for the Savior's own Apostles to master, both during and immediately after His mortal ministry, when He became the first fruits of the resurrection. (See Jacob 4:11).

It was Alma's faith that "there is a time appointed that all shall come forth from the dead." (Alma 40:4). It was not important to him to know specifically when that time was. Although he lived before the mortal ministry of Christ, he had developed an eternal perspective, and knew that "time only is measured unto men." (Alma 40:8). For God resides "on a globe like a sea of glass and fire, where all things are manifest, past, present, and future, and are continually before the Lord." (D&C 130:7).

The scriptures make a valiant effort to describe God's perspective. But it remains that, trapped in time, we can only indirectly appreciate the eternities. "Even now, time is clearly not our natural dimension," said Neal A. Maxwell. "Thus it is, that we are never really at home in time. Alternately, we find ourselves impatiently wishing to hasten the passage of time, or to hold back the dawn. We can do neither, of course. Whereas, the bird is at home in the air, we are clearly not at home in time, because we belong to eternity. Time, as much as any one thing, whispers to us that we are strangers here. If time were natural to us, why is it that we have so many clocks and wristwatches?" ("B.Y.U. Speeches of The Year," 1979).

"Concerning the state of the soul between death and the resurrection," Alma had a clear vision, teaching "that the spirits of all men, as soon as they are departed from this mortal body, yea, the spirits of all men, whether they be good or evil, are taken home to that God who gave them life." (Alma 40:11). Nevertheless, they are not immediately taken into the actual presence of God. Rather, "the spirits of those who are righteous are received into a state of happiness, which is called paradise, a state of rest, a state of peace, where they shall rest from all their troubles and from all care, and sorrow." (Alma 40:2). Paradise is not a state of perfect happiness, for that is possible only in the resurrection. As the Lord said, "The elements are eternal, and (only) spirit and element inseparably connected, receive a fulness of joy, and when separated, man cannot receive a fulness of joy." (D&C 93:23-24).

It was Alma's correct opinion that "the souls and the bodies (of the righteous) are reunited at the resurrection of Christ, and his ascension into heaven." (Alma 40:20). We learn from other scripture that the wicked, though, will be resurrected only at the end of the Millennium. (See D&C 76:81-85, & 88:100-101).

"And the righteous shall be gathered on my right hand unto eternal life; and the wicked on my left hand will I be ashamed to own before the Father. Wherefore I will say unto them - Depart from me, ye cursed, into everlasting fire, prepared for the devil and his angels." (V. 27-28). This is the second death. (See Revelation 20:14). The fate or destiny of these Sons of Perdition will not be revealed to any except those who are made partakers thereof.

In vision, John foresaw that "He that overcometh shall inherit all things," but "whosoever was not found written in the book of life was cast into the lake of fire." (Revelation 21:7 & 20:15). For "the fearful, and unbelieving, and the abominable, and murderers, and whoremongers, and sorcerers, and idolaters, and all liars, shall have their part in the lake which burneth with fire and brimstone: which is the second death." (Revelation 21:8).

"Never at any time have I declared from mine own mouth that they should return, for where I am they cannot come, for they have no power." (V. 29). It has been argued that the time when we may elect to live a celestial law has passed when we are judged and assigned to a lesser kingdom of glory. According to this scenario, we may thereafter progress only within the limitations of whichever kingdom we are in. Our progression is not to the extent that would ever lead us to live a celestial law. To put it another way, we may lose our ability to exercise our capacity to become as God is, because we neglected to do so while the opportunity was available to us. The opportunity of a lifetime must be taken during the lifetime of the opportunity.

At least one thing does seem certain: If we are to obtain exaltation and eternal life in the Celestial Kingdom, we must do more than just acknowledge, or confess, that Jesus Christ is Lord. The critical point of our conversion, beyond which lie the encircling flames of the Celestial Kingdom of God, rests in our making a conscious decision to accept not only Jesus Christ, but the on-going performance demands of His gospel as well.

A simple and yet uncommitted recognition of Jesus will not qualify us for admittance to the Celestial Kingdom. If we are only Christians of convenience, we will lack the fire that the demands of discipleship require. Many honorable people who accept Jesus will still go to the Terrestrial Kingdom. According to the scriptures, these are they who "received not the gospel, neither the testimony of Jesus, neither the prophets, neither the everlasting covenant. Last of all, these are all they who will not be gathered with the Saints, to be caught up unto the Church of the Firstborn, and received into the cloud." (D&C 76:101-102).

Only if we passionately embrace the gospel with its ordinances and covenants, and then partake of the divine nature, will we enjoy the highest degree of glory and live in the presence of God Himself. "These are they who are priests and kings, who have received of his fulness, and of his glory; and are priests of the Most High, after the order of Melchizedek, which was after the order of Enoch, which was after the order of the Only Begotten Son. Wherefore, as it is written, they are gods, even the sons of God." (D&C 76:56-58).

This distinction becomes vitally important to those billions of souls whose improvement would seem to halt at the Last Judgment, because of the poor decisions they made in mortality. The Plan introduced by Heavenly Father to His spirit children was so magnificent that when the "foundation of the earth" was laid, "the morning stars sang together, and all the sons of God shouted for joy." (Job 38:7-8). It is inconceivable that a Plan of such transcendent perfection would have been consciously designed to save only a small percentage of His spirit children in the Celestial Kingdom.

The question remains: Are our actions during mortality so significant that they will determine our status forever? Before the Fall, Adam lived in the Garden of Eden in a morally static, vegetative state. It seems satanic to argue that most of his posterity will do so again, in a mind-numbing telestial existence. After all, it was the devil himself who sought "that all men might be miserable like unto himself." (2 Nephi 2:27). Will he be declared the ultimate winner, by default, in the ideological conflict that commenced in heaven so long ago?

Perhaps God will only leave his unrighteous and disobedient children in the so-called Spirit Prison of the Unjust long enough for them to recognize the error of their ways, that they might make behavioral changes consistent with the teachings of the gospel of Jesus Christ. (See "Doctrines of the Gospel Student Manual, (2000), p. 87–89, D&C 76:73, 88:97-102, Alma 40:11-14, & Moses 7:57). Following the recognition of their violation of law, such individuals would be required to pay directly for their sins committed in mortality that had fallen outside the merciful sphere of influence of the Atonement of the Savior. Such a punishment, although admittedly harsh, would be eternally and endlessly in harmony with the Law of Justice.

Perhaps our Father in Heaven wants us to accept His Son and gospel so that we may avoid the "weeping and gnashing of teeth" that accompany the recognition that our "days of probation are past; (when we) have procrastinated the day of (our) salvation until it is everlastingly too late, and (our) destruction is made sure." (J.S.M. 1:54).

When we have sought "all the days of (our) lives for that which (we) cannot obtain, and...have sought for happiness in doing iniquity, which thing is contrary to the nature of that righteousness which is in our great and Eternal Head," we must ultimately face the consequences. (Helaman 13:38). It will then be, in the most difficult circumstances of repentance imaginable, that the necessary reform will be made and the uttermost farthing personally paid.

How much better it would have been to have listened to the prophets. "And in the days of your poverty ye shall cry unto the Lord; and in vain shall ye cry, for your desolation is already come upon you, and your destruction is made sure; and then shall ye weep and howl in that day, saith the Lord of Hosts. And then shall ye lament, and say: O that I had repented, and had not killed the prophets, and stoned them, and cast them out. Yea, in that day ye shall say: ...O that we had repented in the day that the word of the Lord came unto us." (Helaman 13:32-36).

Such a scenario is in harmony with Brigham Young's belief that "all organized existence is in progress either to an endless advancement in eternal perfections, or back to dissolution. There is no period in all the eternities," he believed, "wherein organized existence will become stationary, that it cannot advance in knowledge, wisdom, power, and glory." (J.D., 1:349).

Joseph Smith declared to an assembly of the Saints: "I could explain a hundred-fold more than I ever have of the glories of the kingdoms manifested to me in vision, were I permitted, and were the people prepared to receive them." (H.C., 5:402) After all is said and done, when all the leaders of the church have been quoted, and the supporting scriptures cited, the fact remains that we have not been given the revelation that answers the question regarding the ultimate state in the eternities of those who fell short of exaltation following their mortal probation.

"But remember that all my judgments are not given unto men; and as the words have gone forth out of my mouth even so shall they be fulfilled, that the first shall be last, and that the last shall be first in all things whatsoever I have created by the word of my power, which is the power of my Spirit." (V. 30). This is the expression of the operation of a divine principle that illustrates the impartiality of God.

"For by the power of my Spirit created I them; yea, all things both spiritual and temporal - First spiritual, secondly temporal, which is the beginning of my work; and again, first temporal, and secondly spiritual." (V. 31-32). When this revelation was given, the members of the church were being taught for the very first time something about their life before the earth was organized! It seems axiomatic to us, but for the Saints in 1830, it would be three more years before the Lord would make known that He was the Firstborn of Heavenly Father's children (D&C 93:21) and that the rest of the human race was also in the beginning with the Father. (D&C 93:23, see D&C 77:2, & Moses 3:15). In these revelations, we see the principles of the Restoration unfolding before our eyes.

Today, these doctrines seem very natural to us. Elohim is our Heavenly Father. We were born of Him as His spirit children. We acquired His spiritual qualities and characteristics and were raised by Him to spiritual maturity, until we could progress no more. As spirit children, there were some laws that pertain only to mortality that we could not have the opportunity to obey, and so there were some blessings that were unavailable to us. Therefore, we left His presence to fulfill a mission on earth. Even now, living in a foreign land, we are yet His spirit sons and daughters who enjoy a measure of His divine nature. If we continue to develop His characteristics during this period of probation, we will eventually become as He is. We will assume both His image and likeness. But for the Saints in 1830, these concepts were a revelatory thunder and lightning storm.

"We learn from the word of the Lord to Moses that He selected a place for the children of Israel, even before they were born. He indicated the number of spirits who were assigned to become the descendants of Jacob. We may well believe that the Lord also parceled out the surface of the earth for all other peoples." (Joseph Fielding Smith, Jr., "Answers to Gospel Questions," 4:11-12, see Deuteronomy 32:8).

In The Book of Mormon, probably the clearest affirmation that we lived before our birth is found in Alma 13:3. It states that those who in mortality receive the Melchizedek Priesthood were foreordained from the foundation of the world. In our pre-mortal life, where both agency and opposition thrived because of the ideological war that had taken place following the Council, they chose the better part. In mortality they "are called with a holy calling." For Alma, Melchizedek epitomized a practical realization that each of us has potential from the foundation of the world that is realized in mortality, when we recognize and respond to the voice of the Lord.

"And thus," Alma explained, "they have been called to this holy calling on account of their faith," with history as a precedent, as well as with prophecy as a promise. These may provide a foundation for the way that we are called to positions within the church today. (Alma 13:4). "I like to think," said J. Reuben Clark, Jr., "that perhaps in that Grand Council something was said to us indicating what would be expected of us of lesser calling and lesser stature, and empowering us, subject to reconfirmation here, to do certain things in building up the Kingdom of God on earth." (C.R., 10/1950).

As a matter of fact, the scriptures teach that righteousness and obedience gave all of Heavenly Father's spirit children an equal opportunity to progress in their pre-earth life, and that faithful men who exercised priesthood power and authority in that first estate, do so again in mortality. Abraham was told: "And they who keep their first estate shall be added upon; and they who keep not their first estate shall not have glory in the same kingdom with those who keep their first estate; and they who keep their second estate shall have glory added upon their heads for ever and ever." (Abraham 3:26). Paul taught that "before the world began" God promised His spirit children that they would be provided with the opportunity to enjoy eternal life. (Titus 1:2).

Henry D. Moyle said: "We might well be assured that we had something to do with our allotment, in our pre-existent state. This would be an additional reason for us to accept our present condition and make the best of it. It is what we agreed to do. We unquestionably knew before we came to this earth the conditions under which we would here exist, and live, and work. So little wonder that Alma said that we sin in the thought, or in the desire, or in the wish that we were someone other than ourselves." (C.R., 10/1952).

These "great and eternal purposes were prepared from the foundation of the world," that "mercy claimeth the penitent, and mercy cometh because of the atonement; and the atonement bringeth to pass the resurrection of the dead; and the resurrection of the dead bringeth back men into the presence of God. For behold, justice exerciseth all _his_ demands, and also mercy claimeth all which is _her_ own; and thus, none but the truly penitent are saved." (Alma 42:23-24 & 26, underlining mine).

The Law of Justice made the Atonement of Jesus Christ necessary, while the Law of Mercy made it possible. The two laws are in complete harmony, with Mercy introducing the possibility of vicarious payment for the required punishment in consequence of laws that have been transgressed. Intriguingly, In the scripture just cited, Alma seemed to treat mercy and justice as counterpoints, if not outright opposites, in the grand scheme of the Plan of Salvation. This scripture brings to mind Lehi's hokmah, or truism, that there must needs be opposition in all things. Apparently, this includes foundation principles of the Plan, as well as gender assignment that makes those principles easier to comprehend. It is possible that Alma consciously used the natural differences between men and women to intentionally illustrate, against the backdrop of masculinity and femininity, the unique individuality of Justice on the one hand, and Mercy on the other.

"Our birth," wrote William Wordsworth, "is but a sleep and a forgetting. The soul that rises with us, our life's star, hath had elsewhere its setting, and cometh from afar. Not in entire forgetfulness, and not in utter nakedness, but trailing clouds of glory do we come, from God, who is our Home." ("Ode: Intimations of Immortality").

The Savior explained to the Saints: I speak "unto you that you may naturally understand; but unto myself my works have no end, neither beginning; but it is given unto you that ye may understand." (V. 33). To Latter-day Saints, Christ is the personification of the Rock of Revelation. He is the physical expression of the One Eternal God. The message He gives to His people is "the doctrine of Christ, and the only and true doctrine of the Father, and of the Son, and of the Holy Ghost, which is one God, without end." (2 Nephi 31:21).

Because faithful Saints hold to the iron rod, "no unhallowed hand can stop the work from progressing; persecutions may rage, mobs may combine, armies may assemble, calumny may defame, but the truth of God will go forth boldly, nobly, and independent, until it has penetrated every continent, visited every clime, swept every country, and sounded in every ear, 'til the purposes of God shall be accomplished and the Great Jehovah shall say 'The work is done.'" (Joseph Smith, in "The Wentworth Letter," H.C., 4:540).

For "God doth not walk in crooked paths, neither doth He turn to the right hand nor to the left, neither doth He vary from that which He hath said, therefore His paths are straight, and His course is one eternal round." (D&C 3:2).

It is worth noting that the religious views of The Church of Jesus Christ of Latter-day Saints are based almost entirely on a great mass of new revelation given to Joseph Smith between 1820 and 1844. We can be sure, however, that the doctrines we have accepted will continue to be compatible with truth, even hidden truth, for example, that which is contained within the sealed portion of The Book of Mormon.

After all, a basic tenet of our faith affirms that "we believe all that God has revealed, all that He does now reveal, and we believe that He will yet reveal many great and important things pertaining to the Kingdom of God." (9th Article of Faith).

Our introduction to these revelatory doctrines allows us to catch a glimpse of heaven. In our study of the Doctrine & Covenants, we sometimes dream about "stepping on shore, and finding it heaven! Of taking hold of a hand, and finding it God's hand. Of breathing a new air, and finding it celestial air. Of feeling invigorated, and finding it immortality. Of passing from storm and tempest to the unbroken calm of God's Rest. Of waking up, and finding it Home." (Anonymous).

When the scriptures encourage us to find wisdom and great treasures of knowledge, even hidden treasures, they are suggesting the need to search for those pearls that may not be readily discernible after only a cursory glance. It is dangerous to summarily dismiss as things of no consequence doctrine that is interwoven into the tapestry of our being. "And all they who receive the oracles of God, let them beware how they hold them lest they are accounted as a light thing, and are brought under condemnation thereby, and stumble and fall when the storms descend, and the winds blow, and the rains descend, and beat upon their houses." (D&C 90:5). Those who have access to the revelations through the prophets, but who do not take them seriously, will not be able to withstand life's trials. Joseph Smith wrote: "There are but a very few beings in the world who understand rightly the nature of God, (and) if men do not understand the character of God they do not comprehend themselves." ("Teachings," p. 343).

"Wherefore, verily I say unto you that all things unto me are spiritual, and not at any time have I given unto you a law which was temporal; neither any man nor the children of men; neither Adam, your father whom I created." (V. 34). Here, Christ is speaking for the Father, by divine investiture of authority. Everything He says or does is exactly and precisely what the Father would say and do under the same circumstances.

From the Savior's perspective, everything in temporal existence enjoys a seamless spiritual symmetry. As such, all of God's creations testify of His divinity. The Plan of Salvation so perfectly harmonizes the temporal with the spiritual, that perfect obedience obliterates any distinction between the two. Every principle of the gospel has an associated component associated with obedience. As consequence follows action, so blessings follow obedience. As Alma explained, "All men that are in a state of nature, or I would say, in a carnal state, are in the gall of bitterness and in the bonds of iniquity; they are without God in the world, and they have gone contrary to the nature of God; therefore, they are in a state contrary to the nature of happiness." (Alma 41:11).

The difference between a spiritual and a natural man is one of generation, and not just of maturation. The transformation involves a change of heart so profound that the scriptures liken the process to being "born again." When we catch the vision, we have no more disposition to sin, so ennobling is our sanctification by the Spirit. It is then that we realize that "earth is crammed with heaven, and every common bush with fire of God. But only those who see, take off their shoes. The rest stand around picking blackberries." (Elizabeth Barrett Browning).

"I gave unto him that he should be an agent unto himself." (V. 35). Disciples of Christ do not have the option to walk "in (their) own way, and after the image of (their) own god, whose image is in the likeness of the world, and whose substance is that of an idol." (D&C 1:16). Those who have consecrated their time, talents, energies, and their very lives to the Kingdom of God, have long since 'crossed over Jordan.' They stand with Joshua, who declared: "Choose you this day whom ye will serve; whether the gods which your fathers served that were on the other side of the flood, or the gods of the Amorites, in whose land ye dwell: but as for me and my house, we will serve the Lord." (Joshua 24:15).

In all ages, there have been many who have said: "Eat, drink, and be merry, for tomorrow we die; and it shall be well with us." (2 Nephi 28:7). This is their supposed justification of unrighteous conduct, and perhaps it is the ultimate rationalization. When people believe there are no consequences, their capacity to make correct choices diminishes, their desire to act with moral responsibility wavers, and their apprehension at doing wrong evaporates. Only sentient beings, who are truly self-aware, have true moral agency with the capacity to make choices, and only when the principles of Justice and Mercy are clearly understood can they work in concert to help shape behavior.

The Plan of Salvation preserves the principle of opposition because choice is critical to our development. How we deal with our experiences allow us to grow in spiritual stature, as we grapple with happiness and misery, good and evil, truth and error, freedom and captivity, life and death, pleasure and pain, and light and darkness.

"I gave unto him commandment, but no temporal commandment gave I unto him, for my commandments are spiritual; they are not natural nor temporal, neither carnal nor sensual." (V. 35). "The Latter-day Saints believe not only in the gospel of spiritual salvation, but in the gospel of temporal salvation, as well. The temporal and spiritual are blended. One cannot be carried on without the other, so long as we are here in mortality." (Joseph F. Smith, "Gospel Doctrine," p. 208).

"And it came to pass that Adam, being tempted of the devil - for behold, the devil was before Adam, for he rebelled against me, saying Give me thine honor, which is my power; and also a third part of the hosts of heaven turned he away from me because of their agency." (V. 36). The origin of Satan's rebellion, the number of spirits who followed him, the reality of agency as a principle in the pre-earth existence, the eventual home of the devil's angels, and the place of his operations in the lives of those in mortality, are all alluded to in verses 36-39.

"And there appeared another wonder in heaven: and behold a great red dragon... and his tail drew the third part of the stars of heaven, and did cast them to the earth. And there was war in heaven: Michael and his angels fought against the dragon; and the dragon fought and his angels, and prevailed not; neither was their place found any more in heaven." (Revelation 12:3-4). "And they were thrust down, and thus came the devil and his angels." (V. 37). And the great dragon was cast out, that old serpent, called the Devil, and Satan, which deceiveth the whole world: he was cast out into the earth, and his angels were cast out with him." (Revelation 12:7-9).

"And, behold, there is a place prepared for them from the beginning, which place is hell." (V. 38). The wicked are evil. They "have no part nor portion of the Spirit of the Lord," and are cast into outer darkness, which is "a state of awful, fearful looking for the fiery indignation of the wrath of God." (Alma 40:13-14). The wicked will remain in this state until the time of their resurrection. What is commonly called "the Spirit Prison of the Unjust is a place of correction for those who have committed all but the unpardonable sin. (See "Doctrines of the Gospel Student Manual, (2000), p. 87–89, D&C 76:73, 88:97-102, Alma 40:11-14, & Moses 7:57). When the penalty has been paid, and Justice has been satisfied, the sinner will be released from hell, prepared to be resurrected to a kingdom of glory." (James E. Talmage, "The Vitality of Mormonism," p. 264, see Alma 40:11-14). The devil and his angels, however, "shall be cast away into their own place, that they shall not have power over the Saints any more, at all." (D&C 88:114).

And it must needs be that the devil should tempt the children of men, or they could not be agents unto themselves; for if they never should have bitter they could not know the sweet." (V. 39). "Woe to the inhabiters of the earth and of the sea! For the devil is come down unto you, having great wrath, because he knoweth that he hath but a short time" left, until he will be bound by the righteousness of the people. (Revelation 12:12, see Revelation 20:2, & 1 Nephi 22:26).

It is Christ's way for men to act for themselves. It is Satan's way for them to be acted upon. The 'perfect law of liberty' requires that we be free according to the flesh. (See James 1:25). Our choice is between liberty and eternal life, or captivity and spiritual death. But all of our actions must be carried out within the context of the gospel and its laws, otherwise, our unbridled freedom would lead to tyranny. We are free to choose, but we cannot choose to escape the consequences of our poor choices.

Satan's tactics and plan would deny free will, require obedience, and rely on compulsion. When we forfeit our agency to the devil, we find ourselves in his snares, in the grip of bad habits, bound by his strong chains, and we feel his heavy cords around our necks that restrict our ability to move about freely, as they drag us down to hell. It is very hard for us to break our bad habits, because we have given up our agency in order to acquire them. We have sold our birthright, to choose for ourselves, (see Moses 3:17), for a mess of pottage.

Heavenly Father does not operate this way. He always honors the eternal principle of agency. It is riskier this way, but it is the only way. Rather than enslaving us in good habits, He repeatedly gives us the opportunity to recommit ourselves to our covenants of obedience to true and eternal principles, as we receive the Sacrament on a weekly basis. This is one of the most important reasons why church membership, and faithful participation in the on-going activities of the household of God, in particular Sacrament Meeting and temple attendance, is vital to our spiritual well-being.

"The spirit is pure, and (is) under the special control and influence of the Lord, but the body is of the earth, and is subject to the power of the devil, and is under the mighty influence of that fallen nature that is of the earth. If the spirit yields to the body, the devil then has power to overcome the body and spirit of that man, and he loses both." (Brigham Young, D.B.Y., p. 69-70).

"Wherefore, it came to pass that the devil tempted Adam." (V. 40). Not knowing the mind of God, that there must needs be opposition in all things, Satan sought what he thought would be the misery of all mankind, and with his congenital short-sightedness and his typical stratagem of promoting half-truths, he offered the forbidden fruit to Eve. "Ye shall be as God, knowing good and evil," he promised. (2 Nephi 2:18).

"And he partook of the forbidden fruit and transgressed the commandment." (V. 40). But Adam was not deceived. His was a conscious decision, the result of his intuitive understanding of the requirements of the gospel Plan. "Adam fell that men might be." (2 Nephi 2:25). A correct concept of the Fall of Adam is necessary if we are to understand the basic claims of Christianity. There was opposition from the beginning, for that is a principle of the Plan, but in the Garden of Eden, Adam and Eve did not have true moral agency before they yielded to the enticements of

Satan, for their eyes were not yet opened. (See Genesis 3:5). Therefore, the violation of law by Adam and Eve is characterized as a transgression, rather than a sin, in the normal sense of the word. See the 2nd Article of Faith).

"He became subject to the will of the devil, because he yielded unto temptation." (V. 40). Adam was deceived only in the sense that he was told of consequences that likely had no meaning to him, for he had no frame of reference. He had been told by God that should he partake of the forbidden fruit, he would die. This was a state of existence that was alien to him, for he was immortal, and not yet subject to death. We do not know what conditions were like outside the borders of the Garden, but we do know that no living thing in Eden had died or decayed. So Adam had no direct experience with death.

Then, he was told by the devil that he should not die, but that there should be a beneficial consequence following the transgression of the law. He was led to believe that he should be as the gods, knowing good and evil. (See Genesis 3:5 & Moses 4:11). Being innocent, he was caught in a quandary, with two incompatible alternatives laid out before him.

Adam and Eve had been told to be fruitful, and multiply, and replenish the earth, (see Genesis 1:28), but they had also been told not to partake of the fruit of the tree of knowledge of good and evil. (See Genesis 2:17, Moses 3:17, & Abraham 5:13). Opposition is a good thing, but Adam and Eve were in a conundrum from which there seemed to be, from their perspective, no way out. Ultimately, they partook of the forbidden fruit, that man might be. (See Genesis 3:6). Of course, God had foreseen the outcome of their encounter with Satan in the Garden, and had provided a Savior for them, (see Moses 1:6 & 1 John 4:14), that they might still enjoy eternal life in the Celestial Kingdom if they would submit themselves to the requirements of the Plan of Salvation. (See Moses 3:31).

The devil, not knowing the mind of God, unwittingly provided the way for Adam and Even to experience the joys and sorrows of mortality, and at the same time facilitated the introduction of moral agency into the world. Adam and Eve would have the opportunity to choose. Free will, that was so repugnant to Satan, would be the engine that would drive the Plan of Salvation forward. The transgression of Adam became the catalyst that generated that part of the Plan that would be carried out on the earth.

These verses put in proper perspective the expulsion of Adam and Eve from the Garden. They teach that "the Fall of Adam" was a blessing in disguise, by which the spirit sons and daughters of God, the posterity of Adam and Eve, would be given additional opportunities for progression that lay beyond the scope of the pre-mortal world. For "death hath passed upon all men, to fulfill the merciful plan of the great Creator." (2 Nephi 9:6).

"Wherefore, I, the Lord God, caused that he should be cast out from the Garden of Eden, from my presence, because of his transgression." (V. 41). There was no need for God to offer an apology for His action. What He did was never characterized as a punishment; rather, it was a policy decision that was critical to the successful execution of the Merciful Plan of the Great Creator. (See Abraham 3:25). The transgression of Adam resulted in spiritual death, that set the stage for moral development. The result of the Fall was the establishment of "the family of all the earth." (2 Nephi 2:20). The scriptures clearly teach that Adam and Eve were the first of Heavenly Father's children to live on this earth. "Father Adam, (was) the Ancient of Days, and father of all, (and so, too, was) our glorious Mother Eve." (D&C 138:38-39).

"Wherein he became spiritually dead, which is the first death." (V. 41). These first generations of mankind lived to great age, so that they might have time to repent. "And the days of the children of men were prolonged, according to the will of God, that they might repent while in the flesh; wherefore, their state became a state of probation, and their time was lengthened, according to the commandments which the Lord God gave unto the children of men: For he gave commandment that all men must repent." (2 Nephi 2:21). As Hugh Nibley said: "When the day of repentance is past, so is the day of grace. The ominous sign today is not that men do wrong, for they always have, but that they have no intention of repenting." ("Beyond Politics").

Mortality thus became a time of probation, of testing, or of putting to the proof. Always at issue is the question: "Will we repent?" If not, we must be lost, because of the transgression of Adam and Eve, that brought temporal and spiritual death to mankind; temporal death because of the separation of the body from the spirit at the close of mortal existence, and spiritual death because of the alienation of the Spirit from God in the absence of an Atonement, at the time of the Judgment.

What is called "the Fall of Adam" is really a means of giving further opportunities for the progression of the spirit sons and daughters of God. Spiritual death is banishment from God's presence, due to sin after the age of accountability. Temporal death is separation of the body from the spirit at the close of the mortal experience.

The purpose of the Fall was to give the children of Heavenly Father the opportunity to prepare for a resurrection. "And we see that death comes upon mankind...which is the temporal death; nevertheless there was a space granted unto man in which he might repent; therefore this life became a probationary state; a time to prepare to meet God; a time to prepare for that endless state which has been spoken of by us, which is after the resurrection of the dead." (Alma 12:24). Through the Atonement, we will be raised in the resurrection with the kinds of bodies that we will need in order to dwell in the degree of glory we have merited.

After the Fall, and because of the requirements of the Law of Justice, Adam and Eve and their posterity suffered spiritual death, that was a temporary alienation from the Spirit of God. Spiritual death occurs when we die "as to things pertaining unto righteousness." (Alma 12:16). The first individual spiritual death occurs when we commit sin after the age of accountability. In the scriptures, this is called "the first spiritual death." (See D&C 29:41). Fortunately, we can be spiritually born again through the cleansing action of the Holy Ghost, after repentance, and baptism of water and the Spirit.

"Even that same death which is the last death, which is spiritual, (the second spiritual death), which shall be pronounced upon the wicked when I shall say: Depart, ye cursed." (V. 41). The second spiritual death is an entirely different beast, however. It is an eternal separation from the presence of God, but it only occurs if we pass from mortality without having participated in the ordinances of the Priesthood, or when we willingly decline the vicarious ordinances performed on our behalf in the temples of the Lord.

Life is short, and yet all that is required may be accomplished within the parameters of the Plan. Death is essential to its successful execution. The transgression of Adam was an integral part of the Plan, inasmuch as it gave his posterity the opportunity to be born into this world, to live, and to die. Adam did not sin in the Garden of Eden, in the classical sense, for he did not have true moral agency. The scriptures refer only to his "transgression," and as mentioned above, the 2nd Article of Faith makes a specific distinction between it and our "sins." Mortality, that was the consequence of his transgression, was not a punishment for sin.

An Atonement was required to activate the Plan, and to give it vitality. The Atonement removed the permanent effects of physical death, and gave everyone the opportunity to have the effects of spiritual death removed through repentance. The Atonement can literally save us from becoming devils or angels to devils. It does this by bringing the Law of Mercy on-line, mitigating for those who conform to its requirements the effects of the first Law, that demands Justice.

"I, the Lord God, gave unto Adam and his seed, that they should not die as to the temporal death, until I, the Lord God, should send forth angels to declare unto them repentance and redemption, through faith on the name of mine Only Begotten Son," that they might become once again become spiritually alive. (V. 42). Adam was promised that he would have the opportunity to accept the gospel, so that the negative effects of spiritual death might be eliminated. He would die physically and experience a separation of his body and spirit until the resurrection, but he would not die suffer an interminable spiritual death.

Had Adam not transgressed the Law in the Garden, he would have vegetated there forever. Life in Eden was not an ideal existence, but was instead morally static. Our Father knew that Adam must fall as a critically operative part of the Plan of Salvation, but Satan had no such knowledge. Lehi's declaration that "Adam fell that men might be, and men are that they might have joy," is a grand summary of the doctrine concerning opposition and the Fall of Adam. (2 Nephi 2:25). This simple aphorism speaks volumes, and is one of the basic messages of the Restoration. When the Fall of Adam is considered in conjunction with the Atonement of Christ, it is clear that both are part of God's Plan of Eternal Progression for His children, who could only attain a fulness of joy in the presence of the Father in a personal, tangible, resurrection. "For man is spirit, the elements are eternal, and spirit and element, inseparably connected, receive a fulness of joy." (D&C 93:33).

The Plan of Salvation is the Plan of Redemption, and it makes possible the resurrection of otherwise imperfect mortals to an eternal life of glory. "Now, if it had not been for the plan of redemption, which was laid from the foundation of the world, there could have been no resurrection of the dead; but there was a plan of redemption laid, which shall bring to pass the resurrection of the dead." (Alma 12:25).

In the absence of repentance for our sins, and without the benefit of the gospel Plan of Salvation, we must ultimately be miserable, living forever in our sins. "And now behold, if it were possible that our first parents could have gone forth and partaken of the tree of life they would have been forever miserable, having no preparatory state; and thus the plan of redemption would have been frustrated, and the word of God would have been void, taking none effect." (Alma 12:26).

If one in that condition, having transgressed the law of God without the opportunity to exercise repentance unto forgiveness through the Atonement, were to unworthily partake of the fruit of the Tree of Life, which is eternal life, or the highest expression of the love of God, it would not be possible to sustain a celestial existence, inasmuch as one would not have aforetime demonstrated the capacity to be eternally obedient to celestial principles. Partaking of the fruit (eternal life), without having first learned to rely upon the merits of Christ (the Atonement), would have condemned Adam and Eve to live forever in their sins. Thus, the Plan of Salvation would have been frustrated, since Atonement and Redemption would have been nullified.

However, that scenario was not to be the case. Satan, who was a liar from the beginning, stormed out of the Council in Heaven and attempted to foil the proposed Plan of Salvation by substituting a counterfeit, unworkable plan, but His efforts were thwarted. Instead, the Lord appointed "unto man the days of his probation - that by his natural death he might be raised in immortality unto eternal life, even as many as would believe." (V. 43). The body and spirit would never again be separated, and would live forever in the presence of God, in eternal harmony with the principles that govern His kingdom.

Because of the resurrection of Christ, all mankind will pass from physical death to immortality, which is the condition of the body when reunited eternally with the spirit. This will come as a free gift to all who have ever lived on the earth.

We have been placed in a mortal condition with death our only exit. No-one is going to get out of this alive. "It was appointed unto men that they must die; and after death, they must come to judgment." (Alma 12:27). This judgment will come only after we have been given the opportunity to conform our lives to the principles of the Plan of Redemption. "It was expedient that man should know concerning the things whereof (God) had appointed unto them. Therefore, he sent angels to converse with them. ...And they began from that time forth to call on his name; therefore God conversed with men, and made known unto them the plan of redemption, which had been prepared from the foundation of the world; and this he made known unto them according to their faith and repentance and their holy works." (Alma 12:28-30).

We have agency to act for ourselves, and if we violate the commandments, we are to commanded to repent. Thus, we become "as Gods, knowing good from evil," and we live "in a state to act according to (our) wills, and pleasures, whether to do evil or to do good." (Alma 12:31).

In the clarifying light of latter-day revelation, we are taught that the violation of the commandments will result in "a second death, which was an everlasting death as to things pertaining unto righteousness; for on such the plan of redemption could have no power, for the works of justice could not be destroyed, according to the supreme goodness of God." (Alma 12:32). God will not nullify the demands of Justice, even if we choose to unwisely use our freedom to act independently.

Therefore, He has provided a safety net for us; another way for us to partake of the fruit of the Tree of Life. He "did call on men, in the name of his Son, (this being the plan of redemption which was laid) saying: If ye will repent, and harden not your hearts, then will I have mercy on you, through mine Only Begotten Son." (Alma 12:33).

If we execute the Plan, exercise faith in Christ and repent, we will gain a remission of our sins, because of our claim on Mercy through the Atonement of the Only Begotten Son of the Father. Those who refuse to repent because of the hardness of their hearts will not be able to enter into God's Rest, which is the fulness of His glory.

All of us will pass, at least temporarily, from spiritual death and have the opportunity to meet God at the Judgment Bar. Thus, the effects of the Fall, that are physical and spiritual death, are automatically and totally overcome by the Resurrection. At least briefly, we will come back into the presence of God, to be judged. However, those who have refused to repent will be banished from His presence as a matter of practicality, for they could not endure His glory. But for the righteous, the judgment will be "the pleasing bar of the great Jehovah," because it will be a comfortable, supportive, and uplifting experience. (Moroni 10:34).

Those who have not been cleansed in the blood of the Lamb, in the sense that they have not taken the opportunity to rely upon the merits of Christ and the power of His Atonement through the first principles and ordinances of the gospel, are described as being "filthy." (2 Nephi 9:16). From their perspective, the wind has been taken out of the sails of the Atonement, because they will not allow it to display its power to pay the penalty for their sins. They have not frustrated the sacrifice of the Savior, but for them, the Law of Mercy can be of no effect. They must submit themselves, instead, to the Law of Justice, as if there had been no Atonement made, and the torment that follows is symbolically described "as a lake of fire and brimstone, whose flame ascendeth up forever and ever and has no end." (2 Nephi 9:16).

Only those who refuse to believe, will be condemned to an existence of "eternal damnation; for they cannot be redeemed from their spiritual fall, because they repent not; for they love darkness rather than light, and their deeds are evil, and they receive their wages of whom they list to obey." (V. 44-45). The wicked never seem to learn from the mistakes of the past. Because they are faithless, they are doomed to watch history repeat itself. They can see no alternative but to rely on the arm of flesh. After all, it is the natural thing to do. To Nephi, they said: "We are powerful, and our cities great, therefore our enemies can have no power over us." (Helaman 8:6). Those who suffer from congenital short sightedness and are blinded to any sense of historical perspective, find it impossible to recognize the irony of such arrogant boasting. Their only hope is to have a spiritual heart transplant, and the irony of the situation is that a perfect match has already been found in the genome and blood type of the Savior of the world.

"And thus we see the end of (those) who perverteth the ways of the Lord; and thus we see that the devil will not support his children at the last day, but doth speedily drag them down to hell." (Alma 30:60). The adversary finally betrays his followers, because he cannot deliver on his promises. His enticements lead Father's children into conceptual cul-de-sacs, telestial traffic circles, and doctrinal dead-ends from which there is no exit except retreat. His cunning caresses entice the weak to plunge into a perceived freedom that is really a bottomless pit of misery. In a perverted, twisted way, "the devil seeks that all men might be miserable like himself." (2 Nephi 2:27).

TThe only individuals over whom Satan has any power are the wicked, who have surrendered their agency for the fleeting adrenalin rush of telestial temptations. His dominion over them is selfish, and he uses them as his pawns to lash out at anything that is good. He esteems them as nothing. His hatred, even for the wicked, is all-consuming, typified by a complete and utter darkness. Ultimately, he has no use even for the wicked, because they distantly remind him of his heavenly home and the associations he had there. There is something that lingers even in the nature of the wicked with which the devil is extremely uncomfortable.

The righteous, however, by their actions, entirely escape the negative consequences of his influence. They are only his adversaries in the sense that they do not yield to his temptations. Picking a fight with the devil is foolish because it requires that the righteous move off the secure foundation of gospel principles onto his unstable telestial turf.

The righteousness of heaven extends its reach to little children, who are redeemed from the foundation of the world through the Only Begotten. "Wherefore, they cannot sin, for power is not given unto Satan to tempt little children until they begin to become accountable before me." (V. 46-47). Little children do not need the ordinance of baptism, for they "have eternal life." (Mosiah 15:25). "All children who die before they arrive at the years of accountability are saved in the Celestial Kingdom of heaven." (D&C 137:10). In other words, provision for their exaltation was made at the Grand Council in Heaven, even before the world was. "Little children cannot (or need not) repent; wherefore, it is awful wickedness to deny the pure mercies of God unto them, for they are all alive in Him because of His mercy." (Moroni 8:19).

As children advance in years, they "become accountable." This suggests developing culpability, as children mature to finally assume complete control over their actions. "Heaven lies about us in our infancy," wrote William Wordsworth. "Shades of the prison house begin to close upon the growing boy, but he beholds the light and whence it flows. He sees it in his joy. The youth, who daily farther from the east must travel, still is nature's priest, and by the vision splendid, is on his way attended. At length, the man perceives it die away, and fade into the light of common day." ("Ode: Intimations of Immortality").

"Since "children shall be baptized for the remission of their sins when eight years old," it seems that this is the age of accountability. (D&C 68:27). Jehovah told Abraham: "And I will establish a covenant of circumcision with thee, and it shall be my covenant between me and thee, and thy seed after thee, in their generations; that thou mayest know for ever that children are not accountable before me until they are eight years old." (J.S.T. Genesis 17:11).

The practice of infant baptism in the various sects of Christianity in the Last Days, and the differences of opinion regarding the correct method of baptism in Joseph Smith's day, in particular, made the restoration of the gospel and of the true church imperative. It is critical that the ordinance that admits an applicant into the fold of Christ be carried out according to His instruction, for there is only "one Lord, one faith, (and) one baptism." (Ephesians 4:5). "Except a man be born of water and of the Spirit," declared the Savior, "he cannot enter into the kingdom of God." (John 3:5).

Mormon had a correct understanding of the mission of the Redeemer, and knew that He had come "into the world not to call the righteous but sinners to repentance; the whole need no physician, but they that are sick; wherefore little children are whole, for they are not capable of committing sin." (Moroni 8:8). Therefore, he said, "it is solemn mockery before God, that ye should baptize little children," because to do so denies the power of the Atonement. (Moroni 8:9).

The doctrine of infant baptism denies that Jesus Christ atoned for the "original sin" of Adam, and refutes the concept of individual accountability. It demands that little children who die without baptism cannot enter heaven. But the Atonement did redeem them from the Fall. They are capable of actions that are inconsistent with obedience to gospel principles, but they are not counted against them as sins. They are not culpable.

Rather, Mormon wrote: "This thing shall ye teach - repentance and baptism unto those who are accountable and capable of committing sin; yea, teach parents that they must repent and be baptized, and humble themselves as their little children, and they shall all be saved with their little children." (Moroni 8:10). Then, for added emphasis, he declared: "Little children need no repentance, neither baptism. Behold, baptism is unto repentance to the fulfilling the commandments unto the remission of sins. But little children are alive in Christ, even from the foundation of the world," when the doctrine must have been clearly articulated, and discussed, at the Council. (Moroni 8:11).

It was an integral part of the Plan of Salvation, ordained in Heaven before the world was, that little children who died before the age of accountability would be saved in the Celestial Kingdom by the power of the infinite Atonement. "If not so, God is a partial God, and also a changeable God, and a respecter of persons; for how many little children have died without baptism!" (Moroni 8:12). Those who labor under the burden of a belief in infant baptism are in the gall of bitterness, for how could a just and loving Father in Heaven consign so many of His innocent children to an eternal fate that, on their own merits, they did not deserve? Infant baptism is repugnant because it denies the efficacy of free will, that is the engine that drives the Plan of Salvation forward.

Unenlightened individuals who advocate infant baptism are in the bonds of iniquity in the sense that they must experience despair, or a sense of hopelessness regarding their little ones who have died without the ordinance. "Despair cometh because of iniquity," because when sin clouds vision, unrepentant sinners can see no way out of their miserable situations. (Moroni 10:22). Apostate teachings leave no alternative but to suggest that "if little children could not be saved without baptism, these must have gone to an endless hell." (Moroni 8:13).

Mormon would have us recognize the doctrine of infant baptism for the damnable heresy that it is. He wrote that those who persist in this practice "must go down to hell." (Moroni 8:14). "For awful is the wickedness to suppose that God saveth one child because of baptism, and the other must perish because he hath no baptism. Wo be unto them that shall pervert the ways of the Lord after this manner, for (after they understand the role of accountability, its effects on the fall of Adam, and the necessity of the Savior's redemption) they shall perish, except they repent." (Moroni 8:15-16).

Whereas those who teach the doctrine of infant baptism believe that those children who die without the ordinance will go to hell, the truth is that "they (the professors of the doctrine, are the ones who) are in danger of death, hell, and an endless torment." (Moroni 8:21). Mormon knew that he was speaking boldly, but God had commanded him to do so. Indeed, our eternal welfare depends upon our correct understanding of this doctrine.

Because little children are so precious to God, "great things may be required at the hand of their fathers," who have a solemn responsibility regarding the salvation of their little children. (V. 48). The Restoration has provided clarity to the concept of the family, both on earth and in heaven. As a matter of fact, heaven is described in the scriptures as "worlds without end" or "eternal lives." Heaven is thus equated with home and family. Those in heaven enjoy a many-fold increase of the best qualities of family life. The temple endowment and temple marriage clearly define the basis for happiness, as they teach principles of obedience, sacrifice, consecration, and love, all within the context of the family. The ordinances of the temple provide the mortar that holds together the basic building blocks of the Celestial Kingdom, which is the family.

The priesthood facilitates unity within the family by administering gospel ordinances in the temple, where God's children enter into the patriarchal order of celestial marriage and are organized into eternal family units. In the temple, we learn to govern temporally and spiritually, and we covenant to consecrate our time and talents to the church and kingdom, and to lend our efforts to the preparation of the earth for the millennial reign of Christ. These priesthood powers include the means to gain eternal life, or the kind of life that God lives. We have been promised that we will be fruitful, and multiply, and replenish the earth, (see Genesis 1:28), and that we will have joy in our posterity, (see Moses 5:10), and we have also been promised that we will receive kingdoms, thrones, principalities, powers, dominions, and exaltations, with all the blessings of Abraham, Isaac, and Jacob. (See Moses 4:26).

But "he that hath no understanding, it remaineth in me to do according as it is written." (V. 50). Developmentally challenged individuals seem to be in the same class as children who have not yet reached the age of accountability: "They are blameless before God." (Moroni 8:22). Mormon explained that "little children cannot repent." (Moroni 8:19). They are not accountable, because the Plan ordained "that all little children are alive in Christ, and also all they that are without the law." (Mormon 8:22). Without sin, there is no need for repentance or for baptism. "For the power of redemption cometh on all them that have no law; wherefore, he that is not condemned, or he that is under no condemnation, cannot repent; and unto such baptism availeth nothing." (Mormon 8:22).

One of the greatest contributions of Joseph Smith was to share with the world his knowledge of what is to come after death. He clarified our understanding of heaven, and taught that it was an attainable goal. He created desire in the hearts of millions to follow the difficult road to Gethsemane. What he did validated the promises made by the Father to each of us, that our struggles would be worth every effort, and that we would look back upon our experiences in appreciation for the personal growth and development that occurred because we energetically participated in the Plan. But only if the drama is played out within the context of the gospel, according to the rules established by the Plan, will the anticipated blessings come. There is no other way.

This has been the pattern from the foundation of the world. "And thus the gospel began to be preached, from the beginning, being declared by holy angels sent forth from the presence of God, and by his own voice, and by the gift of the Holy Ghost. And thus all things were confirmed unto Adam, by an holy ordinance, and the gospel preached, and a decree sent forth, that it should be in the world, until the end thereof; and thus it was. Amen." (Moses 5:58-59).

# Section 30

## (Instructions in 1830 to the newly organized church in New York).

"Originally this material was published as three revelations. It was combined into one section by the Prophet for the 1835 edition of the Doctrine & Covenants." (Superscript).

David Whitmer followed the example of Hyrum Page, who had been expounding false prophecy, (D&C 28), and so the Lord rebuked him, saying: "You have feared man and have not relied on me for strength as you ought. But your mind has been on the things of the earth more than on the things of me, your Maker, and the ministry whereunto you have been called; and you have not given heed unto my Spirit, and to those who were set over you, but have been persuaded by those whom I have not commanded." (V. 1-2). "How carefully most men creep into nameless graves, while now and again one or two forget themselves into immortality." (Phillips Brooks).

Ideally, we are spiritual beings having mortal experiences. In practical terms, though, in the mission field of mortality we are constantly buffeted by the influences of carnality, sensuality, and devilishness. There can be a wide gulf separating the spiritual from the temporal. The purpose of the Plan of Salvation is to reconcile the two, and bring us into a state of holiness, richer for having had the experiences of mortality. We are not to be worn down by life, but rather to be refined and polished by adversity. This was David Whitmer's challenge.

Truman Madsen once wrote: "We have intelligent initiative that can go astray. In this realm, the role of Christ is to break the bonds of our diminishing freedom and re-enthrone our becoming. In critical ways, only He can do this. Freely, we must face it. Out of the eternities, we chose and were chosen for light and Divine Sonship. Only if we become determined against such a glorious destiny will we avoid the over-arching decisions of direction that bring total freedom. For if we will, our destiny is to become more and more free in the widening circles of fulfillment called Eternal Life." ("Eternal Man," p. 69-70).

Mormon recognized "the unsteadiness of the hearts of the children of men." (Helaman 12:1). At the same time, he also saw the fulfillment of a grand principle of the gospel, namely, that "there is a law, irrevocably decreed in heaven before the foundations of this world, upon which all blessings are predicated, and when we obtain any blessing from God, it is by obedience to that law upon which it is predicated." (D&C 130:20-21). David Whitmer, like any other member of the church, had within himself the capacity to so order his life that he might rightfully claim the blessings that are tied to obedience.

When we respond to the whisperings of the Spirit, we grow into our potential, and become worthy of the description attributed by William Shakespeare to humanity: "What a piece of work is man! How noble in reason! How infinite in faculty! In form and moving, how express and admirable! In action, how like an angel! In apprehension, how like a god! The beauty of the world! The paragon of animals!" ("Hamlet," Act 2, Scene 2).

The irony of it all is that "at the very time when (Heavenly Father) doth prosper his people, then is the time that they do harden their hearts, and do forget the Lord their God, and do trample under their feet the Holy One - yea, and this because of their ease, and their exceedingly great prosperity." (Helaman 12:2). It has ever been so.

It seems that unless the Lord chastens his people, they will not remember him. Adversity is part of our mortal experience, and it can serve a useful purpose. it is not in vain. Even Joseph Smith was comforted with these words of the Savior: "Know thou, my son, that all these things shall give thee experience, and shall be for thy good." (D&C 122:7).

In mortality, how quickly are we "lifted up in pride; yea, how quick to boast, and do all manner of that which is iniquity; and how slow are (we) to remember the Lord (our) God, and to give ear unto his counsels, yea, how slow to walk in wisdom's paths!" (Helaman 12:5).

It is so easy to be influenced by the adversary. Our natural tendency seems to be to make mistakes, violate law, and suffer the consequences. It must be one of the critical experiences of mortality, to deal with opposition, exercise agency, and enjoy the natural and inevitable consequences of independent action.

But central to the Plan of Salvation is complete and unequivocal dependence upon God. It is only the disobedient who "do not desire that the Lord their God, who hath created them, should rule and reign over them; notwithstanding his great goodness and his mercy towards them, they do set at naught his counsels, and they will not that he should be their guide." (Helaman 12:6).

To Peter Whitmer, Jr., the Lord said: "Wherefore, you are left to inquire for yourself... and ponder upon the things which you have received." (V. 3). Those who believe in God, and are obedient to His will, "hope for a better world, yea, even a place at the right hand of God, which hope cometh of faith, maketh an anchor to the souls of men, which would make them sure and steadfast, always abounding in good works, being led to glorify God." (Ether 12:4). This is a tremendous promise, and it is all the more powerful because of its brevity. It succinctly defines the Plan of the Father, and harmonizes beautifully with His Own "mission statement," which is to bring to pass our immortality and eternal life. (See Moses 1:39).

In every dispensation, there are those who cannot see the forest for the trees, that the messages of the prophets are essential to salvation. Such individuals are spiritually blind, and cannot seem to "catch the vision." The standard of the world is: "Seeing is believing." But seeing is not only irrelevant to the acquisition of faith, it is often the wrong answer to our inquiry. Harold B. Lee taught: "You must learn to walk to the edge of the light, and then take a few steps into the darkness; then the light will appear and show the way before you." (Quoted by Boyd K. Packer, BYU Magazine, "The Edge of The Light," 3/1991). This is the way faith is developed and strengthened.

There are probably three classic definitions of faith in the scriptures. They are:

One: "Faith is not to have a perfect knowledge of things; therefore if ye have faith ye hope for things which are not seen, which are true." (Alma 32:21). This is correct in the ultimate sense. In Alma's usage, the verse might more clearly read: "Faith is not to have a perfect knowledge of things gained through our own experiences." It is important to remember the context in which Alma taught this principle to his Zoramite audience. Alma vividly remembered his recent experience with Korihor, and how his demand for a sign had been the condition for his faith, since he trusted only his physical senses. This rational approach is always prone to be the enemy of faith. Some things need to be believed to be seen.

Two: "Now faith is the substance of things hoped for, the evidence of things not seen." (Hebrews 11:1). In this context, faith is not to receive a sign from heaven. As Alma told the Zoramites, "If a man knoweth a thing he hath no cause to believe, for he knoweth it." (Alma 32:18). No exercise of faith is necessary to receive a sign from heaven. When the sign is given, we might have a sure knowledge of the event, but no expenditure of faith has been made to produce it. Under proper circumstances, though, "by doing our duty, faith increases until it becomes perfect knowledge." (Heber J. Grant, C.R., 4/1934). Once again, initially, faith is to believe what we do not see, and the reward of faith is to see what we believe.

Three: "Faith is things which are hoped for and not seen; wherefore, dispute not because ye see not, for ye receive no witness until after the trial of your faith." (Ether 12:6). It is important to remember that, in matters of faith, the Lord is not on trial. At the Bar of Justice, the Judge will receive the evidence, and our previous acceptance or rejection of that evidence will determine our reward or punishment. The trial of our mortal experience is eminently fair because the burden of proof rests squarely upon our own shoulders.

Peter Whitmer had been asked by the Lord to fulfill a mission for the church, in part, so that he could develop faith unto salvation. "The time has come," the Lord said, "that it is expedient in me that you shall open your mouth to declare my gospel." (V. 5). The process by which real faith, or power, is developed is one of testing. The Lord gives certain principles, and by obedience to them, blessings and power follow. But we have no proof of that promise until we act on the basis of trust or belief. Then comes the confirmation of that reality. That is why James taught that "faith if it hath not works, is dead, being alone." (James 2:17).

"Faith cometh not by signs, but signs follow those that believe." (D&C 63:9). When we understand this process, we can see why sign seeking is condemned. Someone who demands outward evidence of the power of God as a condition for his belief is really seeking to circumvent the process by which faith is developed. He wants proof without paying the price. As with the adulterer, he seeks the result without accepting the responsibility. What better way could there be for the Lord to instill faith in His children than to ask them to serve Him as missionaries?

Therefore, John Whitmer was also commanded by the Lord: "Proclaim my gospel, as with the voice of a trump...not fearing what man can do, for I am with you." (V. 9 & 11). The missionaries were to go forth, full of the Spirit of God like a burning fire, to preach the gospel. As Zenos had prophesied in his allegory, "And it came to pass that the servants did go and labor with their mights, and the Lord of the vineyard labored also with them; and they did obey the commandments of the Lord of the Vineyard in all things." (Jacob 5:72). "Send forth the elders of my church unto the nations which are afar off," declared the Lord in 1831, "unto the islands of the sea; send forth unto foreign lands; call upon all nations, first upon the Gentiles, and then upon the Jews." (D&C 133:8).

The missionaries were not to fear the arm of flesh, for those who had been cast out of the vineyard were telestial individuals who could not endure "the brightness of His coming." (2 Thessalonians 2:8). The glory of God is like a burning fire that cleanses and purges out all impurity. In a refining process, if imperfections exist, metal has no value. Good for nothing, it must be cast upon the scrap heap. Only if no impurities exist, can it be fashioned into a thing of value, will it stand up under punishing use, and with proper care give many years of reliable service.

God is merciful, because in spite of Israel being stiff-necked and gainsaying, or contradictory, His hand is stretched forth unto them "all the day long." (Jacob 6:4). If only we will not harden our hearts, that we are no longer teachable, He will yet save us in His kingdom. When we have full purpose of heart, and rely completely upon the merits of Christ's Atonement, our repentance, and His forgiveness, are possible.

# Section 31
## (Instructions in 1830 to the newly organized church in New York).

This revelation was "given through Joseph Smith the Prophet to Thomas B. Marsh, September 1830, who had been baptized earlier in the month, and had been ordained an elder in the church before this revelation was given." (Superscript). Brother Marsh would later be called to the Quorum of The Twelve Apostles, and would serve as its senior member, or president. In order of succession, he stood next in line to preside over the church, after Joseph Smith, as prophet, seer, and revelator. But in 1838, Thomas B. Marsh was caught in the crucible of the refiner's fire in Missouri, and he lost his standing and even his membership in the church. Another Apostle took his place at the head of the Quorum, and later observed: "The spirit is pure, and under the special control and influence of the Lord, but the body is of the earth, and is subject to the power of the devil, and is under the mighty influence of that fallen nature that is of the earth. If the spirit yields to the body, the devil then has power to overcome the body and spirit of that man, and he loses both." (Brigham Young, D.B.Y., 69-70).

The Lord knew Thomas B. Marsh, and that he would need to stay focused, lest he lose his way. "You have had many afflictions because of your family," he was told. (V. 2). Years later, Brother Marsh reflected: "Let no one feel too secure; for before you think of it, your steps will slide. You will not then think or feel for a moment as you did before you lost the Spirit of Christ; for when men apostatize, they are left to grovel in the dark. Do not let the seeds of apostasy make their appearance, but nip that spirit in the bud, for it is misery and affliction in this world, and destruction in the world to come." (Remarks at his re-baptism, in 1857, in Utah).

"You shall declare glad tidings of great joy unto this generation." (V. 3). "The seed of Christ" or "the heirs of the kingdom of God" are "they who have published peace." (Mosiah 15:11 & 14). In so doing, they experience joy, even its fulness. Jesus revealed something of His character, and taught a marvelous lesson as well, when He declared to His Nephite disciples: "And now, behold, my joy is great, even unto fulness." (3 Nephi 27:30). Here is a key to an understanding of the

Lord, Who is our Savior and Redeemer. He did the work His Father gave to Him, because He loved us so much. In its performance, He received a fulness of joy. His message to us is that if we follow His lead, we too can enjoy this consummate reward for missionary work well done, which is the ultimate work of salvation and is a manifestation of pure, unselfish love.

The Lord is "the founder of peace." (Mosiah 15:18). "My peace I give unto you," promised the Savior, "not as the world giveth, give I unto you." (John 14:27). His peace "is not the peace of the world, of ease, of luxury, idleness, absence of turmoil, and strife, but the peace born of the righteous life, the peace that lifts the soul, that day by day brings us closer to the home of Eternal Peace, the dwelling place of our Father." (J. Reuben Clark, Jr.).

"The field...is white already to be burned." (V. 4). Upstate New York in the 1830s was the scene of religious fervor, and tent meetings were regularly held at chautauquas throughout the region. It was called the 'Burned Over District' because of the intensity of its religious revivalism. What a wonderful setting this would be for the missionary harvest of souls that was about to take place!

Ammon had metaphorically described the harvest to illustrate for his brethren, the Sons of Mosiah, how thousands had been gathered through their missionary efforts. "Behold, the field was ripe," he said, "and blessed are ye, for ye did thrust in the sickle, and did reap with your might, yea, all the day long did ye labor; and behold the number of your sheaves!" (Alma 26:5). Those in his party had come up out of the Land of Zarahemla into the highlands of Nephi to bring a message of love to their brethren, who had heretofore been strangers to God, but who would henceforth be no more "foreigners, but fellowcitizens with the Saints, and of the household of God." (Ephesians 2:19).

It was critical to the spiritual well-being of Thomas B. Marsh that he be enlisted into a similar missionary army. "Thrust in your sickle with all your soul," the Lord commanded him, "and your sins are forgiven you.... Wherefore, your family shall live." (V. 5). God "looketh down upon all the children of men; and he knows all the thoughts and intents of the heart; for by his hand were they all created from the beginning." (Alma 18:32). The Savior was the elder brother of Thomas B. Marsh; they were both spiritual children of our Heavenly Father. Missionary service would make it possible for Marsh and his family to be born again, and become, in turn, the spiritual children of Christ. The steps in his conversion process would require a clear realization of his iniquities, and consequently a deep godly sorrow for sin. Then, when he had appealed to the Savior, he would receive forgiveness, spiritual enlightenment, and great joy. Finally, for his faithfulness and obedience, he would be rewarded with the opportunity to enjoy a life of righteousness and service. He would be saved by the grace of God, after all he had done.

"Go from them only for a little time, and declare my word, and I will prepare a place for them." (V. 6). The gospel gives each of us an equal opportunity to qualify for eternal family life, and to preside over kingdom, thrones, dominions, principalities, powers, and exaltations, in the eternities. Only a few years after this revelation was given, the blessings of the temple became available to the Latter-day Saints. There, God's children could enter into the patriarchal order of celestial marriage and into eternal family units. In the temple, the Saints would get their bearings on eternity, learn to govern spiritually and temporally, consecrate their time and talents to the church and kingdom, and lend their efforts to the preparation of the earth for the millennial reign of Jesus Christ, after His Second Coming.

"I will open the hearts of the people, and they will receive you." (V. 7). As Alma had said of the marvelous power of Christ: "He changed their hearts and they awoke unto God. Behold, they were in the midst of darkness; nevertheless, their souls were illuminated by the light of the everlasting word." (Alma 5:7).

"And you shall strengthen them and prepare them against the time when they shall be gathered.... You shall be a physician unto the church, but not unto the world, for they will not receive you." (V. 8 & 10). Through the efforts of the early missionaries of the church, many would be brought out of the world, from their stressful, disorganized, and disoriented existence into the marvelous light of God. Bathed in the stunning clarity of the missionary message, those taught would stare in wide-eyed wonder at the beautiful simplicity of the tapestry of gospel principles that adorn the Plan of Happiness. This would be in sharp contrast to the slit-eyed skepticism with which the unrepentant and hard hearted would greet the light of truth.

"Be patient in afflictions, revile not against those that revile. Govern your house in meekness, and be steadfast." (V. 9). Thomas B. Marsh had difficulty helping his wife to reconcile certain of her personality traits with gospel principles. Basically, she had trouble maintaining humility. Consequently, she exercised undue self-assertiveness, and was haughty and aggressive in her interactions with others. She failed to submit to proper authority, and lacked modesty and meekness. She forgot that the hand of divine Providence had smiled upon her most pleasantly.

Had she not abandoned her core values, surely she would have understood that God could not justify her obsessive desire for telestial trivia. Ezra Taft Benson made the condemnation of selfishness and of pride the centerpiece of several of his last sermons. Drawing on Book of Mormon teachings, he called it "the universal sin, the great vice" and identified its central feature as "enmity toward God and enmity toward our fellowmen." The insidiously evil and destructive quality of pride, he said, is that it "is essentially competitive in nature, arising when individuals pit their will against God's, or their intellects, opinions, works, wealth, and talents against those of other people." He warned the Latter-day Saints that "pride is a damning sin" that "adversely affects all our relationships" and "limits or stops our progression." (C.R., 4/1989).

"Pray always, lest you enter into temptation and lose your reward." (V. 11). The Atonement of Christ takes into account the reality that we will yield in varying degrees to carnality, sensuality, and devilish enticements. But the gospel of Jesus Christ, that is the Plan of Salvation, provides a way for us to learn from our mistakes by relying upon the sacrifice of the Savior, so that we may be justified by the Spirit. That is to say, we may yet be found worthy to enter into God's Rest, even after having endured bruising experiences in this telestial world.

President Benson warned that pride can infect those who are otherwise active, participating members in full fellowship in the church, for it includes "faultfinding, gossiping, living beyond our means, envying, coveting, withholding gratitude, and being unforgiving and jealous." ("Encyclopedia of Mormonism," V. 3).

When we have shorn ourselves of pride and other character crippling personality traits, and we have obtained the kingdom while yet on earth, God will grant us those temporal blessings necessary to "clothe the naked, and to feed the hungry, and to liberate the captive, and administer relief to the sick and the afflicted." (Jacob 2:19). We might ask ourselves: "How may we accomplish these things today as individuals and as a church?"

After the apostasy of Thomas B. Marsh in 1838, he swore an affidavit against Joseph Smith and the church in Missouri, that ultimately resulted in issuance of the infamous Extermination Order. His example illustrates that the effect of sin on those who have been taught the gospel is that the guidance of the Spirit is withdrawn, and they are left alone to grope in darkness. Guilt causes them to shrink from church activity, and in the absence of the Spirit, unrepentant sinners have no claim on priesthood power, prosperity, or preservation. In their miserable circumstances, such individuals descend into a pit of despair that is accurately described as hell on earth. Tragically, feeling uncomfortable in proximity to spiritual experiences, they withdraw to lifestyles devoid of such associations. Thus begin downward spirals that gain momentum as sinful practices, more easily committed, become entrenched.

Joseph Fielding Smith wrote: "When the Spirit is withdrawn, darkness supersedes the light, and apostasy will follow. This is one of the greatest evidences of the divinity of the Latter-day work. In other organizations, men may commit all manner of sin, and still retain their membership, because they have no companionship with the Holy Ghost to lose, but in the church, when a man sins and continues without repentance, the Spirit is withdrawn, and when he is left to himself, the adversary takes possession of his mind, and he denies the faith." ("Doctrines of Salvation," 3:309). Those who break windows enjoy throwing stones and the sound of shattering glass more than they do fresh air, and "the man that doeth this, the same cometh out in open rebellion against God." (Mosiah 2:37).

"These words are not of man nor of men, but of me, even Jesus Christ, your Redeemer." (V. 13, see D&C 18:34). "The first issue of 'The Times and Seasons' contained a lead editorial to the elders: 'Be careful that you teach not for the word of God, the commandments of men, nor the doctrines of men, nor the ordinances of men. Study the word of God and preach it and not your own opinions, for no man's opinion is worth a straw." (Quoted by Hugh Nibley, in "Beyond Politics," p. 299).

Harold B. Lee told the Saints after a General Conference of the church: "If you want to know what the Lord has for this people at the present time, I would admonish you to get and read the discourses that have been delivered at this conference, for what these brethren have spoken by the power of the Holy Ghost is the mind of the Lord, the will of the Lord, the word of the Lord, and the power of God unto salvation." (CR, 4/1973). That would have been good counsel for Thomas Marsh to heed. It certainly is for us.

# Section 32
## (Instructions in 1830 to the newly organized church in New York).

"Great interest and desires were felt by the elders respecting the Lamanites, of whose predicted blessings the church had learned from The Book of Mormon." (Superscript). "How glorious it would be," Spencer W. Kimball mused in 1975, "if a million Latter-day Saints were on their knees daily, asking in faith that the work among these their brethren would be hastened, that the doors might be opened." ("Ensign," 12/1975).

On another occasion, he declared: "I am positive that the blessings of the Lord shall attend every country which opens its gates to the gospel of Christ. Their blessings will flow in education, and culture, and faith, and love. There will come prosperity to the nations, comfort and luxuries to the people, joy and peace to all recipients, and eternal life to those who will accept and magnify it. I believe the time has come when we must change our goals and raise our sights." ("When The World Will Be Converted," "Ensign," 10/1974).

"And now, concerning my servant Parley P. Pratt, behold I say unto him that, as I live, I will that he shall declare my gospel and learn of me, and be meek and lowly of heart." (V. 1). At the time this revelation was given, Parley P. Pratt had been a member of the church for just one month, but he had already demonstrated his meekness and humility. The meek are not weak, but rather neither take nor give offense. When faced with the challenge of adversity, they become "Pro-Gospel" rather than "Anti-Enemy."

The meek delight in the grace of God, for they understand what the Lord meant when He said: "If men come unto me I will show unto them their weakness. I give unto men weakness that they may be humble; and my grace is sufficient for all men that humble themselves before me; for if they humble themselves before me, and have faith in me, then will I make weak things become strong unto them." (Ether 12:27). Those who develop meekness will qualify to inherit the celestialized earth.

"And that which I have appointed unto him is that he shall go with my servants, Oliver Cowdery and Peter Whitmer, Jun., into the wilderness among the Lamanites. And Ziba Peterson also shall go with them; and I myself will go with them, and be in their midst; and I am their advocate with the Father, and nothing shall prevail against them." (V. 2-3). Moroni wrote of such individuals: "The office of their ministry is to call men unto repentance, and to fulfill and to do the work of the covenants of the Father, which he hath made unto the children of men, to prepare the way among the children of men, by declaring the word of Christ." (Moroni 7:31).

On their way, the missionaries stopped in Kirtland, Ohio, and taught the gospel to a minister there by the name of Sydney Rigdon, and to his congregation, as well. The Lord later spoke to Sydney Rigdon through the Prophet Joseph Smith, saying: "I have looked upon thee and thy works. I have heard thy prayers, and prepared thee for a greater work. Thou art blessed, for thou shalt do great things. Behold, thou wast sent forth, even as John, to prepare the way before me, and before Elijah which should come, and thou knewest it not. Thou didst baptize by water unto repentance, but they received not the Holy Ghost. But now I give unto thee a commandment, that thou shalt baptize by water, and they shall receive the Holy Ghost by the laying on of the hands, even as the apostles of old." (D&C 35:3-6).

"And they shall give heed to that which is written, and pretend to no other revelation, and they shall pray always that I may unfold the same to their understanding." (V. 4). Full of the Spirit of the Lord, these missionaries would be as Jeremiah, who said of his own preparation: "His word was in mine heart as a burning fire shut up in my bones, and I was weary with forbearing, and I could not stay." (Jeremiah 20:9).

"And they shall give heed unto these words and trifle not." (V. 5). The Lord desires that we hearken to Him, or pay strict attention, and open our ears, or listen carefully, and our hearts, to feel the spirit of His messages, and our minds, to invite understanding. When we approach gospel study with this level of preparation, the mysteries of God may be unfolded to our view.

Nephi taught: "If ye shall press forward" with complete dedication, "feasting upon the word of Christ" or receiving physical and spiritual strength and nourishment, "and endure to the end" with continuing responsibility and accountability, "behold, thus saith the Father: Ye shall have eternal life," which is the greatest of God's gifts. (2 Nephi 31:20).

The Lord said that we should "seek not for riches, but for wisdom; and, behold, the mysteries of God shall be unfolded unto you, and then shall you be made rich.

Behold, he that hath eternal life is rich." (D&C 11:7). The mysteries of God are those truths that can only be known by revelation from the Holy Ghost. When we hunger and thirst after righteousness, the doctrine of the priesthood will distill upon our souls as the dews from heaven, and the Holy Ghost will be our constant companion. (See D&C 121:45-46).

That Parley P. Pratt was faithful to his calling is evidenced by his later declaration, made in Salt Lake City: "I have received the Holy Anointing and I can never rest until the last enemy is conquered, death destroyed, and truth reigns triumphant." ("Deseret News," 4/30/1853).

# Section 33
## (Instructions in 1830 to the newly organized church in New York).

The word of the Lord is "quick and powerful, sharper than a two-edged sword, to the dividing asunder of the joints and marrow, soul and spirit." (V. 1). It is living, in a biblical sense. It is a source of life and energy, and penetrates to our innermost parts.

The Lord is "a discerner of the thoughts and intents of the heart." (V. 1). At the Judgment Bar, "our words will condemn us, yea, all our works will condemn us and our thoughts will also condemn us." (Alma 12:14). "In the armory of thought, we forge the weapons by which we destroy ourselves," said Spencer W. Kimball. "We also fashion the tools with which we build for ourselves heavenly mansions of joy and strength and peace. Between these two extremes are all grades of character, and we are their maker. We are the masters of thought, the shapers of condition, environment, and of destiny." ("The Miracle of Forgiveness," p. 103).

King Benjamin had told his people that there are many ways to commit sin. (Mosiah 4:29). There is a rule, however, that is the foundation for purposeful living, and the order of counsel is significant. When we have been taught the truth, and have a firm knowledge of that which is good, we must take care to watch 1) our thoughts, 2) our words, and 3) our deeds. (See Mosiah 4:30, & Alma 12:14). When we are taught correct principles, we are left to govern our own behavior, according to the light and knowledge we have received. (See D&C 58:26). Usually, the Lord gives us the overall objectives to be accomplished and some guidelines to follow, but He expects us to work out most of the details ourselves. These are developed through study and prayer, and the unmistakable promptings of the Spirit.

If we stand condemned, "we would fain be glad if we could command the rocks and the mountains to fall upon us to hide us from his presence." (Alma 12:14). "In the last days, an angel will sound his trump," and reveal our secret acts, "and the thoughts and intents of (our) hearts." (D&C 88:109). The Last Judgment will have begun.

Even if we stand unrepentant at the Bar, in the presence of God "in his glory, and in his power, and in his might, majesty, and dominion," we will still have to acknowledge His justice and mercy. (Alma 12:15). God, Who is the Author of Salvation and the Builder of the universe and all things therein, including the Pillars of Creation, will be able to read the blueprint of our lives with unerring accuracy. In a sense, it would seem that we are, after all is said and done, the architects of our own fate. Therefore, we should be vigilant to see that we are building temples for the eternal dwelling place of our souls, and not rickety shanties that will not stand the test of time, let alone eternity. Life should be more than just an overnight stay in a cheap, second class hotel room.

"Ye are called to lift up your voices as with the sound of a trump." (V. 2). Trumpets were used anciently to sound the alarm and signal for battle, or to announce the coming of royalty. "Blow ye the trumpet in Zion, and sound an alarm in my holy mountain: let all the inhabitants of the land tremble: for the day of the Lord cometh." (Joel 2:1-2). It will be a day of thick darkness and gloominess for the wicked, when even the sun and the moon and the stars of heaven obey the voice of the Master. "For the stars of heaven and the constellations thereof shall not give their light; the sun shall be darkened in his going forth, and the moon shall not cause her light to shine." (Isaiah 13:10). For the purpose of the day of the Lord is to "destroy the sinners thereof out of (the land)." (Isaiah 13:9). They will be punished for the iniquity, arrogance, pride, and haughtiness, that were hastily thrown up barriers to their progression, and stood in the way of their repentance.

In that day, a righteous man will be "more precious than fine gold." (Isaiah 13:12). This might be because they are few in number, or it could be because the true value of righteousness, when compared to the insignificance of the treasures of the earth, will be apparent. Even the wealth of the Golden Wedge of Ophir will pale in comparison to one righteous individual. (See Isaiah 13:12).

The Lord called Ezra Thayre and Northrop Sweet to declare His gospel "to a crooked and perverse generation." (V. 2). Missionaries in all ages have been shocked by the distorted understanding of the spiritually illiterate. B.H. Roberts related an experience he had as a young Elder while serving in the Southern States Mission: "As Brother Palmer and I stepped into the church, we found the pastor engaged in prayer, and what was my surprise to hear him say: 'O Lord, help us to understand that we have enough of Thy word; that the canon of scripture is full. Help us to believe, O Lord, that the awful voice of prophecy will no more be heard; help us to believe that revelation has ceased, that Thou wilt no more speak to man.' Well, thought I, there is a wide difference between the ideas contained in that person's prayer and what we are going to preach!" ("Defender of The Faith," p. 108).

Expressions of false doctrine pepper memorized prayers with the elements of apostasy. Some believe that God is a Spirit. Others believe in pre-destination. For many, only a confession of faith is necessary to gain the favor of the Lord, and salvation. Weekday activities may be uninfluenced by belief in God, for whatever faith is possessed may lie dormant. When religious thoughts are confined to the Sabbath, they can become sterile, or devoid of vitality. Their expressions may be impotent, or without power. With this in mind, James taught: "Faith without works is dead, being alone." (James 2:14). Such a stylistic ritual in prayer is astonishing to those who are accustomed to conversations with God that are on more intimate levels.

In a sense, the seeds of apostasy do not naturally occur in nature. As Paul taught, some things have been given up "unto vile affections," so that their intended use may be changed "into that which is against nature." (Romans 1:26). These are the genetically modified organisms that have been synthesized by Satan, and formulated in the alchemist's laboratory into an arresting aerosol that may be more easily scattered about by the dry winds of a famine in the land. (See Amos 8:11).

Just after the organization of the church, Ezra Thayre and Northrop Sweet may have looked forward with great anticipation to a Zion society, but they may have overlooked the Apostles' warning that the Restoration would come at a great cost. "Be not soon shaken in mind," Paul had written, "as that the day of Christ is at hand...for that day shall not come, except there come a falling away first." (2 Thessalonians 2:3). "This know also," he had written to Timothy, "that in the last days perilous times shall come. For men shall be...ever learning, and never able to come to the knowledge of the truth...having a form of godliness, but denying the power thereof." (2 Timothy 3:1-2, 7 & 5). With soberness, Ezra Thayre and Northrop Sweet must have known that the devil himself would muster his forces to "make war with the Saints, and to overcome them," unless they would be exacting in their obedience. (Revelation 13:7). The missionaries would have to deal with these issues, if they were to assist in the gathering of the Saints and the establishment of Zion.

The famine in the land has resulted, in part, from deliberate attempts to distort the doctrines, and the 'burned over district' of western New York in 1830 seemed to be in the tight grip of ignorance of the truth. Moroni pleaded with those in the Last Days who would "transfigure the holy word of God," or who would change the appearance and substance of the scriptures, and so bring damnation upon their souls. (Mormon 8:33). For Moroni, the simple doctrine of Jesus Christ found in latter-day scripture and revelation was clearly "the way, the truth, and the life." (John 14:6).

In vision, Nephi had beheld the Bible itself, and wrote that at the time that "it proceeded forth from the mouth of a Jew, it contained the fulness of the gospel of the Lord." (1 Nephi 13:24). In older editions of The Book of Mormon, this verse was rendered "...the plainness of the gospel." The fulness of the gospel is the Plan of Salvation, which is a more accurate description of the Bible's doctrinal teachings before the plain and most precious parts were removed.

Nephi characterized as 'abominable' the actions of those who had thus tampered with the holy scriptures. "For behold, they have taken away from the gospel of the Lamb many parts which are plain and most precious; and also many covenants of the Lord have they taken away." (1 Nephi 13:26).

Section 29:12 is the only instance in the Doctrine & Covenants where the term 'great and abominable church' is employed, although it is used twelve times in The Book of Mormon, in 1 Nephi 4:3, 9, 15, & 17, 1 Nephi 13:6, 8, 26 & 28, 1 Nephi 22:13 & 14, 2 Nephi 6:12, & 2 Nephi 28:18. That is enough, however, to entrench the phrase in our lexicon. Nephi was given, in vision, a broad view of the state of the world in the Last Days, and clearly saw "the great persecutor of the church, the apostate, the whore, even Babylon, that maketh all nations to drink of her cup, in whose hearts the enemy, even Satan, sitteth to reign." (D&C 86:3).

When the scriptures are no longer a witness for Christ, and the ordinances of salvation and exaltation are no longer part of our personal protocol for perfection, it is an abomination because the snares of misunderstanding and false doctrine jeopardize our progression. The purpose of mortality in the great Plan of Salvation is thereby compromised. With this in mind, the "Church News" reported: "The witness for Christ was the most important thing in that ancient record." (1/1966). Without a vibrant testimony of Christ, the Old Testament loses much of its purpose and power. "And all this have they done that they might pervert the right ways of the Lord," wrote Nephi, "that they might blind the eyes and harden the hearts of the children of men." (1 Nephi 13:27).

Nevertheless, times of crisis create opportunity, and the apostasy allowed the Restoration to stand out like a breath of fresh air against the backdrop of those 'dry winds of famine' that were raking across the land. The Book of Mormon, in particular, would prove to be one of the greatest weapons in the spiritual arsenal of the missionaries. Its teachings would bridge the gap between apostasy and illumination by the Spirit, and lead to doctrinal understanding. In addition, Ezra Thayre and Northrop Sweet could not have known that their divine commission to preach the gospel would become part of the Doctrine & Covenants of the church, that would in turn guide the faithful through the formative years of the Restoration, and beyond.

"For behold, the field is white already to harvest; and it is the eleventh hour, and the last time that I shall call laborers into my vineyard." (V. 3, see v. 7). This is the Parable of the Laborers in the Vineyard in the Dispensation of the Fulness of Times. The Lord numbers His children by their willingness to accept covenants. The missionary efforts of members of the church in the conversion process is really quite simple. Their commission is to find those who have been prepared to receive the oil of gladness, and teach them by the Spirit. (Hebrews 1:9). "And ye are called to bring to pass the gathering of mine elect," declared the Lord, "for mine elect hear my voice and harden not their hearts." (D&C 29:7).

When the missionaries are faithful, their continuing focus of attention on their less fortunate brethren has the power to eventually bring God's children into complete harmony with His attributes. "And ye shall be even as I am, and I am even as the Father, and the Father and I are one," said the Savior to the Three Nephites. (3 Nephi 28:10).

The vineyard had become corrupted in "every whit...because of priestcrafts, all having corrupt minds." (V. 4). False doctrine comes about because of "the loftiness of (the) vineyard," or the haughtiness and pride of the world. It occurs when the people raise themselves above the word of the Lord, and "look beyond the mark" which is Jesus Christ. It happens when members of the church pay no heed to the teachings of the gospel, but follow their own agenda, and establish their own values on the shifting sands of expediency, rather than on the bedrock of Christ. It is because even church members sometimes exercise unrighteous dominion, or take "strength unto themselves." It is then that we try to bring the world into the gospel, rather than the gospel into the world. (Jacob 5:48).

The Lord rhetorically asked: "What could I have done more for my vineyard?" (Jacob 5:49). This question is all the more penetrating when we realize that the Master Who is in control is wise, benevolent, and knows our individual and collective weakness; and yet His grace is sufficient for all those who simply humble themselves before Him. (See Ether 12:27).

Therefore, it was "out of the wilderness" of apostasy that the restoration of the gospel emerged. (V. 5). Even as the wicked grope about blindly, the Lord described the Restoration as "the beginning of the rising up and the coming forth of my church out of the wilderness - clear as the moon, and fair as the sun, and terrible as an army with banners." (D&C 5:14, see Song of Solomon 6:10). The Savior indicated to the Nephites that in the day when the latter-day Restoration would burst upon the world stage, it would be of such significance "that kings shall shut their mouths." (3 Nephi 21:8). Its destiny is to become the greatest power the world has ever known.

"For in that day," declared the Savior, "shall the Father work a work, which shall be a great and marvelous work among them." (3 Nephi 21:9).

"The elect...even as many as will believe in me, and hearken unto my voice," will be gathered to the church that is the fruits of the Restoration. (V. 6). It is the mission of The Church of Jesus Christ of Latter-day Saints to preach the gospel throughout the world because the blood of Israel is there, and they need the "roots" that are the foundation covenants that are anchored in rich gospel soil. We do not preach the gospel so that people can enjoy a better life. We do it so that they can be saved in the Celestial Kingdom of God.

"Open your mouths and they shall be filled" through the prompting of the Holy Ghost." (V. 8). The Lord asks only that we establish a spiritual rapport with Him by developing a relationship that is at first initiated, and then sustained, through intimate conversation. We do not draw near to God by crafting eloquent prayers or constructing elaborate edifices in which to recite them by rote. The world's misconception relating to the nature of God is characterized by its secularization of the divine model, first represented by the ancient ziggurat of Babel, that the people built in the false hope that the top thereof would reach all the way to heaven. (See Genesis 11:4). But Heavenly Father's children do not approach Him that way. Holy sanctuaries can more easily be quiet stands of trees than piles of stone, glaring gargoyles, elaborate cathedra, censers of burning incense, or stained glass windows.

In the words of Mother Teresa of Calcutta: "Do not search for Jesus in far off lands. He is in you. Just keep the lamp burning, and you will always see Him. Give Jesus not only your hands to serve, but your heart to love. Pray with absolute trust in God's loving care for you. Let Him use you without consulting you. Let Jesus fill you with joy, that you may preach without preaching." ("Love: A Fruit Always in Season, Daily Meditations").

Those who practice priestcraft and who are engaged in idolatry are more prone to focus their worship on their "elegant and spacious buildings and fine work of wood, and all manner of precious things." (Mosiah 11:8-11). We are reminded of the Emperor Justinian, who "began a new St. Sophia (or Hagia Sophia). He summoned the most famous of architects to plan and superintend the work. Abandoning the traditional basilican form, they conceived a design whose center would be a spacious dome resting not on walls but on massive piers, and buttressed by a half dome at either end. Ten thousand workmen were engaged, and 320,000 pounds of gold were spent on the enterprise. In five years and ten months the edifice was complete, and on December 26, 537 A.D., the emperor led a solemn inaugural procession to the resplendent cathedral. Justinian walked alone to the pulpit, and lifting up his hands, cried out: "Oh Solomon! I have vanquished you!" (Will Durant, "The Lessons of History," 4:130).

Today, when we study the archaeological evidences of ancient Meso-American cultures, we are probably seeing the remnants of similarly self-absorbed Lamanite civilizations, since it was they who worshipped gods of wood and of stone and focused their attention on the temporal monuments to their profane deities. (See Ezekiel 20:32). Jeremiah might have asked of these apostates: "Shall a man make gods unto himself, and they are no gods?" (Jeremiah 16:20).

As Truman Madsen so keenly observed, the avenue through which we may approach our Father is intimate and heart-felt prayer, acting no hypocrisy. "At one level," he said, "we all indulge the daily clichés, and more or less mean them: 'Forgive us,' or 'Help us to overcome our weaknesses.' At a deeper level, we voice actual present feelings, even when they are raw, ugly, miserable ones: 'Father, I feel awful,' or 'I am racked with anxiety.' But there is a deeper level, the inmost of which often defies words, even feeling words. This level may be likened to what the scriptures call "groanings which cannot be uttered." (Romans 8:26). Turned upward, they become the most powerful prayer-thrusts of all. There is a wordless center in each of us." ("Christ & The Inner Life," p. 17-18).

As we do this, the Lord promised that we "shall become even as Nephi of old." (V. 8). He "was an extraordinary man. He was firm and as unflinching as a rock in standing up for the right. He was full of faith, and uncomplaining in the face of adversity, and yet was as humble and tender as a child. The Holy Ghost seems constantly to have attended him and instructed him. He is one of the very greatest spiritual characters of The Book of Mormon." (Sydney B. Sperry, "Book of Mormon Compendium," p. 253).

Nephi set a tremendous example for those who would follow him. He was self-effacing, and would have been embarrassed to know that one day he would be held up as a role model. His Exemplar was Jesus Christ, and he would count his ministry a failure if it proved unable to deepen our commitment to the Savior, and strengthen our testimony of the principles of His gospel. The Tree of Life was very real to Nephi, and his constant prayer must have been to be sensitive to the whisperings of the Spirit, so that he might help as many as possible to make their way along the path, through mists of darkness, and past great and spacious buildings, while braving torrents of filthy water, to be introduced, almost at the point of exhaustion, to the delicious fruit of the tree.

We could also pattern our lives after that of Captain Moroni, of whom Mormon wrote: "Yea, verily, verily I say unto you, if all men had been, and were, and ever would be, like unto Moroni, behold, the very powers of hell would have been shaken forever; yea, the devil would never have power over the hearts of the children of men." (Alma 48:17). He had humility, but he was so outwardly focused on the peaceable things of the kingdom that he had no time to notice.

When our lives conform to the principles that shaped Nephi and Moroni, we follow Jesus Christ, and cry: "Repent, repent, and prepare ye the way of the Lord, and make his paths straight; for the kingdom of heaven is at hand." (V. 10). We acknowledge His sovereignty and make all necessary preparations for His reception as King of kings and Lord of lords. (See Revelation 19:16).

Faith and repentance lead us to the strait gate of baptism. Baptism serves at least nine purposes: 1) We are baptized to demonstrate our obedience, and 2) to follow in the footsteps of the Savior. 3) We are baptized to fulfill all righteousness. 4) Baptism allows us to receive a remission of our sins if we have reached the age of accountability. 5) Baptism enables us to gain admission to the Lord's church, "the only true and living church upon the face of the whole earth" with which the Lord is pleased. (D&C 1:31). 6) Baptism provides us with the opportunity to be personally sanctified through fire and the Holy Ghost. 7) It is outwardly symbolic of our rebirth, as we pass through a tangible portal that is in the similitude of the grave. 8) It is the gateway ordinance leading to the blessings reserved for the faithful that are only found in the other ordinances of the gospel, and 9) it sets us squarely on the path that leads to the Celestial Kingdom of God, and gets us up and moving forward, toward our destiny. It enables us to lose ourselves in visions of glory.

When we pass through its threshold, we will find that the path of eternal progression is strait and narrow. The gospel standard is undeviating, with no room for rationalization or compromise. There is no latitude in God's declaration, when He said: "For I the Lord cannot look upon sin with the least degree of allowance." (D&C 1:31).

"This seems a harsh scripture, for it clearly states that God cannot tolerate sin or sinfulness in any degree. He can't wink at it, or ignore it, or turn and look the other way. He won't sweep it under the rug or say, 'Well, it's just a little sin. It'll be all right.' God's standard, the celestial standard, is absolute, and it allows no exceptions. There is no wiggle room. Many people seem to have the idea that the Judgment will somehow involve weighing or balancing, with their good deeds on one side of the scales and their bad deeds on the other. If their good deeds outweigh their bad, or if their hearts are basically good and outweigh their sins, then they can be admitted into the presence of God. This notion is false. God cannot, will not, allow moral or ethical imperfection in any degree whatsoever to dwell in his presence. He cannot tolerate sin 'with the least degree of allowance.' It is not a question of whether our good deeds outweigh our sins. If there is even one sin on our record, we are finished. The celestial standard is complete innocence, pure and simple, and nothing less will be tolerated in the kingdom of God." (Stephen Robinson, "Believing Christ," p. 1-2).

"Yea, repent and be baptized, every one of you, for a remission of your sins; yea, be baptized even by water, and then cometh the baptism of fire and of the Holy Ghost. ...This is my gospel." (V. 11-12). All of our teaching should be geared to motivate repentance. "Behold," said the Lord, "this is my doctrine - whosoever repenteth and cometh unto me, the same is my church." (D&C 10:67). Moroni offered the same message: "Be wise in the days of your probation," he cautioned. "Strip yourselves of all uncleanness... Ask with a firmness unshaken, that ye will yield to no temptation, but that ye will serve the true and living God." (Mormon 9:28).

The spirit of revelation impresses upon those who are pure in heart the principles of the gospel that are revealed in the scriptures. "And upon this rock" of revelation "I will build my church; yea, upon this rock ye are built, and if ye continue, the gates of hell shall not prevail against you." (V. 13). The key to an understanding of the mysteries of God is the softening of our hearts that leads to the spiritual illumination of our minds. Of secular Christianity, B.H. Roberts once wrote: "In their efforts to clarify (their consideration of Christ) they were often simply multiplying mirrors and studying angles without increasing the light. The New Dispensation brought a flood of light that did not simply replace the darkness, but illuminated elements and principles, and their relationships, that heretofore had been (only) dimly perceived." ("The Truth, The Way, The Life," p. 263).

Under most circumstances, though, the people to whom the glad message is offered "will not seek wisdom, neither do they desire that she should rule over them!" Under those circumstances, "how blind and impenetrable are the understandings of the children of men." (Mosiah 8:20).

On the college portals in Moorish Granada (1300 – 1492) were inscribed these words: "The world is supported by four things, the learning of the wise, the justice of the great, the prayers of the good, and the valor of the brave." The real casualties of every dispensation are those who substitute intellect for intelligence, those who suppose that, because they live in a telestial landscape, they can rationally judge both the truth and the morality of the word of the Lord and of His prophets. In a society of Saints, however, people will gain knowledge and skill by both study and faith, and will not confuse the two.

In addition, the Lord revealed that it would be necessary for every faithful Latter-day Saint to "remember the church articles and covenants to keep them." (V. 14). Doctrine and Covenants Section 20, a revelation on Church Organization and Government, and Section 22, that deals with the New and Everlasting Covenant, were accepted by the membership of the church at its first conference, in June 1830, and constituted the Church Articles and Covenants, that was really the first general handbook of instructions of the priesthood.

Of the occasion of the organization of the church two months earlier, the Prophet Joseph Smith had written: "After a happy time spent in witnessing and feeling for ourselves the powers and blessings of the Holy Ghost, through the grace of God bestowed upon us, we dismissed with the pleasing knowledge that we were now individually members of, and acknowledged of God, 'The Church of Jesus Christ.'" (H.C., 1:79). It must have been a very good feeling!

In addition to the revelations dealing with church organization and government, and the New and Everlasting Covenant, the members were to be guided by the Holy Ghost. Therefore, the Lord instructed: "Whoso having faith you shall confirm in my church, by the laying on of the hands, and I will bestow the gift of the Holy Ghost upon them." (V. 15). "The world does not have the guidance of the Holy Ghost, but is blessed with the Light of Christ as a guide, which, if they are humble and seek the light, will lead them to the (greater) light." (Joseph Fielding Smith, Jr.).

"The Book of Mormon and the holy scriptures are given of me for your instruction; and the power of my Spirit quickeneth all things." (V. 16). These are the tools of conversion and the particles of our faith. The scriptures are the great equalizer, for the past is prologue, and holy writ can be individually tailored to fit the circumstances of each of us who ponders its messages.

Marion G. Romney once told the Saints: "I don't know much about the gospel other than what I've learned from the Standard Works. When I drink from a spring, I like to get the water where it comes out of the ground, not down the stream, after the cattle have waded in it. I appreciate other people's interpretation, but when it comes to the gospel, we ought to be acquainted with what the Lord says." (C.R., 4/1975).

Dallin Oaks very insightfully wrote the following: "Latter-day Saints know that learned or authoritative commentaries can help us with scriptural interpretation, but we maintain that they must be used with caution. Commentaries are not a substitute for the scriptures any more than a good cookbook is a substitute for food. (When I refer to commentaries, I refer to everything that interprets scripture, from the comprehensive book-length commentary to the brief interpretation embodied in a lesson or an article, such as this one.)

One trouble with commentaries," he continued, "is that their authors sometimes focus on only one meaning, to the exclusion of others. As a result, commentaries, if not used with great care may illuminate the author's chosen and correct meaning, but close our eyes and restrict our horizons to other possible meanings. Sometimes, those other, less obvious meanings can be the ones most valuable and useful to us as we seek to understand our own dispensation and to obtain answers to our own questions. This s why the teaching of the Holy Ghost is a better guide to scriptural interpretation than even the best commentary." ("Scripture Reading and Revelation," "Ensign," 1/1995).

Spencer W. Kimball said: "I ask us all to honestly evaluate our performance in scripture study. It is a common thing to have a few passages of scripture at our disposal, floating in our minds, as it were, and thus to have the illusion that we know a great deal about the gospel. In this sense, having a little knowledge can be a problem, indeed. I am convinced that each of us must, at some time in our lives, discover the scriptures for ourselves, and not just discover them once, but rediscover them again and again." ("Teachings of Presidents of The Church: Spencer W. Kimball," p. 59–68).

As President Kimball indicated, the Lord requires that we be in a constant state of spiritual readiness, or in other words, in a constant state of improvement leading to perfection. "Be faithful, praying always, having your lamps trimmed and burning, and oil with you, that you may be ready at the coming of the Bridegroom." (V. 17). Those who continually pray to our Father are not likely to lose sight of their utter dependence on Him for both their temporal and spiritual welfare, nor will they forget from Whom both talents and blessings flow.

Prayer is only "in vain" when it is cursorily performed without effect, or without realistic expectation of the desired or intended result. To pray in vain is to pray without anticipation of success. Using the name of the Lord in vain, during prayer, may even be blasphemous when His name is used casually, without any genuine intention of extending the articulated thanks, or hope of receiving the desired blessing. Those who do so are imposters, invoking the name of Deity in a false, misleading, superficial, and counterfeit way. This is Satan's approach, in contrast to the righteous use of the name of God by those who bear His priesthood authority, are bound by His covenants, and act no hypocrisy.

Nine years after this revelation was received, Joseph Smith pleaded with the church from his confinement in Liberty Jail to develop the behavioral characteristics of our Heavenly Father and Jesus Christ. Remarkably, he implored the Saints: "Let thy bowels also be full of charity towards all men, and to the household of faith," he wrote the Saints, "and let virtue garnish thy thoughts unceasingly; then shall thy confidence wax strong in the presence of God; and the doctrine of the priesthood shall distill upon thy soul as the dews from heaven. The Holy Ghost shall be thy constant companion, and thy scepter an unchanging scepter of righteousness and truth; and thy dominion shall be an everlasting dominion and without compulsory means it shall flow unto thee forever and ever." (D&C 121:45-46).

Nephi had similar concerns about his own brethren. He perceived that they were having difficulty with the doctrine of Christ, because they were not exercising faith sufficient to pray. He equated their acquisition of the knowledge and qualities necessary for salvation with their ability and willingness to pray. His closing remarks to his people contain especially meaningful and inspired counsel on prayer. "If ye would hearken unto the Spirit which teacheth a man to pray," he wrote, "ye would know that ye must pray; for the evil spirit teacheth not a man to pray, but teacheth him that he must not pray. But behold, I say unto you that ye must pray always, and not faint; that ye must not perform any thing unto the Lord save in the first place ye shall pray unto the Father in the name of Christ, that he will consecrate thy performance unto thee, that thy performance may be for the welfare of thy soul." (2 Nephi 32:8-9).

Long ago, the Psalmist wrote: "Evening, and morning, and at noon, will I pray, and cry aloud: and he shall hear my voice." (Psalms 55:17). In the Garden of Gethsemane, the Savior counseled Peter: "Watch and pray, that ye enter not into temptation: the spirit indeed is willing, but the flesh is weak." (Matthew 26:41). The practice of the church to consistently pray makes sense, since its members need regular reinforcement against encroachments by Satan and the tendency to be carnal, sensual, and devilish. Brigham Young once observed that it does not matter if we feel like praying or not; we should nevertheless pray. He said if we wait until we feel like praying, there will not be much prayer in this world. (See D.B.Y., p. 44).

David O. McKay enjoyed quoting a favorite poem: "The builder who first bridged Niagara's gorge, before he swung his cable, shore to shore, sent out across the gulf his venturing kite, bearing a slender cord for unseen hands to grasp upon the further cliff and draw a greater cord, and then a greater yet; 'til at last across the chasm swung The Cable - then the mighty bridge in air! So may we send our little timid thoughts, across the void, out to God's reaching hands. Send our love, and faith, to thread the deep, thought after thought, until the little cord, and we, are anchored to the Infinite! (Edwin Markham).

"The Lord requires His people to bow the knee before Him every night and morning, and to remember Him in their secret prayers. Every Latter-day Saint who neglects this requirement has not that supply of oil that is necessary to prepare him for the Coming of The Son of Man." (Francis S. Lyman, C.R., 4/1901). "For behold, verily, verily, I say unto you, that I come quickly." (V. 18).

# Section 34

## (Instructions in 1830 to the newly organized church in New York).

This is a "revelation given through Joseph Smith the Prophet to Orson Pratt, at Fayette, New York, November 4, 1830. Brother Pratt was nineteen years old at the time. He had been converted and baptized when he first heard the preaching of the Restored Gospel by his older brother, Parley P. Pratt, six weeks before." (Superscript).

We remember the zeal with which Parley P. Pratt embraced the gospel, it is no wonder that he should be the instrument through which his brother would be introduced to the church and kingdom. Both Parley and Orson Pratt would live in the times that try men's souls. They would repeatedly see around them those summer soldiers and sunshine patriots who would, in times of crisis, shrink from their service in the church. They determined to stand fast, not for the love and thanks of man and woman, but because they loved Joseph Smith, they loved the Saints, and they loved the Lord. They knew that ignorance, like hell, would not be easily conquered. Yet, they had this consolation with them, that the harder the conflict, the more glorious would be their triumph. What they obtained too cheaply, they might esteem too lightly. In the fiery crucible of experience, they would learn that it is dearness only that gives everything its value, that heaven knows how to put a proper price upon its goods, and that it would be strange, indeed, if so celestial an article as a knowledge of the Plan of Salvation should not be so highly rated. (Adapted from "The Political Works of Thomas Paine," p. 55, cf. "The Crisis," 12/23/1776).

The Savior addressed Orson Pratt as His "son." (V. 1). Through the spiritual rebirth made possible by Jesus Christ, we acquire His distinctive characteristics, become partakers of His divine nature, and become His sons and daughters. By the covenant of baptism, we take upon ourselves a new name, which is His name, and by our obedience to the principles of His gospel, we enjoy the companionship of His Spirit. This rebirth is equivalent to a spiritual heart transplant; it results in a mighty change in our nature, so that we may become as He is. His heart, as it were, now beats in our chest.

Christ is our Father in the sense that He is the Creator of heaven and earth, and He has assumed the full stature of His own Father, to the end that He possesses the gifts and powers by which all the sons and daughters of God may be brought to perfection. In this sense, Jesus taught: "He that hath seen me hath seen the Father." (John 14:9, see John 1:18, & 12:45).

King Benjamin told his people that because of their covenant with God, they would "be called the children of Christ, his sons and his daughters." (Mosiah 5:7). Just as we are known by the name of our mortal parents, so too are we called by the name of Christ in a familial way. There is a special relationship reserved for the faithful that is in addition to the reality that we are all spirit children of our Father. "For this day He hath spiritually begotten you," explained Benjamin. (Mosiah 5:7). The Saints, in particular, enjoy a special covenant relationship with Jesus Christ, and are thus born of Him. Strictly speaking, "Born Again Christians" are those who are in a special covenant relationship with the Lord, and since only members of Christ's true church can do that through the authority of the priesthood and by continuing revelation, if follows that the only real Born Again Christians must be Latter-day Saints!

But all of us are Christ's children in the sense that He gave us immortality, or life beyond the grave, through the Resurrection. All will be raised from physical death by the power of the Resurrection, and those who call upon His name will be raised from spiritual death by the power of the Atonement. "Surely he hath borne our griefs and carried our sorrows." (Mosiah 14:4). He was "offered to bear the sins of many." (Hebrews 9:28). Thus, He is the Father of all the family of God. Through the sanctifying influence of His Atonement, we may all be spiritually reborn. Thus, He becomes the Father of all who follow His example, and subordinate their will to His guidance and instruction.

We are born of Jesus Christ because He gives birth to our spiritual nature. We are born of Him as we are introduced to righteousness, bear hardship, and endure the refiner's fire. We are born of Him as we carry His testimony in our hearts. We are born of Him as we participate in the creation of a new heaven, and a new earth, and bear our witness of our blessings to others. We are born of God at sacred altars in the House of the Lord.

God's reach extends to all of His children. His spiritual obstetrical skills are granted unto us proportionately as we conform to the standards of personal righteousness that are part of the gospel plan. Thus, we are commanded to "grow in grace" (D&C 50:40) until we have been sanctified and justified "through the grace of our Lord and Savior Jesus Christ." (D&C 20:30-32).

He is our "Redeemer, the light and the life of the world." (V. 3). The light of Christ is the power that controls the order of the universe. "The earth rolls upon her wings," He once declared, "and the sun giveth his light by day, and the moon giveth her light by night, and the stars also give their light, as they roll upon their wings in their glory, in the midst of the power of God. Then shall ye know that ye have seen me, that I am, and that I am the true light that is in you, and that you are in me; otherwise ye could not abound." (D&C 88:45 & 50).

When the "Light of the World" was crucified, all nature found itself in upheaval. Momentarily, the order of the cosmos was thrown into turmoil. When He yielded up the ghost, there were thunderings and lightnings for the space of many hours, and the earth shook and trembled; and the rocks that were upon the face of the earth were broken up. (See Helaman 14:21).

Christ is "a light which shineth in darkness and the darkness comprehendeth it not." (V. 3). He is the life and the light of the faithful, their joy and their salvation, and their redemption from everlasting wo. (See Alma 26:35). Those who receive Him will enjoy kinship with Lamoni, who, in the account of Alma, after welcoming the missionaries into his heart, found that "the dark veil of unbelief was being cast away from his mind, and the light which did light up his mind...was the light of the glory of God...and that the light of everlasting life was lit up in his soul, yea, he knew that this had overcome his natural frame, and he was carried away in God." (Alma 19:6)

The Gospel of John teaches us: "For God so loved the world, that he gave his only begotten Son, that whosoever believeth in him should not perish, but have everlasting life." (John 3:16). But this account in the Doctrine & Covenants goes a step further; it reveals that Christ " so loved the world that he gave his own life" for His brothers and sisters. (V. 3).

In spite of His innocence, He was crucified, and He "gave up the ghost." (Mark 15:37). However, having been born of a mortal mother and an immortal Father, Jesus had inherited power over death. In His genetic makeup, He held the priesthood keys of resurrection. Therefore, He was never subject to the finality of death. He was different from other men. Significantly, Satan must have never considered the possibility that his Elder Brother was not under the spell of Adam's transgression. We scarcely recognize the power in Paul's declaration of fact: "For as in Adam all die, even so in Christ shall all be made alive." (1 Corinthians 15:22).

The heart beating within His chest, and the blood coursing through His veins was different from other men. "For as the Father hath life in himself; so hath he given to the Son to have life in himself." He had the power to lay down His life, and take it up again. For God "hath given him authority to execute judgment also, because he is the Son of man (of Holiness)." (John 5:25-27). Thus, one of His name-titles is "the Resurrection and the Life." (John 11:25). "He opened the door to eternity, to redeem from Satan's power every living creature." (Joseph Fielding Smith, "Man: His Origin & Destiny," p. 379).

No one else among the children of God is capable of eternal life through their own efforts. A greater endowment, or gift of power beyond our own capabilities, is required. The Savior is able to provide that gift for us, for He has been divinely invested with the power of God the Father. He is "the lamb slain from the foundation of the world," and through His Atonement, we are spiritually born of Him. (Revelation 13:8).

"As many as would believe," Orson Pratt was told, would "become the sons of God." (V. 3). Lyman Abbott said: "The brotherhood of man is an integral part of Christianity no less than the Fatherhood of God; and to deny the one is no less infidel than to deny the other." Its "mystic bond makes all men one." (Thomas Carlyle). "The universe is but one great city, full of beloved ones, divine and human, by nature endeared to each other." (Epictetus).

Joseph F. Smith declared: "No man need fear in his heart, when he is conscious of having lived up to the principles of truth and righteousness as God has required it at his hands, according to his best knowledge and understanding." (C.R., 4/1903). When we are diligent in our obedience, our agency enjoys its greatest expression. The perfect law of liberty is one of the hardest things for the unconverted to understand. The Lord knew Orson Pratt, and that when he embraced missionary work, hearts would be touched, lives would be changed on both sides of the equation, and souls would be added to the harvest. "Grace and peace (would be) multiplied unto (him) through the knowledge of God, and of Jesus our Lord." (2 Peter 1:2).

King Benjamin taught his people that because of their covenant with God, they would "be called the children of Christ, his sons and his daughters." (Mosiah 5:7). True Christians recognize that "Jesus Christ (is) the Son of God, the Father of heaven and earth, the Creator of all things." (Mosiah 3:8,). And so they proudly take His name upon themselves.

Only by making covenants with God and Christ can we break the bands of death, and are we made free. "There is no other name given whereby salvation cometh," said Benjamin; "therefore, I would that ye should take upon you the name of Christ, all you that have entered into the covenant with God." (Mosiah 5:8). Is it any wonder that The Church of Jesus Christ of Latter-day Saints is a missionary oriented church, and that Jesus Christ proclaims that it "is the only true and living church upon the face of the whole earth, with which I, the Lord, am well pleased?" (D&C 1:30). No other church possesses within its liturgy this depth of understanding of our relationship with God the Father and His Son Jesus Christ, and no other church is as anxious to share the good news with its neighbors.

Not only the reality of the apostasy, but also the subsequent restoration of priesthood authority is well documented in the scriptures and in the history of the church. No other church exercises this authority to invoke the blessings of companionship with the Holy Ghost, or to bind and ratify the covenants that can be made with God. "By their fruits ye shall know them" is a powerful statement of fact that testifies of the full faith and credit enjoyed by the Lord's church. (Matthew 7:20). No other organization has the power to break the death grip of Satan, who would drag our souls down to hell in an instant, if he were given the opportunity to do so.

"Blessed are you because you have believed; and more blessed are you because you are called to preach my gospel." (V. 4-5). The continuing focus of attention on their less fortunate brethren by those enlisted in the missionary army of Jesus Christ would eventually bring those whom they taught into complete harmony with the attributes of their Father in Heaven, whose similar concern is for the eternal welfare of all of His children. Those entering the fold would be "no more strangers and foreigners, but fellowcitizens with the Saints, and with the household of God." (Ephesians 2:19). "And ye shall be even as I am," promised the Lord, "and I am even as the Father, and the Father and I are one." (3 Nephi 28:10).

Therefore, Orson Pratt was exhorted: "Lift up your voice as with the sound of a trump, both long and loud, and cry repentance unto a crooked and perverse generation." (V. 6). The Savior said: "If thine eye be evil, thy whole body shall be full of darkness. If, therefore, the light that is in thee be darkness, how great is that darkness!" (3 Nephi 14:23). The influence of Satan that gripped Joseph in the Sacred Grove before his deliverance illustrates just how overwhelming the intensity of darkness can be.

Joseph wrote: "I was seized upon by some power which entirely overcame me, and had such an astonishing influence over me as to bind my tongue so that I could not speak. Thick darkness gathered around me, and it seemed to me for a time as if I were doomed to sudden destruction.... I was ready to sink into despair and abandon myself to destruction - not to an imaginary ruin, but to the power of some actual being from the unseen world." (J.S.H. 1:15-16). We are reminded of Lehi's Vision of The Tree of Life, and of those who lost their way in mists of darkness. (See 1 Nephi 8:23).

The Savior taught the great principle that we cannot serve two masters; for either we "will hate the one and love the other, or else (we) will hold to the one and despise the other. We cannot serve God and Mammon." (3 Nephi 14:24). A house divided against itself cannot stand. (See Mark 3:25). The church cannot continually re-adjust its standards by lowering its expectations, so that it becomes popular with the world, for then all hell would want to join it. The Saints cannot hold membership in both the Church of God and the Great and Abominable Church of the Devil. They cannot live in Zion, while maintaining a summer home in Babylon. They cannot journey through Idumea, stopping at every detour along the way to sample its pleasures.

In D&C Section 29:12, we find the only instance in the Doctrine & Covenants where the term 'great and abominable church' is employed, although it is used twelve times in The Book of Mormon, in 1 Nephi 4:3, 9, 15, & 17, 1 Nephi 13:6, 8, 26 & 28, 1 Nephi 22:13 & 14, 2 Nephi 6:12, & 2 Nephi 28:18. That is enough, however, to entrench the phrase in our lexicon. Nephi was given, in vision, a broad view of the state of the world in the Last Days, and clearly saw "the great persecutor of the church, the apostate, the whore, even Babylon, that maketh all nations to drink of her cup, in whose hearts the enemy, even Satan, sitteth to reign." (D&C 86:3).

There is a basic instability associated with hypocrisy, and those who walk what they perceive to be the line between righteousness and wickedness will suffer eternally damaging consequences. They are faced with a conundrum of cosmic proportion. Agency was preserved as the crown jewel of mortality in order to avoid this dilemma. We are free to choose, but choose we must. We are free to follow one lifestyle or another, but not both. That desire is fatally flawed, because it runs counter to the laws of nature. Those who pursue that path travel down a one-way road that leads inevitably to a slippery slope above a personality precipice.

We do not have the option to walk "in (our) own way, and after the image of (our) own god, whose image is in the likeness of the world, and whose substance is that of an idol." (D&C 1:16). Orson Pratt became the grateful recipient of one of the greatest contributions of Joseph Smith, and that was to share his knowledge of what is to come after death. We have all benefited from that instruction. He clarified our understanding of heaven, and made it an attainable goal. He created desire in our hearts to follow the difficult road to Gethsemane. He validated the promises made by the Father that the struggles of mortality would be for but a moment, and that we would look back on our experiences in appreciation for the personal growth and development that occurred only because of our participation in the great Plan of Salvation. Orson Pratt would discover, as we all must, that only if the drama is played out within the context of the gospel, according to the rules that govern the Plan, do the anticipated blessings come. There is no other way.

This has been the pattern from the foundation of the world. "And thus the gospel began to be preached, from the beginning, being declared by holy angels sent forth from the presence of God, and by his own voice, and by the gift of the Holy Ghost. And thus all things were confirmed unto Adam, by an holy ordinance, and the gospel preached, and a decree sent forth, that it should be in the world, until the end thereof; and thus it was." (Moses 5:58-59).

We who have consecrated our time, talents, energy, and our very lives to the kingdom of God, have long since "crossed over Jordan." We stand with Joshua, who declared: "Choose you this day whom ye will serve; whether the gods which your fathers served that were on the other side of the flood, or the gods of the Amorites, in whose land ye dwell: but as for me and my house, we will serve the Lord." (Joshua 24:15).

Orson Pratt was commanded to prepare "the way of the Lord for His second coming." (V. 6). He became one of the original Twelve Apostles, lived longer than any of his colleagues, filled seven missions, and earned a life long reputation as one of the most capable defenders of the faith. He was also responsible for arranging the text of The Book of Mormon and the Doctrine and Covenants into chapters and verses.

"The time is soon at hand that I shall come in a cloud with power and great glory." (V. 7). After Jesus had ministered unto the Nephite Twelve, "there came a cloud and overshadowed the multitude, that they could not see Jesus." (3 Nephi 18:38). This was symbolic of the presence of the Lord. As "the Lord said unto Moses, Lo, I come unto thee in a thick cloud, that the people may hear when I speak with thee, and believe thee for ever." (Exodus 19:9).

Fire and smoke are frequently cited in the scriptures as depictions of the glory of God. In the language of Joseph Smith: "God Almighty Himself dwells in eternal fire. Flesh and blood cannot go there, for all corruption is devoured by that fire. Our God is a consuming fire. Immortality dwells in everlasting burnings." ("Teachings," p. 367). After the Exodus from Egypt, during Israel's sojourn in the wilderness, "mount Sinai was altogether on a smoke, because the Lord descended upon it in fire: and the smoke thereof ascended as the smoke of a furnace, and the whole mount quaked greatly." (Exodus 19:18).

"And it shall be a great day at the time of my coming, for all nations shall tremble." (V. 8). It is a characteristic of the Last Days that our societies are increasingly polarized. It may be somewhat of an oversimplification, but what it comes down to is this: On the one hand is the Kingdom of God, and on the other hand is spiritual Babylon, the whore of the earth. In the judgments that precede the Second Coming, all earthly kingdoms will come to an end, and the kingdom of God will triumph and become the one political power during a thousand years of peace and righteousness. During the time of political upheaval and physical turmoil that will precede the Millennium, "with the sword and by bloodshed the inhabitants of the earth shall mourn; and with famine, and plague, and earthquake, and the thunder of heaven, and the fierce and vivid lightning also, shall the inhabitants of the earth be made to feel the wrath, and indignation, and chastening hand of an Almighty God, until the consumption decreed hath made a full end of all nations." (D&C 87:6).

What are we to do in the face of these judgments that are sure to come? The answer is given by the Lord Himself: "Wherefore, stand ye in holy places, and be not moved, until the day of the Lord come; for behold, it cometh quickly." (D&C 87:8). Holy places have more to do with how we live than where we live. If we enjoy the companionship of a member of the Godhead, the Holy Ghost, then surely we will stand in a holy place at the great day of the Lord. A holy place, then, is anywhere the Spirit and presence of Divinity is enjoyed.

"But before that great day shall come, the sun shall be darkened, and the moon be turned into blood; and the stars shall refuse their shining, and some shall fall, and great destructions await the wicked." (V. 9). "The sun and the moon shall be darkened," prophesied Joel, "and the stars shall withdraw their shining…and the heavens and the earth shall shake: but the Lord will be the hope of his people, and the strength of the children of Israel. So shall ye know that I am the Lord your God, dwelling in Zion, my holy mountain. Then shall Jerusalem be holy." (Joel 3:15-17).

"Wherefore, lift up your voice and spare not, for the Lord God hath spoken; therefore prophesy, and it shall be given by the power of the Holy Ghost." (V. 10). Everyone who remains in Zion or Jerusalem, and whose names are written among the living, or who is approved of God, shall be called holy. (See Isaiah 4:3). The Lord will purge Israel of its moral degradation; the whole earth, and every nation, will be similarly cleansed of unrighteousness. "The Lord shall have washed away the filth of the daughters of Zion, and shall have purged the blood of Jerusalem from the midst thereof, by the spirit of judgment and by the spirit of burning." (Isaiah 4:4).

"And if you are faithful, behold, I am with you until I come." (V. 11). When Orson Pratt came out of spiritual Babylon, he kept his covenants for the remainder of his life. He lived with confidence and high hopes for the future. In 1830, the Lord declared "The day speedily cometh; the hour is not yet, but is nigh at hand, when peace shall be taken from the earth, and the devil shall have power over his own dominion." (D&C 1:35). "But if ye are prepared, ye shall not fear." (D&C 38:30). Orson Pratt discovered that obedience to the principles of the gospel of Jesus Christ was independent of circumstances, and was his key to happiness.

Keeping our own covenants gives us the priesthood and spiritual power necessary to overcome evil and obtain exaltation. "For by doing these things, the gates of hell shall not prevail against you; yea, and the Lord God will disperse the powers of darkness from before you, and cause the heavens to shake for thy good, and His name's glory." (D&C 21:6). The Prophet Joseph Smith said that salvation consists of our being placed beyond the power of our enemies, meaning the enemies of our progression, such as dishonesty, greediness, lying, immorality, and other vices. (Sermon delivered at the Nauvoo temple site on May 21, 1843. Sources: Joseph Smith diary (Willard Richards), Howard and Martha Jane Knowlton Coray Notebook, Franklin D. Richards "Scriptural Items," and James Burgess Notebook. See "Teachings," p. 297-298).

To Orson Pratt, in 1830, the Lord said: "I come quickly." (V. 12). He would come when least expected, preserving for all of God's children their time of probation, of testing, or of putting to the proof the questions: "Will they serve God? Will they recognize Christ as their Savior? Will they exercise faith unto repentance? Will they procrastinate the time of their probation." In each of our individual circumstances, if we fail to do so, it will not matter when the Lord comes, because no matter when that is, it will be inconvenient.

As we look back over the history of the church, we realize that for faithful members like Orson Pratt, the Lord has already come. At the end of his life, he may have recalled the wistful lament of Jacob, who wrote: "The time passed away with us, and also our lives passed away like as it were unto us a dream, we being a lonesome and a solemn people, wanderers cast out from Jerusalem, born in tribulation, in a wilderness, and hated of our brethren, which caused wars and contentions; wherefore, we did mourn out our days. (Jacob 7:26). But he would have also cherished the knowledge that he was a son of God, and not only that, but known by name, and loved of Him.

Orson Pratt did not procrastinate the day of his repentance, nor did he rely upon the false, vain, and foolish doctrine that urges all of us: "Eat, drink, and be merry, for tomorrow we die; and it shall be well with us. (God) will justify in committing a little sin; yea, lie a little, take the advantage of one because of his words, dig a pit for thy neighbor; there is no harm in this; and do all this things, for tomorrow we die; and if it so be that we are guilty, God will beat us with a few stripes, and at last we shall be saved in the kingdom of God." (2 Nephi 28:7-8). Instead, Orson Pratt was as the merchant "who, when he had found one pearl of great price, went and sold all that he had, and bought it." (Matthew 13:46).

# Consummatum Est

# Author's Note

To help defend Jerusalem against attacks by the Assyrians, King Hezekiah ordered that the fountains of the spring of Gihon outside the city walls of Jerusalem be covered, to allow easy access to the water. The waters of the spring were then diverted to the pool of Siloam, inside the city walls. This was done by digging a tunnel through about 1770 feet of limestone rock. Without having this water available from inside the walls of the city, the people of Jerusalem would not have survived the siege by the Assyrians.

Just as the water from the spring of Gihon was vital to the physical survival of Hezekiah's people during their battles with the Assyrians, living water is essential for our spiritual survival during our battles with Satan. The Lord knew that the restoration of the gospel would have to be accompanied by personal and institutional revelation, and lots of it. We see the result of that concern in the Doctrine & Covenants. We are under siege throughout our mortal lives, and our constant access to its living water is our only hope of salvation.

What is this living water that is represented by the revelations? Jesus said to the woman at the well: "Whosoever drinketh of this water shall thirst again: But whosoever drinketh of the water that I shall give him shall never thirst; but the water that I shall give him shall be in him a well of water springing up into everlasting life." (John 4:10-14). The living water that sustains us spiritually is the doctrine of the gospel of Jesus Christ.

Living water is so crucial to our well-being that the Lord has provided a conduit that can penetrate hundreds of feet of solid limestone, as it were, so that it may freely flow into our lives. With great effort, this conduit is chiseled through our rough exterior and stony nature with the tools of faith, obedience, study, prayer, good works, and other healthy lifestyle choices. Latter-day scriptures represent a conduit of living water that nurtures our desire not only to believe, but also to act on our belief by being honest, true, chaste, benevolent, kind, and in doing good to all men. (See the 13th Article of Faith). One of the greatest blessings that are enjoyed by the Saints, is their unshakable faith that God has revealed many great and important things, that He does so now, and that He will continue to do so. (See the 9th Article of Faith).

We receive living water every time we open the scriptures, where we receive instruction, are endowed with power and understanding, and feel peace and joy. The study of God's word was an important protective strategy for the Israelites in Hezekiah's time, and it continues to be an important weapon in our own arsenal of protection. In large part, when we take upon ourselves the whole armor of God, we have the revelations of the Doctrine & Covenants to thank for our clear understanding of the principles of the Plan.

These scriptures instruct us to seek living water "diligently, and (to) teach (each other) words of wisdom; yea, (to) seek...out of the best books words of wisdom; (to) seek learning, even by study and also by faith. (We must) organize (ourselves and) prepare every needful thing; and establish a house, even a house of prayer, a house of fasting, a house of faith, a house of learning, a house of glory, a house of order, a house of God. That (our) incomings may be in the name of the Lord; that (our) outgoings may be in the name of the Lord; that all (our) salutations may be in the name of the Lord, with uplifted hands unto the Most High. Therefore, (in order to be refreshed with living water, it would be well to) cease from all (our) light speeches, from all laughter, from all (our) lustful desires, from all (our) pride and light-mindedness, and from all (our) wicked doings." (D&C 88:118-121).

If we disregard the blessings to be found in the application of the principles that are found in the Doctrine & Covenants, we are guilty of turning our faces away from the habitation of the Lord. Because the people of the Tribe of Judah anciently disregarded these weightier matters of the law, "the wrath of the Lord was upon Judah and Jerusalem, and he...delivered them to trouble, to astonishment, and to hissing.... For, lo, (their) fathers (had) fallen by the sword, and (their) sons and (their) daughters and (their) wives (were) in captivity for this." (2 Chronicles 29:8-9).

Because he realized it was critical to Israel's temporal and spiritual well-being, Hezekiah hoped to re-establish the Covenant with the Lord, by cleansing the temple and preparing it for meaningful worship again. The scriptures record that he declared: "Now it is in mine heart to make a covenant with the Lord God of Israel, that his fierce wrath may turn away from us." (2 Chronicles 29:10). He wanted to keep unclean things out of the temple.

Through Joseph Smith, the Lord has in our day promised to provide living water, as well, that the Saints might be refreshed and rejuvenated. "Inasmuch as my people build a house unto me in the name of the Lord, and do not suffer any unclean thing to come into it, that it be not defiled, my glory shall rest upon it; Yea, and my presence shall be there, for I will come into it, and all the pure in heart that shall come into it shall see God. But if it be defiled I will not come into it, and my glory shall not be there; for I will not come into unholy temples." (D&C 97:15-17).

If we do not qualify by worthiness to partake of the living water found in the scriptures, the Lord has made it clear that we must do as the people of Hezekiah did anciently. The conduit to living water is accessible if we do as Joseph Smith implored at the dedication of the Kirtland Temple. He prayed that "no unclean clean thing (should) be permitted to come into (the House of the Lord) to pollute it; And when thy people transgress, any of them, (that) they may speedily repent and return unto thee, and find favor in thy sight, and be restored to the blessings which thou hast ordained to be poured out upon those who shall reverence thee in thy house." (D&C 109:20-21).

Anciently, when the temple had been cleansed, Hezekiah and the people of Jerusalem "made an end of offering, the king and all that were present with him. (And they) bowed themselves, and worshipped. Moreover Hezekiah the king and the princes commanded the Levites to sing praise unto the Lord with the words of David, and of Asaph the seer. And they sang praises with gladness, and they bowed their heads and worshipped. Then Hezekiah answered and said, Now ye have consecrated yourselves unto the Lord, come near and bring sacrifices and thank offerings into the house of the Lord. And the congregation brought in sacrifices and thank offerings; and as many as were of a free heart burnt offerings." (2 Chronicles 29:29-31).

In our day, Jesus Christ has promised unimpeded access to living water with this instruction: "Thou shalt offer a sacrifice unto the Lord thy God in righteousness, even that of a broken heart and a contrite spirit." (D&C 59:8). Elsewhere, He said: "Verily I say unto you, all among them who know their hearts are honest, and are broken, and their spirits contrite, and are willing to observe their covenants by sacrifice - yea, every sacrifice which I, the Lord, shall command – they are accepted of me." (D&C 97:8).

In order to avoid the spiritual captivity and moral bankruptcy of scriptural illiteracy, Moroni urged us, in the last verses of The Book of Mormon: "And again, I would exhort you that ye would come unto Christ, and lay hold upon every good gift, and touch not the evil gift, nor the unclean thing. And awake, and arise from the dust, O Jerusalem; yea, and put on thy beautiful garments, O daughter of Zion; and strengthen thy stakes and enlarge thy borders forever, that thou mayest no more be confounded, that the covenants of the Eternal Father which he hath made unto thee, O house of Israel, may be fulfilled. Yea, come unto Christ, and be perfected in him, and deny yourselves of all ungodliness; and if ye shall deny yourselves of all ungodliness, and love God with all your might, mind, and strength, then is his grace sufficient for you, that by his grace ye may be perfect in Christ; and if by the grace of God ye are perfect in Christ, ye can in nowise deny the power of God." (Moroni 10:30-32).

Nephi has earlier expressed the common theme that would become the essence of Book of Mormon teaching: "Inasmuch as those whom the Lord God shall bring out of the land of Jerusalem shall keep his commandments, they shall prosper upon the face of this land; and they shall be kept from all other nations." (2 Nephi 1:9). The Lord's introduction to the Doctrine & Covenants warns the world that it has strayed from the ordinances of the Lord and has broken His everlasting covenant. Without the quality of pointed and specific instruction that is found throughout the Doctrine & Covenants, the people would have been left to grope about in the darkness, every one walking in his own way, after the image of his own god, in the likeness of the world. Without a book like the Doctrine & Covenants, even the Saints would have found it difficult to break free from idol worship. (See D&C 1:15-17).

Anciently, those who gave heed to the commandments were promised: "No weapon that is formed against thee shall prosper; and every tongue that shall rise against thee in judgment thou shalt condemn." (Isaiah 54:17). In our day, our Savior has promised us similar protection, if we will nourish ourselves with living water: "Let my army become very great, and let it be sanctified before me, that it may become fair as the sun, and clear as the moon, and that her banners may be terrible unto all nations. That the kingdoms of this world may be constrained to acknowledge that the kingdom of Zion is in very deed the kingdom of God and his Christ; therefore, let us become subject unto her laws." (D&C 105:31-32).

Hezekiah and his people received the Lord's protection because of their righteousness, that was demonstrated by their strict obedience to the commandments. In his Dedicatory Prayer at the Kirtland Temple, Joseph Smith asked our Father in Heaven to bless with the nourishment of living water "the people that shall worship, and honorably hold a name and standing in this thy house, to all generations and for eternity; That no weapon formed against them shall prosper; that he who diggeth a pit for them shall fall into the same himself; That no combination of wickedness shall have power to rise up and prevail over thy people upon whom thy name shall be put in this house; And if any people shall rise against this people, that thine anger be kindled against them; And if they shall smite this people thou wilt smite them; thou wilt fight for thy people as thou didst in the day of battle, that they may be delivered from the hands of all their enemies." (D&C 109:24-28).

Hezekiah was succeeded as king by his son Manasseh and his grandson Amon, and his great-grandson Josiah, who was made king of Judah when he was eight years old. He became a righteous king who ruled in Israel from 641 to 610 B.C., at the very time Lehi was growing up in the land of Jerusalem.

Josiah sought the true God, destroyed idolatry in the kingdom, and sent craftsmen to repair the temple. During its renovation, Hilkiah the high priest "found a book of the law of the Lord (the scriptures) given by Moses." (2 Chronicles 34:14). By this time in Judah's history, the written law apparently had been lost, and was virtually unknown. This is surely why Lehi felt that it was so important for his sons to return to Jerusalem, at great personal risk, to retrieve the Plates of Brass, that would be to them as living water, in the wilderness. As Nephi wrote: "And behold, it is wisdom in God that we should obtain these records, that we may preserve unto our children the language of our fathers; and also that we may preserve unto them the words which have been spoken by the mouth of all the holy prophets, which have been delivered unto them by the Spirit and power of God, since the world began, even down unto this present time." (1 Nephi 3:19-20).

When the book of the law was read to him, Josiah "rent his clothes." (2 Chronicles 34:19). He was distressed to hear what the book of the law contained. The scriptures record his lament: "Great is the wrath of the Lord that is poured out upon us, because our fathers have not kept the word of the Lord, to do after all that is written in this book." (2 Chronicles 34:21). He realized that Israel had polluted the living water that had been provided to sustain Israel during her greatest trials. This begs the question: Have members of the latter-day church jeopardized their standing before the Lord, as well, because of their pollution of the provided living water?

After Josiah found out that his people would be condemned because they had not done as the scriptures instructed, he called all the people to the temple and read the scriptures to them. (2 Chronicles 34:29-30). Spencer W. Kimball warned: "Access to (the scriptures) means responsibility for them. We must study the scriptures according to the Lord's commandment and we must let them govern our lives." ("Ensign," 9/1976). Regarding the living water He has provided the Latter-day Saints, the Lord taught: "These words are given unto you, and they are pure before me; wherefore, beware how you hold them, for they are to be answered upon your souls in the day of judgment." (D&C 41:12).

Because they understood that the living water would save their very lives, while Josiah and his people were at the temple, they approached the altar, where "the king stood in his place, and made a covenant before the Lord, to walk after the Lord, and to keep his commandments, and his testimonies, and his statutes, with all his heart, and with all his soul, to perform the words of the covenant which are written in this book. And he caused all that were present in Jerusalem and Benjamin to stand to it. And the inhabitants of Jerusalem did according to the covenant of God, the God of their fathers. And Josiah took away all the abominations out of all the countries that pertained to the children of Israel, and made all that were present in Israel to serve, even to serve the Lord their God. And all his days they departed not from following the Lord, the God of their fathers." (2 Chronicles 34:31-33).

Just so, in our day we make sacred covenants with the Lord before altars in the temple, the fulfillment of which will bring us earthly blessings and eternal exaltation, and the neglect of which will bring upon us the judgments of God, for God will not be mocked. As we focus our attention on obeying the Lord's commandments and being worthy to enter the temple, our thirst will be quenched with the living water provided by the Doctrine & Covenants.

# About the Author

Phil Hudson and his wife Jan have 7 children and over 20 grandchildren. They enjoy spending time with their family at their cabin nestled in the Selkirk Mountains, on the shores of Priest Lake, the crown jewel of North Idaho. Phil had a successful family dental practice in Spokane, Washington for 43 years, before retiring in 2015. He has an eclectic mix of hobbies, and enjoys riding motorcycles and ATVs. In his free time, he can be found hiking, boating, cycling, snow biking, and traveling with Jan. He always finds time, however, to record his thoughts on his laptop. He understands Isaac Asimov's response when he was asked: "If you knew that you only had 10 minutes left to live, what would you do with your time?" He answered: "I'd type faster."

As this volume was about to be published, Phil and Jan accepted a call to serve as full time missionaries for The Church of Jesus Christ of Latter-day Saints, in the Kingdom of Tonga. While there, they will celebrate their 50th wedding anniversary.

# Opera Additional

# Also by the Author

Essays

- Volume One: Spray from The Ocean of Thought
- Volume Two: Ripples on a Pond
- Volume Three: Serendipitous Meanderings
- Volume Four: Presents of Mind
- Volume Five: Mental Floss
- Volume Six: Fitness Training for the Mind and Spirit

Book of Mormon Commentary

- Born in The Wilderness
- Voices From the Dust
- Journey to Cumorah

Doctrine & Covenants Commentary

- Volume Two

Minute Musings: Spontaneous Combustions of Thought

- Volume One
- Volume Two
- Volume Three

Calendars:

- In His Own Words: Discovering William Tyndale
- As I Think About the Savior
- Daily Inspiration From Scriptural Symbols


Children's Books

- Muddy, Muddy
- We Believe: The 13 Articles of Faith


Diode Laser Soft Tissue Surgery

- Volume One
- Volume Two
- Volume Three


These, and other titles, are available from online retailers.

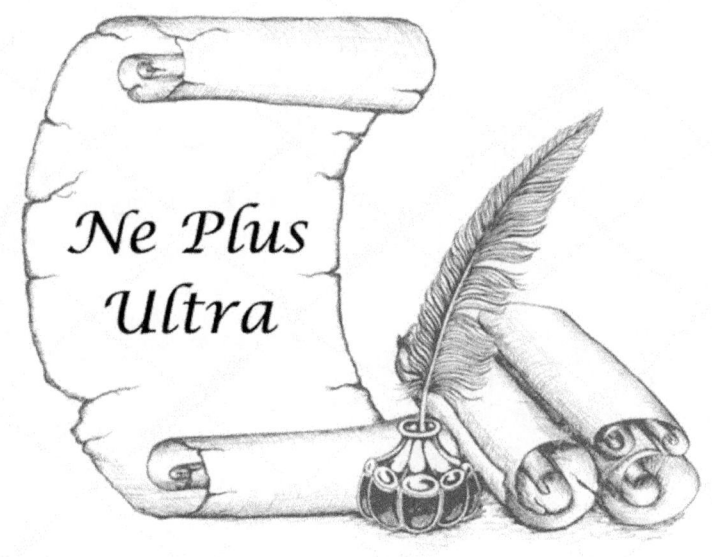

www.ingramcontent.com/pod-product-compliance
Lightning Source LLC
Chambersburg PA
CBHW060505240426
43661CB00007B/918